Dragon Goes House-Hunting

7

Story by
KAWO TANUKI

Art by
CHOCO AYA

CHARACTERS

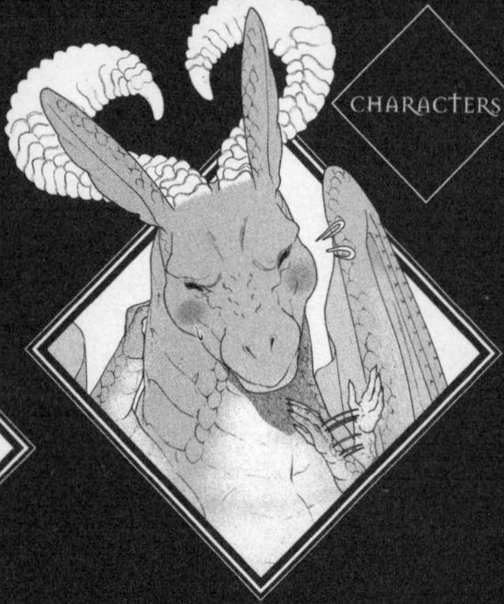

Letty

A weak and cowardly Dragon (♂) who dreams of finding his home sweet home. Also the legendary Flame Dragon King, though he wishes he weren't.

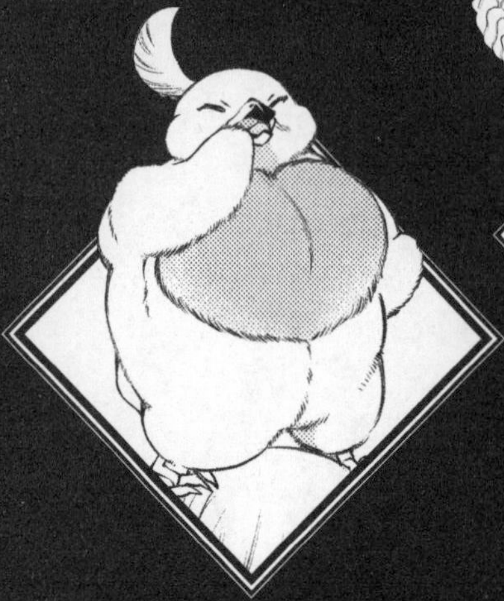

Pip

A Hraesvelgr chick hatched and adopted by Letty. A pampered daddy's boy, but getting stronger every day.

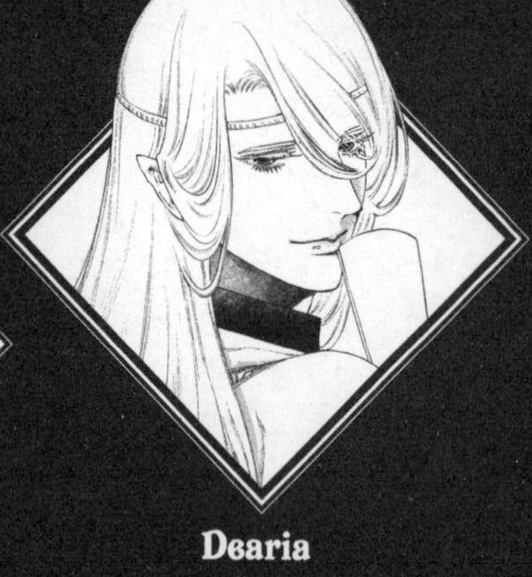

Dearia

A dependable elf-man who knows everything there is to know about homes. A Dark Lord who can defeat ten thousand warriors, he watches over Letty with both warmth and strictness.

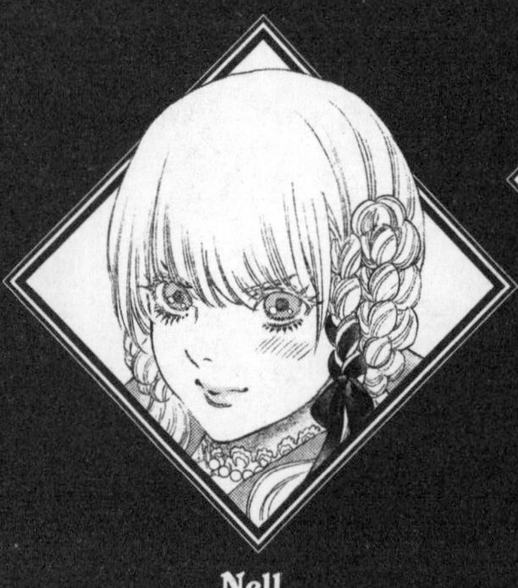

Nell

A kind but tomboyish princess from a human kingdom. Letty rescued her after she ran away from home, and they've been friends ever since.

Although part of the mightiest species of all, Letty is a weak and cowardly dragon. After his family disowned him, he met the elf realtor Dearia and set off on a private viewing journey to find a safe and secure home of his own.

Eventually, Dearia was obliged to go away on business. Standing in was the vampire realtor, Victor. He turned out to be a dishonest operator who only showed defective properties. Things got a bit complicated due to the intervention of the heroic, meddling, and overall useless Yuusha, but Victor was ultimately touched by the kindness in Letty's heart. Victor soon departed as a changed man (or bat), seeking atonement for his past crimes.

With all that business behind them, Letty and company are once again on the hunt for a proper place to call home. Despite his growing legend as the so-called "Flame Dragon King," a good house continues to prove elusive. Day in and day out, Letty's house-hunting journey continues!

Co n t e n t s

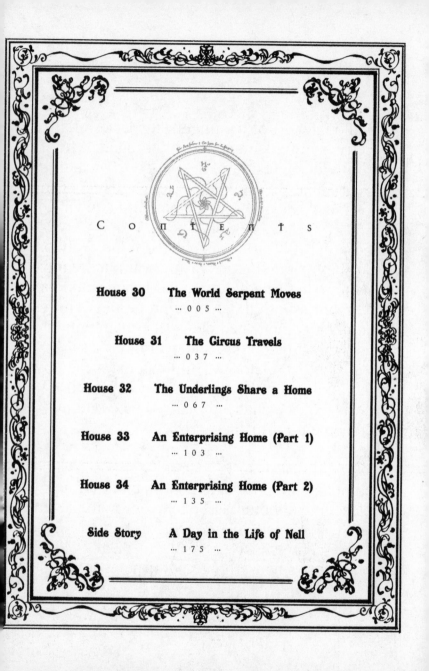

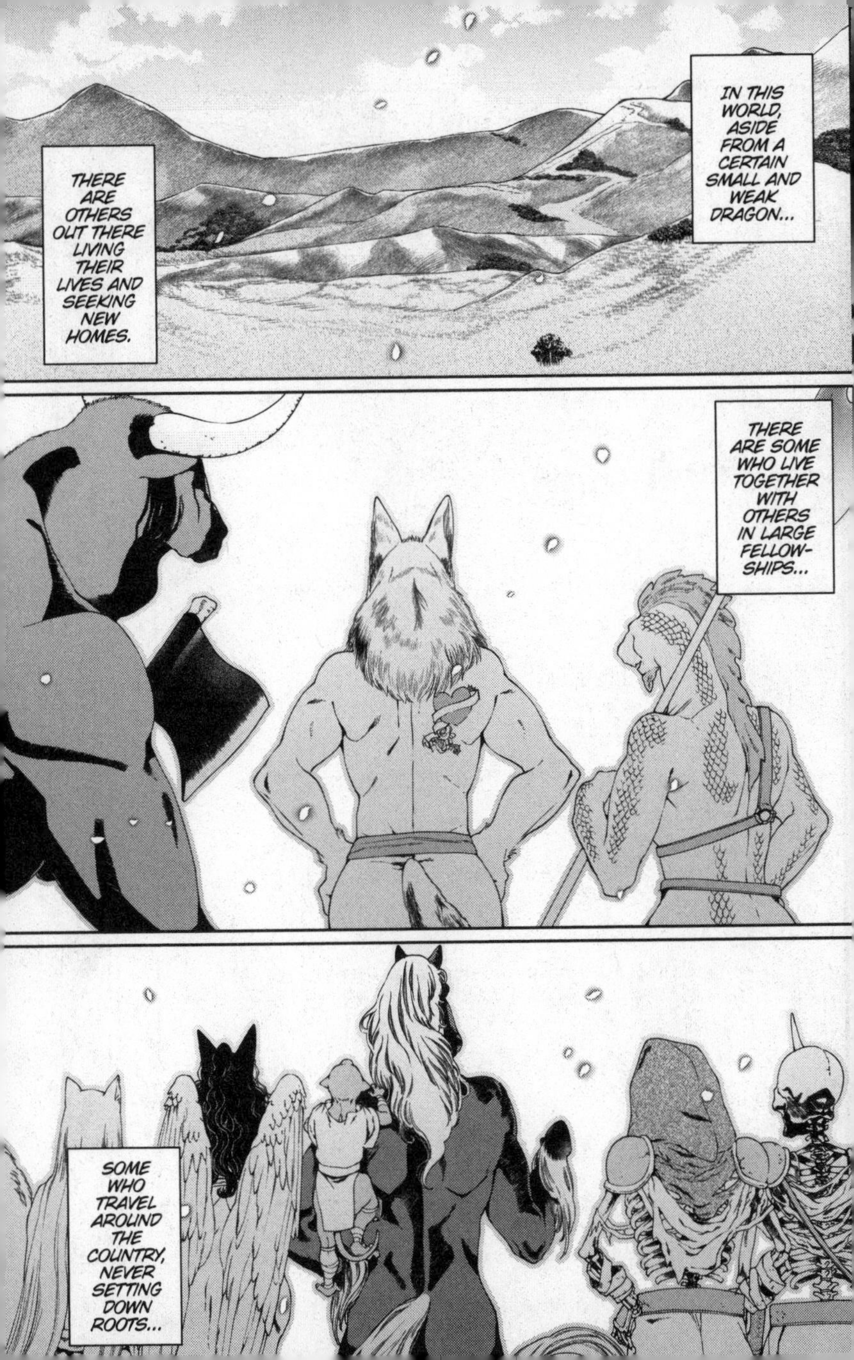
IN THIS WORLD, ASIDE FROM A CERTAIN SMALL AND WEAK DRAGON...
THERE ARE OTHERS OUT THERE LIVING THEIR LIVES AND SEEKING NEW HOMES.
THERE ARE SOME WHO LIVE TOGETHER WITH OTHERS IN LARGE FELLOW-SHIPS...
SOME WHO TRAVEL AROUND THE COUNTRY, NEVER SETTING DOWN ROOTS...

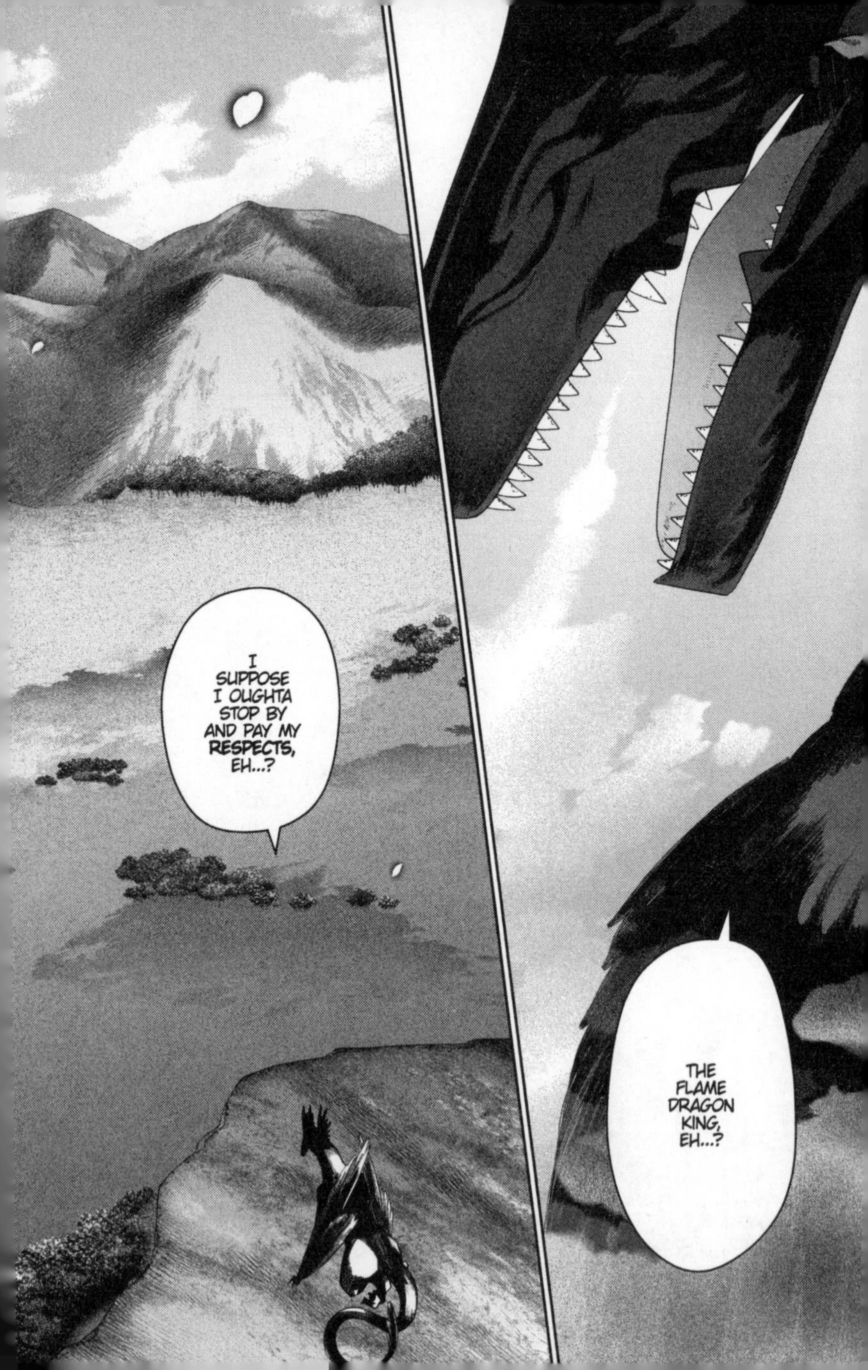
THE FLAME DRAGON KING, EH...?
I SUPPOSE I OUGHTA STOP BY AND PAY MY RESPECTS, EH...?

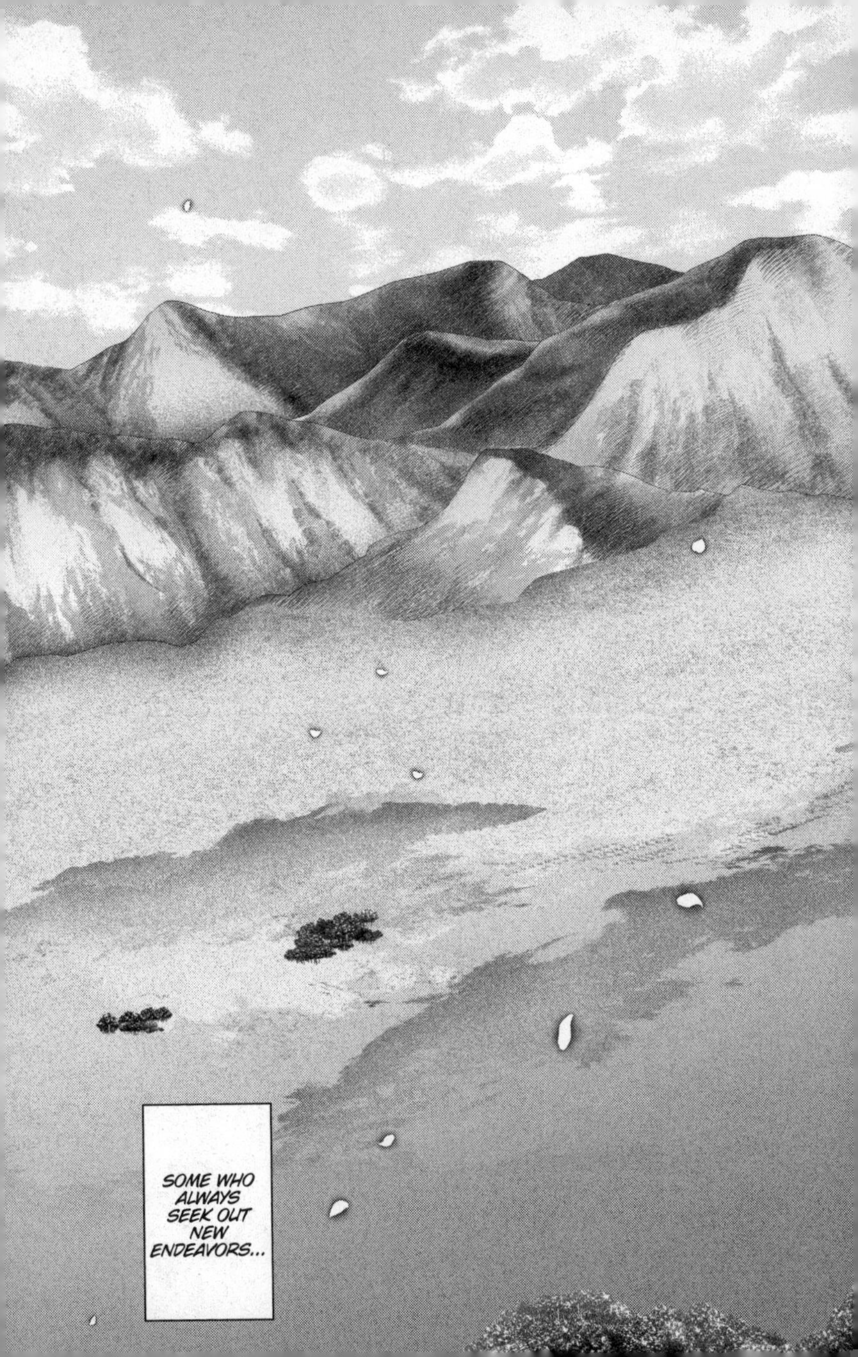
SOME WHO ALWAYS SEEK OUT NEW ENDEAVORS...

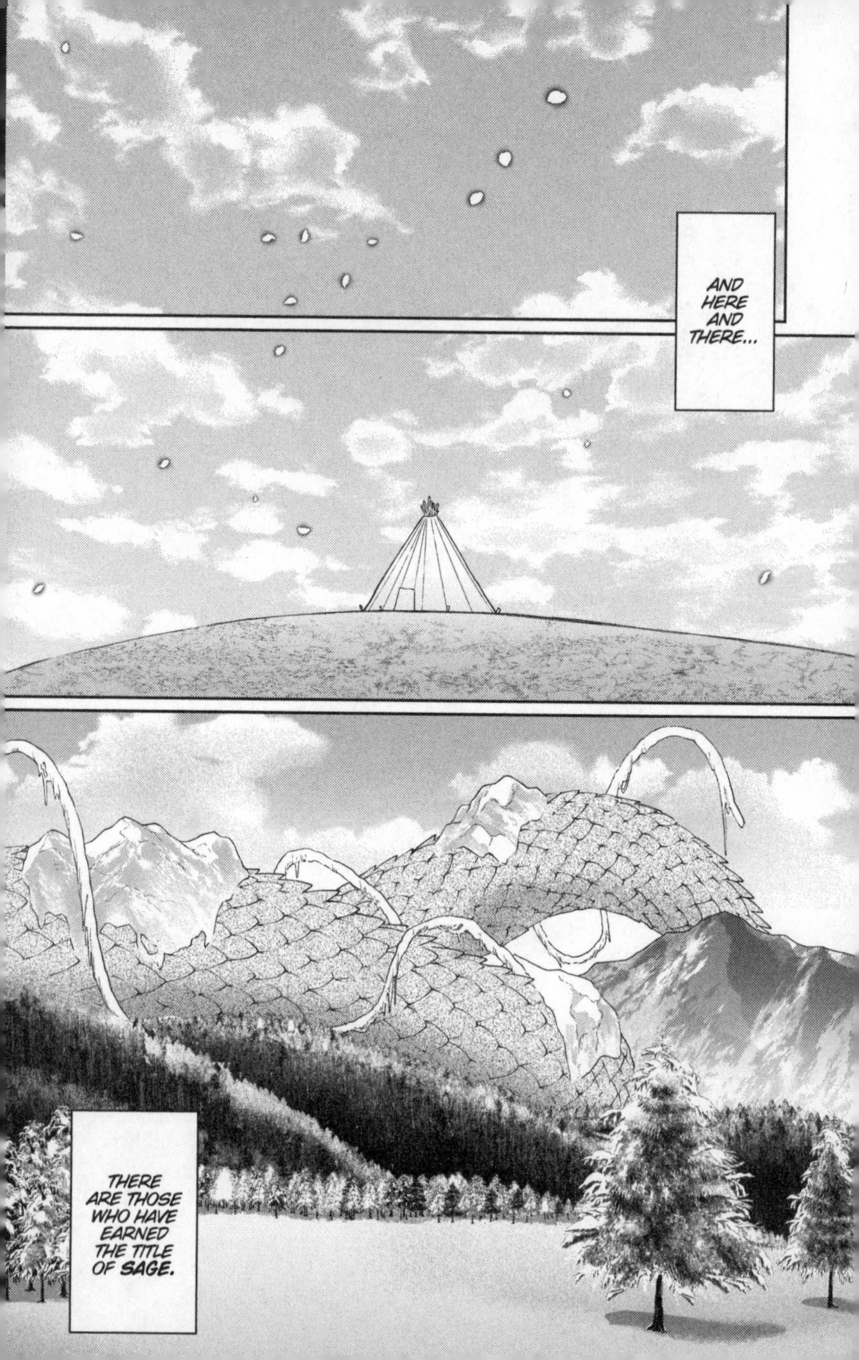
AND HERE AND THERE...
THERE ARE THOSE WHO HAVE EARNED THE TITLE OF SAGE.

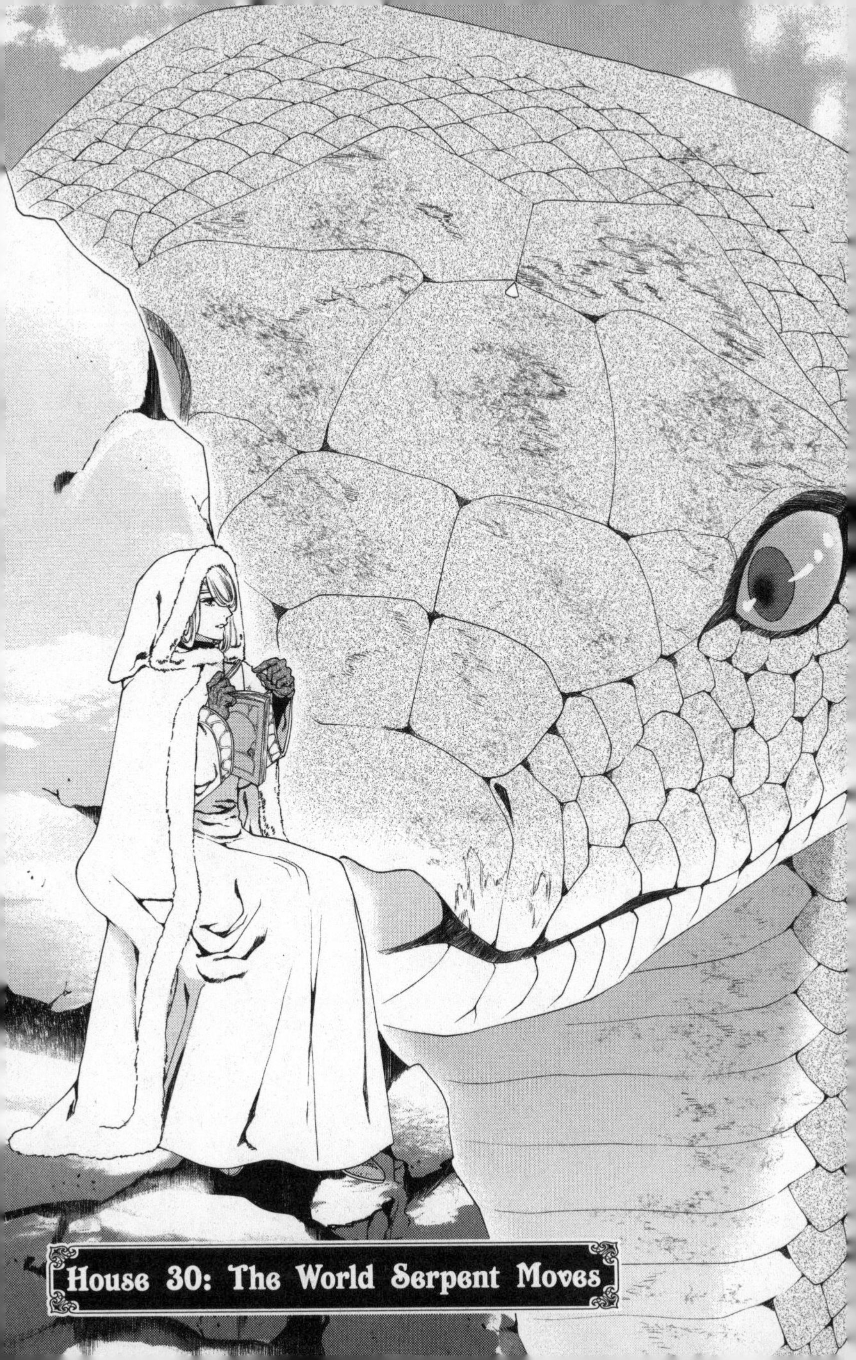
House 30: The World Serpent Moves

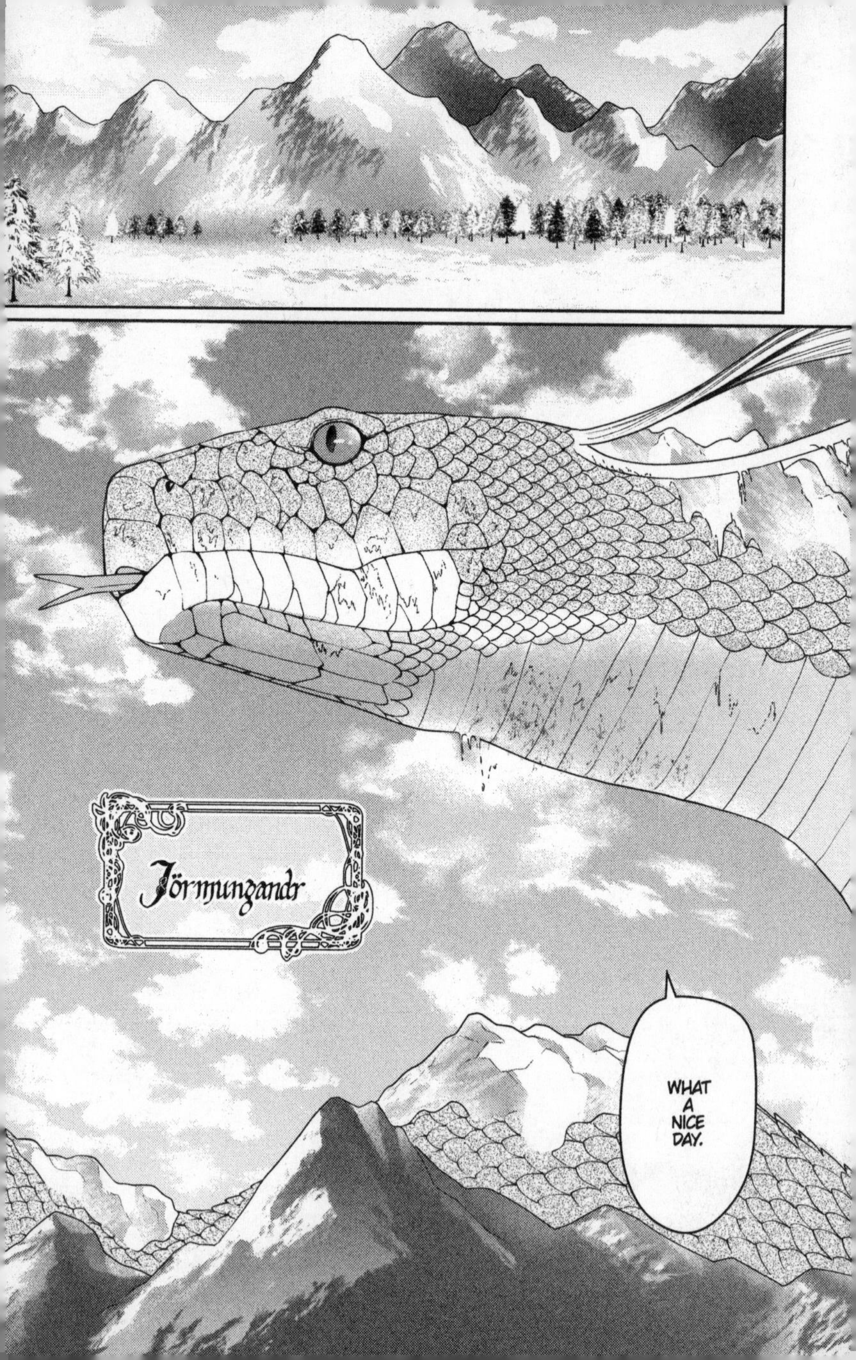
Jörmungandr
WHAT A NICE DAY.

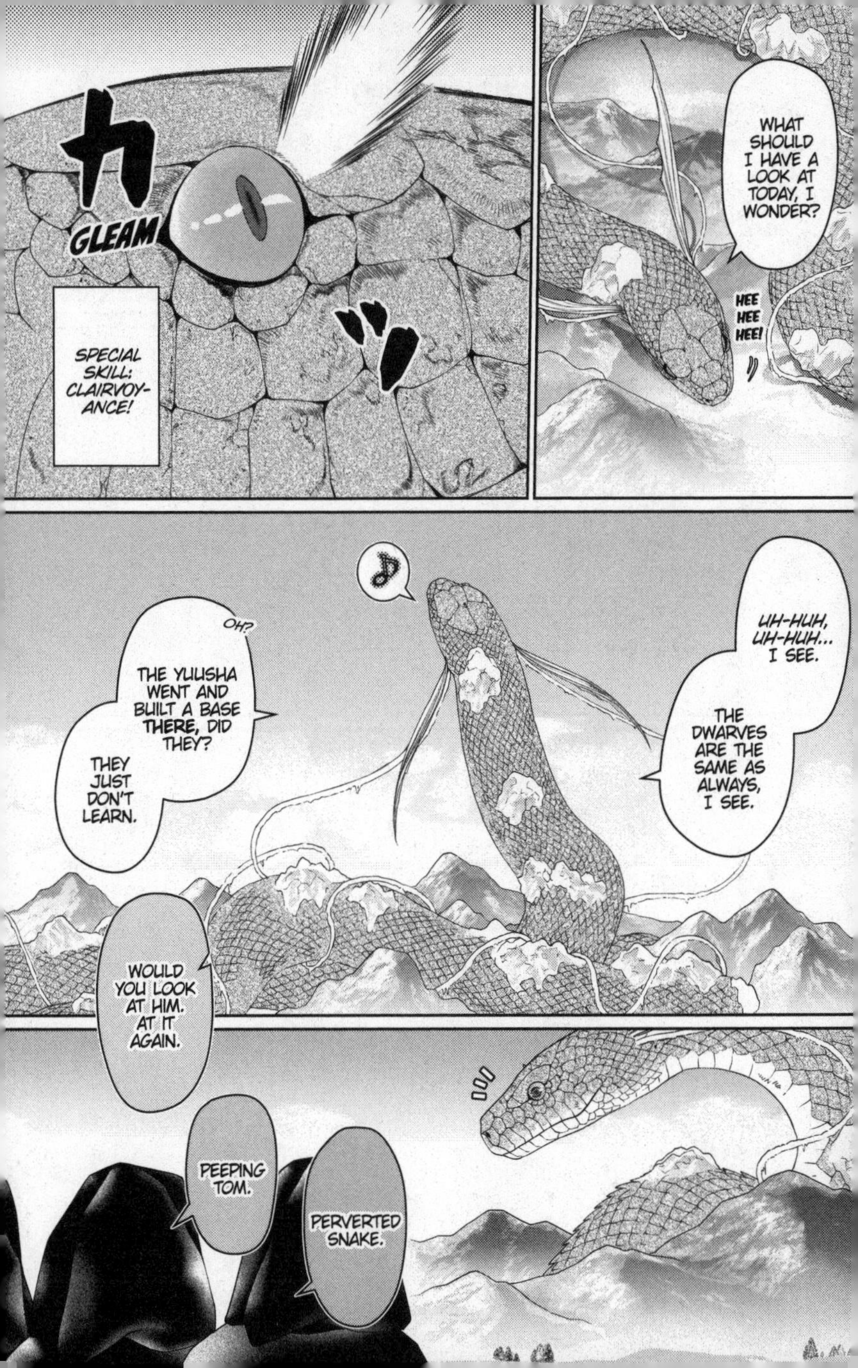
WHAT SHOULD I HAVE A LOOK AT TODAY, I WONDER?
HEE HEE HEE!
カ
GLEAM
SPECIAL SKILL: CLAIRVOYANCE!
UH-HUH, UH-HUH... I SEE.
THE DWARVES ARE THE SAME AS ALWAYS, I SEE.
OH?
THE YUUSHA WENT AND BUILT A BASE THERE, DID THEY?
THEY JUST DON'T LEARN.
WOULD YOU LOOK AT HIM. AT IT AGAIN.
PEEPING TOM.
PERVERTED SNAKE.

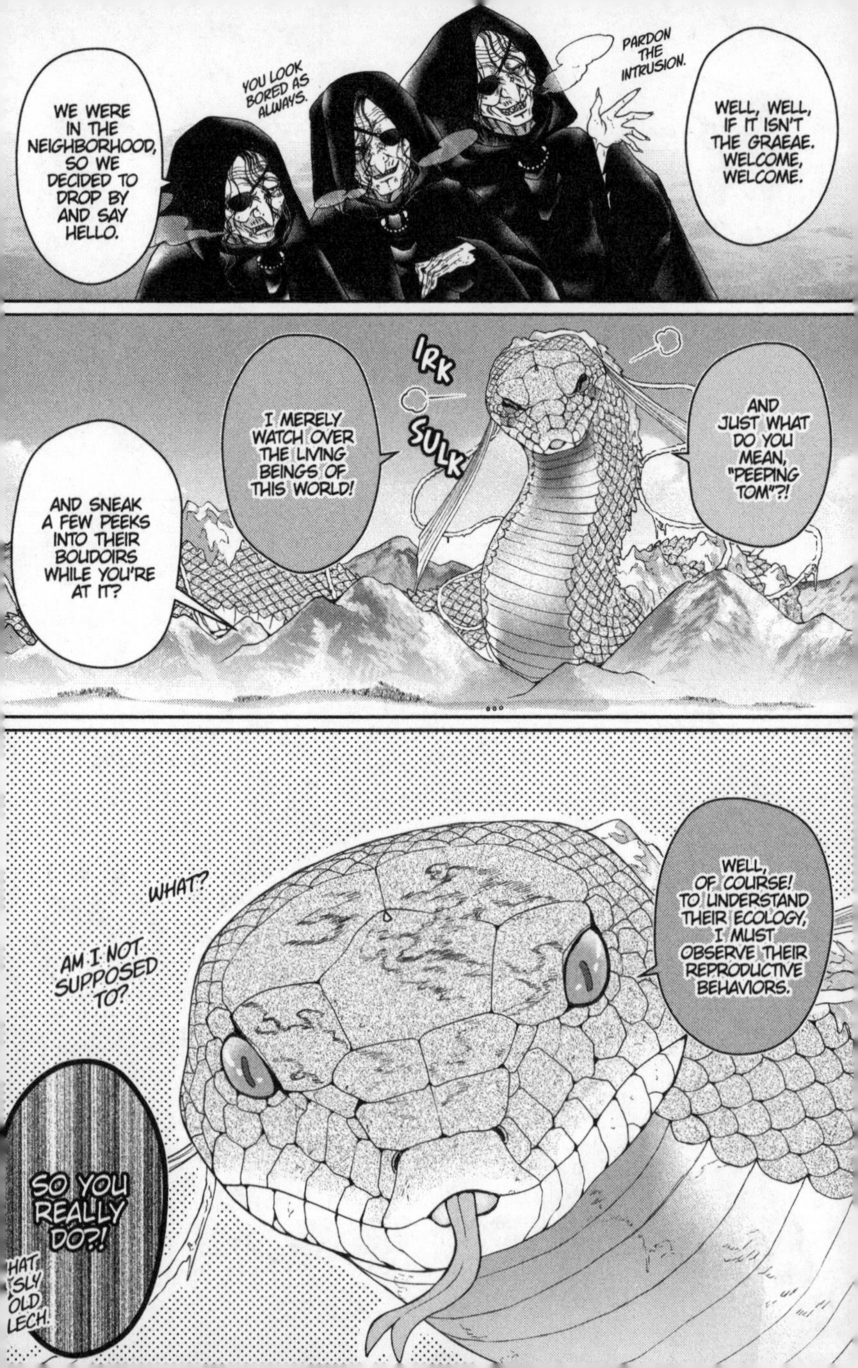
WELL, WELL, IF IT ISN'T THE GRAEAE. WELCOME, WELCOME.
PARDON THE INTRUSION.
YOU LOOK BORED AS ALWAYS.
WE WERE IN THE NEIGHBORHOOD, SO WE DECIDED TO DROP BY AND SAY HELLO.
AND JUST WHAT DO YOU MEAN, "PEEPING TOM"?!
IRK
SULK
I MERELY WATCH OVER THE LIVING BEINGS OF THIS WORLD!
AND SNEAK A FEW PEEKS INTO THEIR BOUDOIRS WHILE YOU'RE AT IT?
WELL, OF COURSE! TO UNDERSTAND THEIR ECOLOGY, I MUST OBSERVE THEIR REPRODUCTIVE BEHAVIORS.
WHAT?
AM I NOT SUPPOSED TO?
SO YOU REALLY DO?!
HAT
ISLY
OLD
LECH.

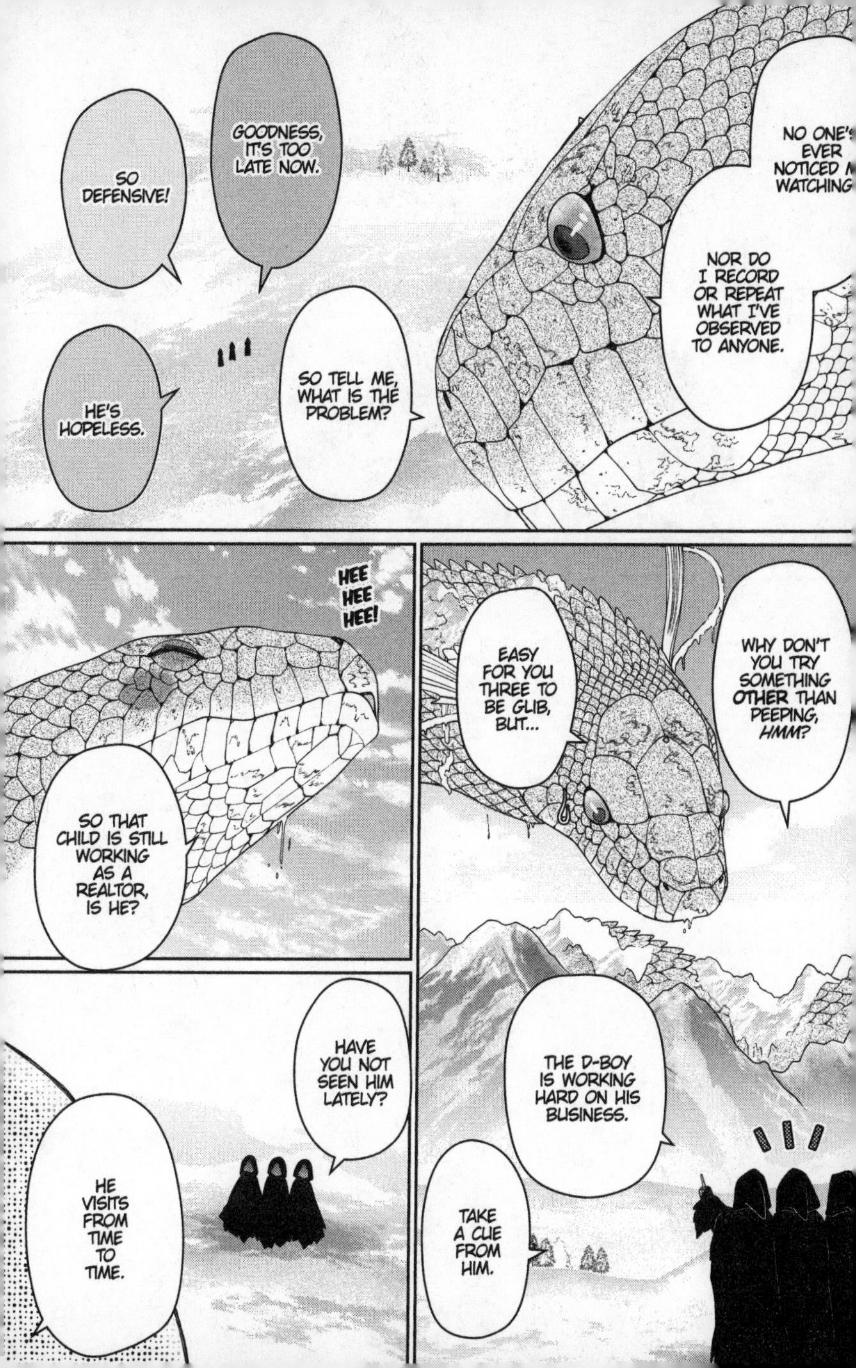
NO ONE'S EVER NOTICED M WATCHING
NOR DO I RECORD OR REPEAT WHAT I'VE OBSERVED TO ANYONE.
GOODNESS, IT'S TOO LATE NOW.
SO DEFENSIVE!
SO TELL ME, WHAT IS THE PROBLEM?
HE'S HOPELESS.
WHY DON'T YOU TRY SOMETHING OTHER THAN PEEPING, HMM?
EASY FOR YOU THREE TO BE GLIB, BUT...
THE D-BOY IS WORKING HARD ON HIS BUSINESS.
TAKE A CUE FROM HIM.
HEE HEE HEE!
SO THAT CHILD IS STILL WORKING AS A REALTOR, IS HE?
HAVE YOU NOT SEEN HIM LATELY?
HE VISITS FROM TIME TO TIME.

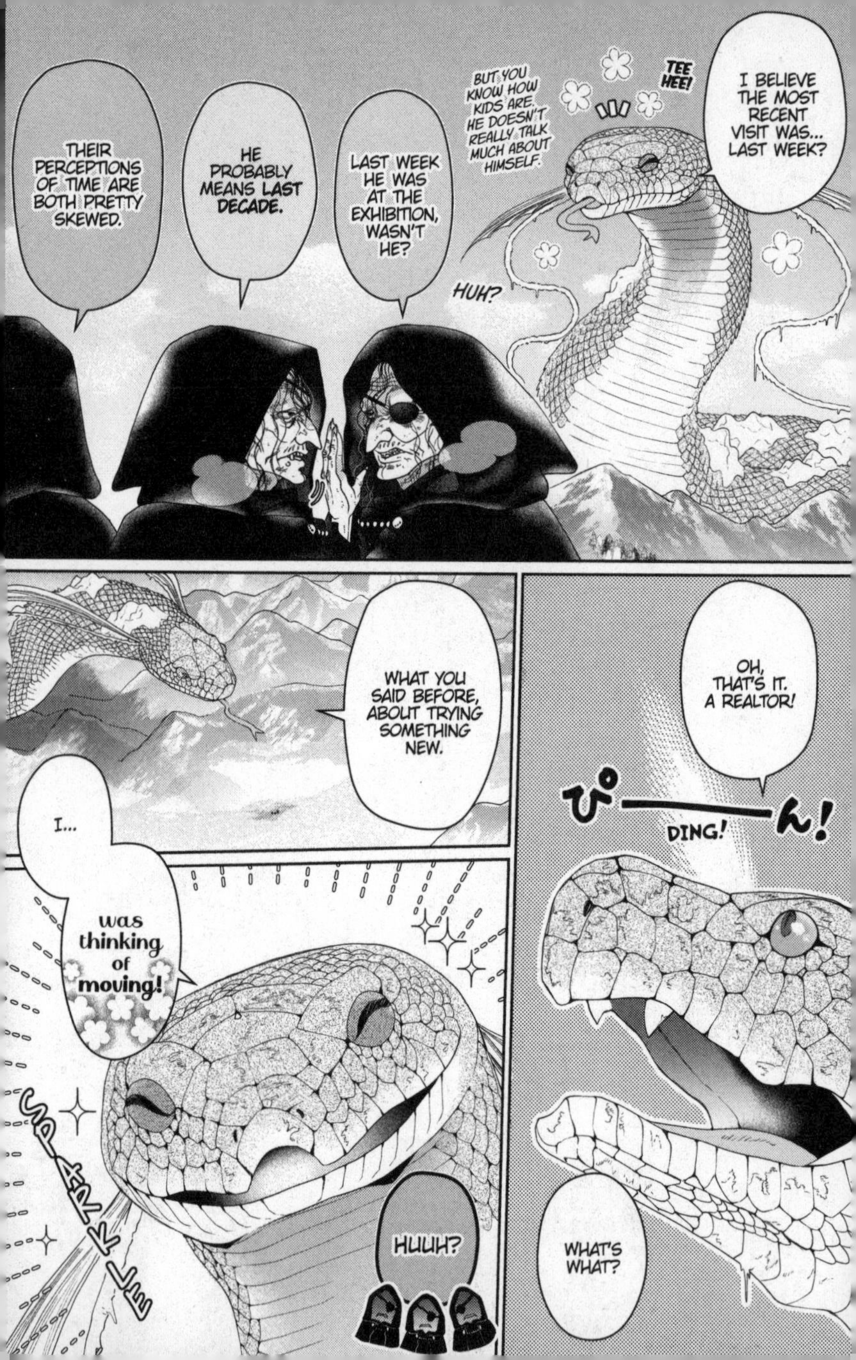
I BELIEVE THE MOST RECENT VISIT WAS... LAST WEEK?
TEE HEE!
BUT YOU KNOW HOW KIDS ARE. HE DOESN'T REALLY TALK MUCH ABOUT HIMSELF.
HUH?
LAST WEEK HE WAS AT THE EXHIBITION, WASN'T HE?
HE PROBABLY MEANS LAST DECADE.
THEIR PERCEPTIONS OF TIME ARE BOTH PRETTY SKEWED.
OH, THAT'S IT. A REALTOR!
ぴーーん!
DING!
WHAT'S WHAT?
WHAT YOU SAID BEFORE, ABOUT TRYING SOMETHING NEW.
I...
was thinking of moving!
SPARKLE
HUUH?

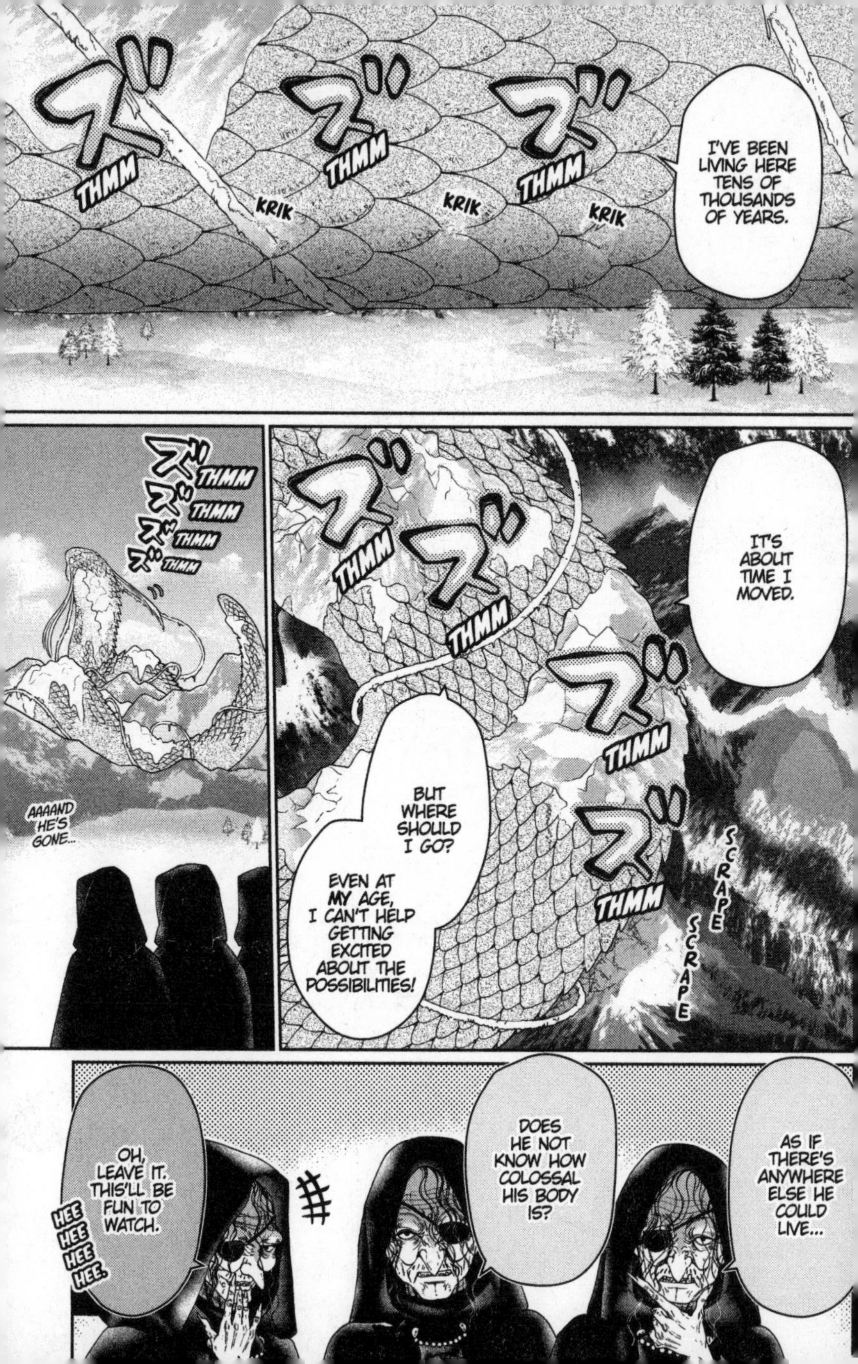
I'VE BEEN LIVING HERE TENS OF THOUSANDS OF YEARS.
THMM
KRIK
THMM
KRIK
THMM
KRIK
IT'S ABOUT TIME I MOVED.
THMM
THMM
THMM
THMM
SCRAPE
SCRAPE
BUT WHERE SHOULD I GO?
EVEN AT MY AGE, I CAN'T HELP GETTING EXCITED ABOUT THE POSSIBILITIES!
THMM
THMM
THMM
THMM
AAAAND HE'S GONE...
AS IF THERE'S ANYWHERE ELSE HE COULD LIVE...
DOES HE NOT KNOW HOW COLOSSAL HIS BODY IS?
OH, LEAVE IT. THIS'LL BE FUN TO WATCH.
HEE HEE HEE HEE.

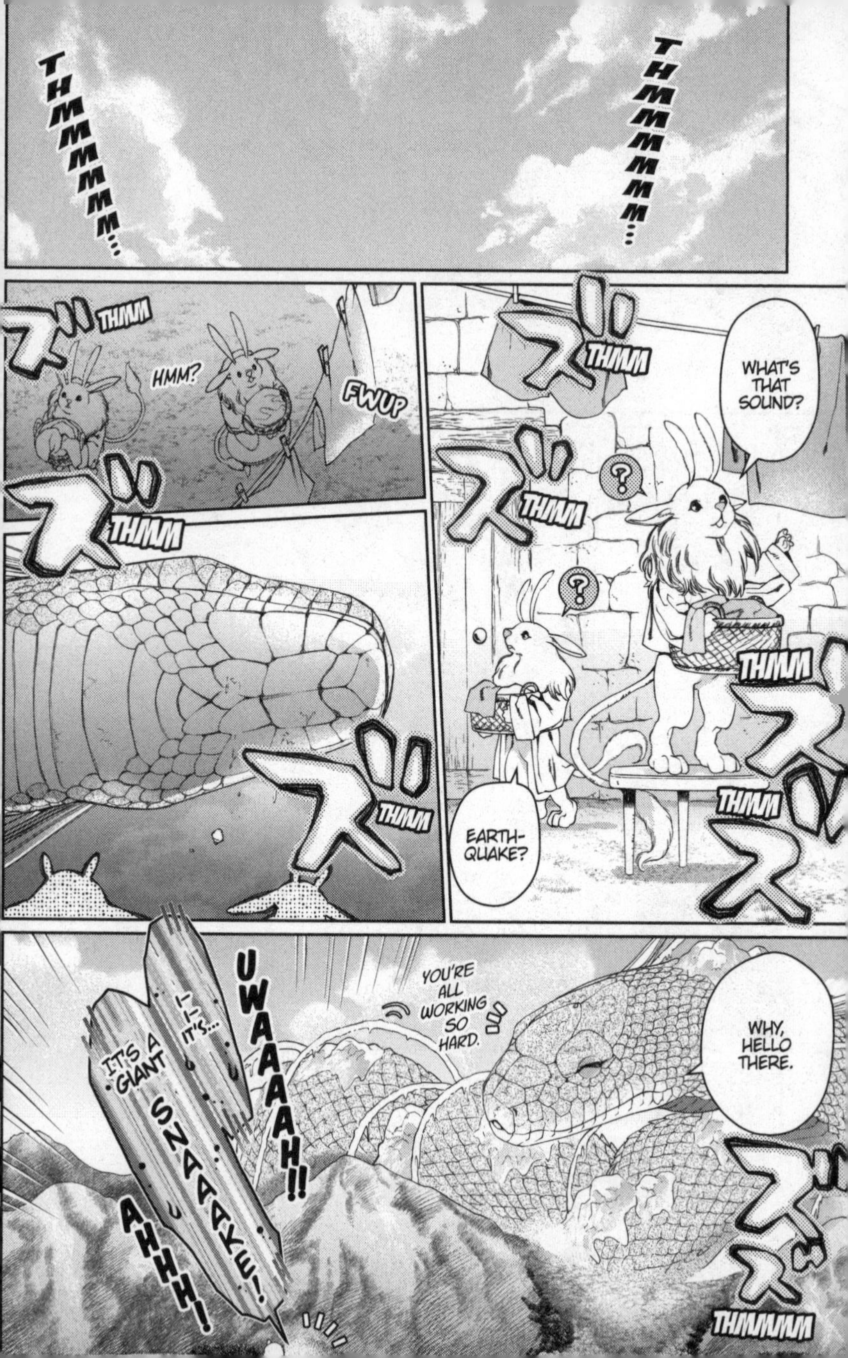

THMMMMMMM...
THMMMMMM...
ズ THMM
WHAT'S THAT SOUND?
ズ THMM
?
?
EARTH-QUAKE?
THMM ズ
THMM ズ
ズ THMM
HMM?
FWUP
ズ THMM
ズ THMM
WHY, HELLO THERE.
YOU'RE ALL WORKING SO HARD.
UWAAAAH!!
I-I-IT'S...
IT'S A GIANT SNAAAAKE!
AHHH!
ズズ THMMMM

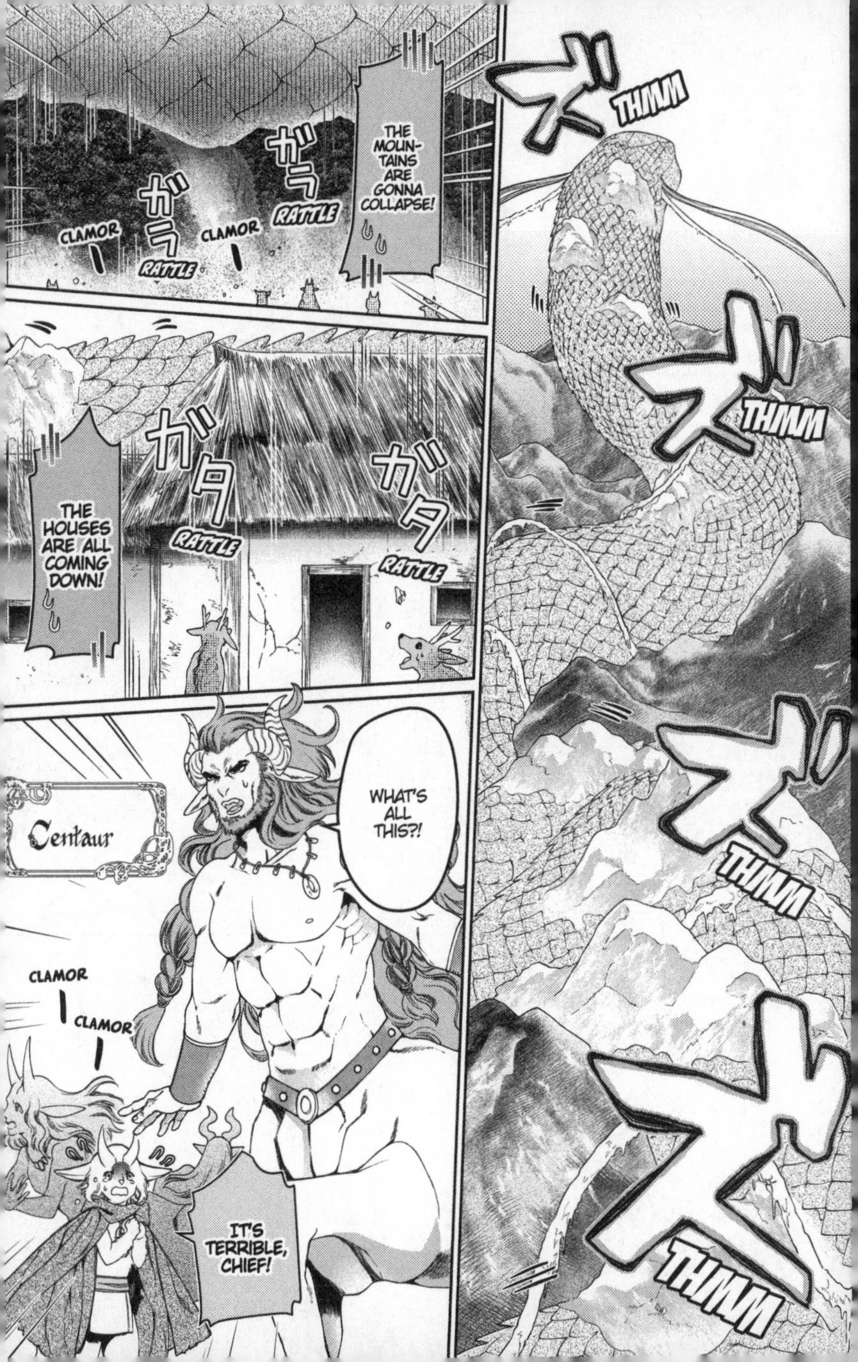
ズ
THMM
ズ
THMM
ズ
THMM
ズ
THMM
THE MOUN-TAINS ARE GONNA COLLAPSE!
ガラ
RATTLE
ガラ
RATTLE
CLAMOR
CLAMOR
ガタ
RATTLE
ガタ
RATTLE
THE HOUSES ARE ALL COMING DOWN!
WHAT'S ALL THIS?!
Centaur
CLAMOR
CLAMOR
IT'S TERRIBLE, CHIEF!

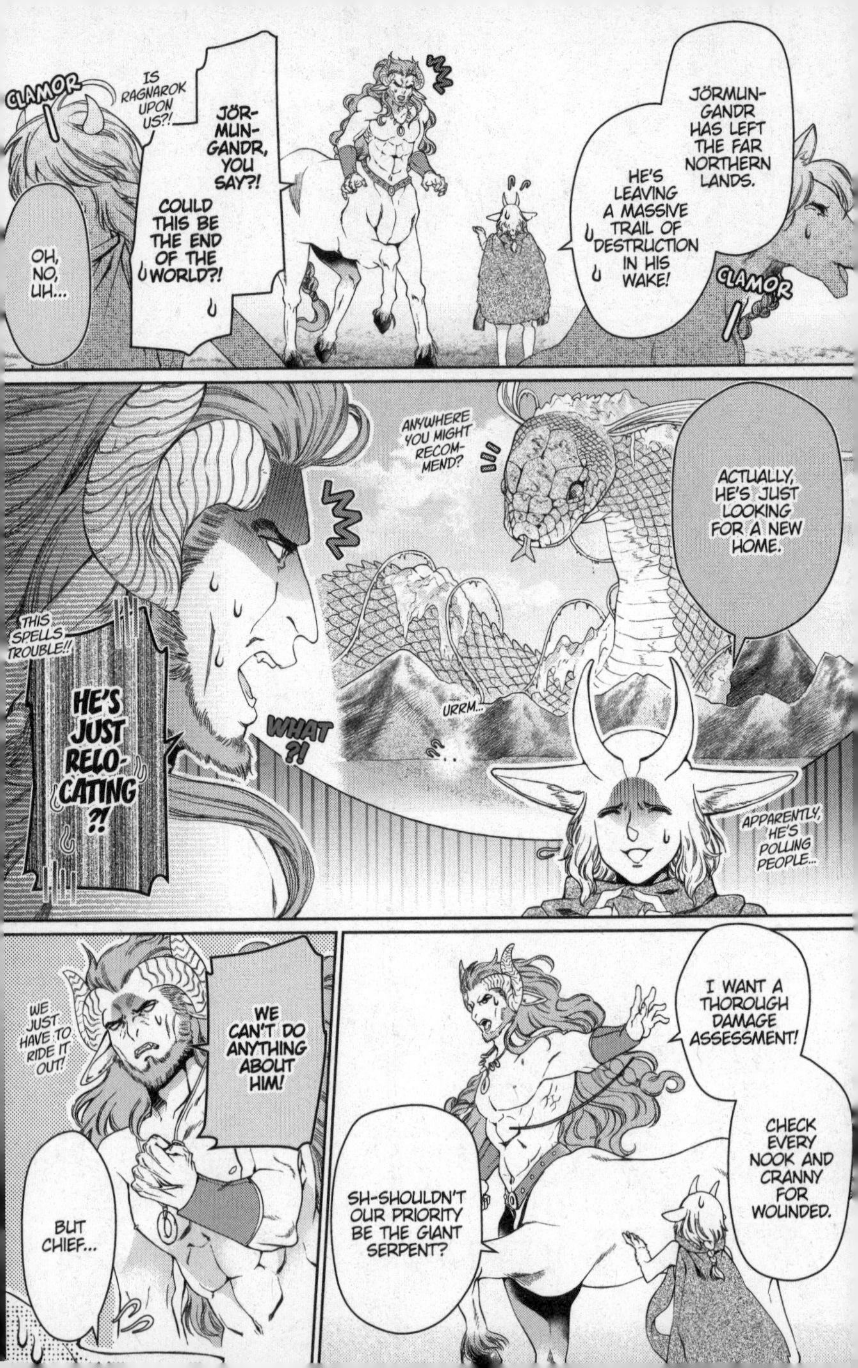
JÖRMUNGANDR HAS LEFT THE FAR NORTHERN LANDS.
HE'S LEAVING A MASSIVE TRAIL OF DESTRUCTION IN HIS WAKE!
CLAMOR
JÖRMUNGANDR, YOU SAY?!
COULD THIS BE THE END OF THE WORLD?!
IS RAGNAROK UPON US?!
CLAMOR
OH, NO, UH...
ACTUALLY, HE'S JUST LOOKING FOR A NEW HOME.
ANYWHERE YOU MIGHT RECOMMEND?
URRM...
APPARENTLY, HE'S POLLING PEOPLE...
WHAT?!
HE'S JUST RELOCATING?!
THIS SPELLS TROUBLE!!
I WANT A THOROUGH DAMAGE ASSESSMENT!
CHECK EVERY NOOK AND CRANNY FOR WOUNDED.
SH-SHOULDN'T OUR PRIORITY BE THE GIANT SERPENT?
WE CAN'T DO ANYTHING ABOUT HIM!
WE JUST HAVE TO RIDE IT OUT!
BUT CHIEF...

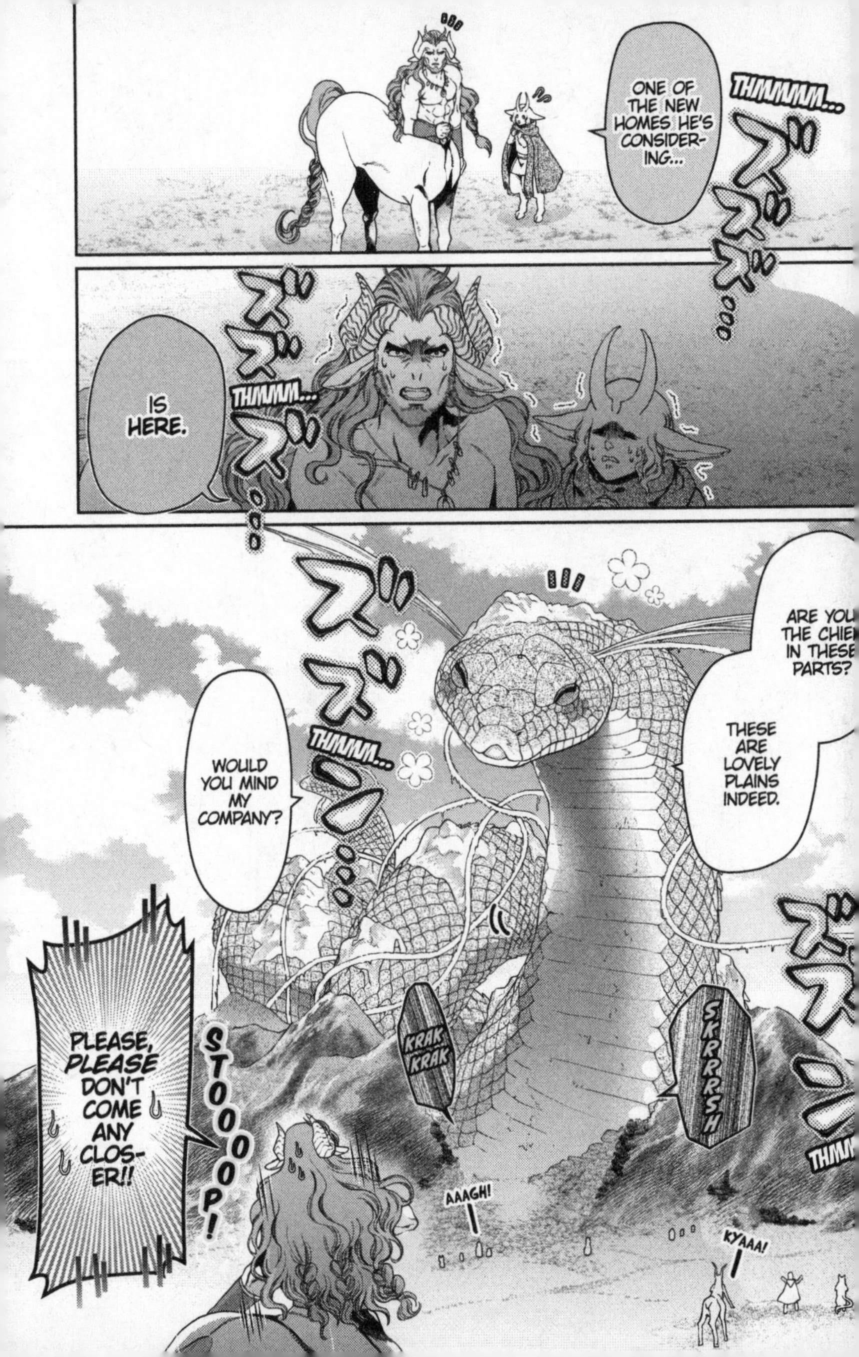
THMMMM...
ONE OF THE NEW HOMES HE'S CONSIDER-ING...
THMMM...
IS HERE.
ARE YOU THE CHIE IN THESE PARTS?
THESE ARE LOVELY PLAINS INDEED.
THMMM...
WOULD YOU MIND MY COMPANY?
SKRRRSH
KRAK KRAK
THMM
STOOOOOP!
PLEASE, PLEASE DON'T COME ANY CLOS-ER!!
AAAGH!
KYAAA!

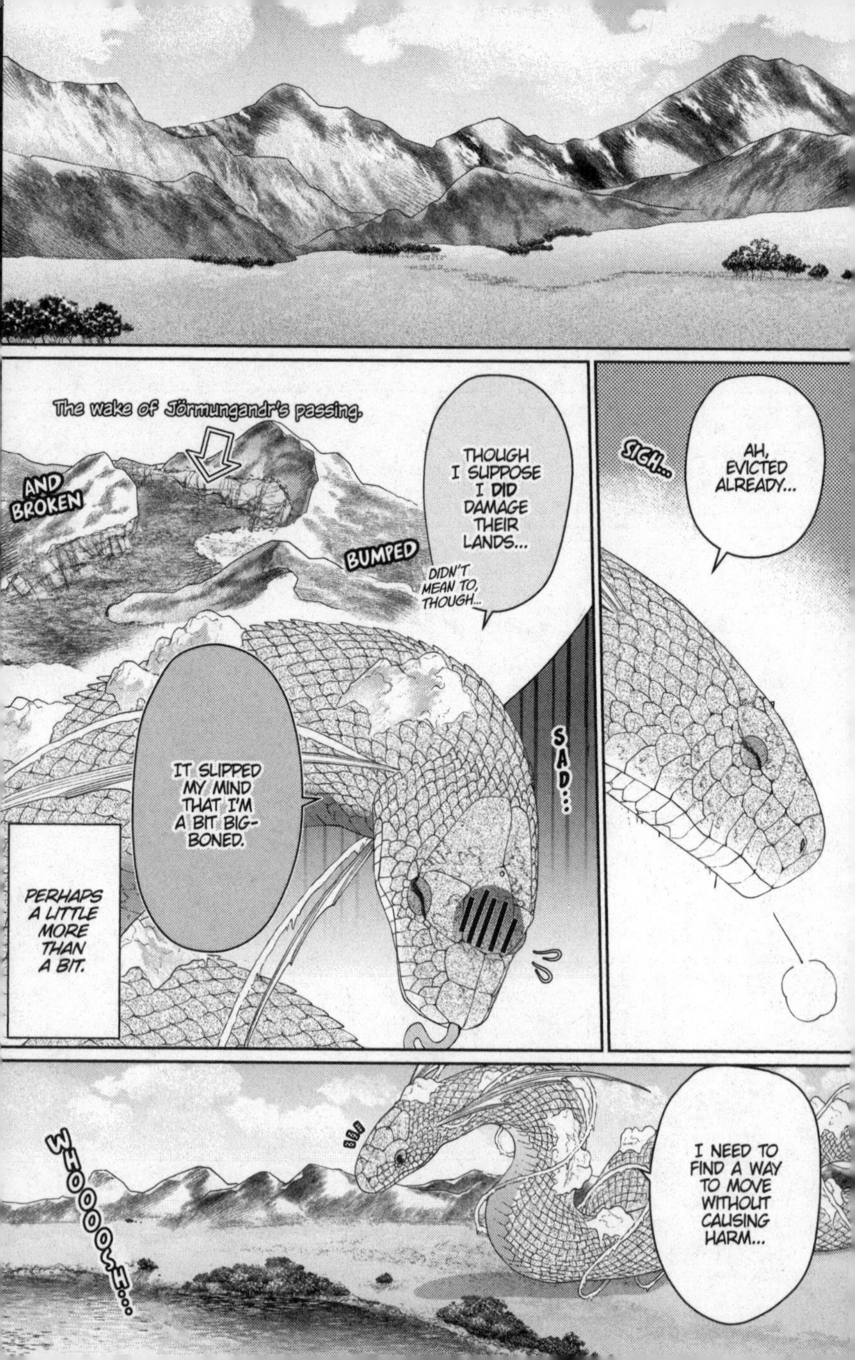
SIGH...
AH, EVICTED ALREADY...
THOUGH I SUPPOSE I DID DAMAGE THEIR LANDS...
DIDN'T MEAN TO, THOUGH...
The wake of Jörmungandr's passing.
BUMPED
AND BROKEN
SAD...
IT SLIPPED MY MIND THAT I'M A BIT BIG-BONED.
PERHAPS A LITTLE MORE THAN A BIT.
I NEED TO FIND A WAY TO MOVE WITHOUT CAUSING HARM...
WHOOOOSH...

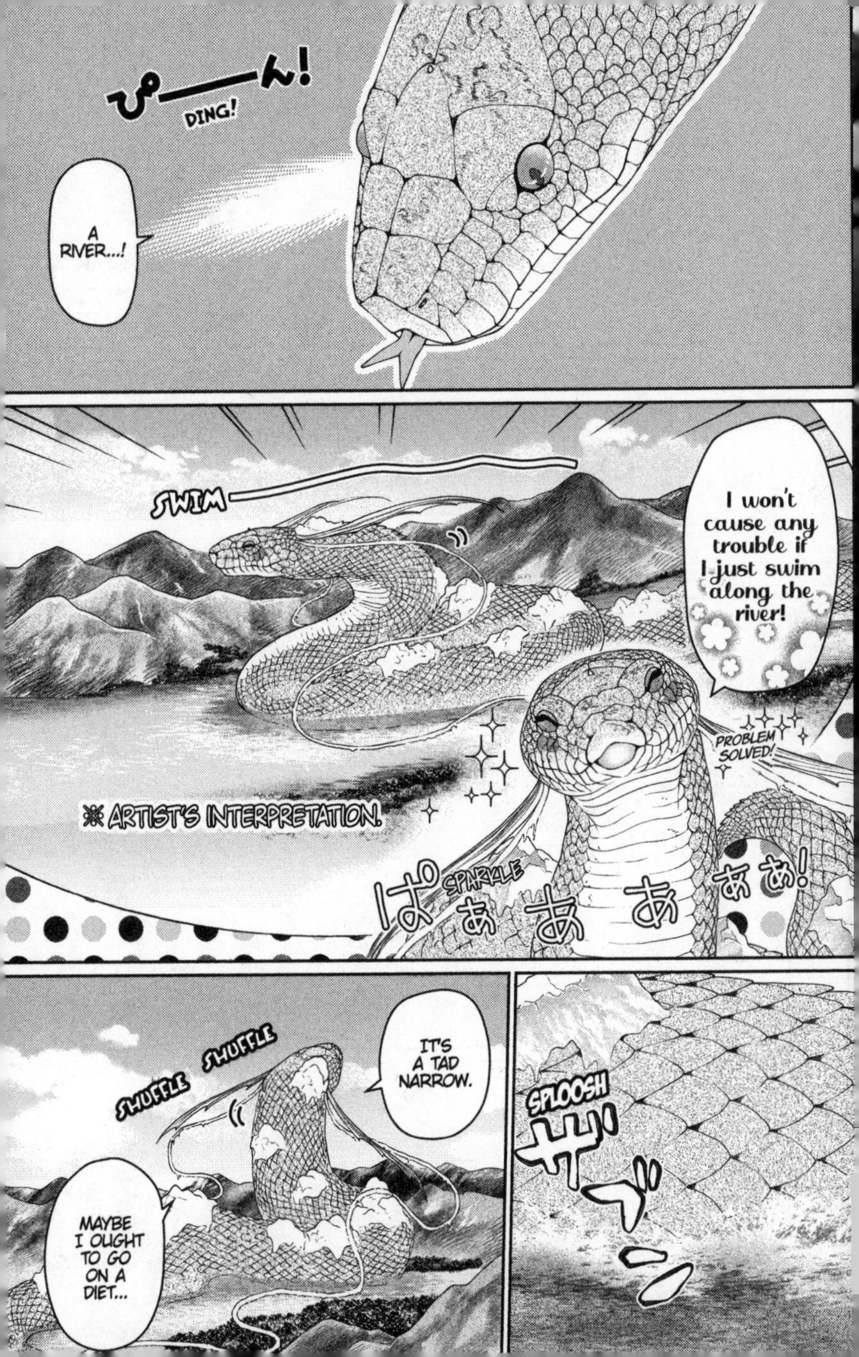
ぴーーん!
DING!
A RIVER...!
I won't cause any trouble if I just swim along the river!
SWIM
PROBLEM SOLVED!
※ARTIST'S INTERPRETATION.
ぱぁあああ!
SPARKLE
SPLOOSH
ザブ
IT'S A TAD NARROW.
SHUFFLE SHUFFLE
MAYBE I OUGHT TO GO ON A DIET...

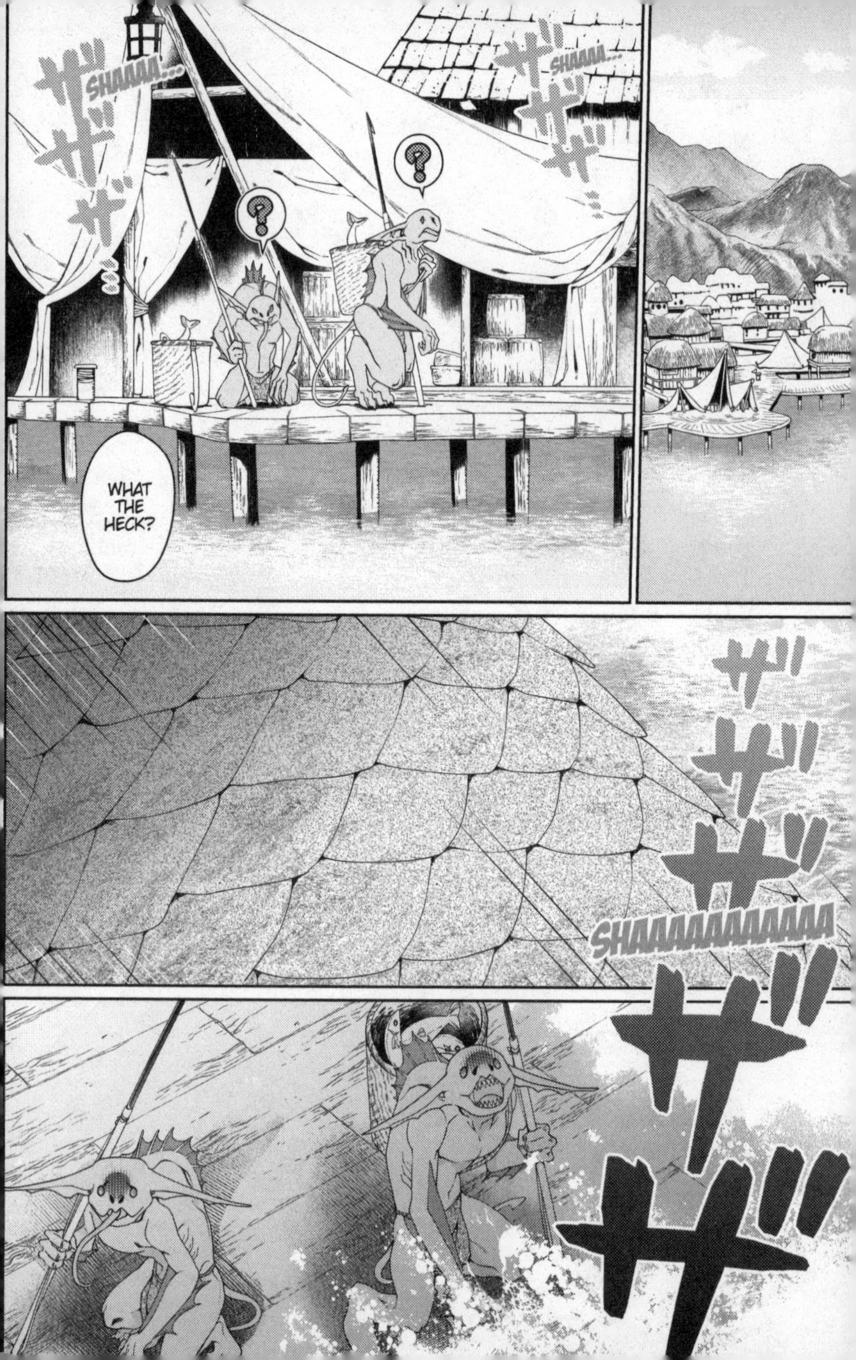
SHAAAA...
SHAAAA...
?
?
WHAT THE HECK?
SHAAAAAAAAAA

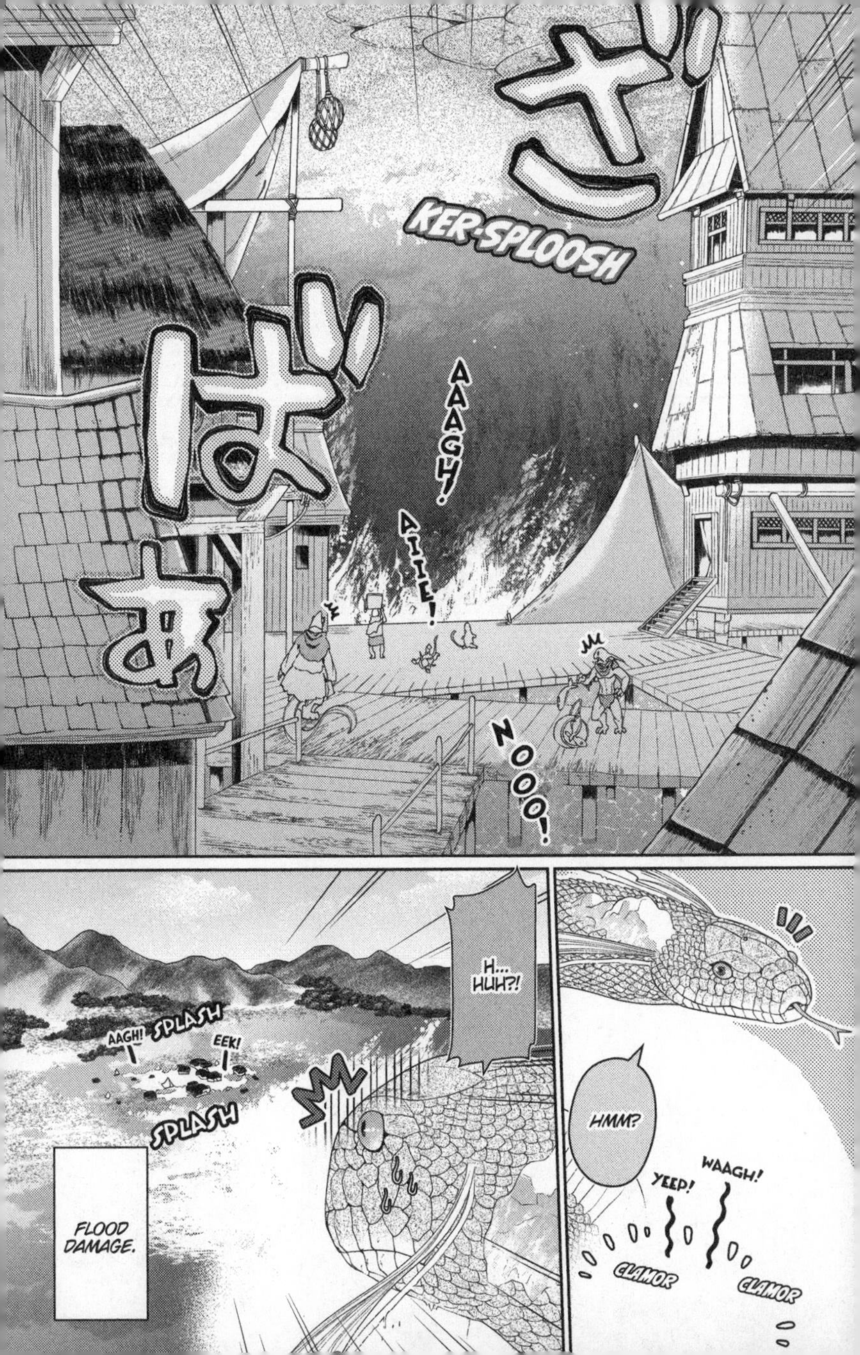
ざばあ
KER-SPLOOSH
AAAAGH!
AIIIE!
NOOOO!
HMM?
WAAGH!
YEEP!
CLAMOR
CLAMOR
H... HUH?!
EEK!
SPLASH
AAGH!
SPLASH
FLOOD DAMAGE.

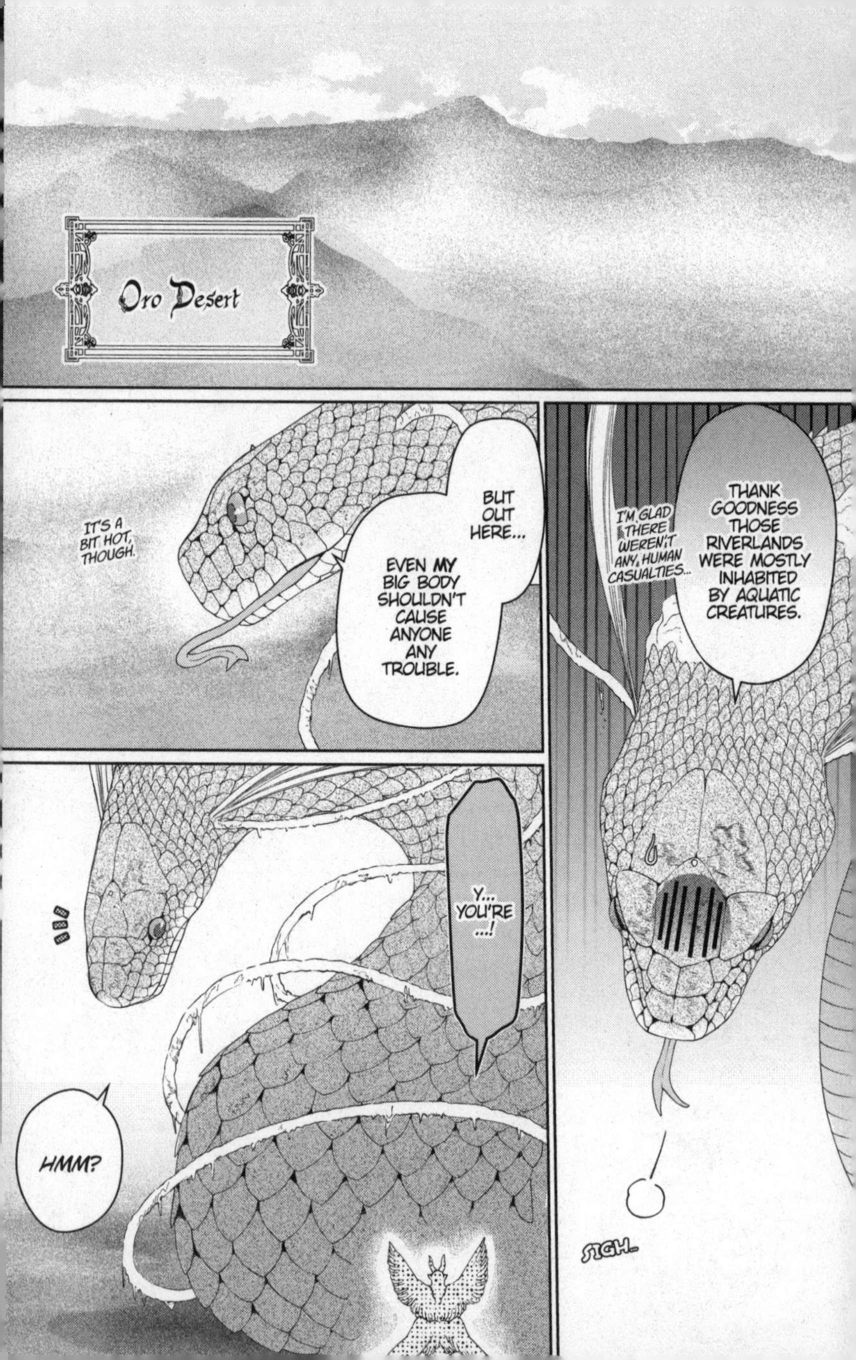
Oro Desert
THANK GOODNESS THOSE RIVERLANDS WERE MOSTLY INHABITED BY AQUATIC CREATURES.
I'M GLAD THERE WEREN'T ANY HUMAN CASUALTIES...
SIGH...
BUT OUT HERE...
EVEN MY BIG BODY SHOULDN'T CAUSE ANYONE ANY TROUBLE.
IT'S A BIT HOT, THOUGH.
Y... YOU'RE ...!
HMM?

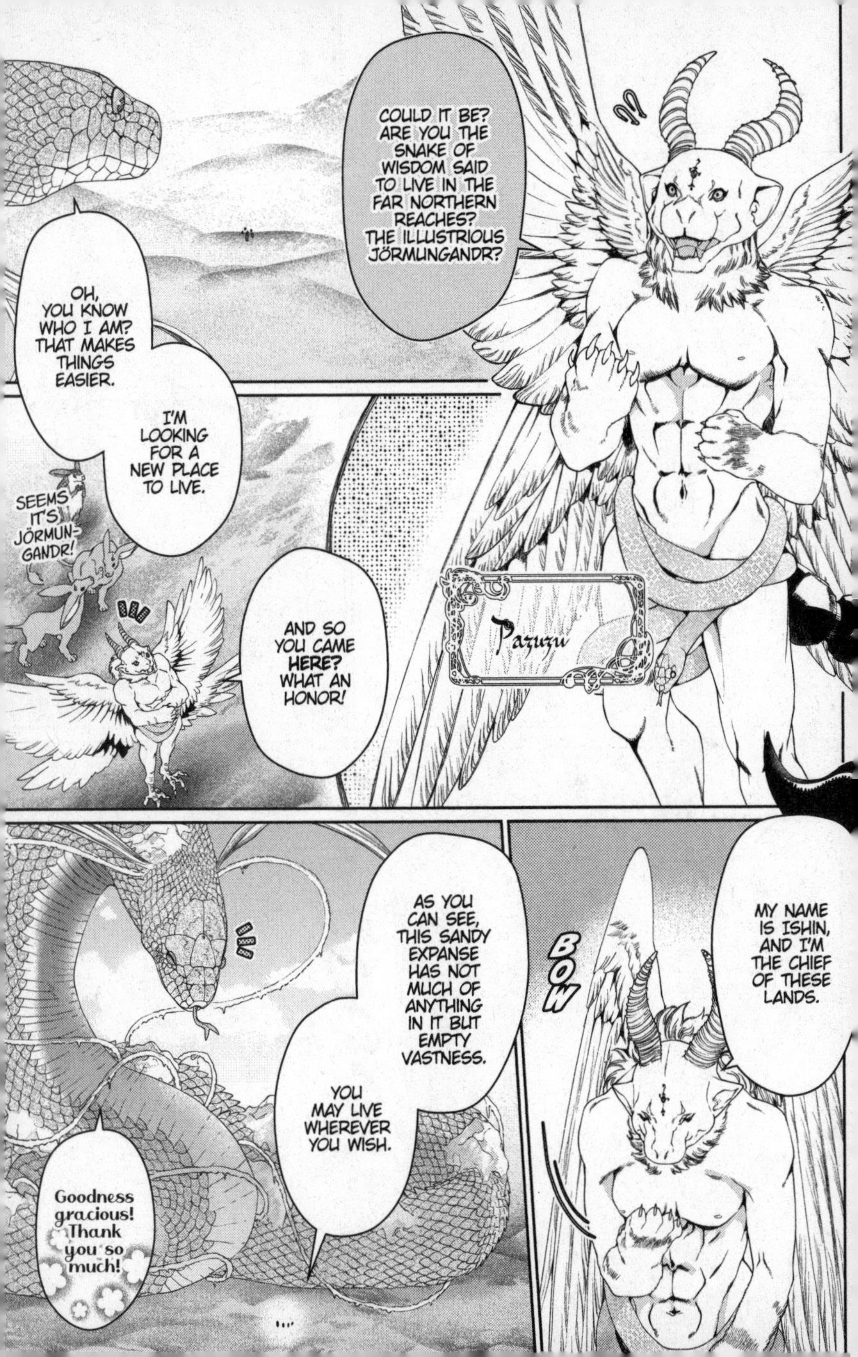
COULD IT BE? ARE YOU THE SNAKE OF WISDOM SAID TO LIVE IN THE FAR NORTHERN REACHES? THE ILLUSTRIOUS JÖRMUNGANDR?
OH, YOU KNOW WHO I AM? THAT MAKES THINGS EASIER.
I'M LOOKING FOR A NEW PLACE TO LIVE.
Pazuzu
AND SO YOU CAME HERE? WHAT AN HONOR!
SEEMS IT'S JÖRMUNGANDR!
BOW
MY NAME IS ISHIN, AND I'M THE CHIEF OF THESE LANDS.
AS YOU CAN SEE, THIS SANDY EXPANSE HAS NOT MUCH OF ANYTHING IN IT BUT EMPTY VASTNESS.
YOU MAY LIVE WHEREVER YOU WISH.
Goodness gracious! Thank you so much!

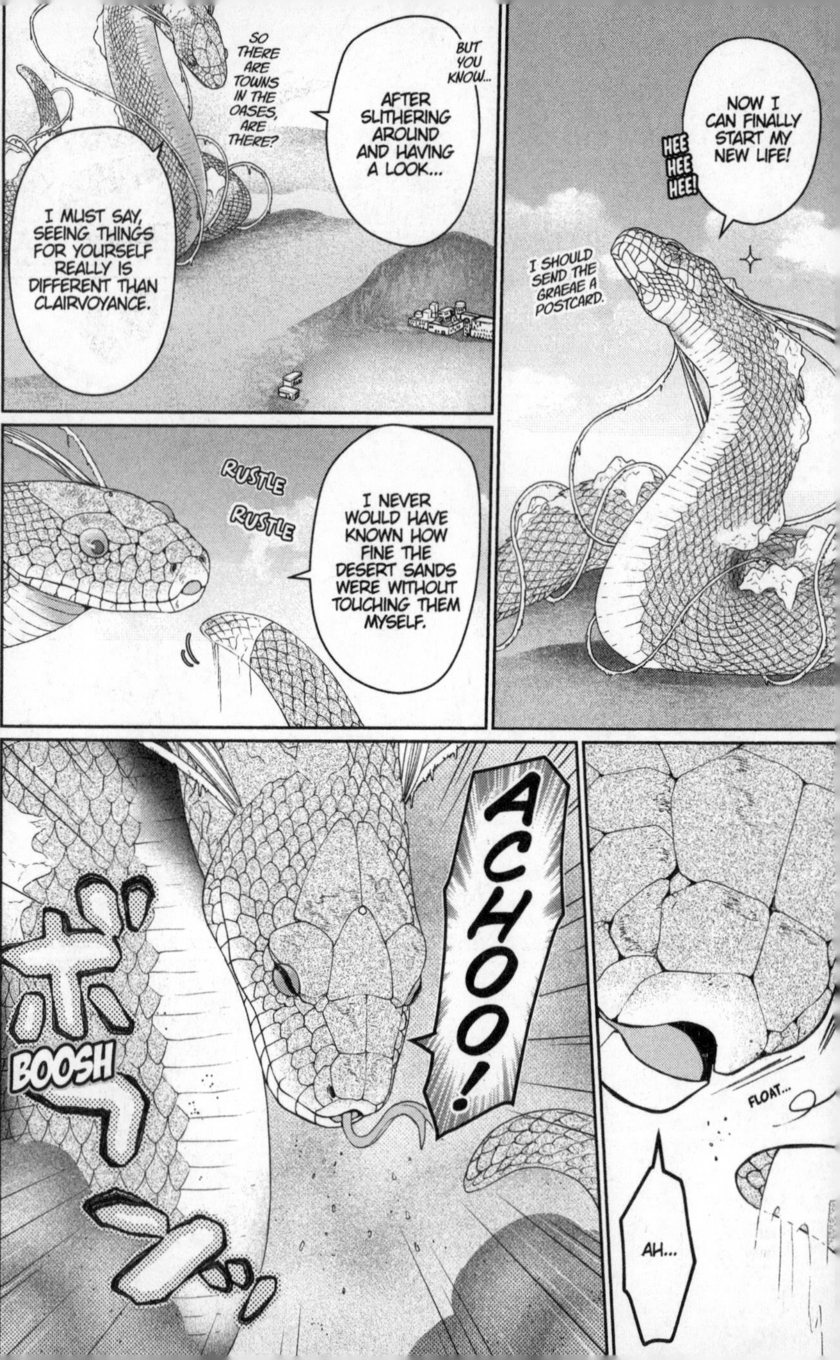

NOW I CAN FINALLY START MY NEW LIFE!
HEE HEE HEE!
I SHOULD SEND THE GRAEAE A POSTCARD.
BUT YOU KNOW...
AFTER SLITHERING AROUND AND HAVING A LOOK...
SO THERE ARE TOWNS IN THE OASES, ARE THERE?
I MUST SAY, SEEING THINGS FOR YOURSELF REALLY IS DIFFERENT THAN CLAIRVOYANCE.
I NEVER WOULD HAVE KNOWN HOW FINE THE DESERT SANDS WERE WITHOUT TOUCHING THEM MYSELF.
RUSTLE
RUSTLE
FLOAT...
AH...
ACHOO!
BOOSH

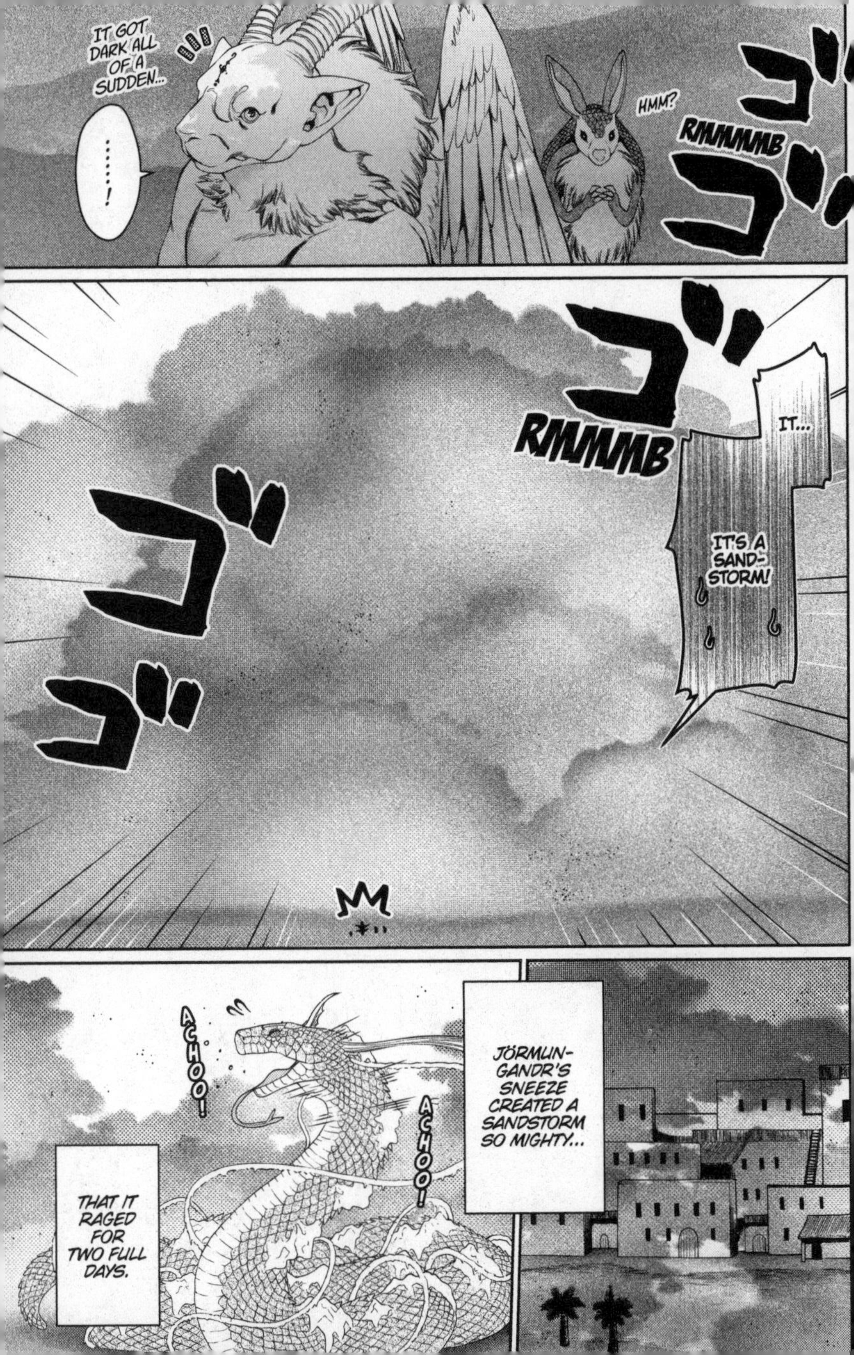
RMMMMB
HMM?
IT GOT DARK ALL OF A SUDDEN...
......!
RMMMMB
IT...
IT'S A SANDSTORM!
JÖRMUNGANDR'S SNEEZE CREATED A SANDSTORM SO MIGHTY...
ACHOO!
ACHOO!
THAT IT RAGED FOR TWO FULL DAYS.

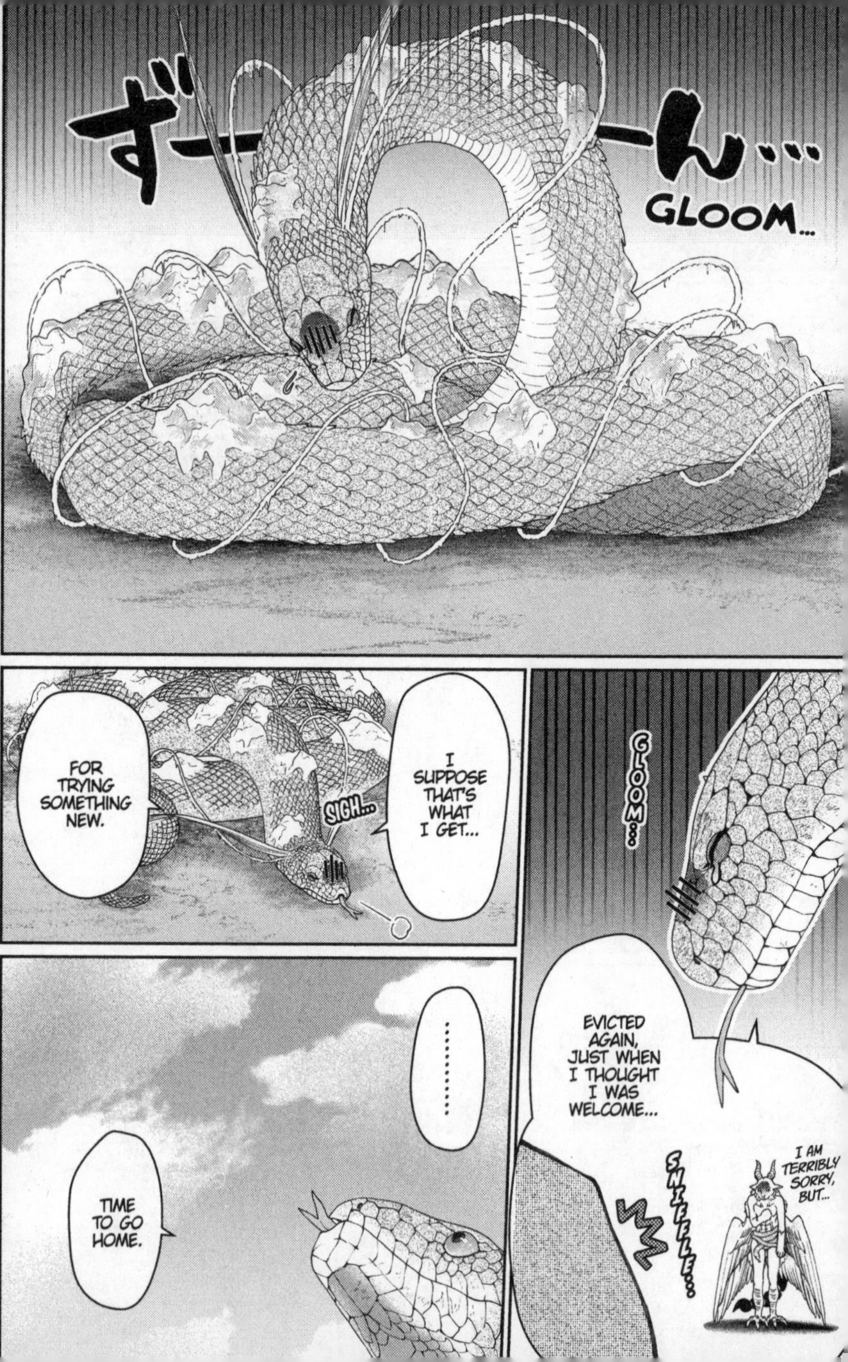
ずーーん…
GLOOM...
GLOOM...
EVICTED AGAIN, JUST WHEN I THOUGHT I WAS WELCOME...
SNIFFLE...
I AM TERRIBLY SORRY, BUT...
I SUPPOSE THAT'S WHAT I GET...
SIGH...
FOR TRYING SOMETHING NEW.
......
TIME TO GO HOME.

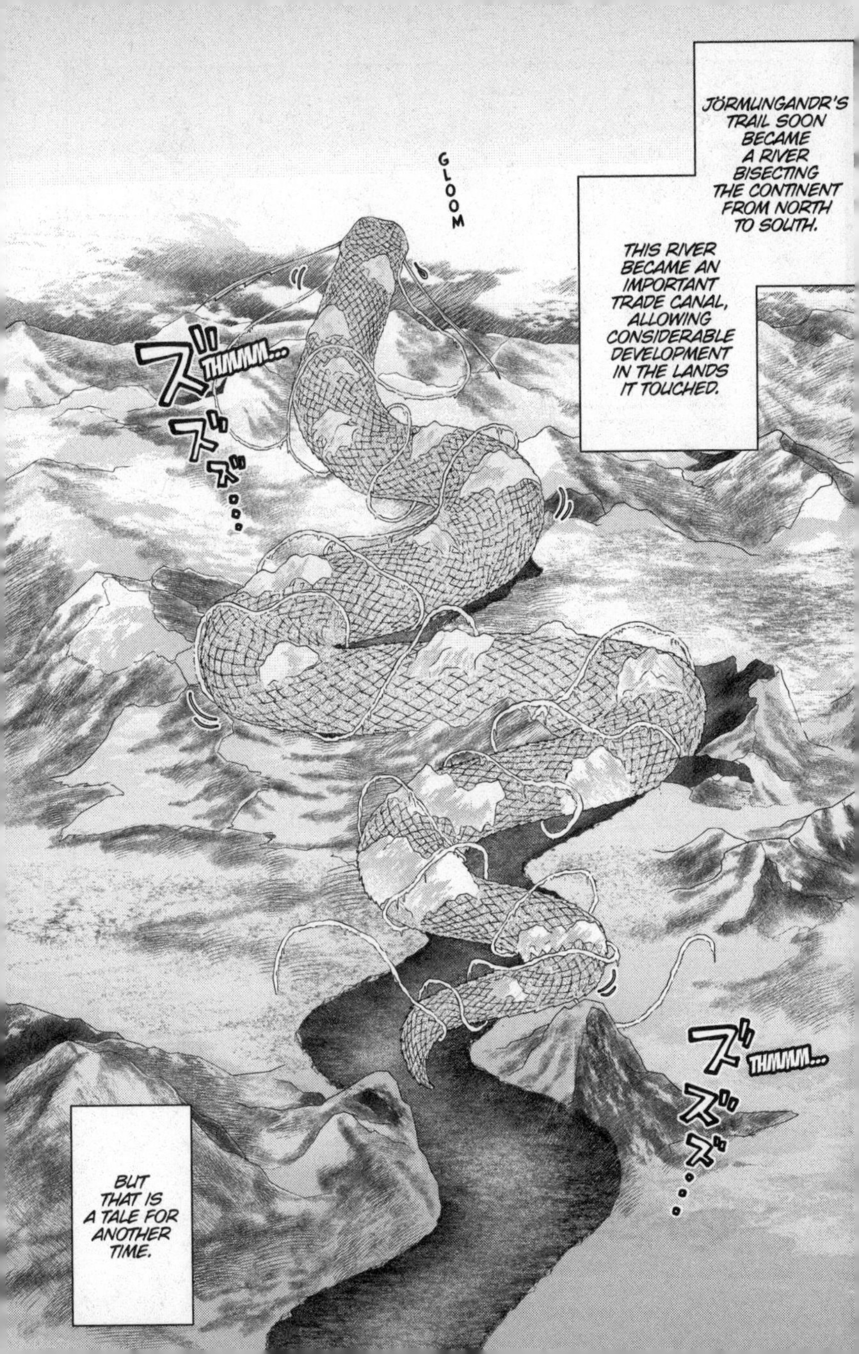
JÖRMUNGANDR'S TRAIL SOON BECAME A RIVER BISECTING THE CONTINENT FROM NORTH TO SOUTH.
THIS RIVER BECAME AN IMPORTANT TRADE CANAL, ALLOWING CONSIDERABLE DEVELOPMENT IN THE LANDS IT TOUCHED.
GLOOM
ズ THMMM...
ズズ...
ズ THMMM...
ズズ...
BUT THAT IS A TALE FOR ANOTHER TIME.

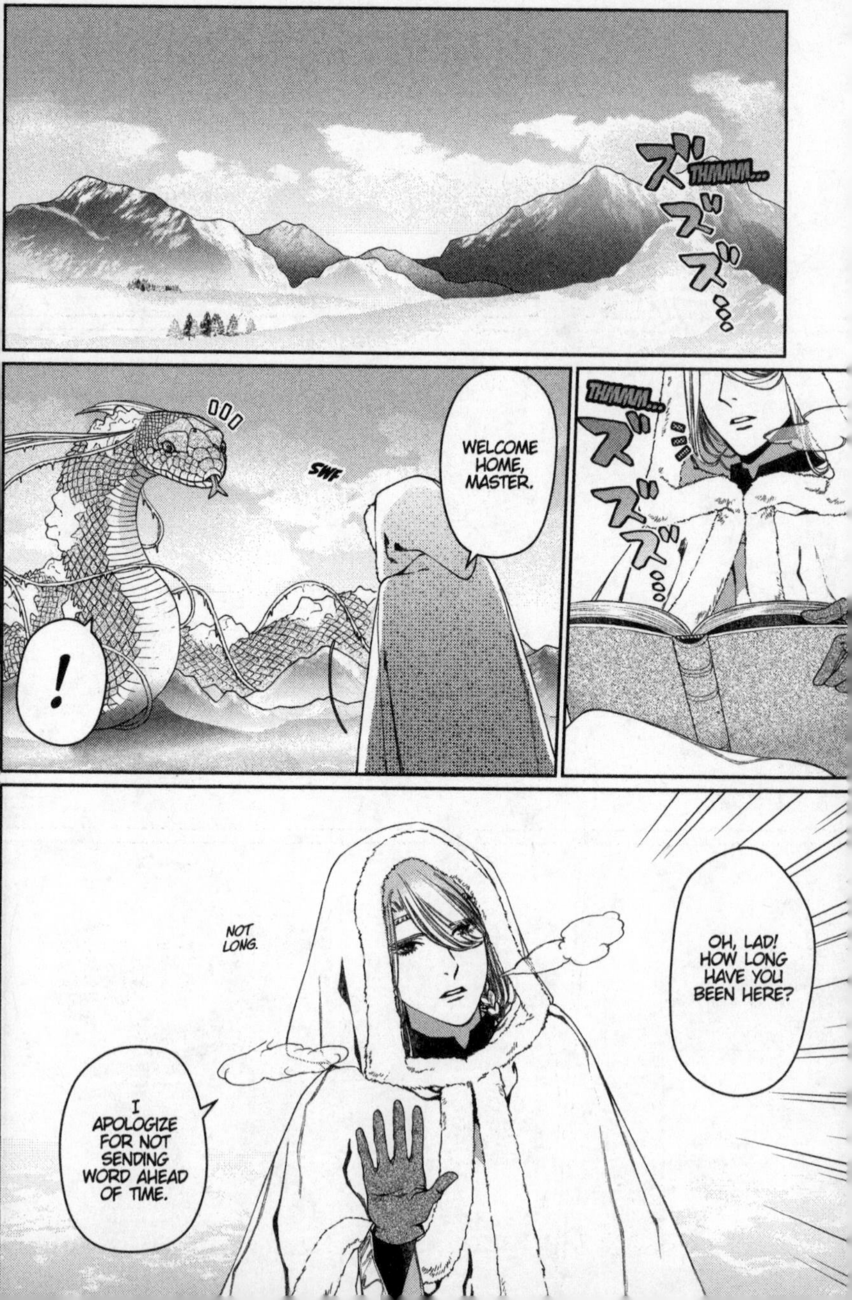
THMMM...
THMMM...
WELCOME HOME, MASTER.
SWF
!
OH, LAD! HOW LONG HAVE YOU BEEN HERE?
NOT LONG.
I APOLOGIZE FOR NOT SENDING WORD AHEAD OF TIME.

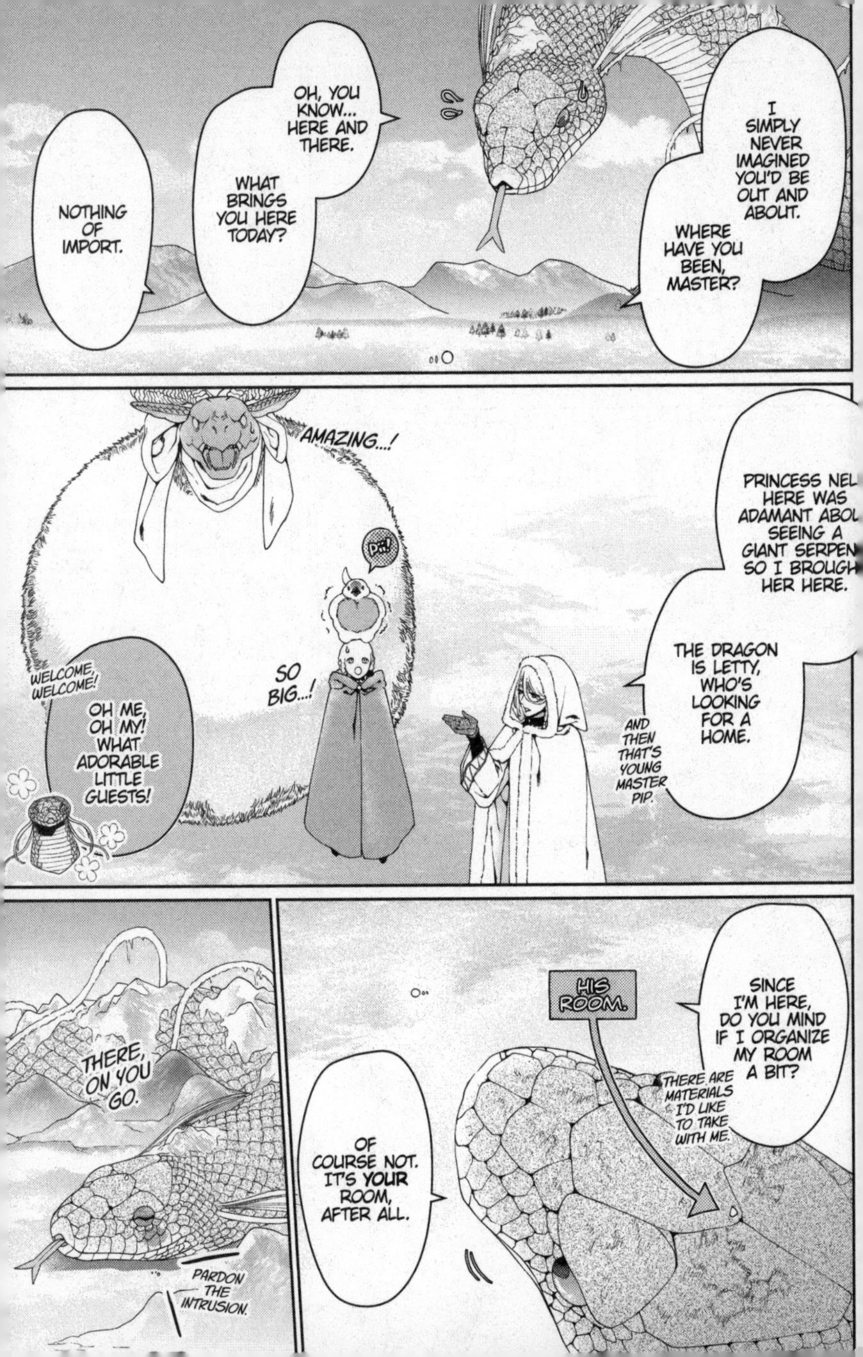
I SIMPLY NEVER IMAGINED YOU'D BE OUT AND ABOUT.
WHERE HAVE YOU BEEN, MASTER?
OH, YOU KNOW... HERE AND THERE.
WHAT BRINGS YOU HERE TODAY?
NOTHING OF IMPORT.
PRINCESS NEL HERE WAS ADAMANT ABOL SEEING A GIANT SERPEN SO I BROUGH HER HERE.
THE DRAGON IS LETTY, WHO'S LOOKING FOR A HOME.
AND THEN THAT'S YOUNG MASTER PIP.
AMAZING...!
SO BIG...!
OH ME, OH MY! WHAT ADORABLE LITTLE GUESTS!
WELCOME, WELCOME!
SINCE I'M HERE, DO YOU MIND IF I ORGANIZE MY ROOM A BIT?
THERE ARE MATERIALS I'D LIKE TO TAKE WITH ME.
HIS ROOM.
OF COURSE NOT. IT'S YOUR ROOM, AFTER ALL.
THERE, ON YOU GO.
PARDON THE INTRUSION.

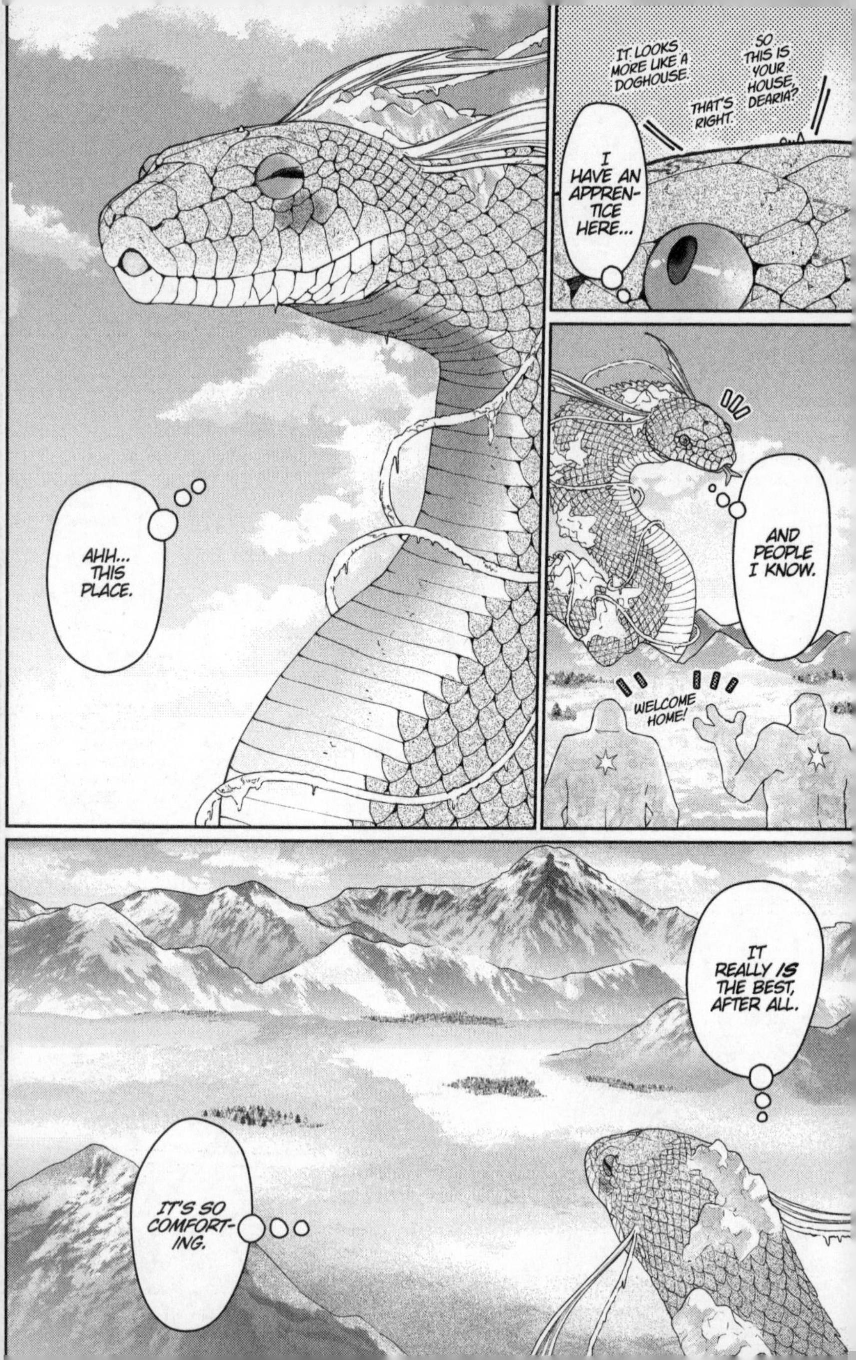
SO THIS IS YOUR HOUSE, DEARIA?
THAT'S RIGHT.
IT LOOKS MORE LIKE A DOGHOUSE.
I HAVE AN APPRENTICE HERE...
AND PEOPLE I KNOW.
WELCOME HOME!
AHH... THIS PLACE.
IT REALLY *IS* THE BEST, AFTER ALL.
IT'S SO COMFORTING.

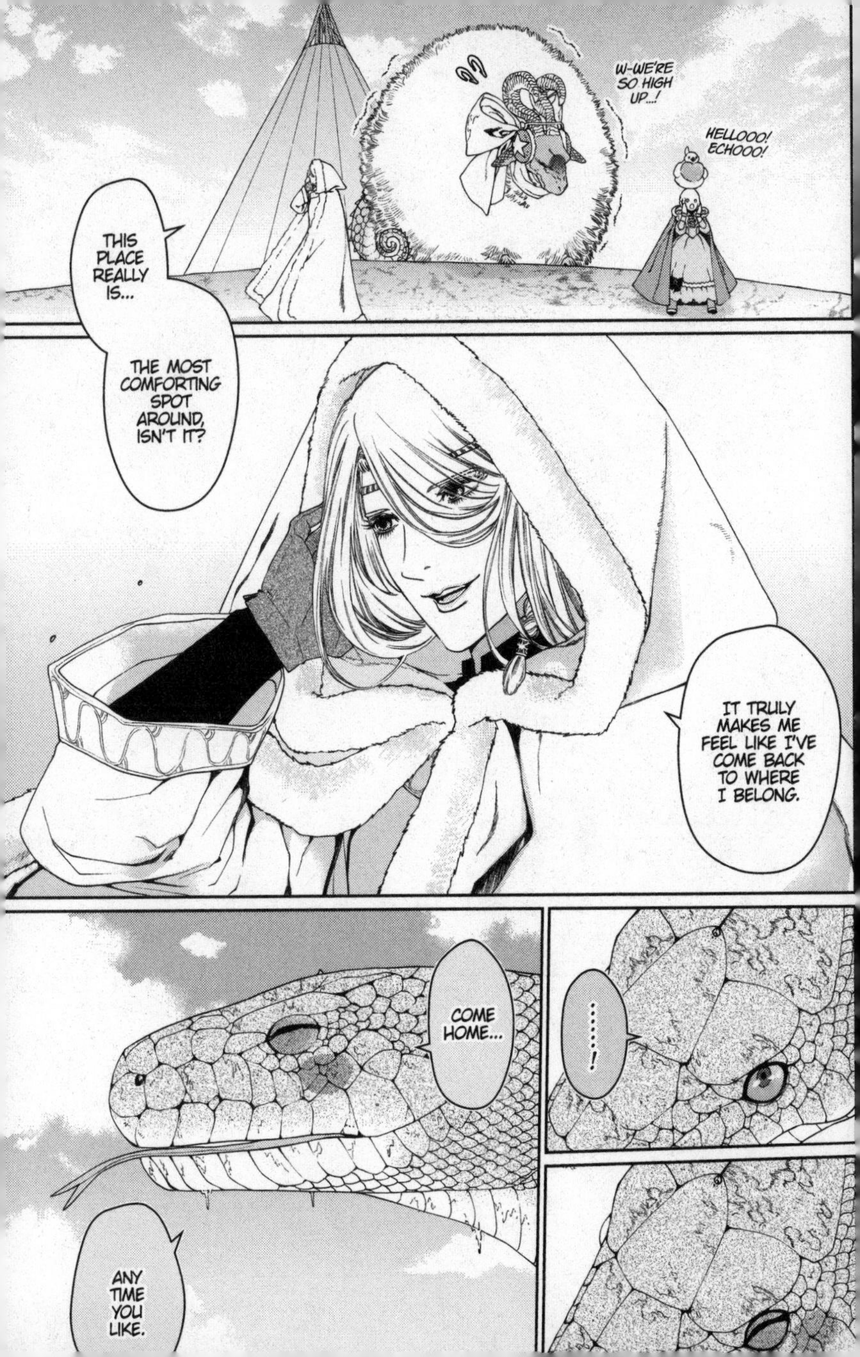
HELLOOO! ECHOOO!
W-WE'RE SO HIGH UP...!
THIS PLACE REALLY IS...
THE MOST COMFORTING SPOT AROUND, ISN'T IT?
IT TRULY MAKES ME FEEL LIKE I'VE COME BACK TO WHERE I BELONG.
......!
COME HOME...
ANY TIME YOU LIKE.

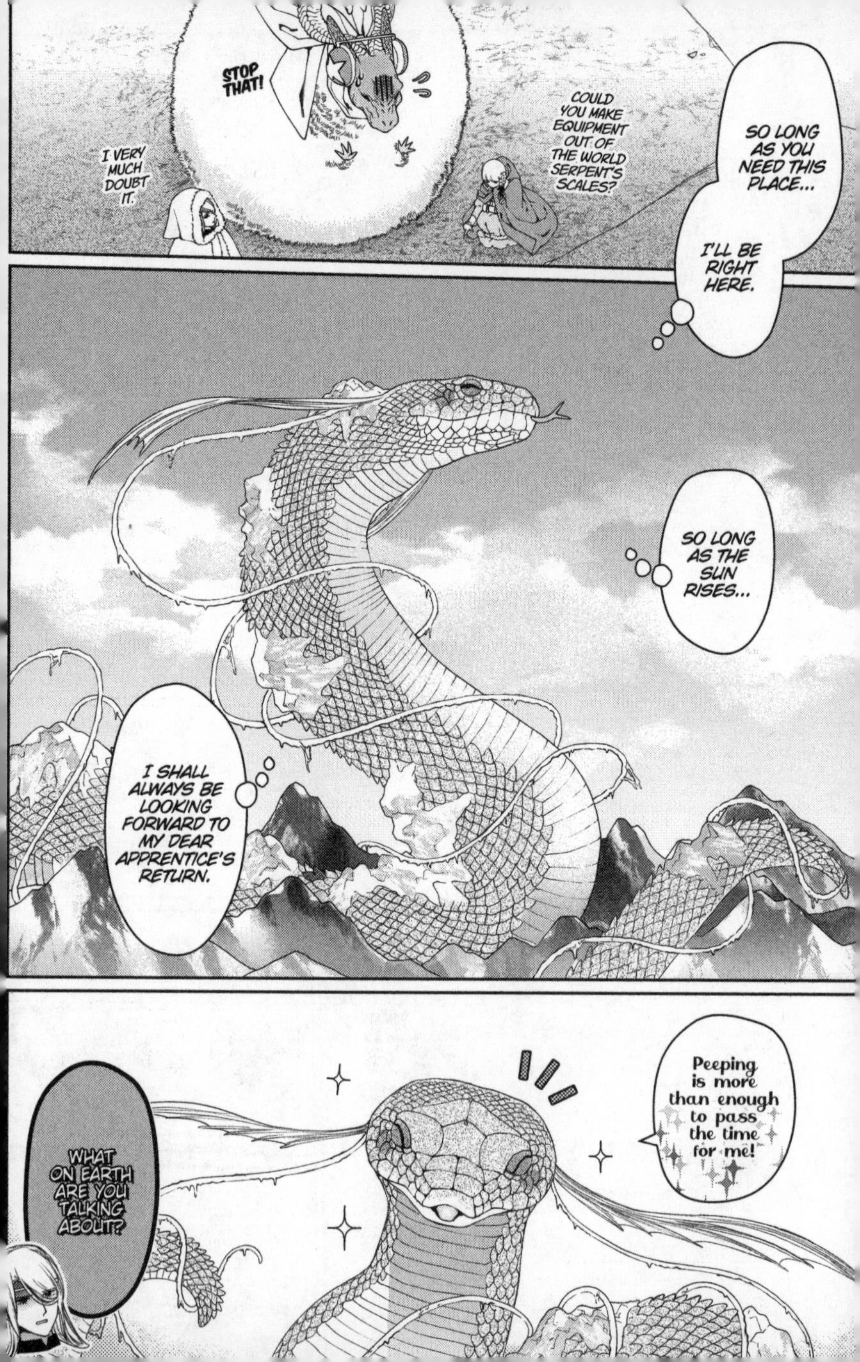
COULD YOU MAKE EQUIPMENT OUT OF THE WORLD SERPENT'S SCALES?
STOP THAT!
I VERY MUCH DOUBT IT.
SO LONG AS YOU NEED THIS PLACE...
I'LL BE RIGHT HERE.
SO LONG AS THE SUN RISES...
I SHALL ALWAYS BE LOOKING FORWARD TO MY DEAR APPRENTICE'S RETURN.
Peeping is more than enough to pass the time for me!
WHAT ON EARTH ARE YOU TALKING ABOUT?

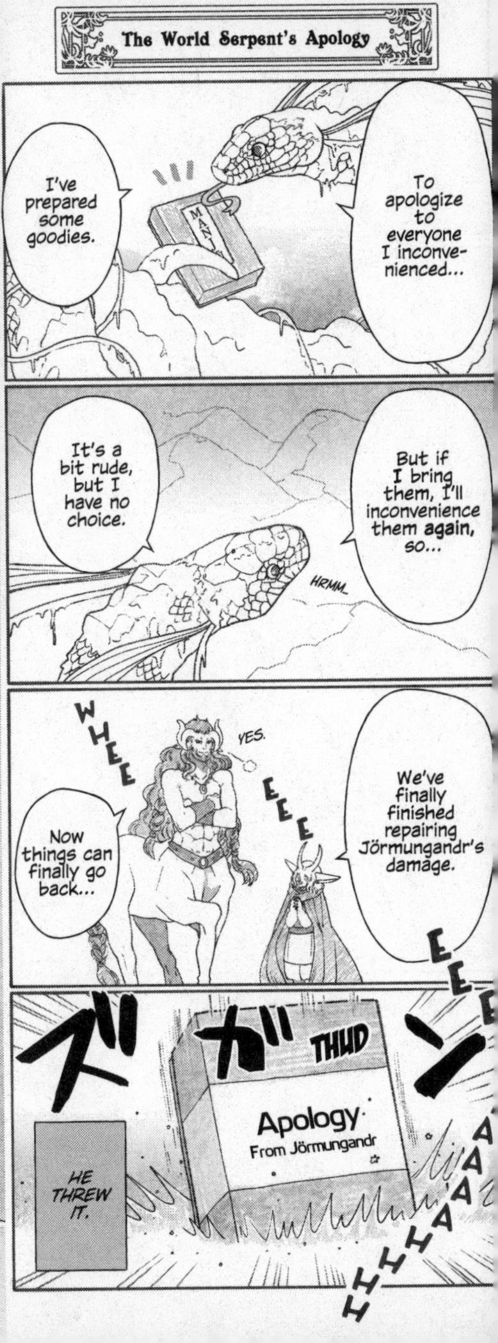
The World Serpent's Apology
To apologize to everyone I inconvenienced...
I've prepared some goodies.
MANJU
But if I bring them, I'll inconvenience them again, so...
HRMM
It's a bit rude, but I have no choice.
We've finally finished repairing Jörmungandr's damage.
YES.
Now things can finally go back...
WHEEE
EEE
EEE
ズガーン
THUD
Apology
From Jörmungandr
AAAAAHHHHHH
HE THREW IT.
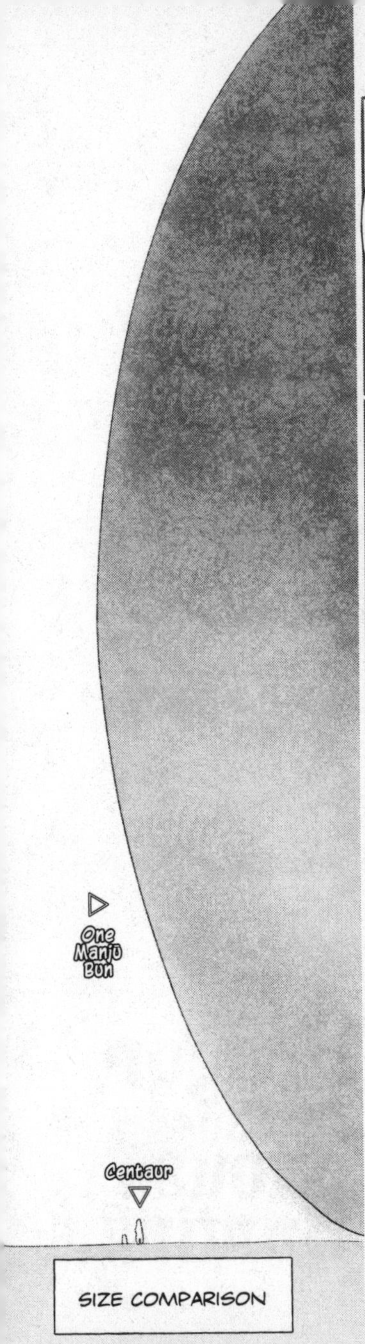
One Manjū Bun
Centaur
SIZE COMPARISON

Dragon
Goes
House-
Hunting

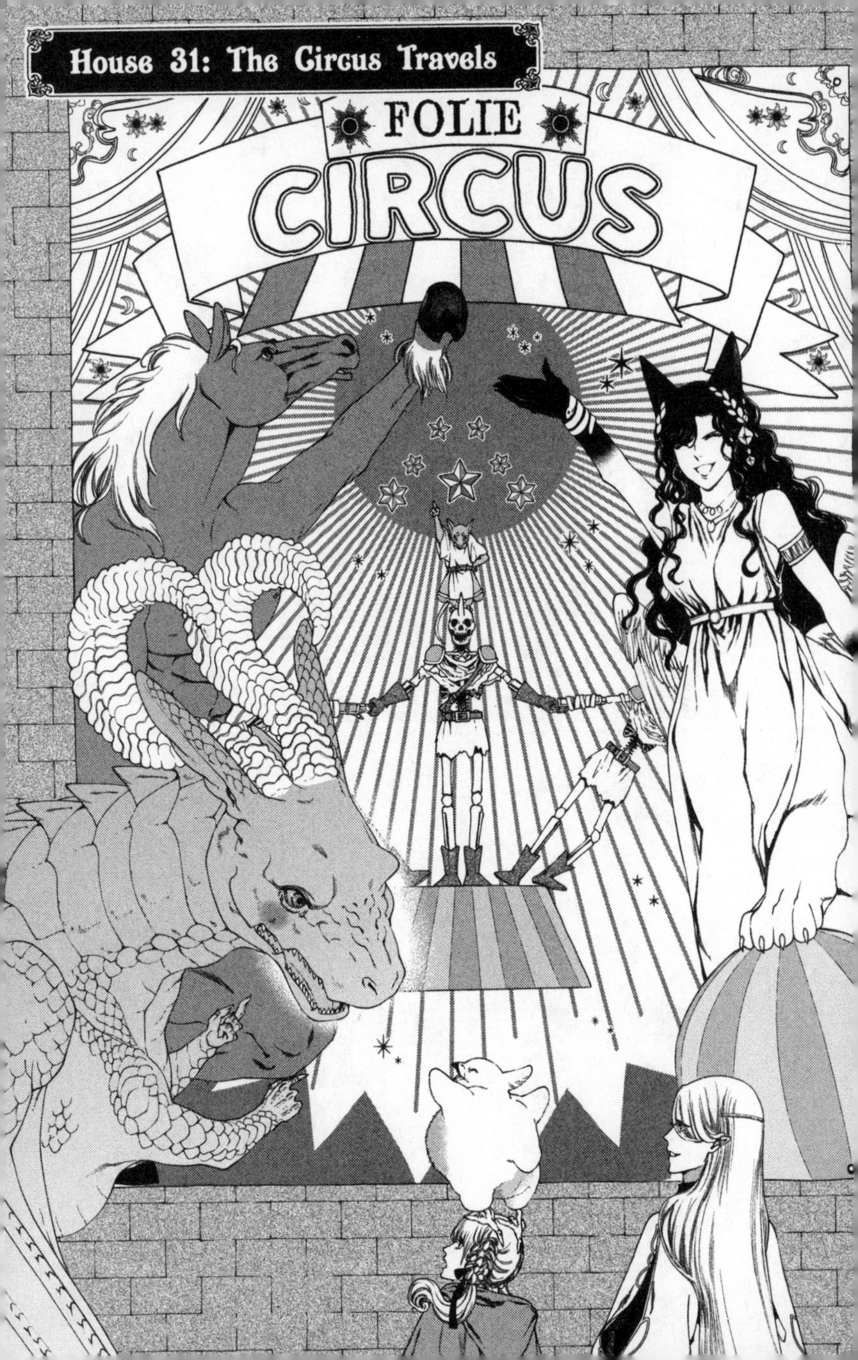
House 31: The Circus Travels
FOLIE
CIRCUS

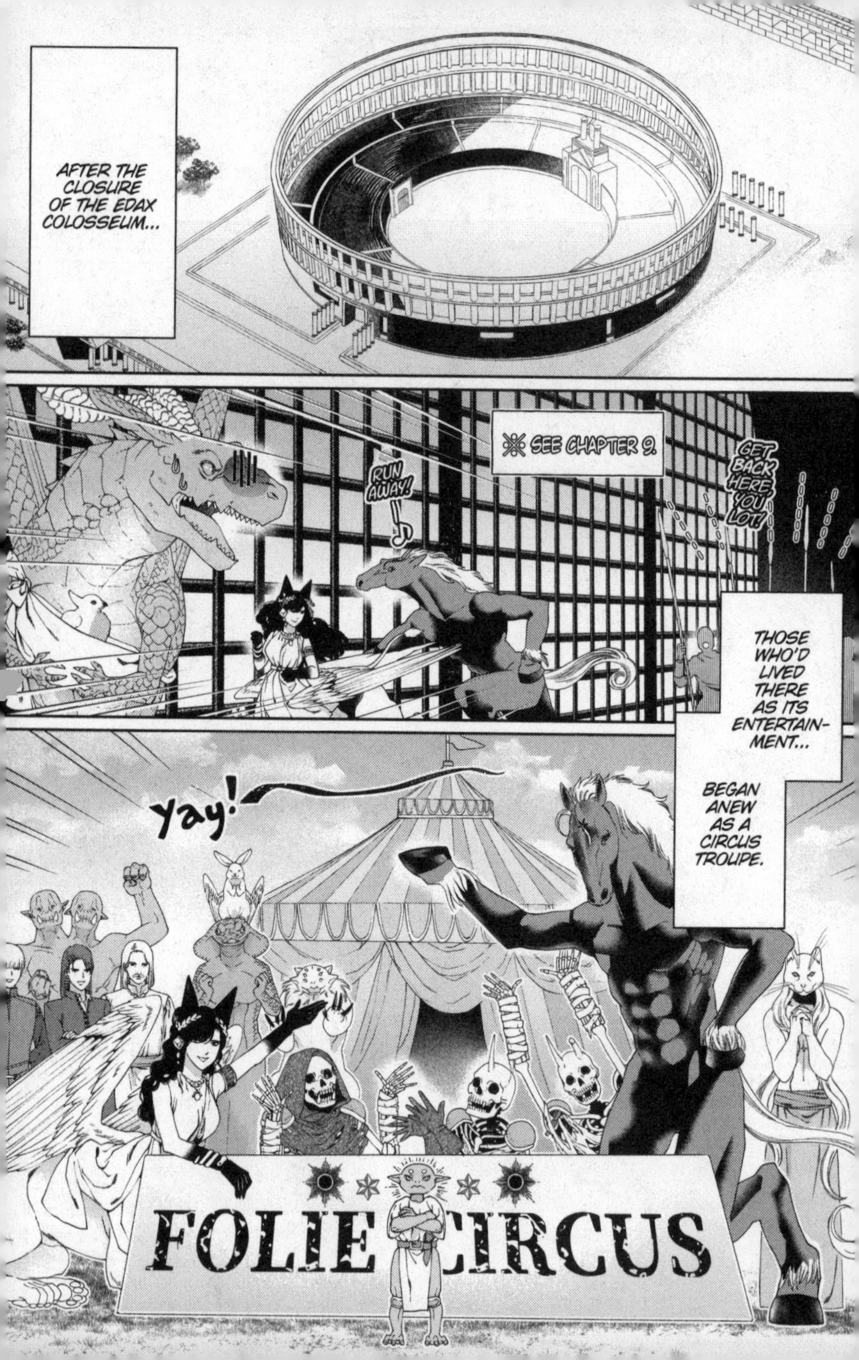
AFTER THE CLOSURE OF THE EDAX COLOSSEUM...
GET BACK HERE, YOU LOT!
※ SEE CHAPTER 9.
RUN AWAY!
THOSE WHO'D LIVED THERE AS ITS ENTERTAINMENT...
BEGAN ANEW AS A CIRCUS TROUPE.
yay!
FOLIE CIRCUS

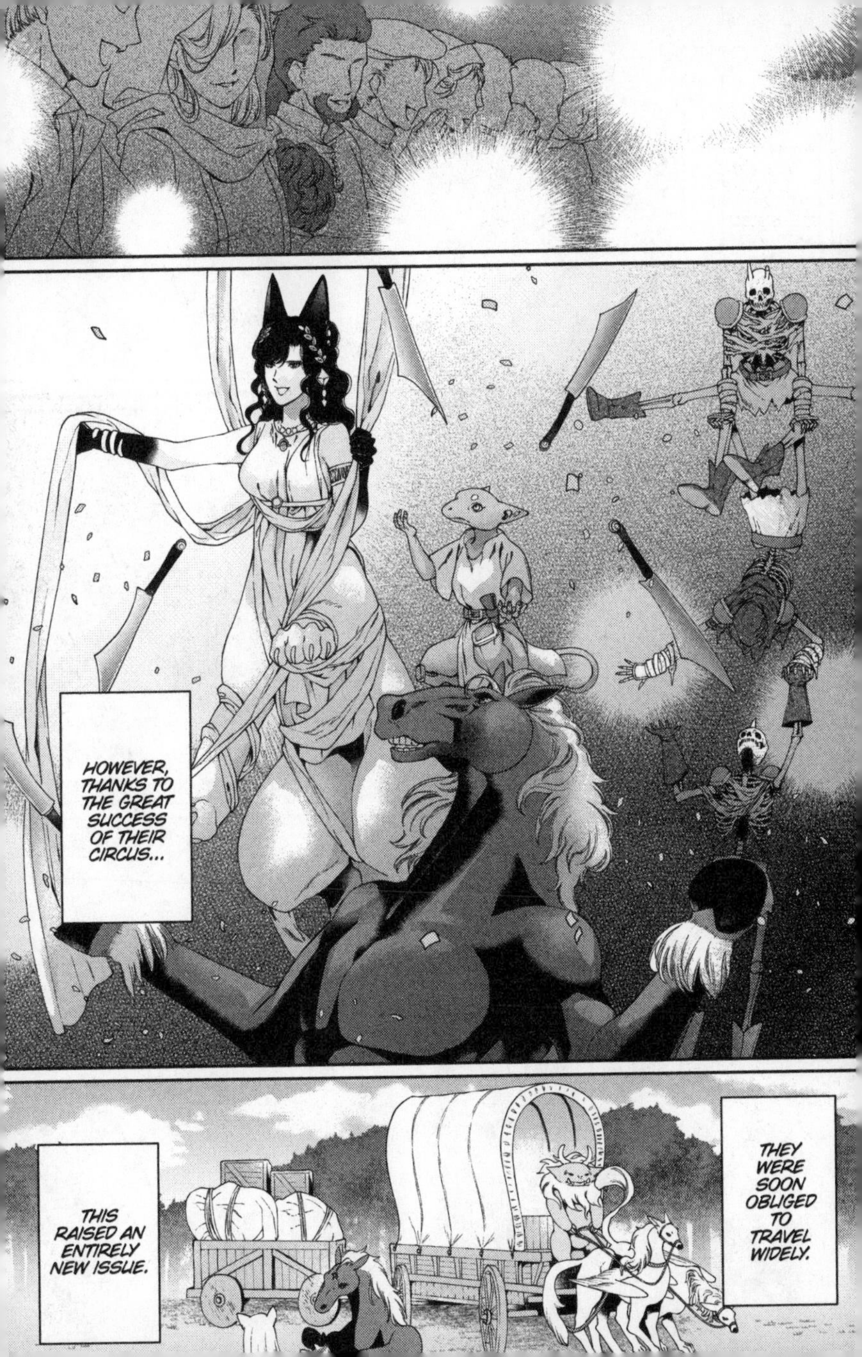
HOWEVER, THANKS TO THE GREAT SUCCESS OF THEIR CIRCUS...
THEY WERE SOON OBLIGED TO TRAVEL WIDELY.
THIS RAISED AN ENTIRELY NEW ISSUE.

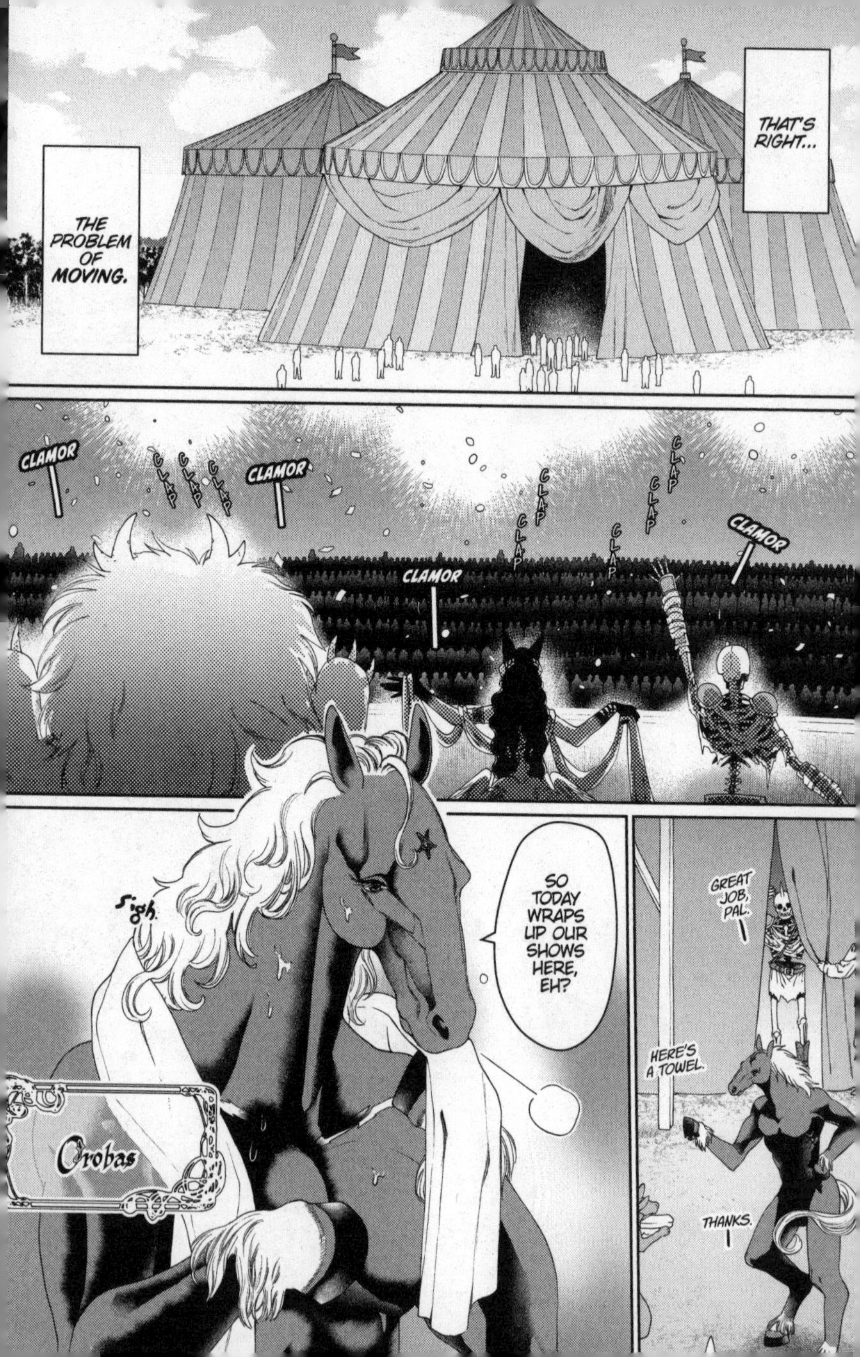
THAT'S RIGHT...
THE PROBLEM OF MOVING.
CLAP
CLAP
CLAMOR
CLAP
CLAP
CLAP
CLAMOR
CLAMOR
CLAP
CLAP
CLAP
CLAMOR
GREAT JOB, PAL.
HERE'S A TOWEL.
THANKS.
SO TODAY WRAPS UP OUR SHOWS HERE, EH?
Sigh.
Orobas

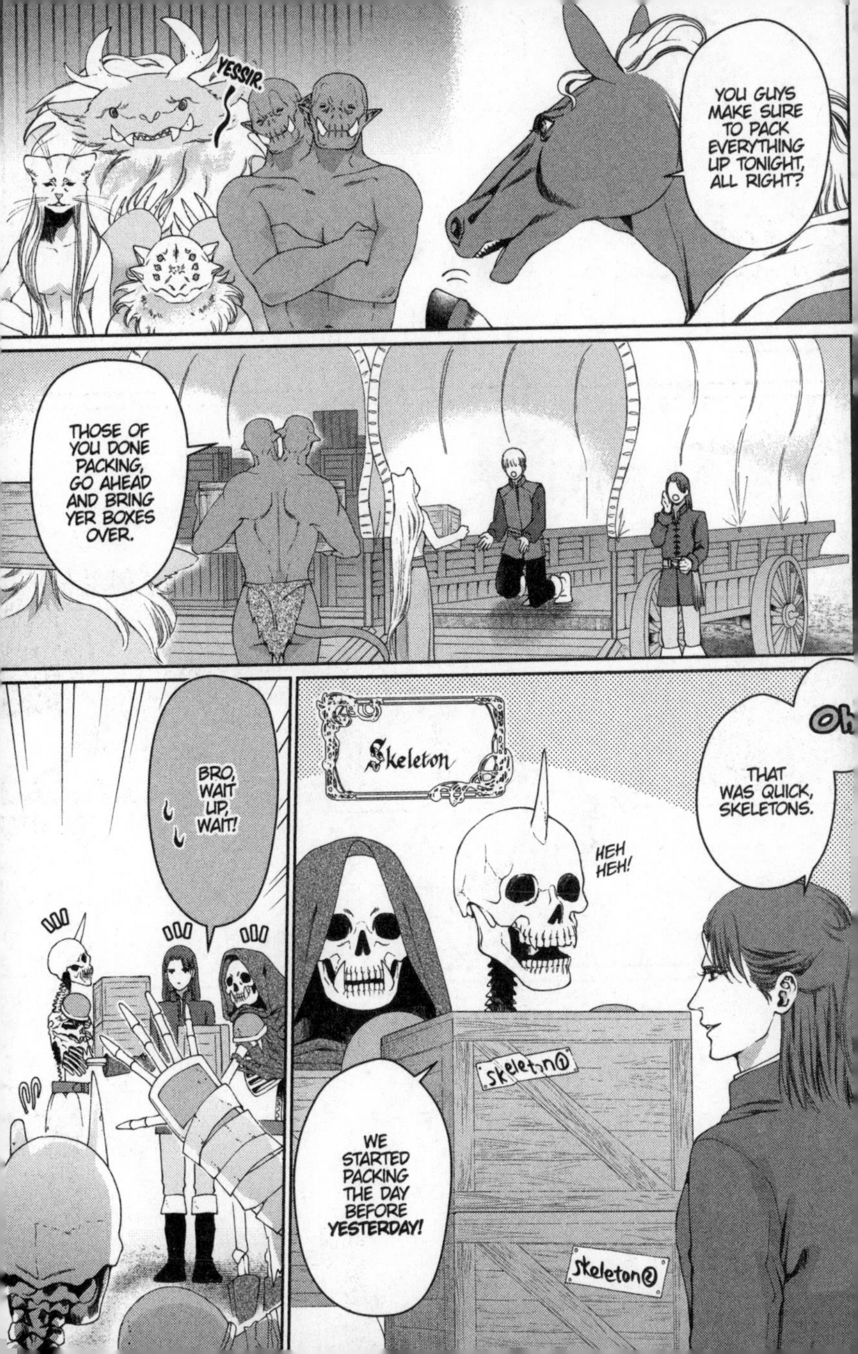
YOU GUYS MAKE SURE TO PACK EVERYTHING UP TONIGHT, ALL RIGHT?
YESSIR.
THOSE OF YOU DONE PACKING, GO AHEAD AND BRING YER BOXES OVER.
Oh
THAT WAS QUICK, SKELETONS.
Skeleton
HEH HEH!
WE STARTED PACKING THE DAY BEFORE YESTERDAY!
skeleton①
skeleton②
BRO, WAIT UP, WAIT!

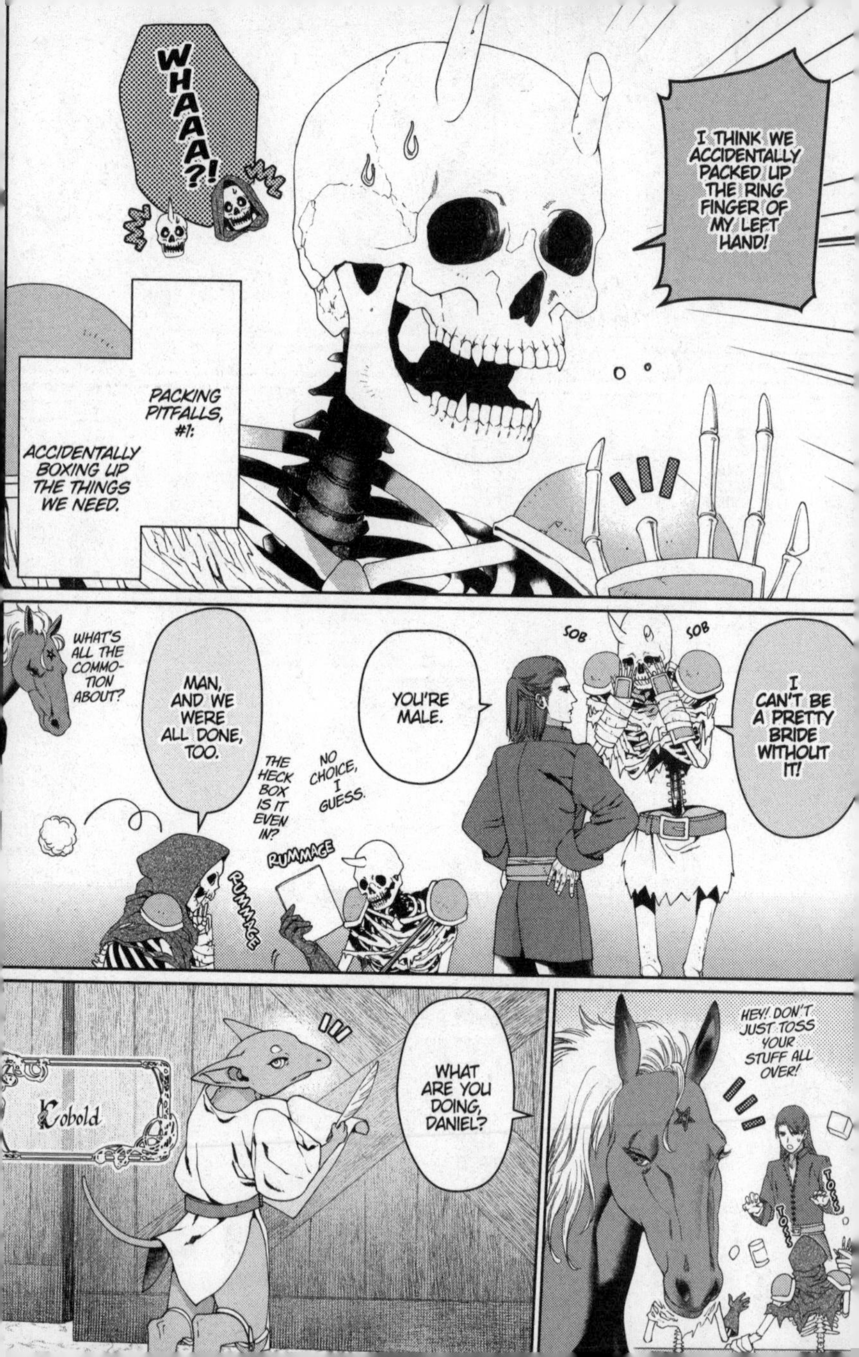

I THINK WE ACCIDENTALLY PACKED UP THE RING FINGER OF MY LEFT HAND!
WHAAA?!
PACKING PITFALLS, #1:
ACCIDENTALLY BOXING UP THE THINGS WE NEED.
I CAN'T BE A PRETTY BRIDE WITHOUT IT!
SOB
SOB
YOU'RE MALE.
NO CHOICE, I GUESS.
THE HECK BOX IS IT EVEN IN?
RUMMAGE
RUMMAGE
MAN, AND WE WERE ALL DONE, TOO.
WHAT'S ALL THE COMMOTION ABOUT?
HEY! DON'T JUST TOSS YOUR STUFF ALL OVER!
TOSS
TOSS
WHAT ARE YOU DOING, DANIEL?
Kobold

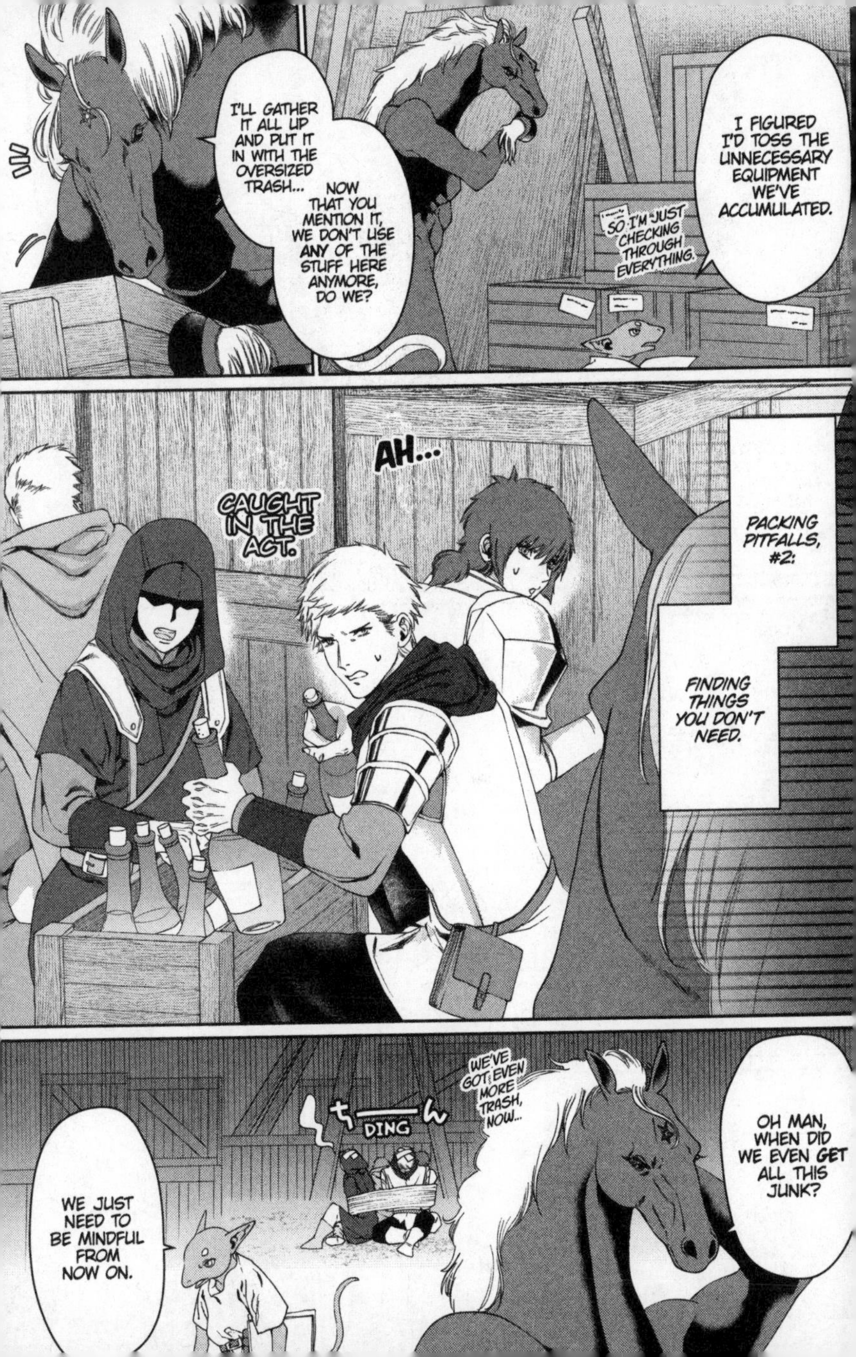
I FIGURED I'D TOSS THE UNNECESSARY EQUIPMENT WE'VE ACCUMULATED.
SO I'M JUST CHECKING THROUGH EVERYTHING.
I'LL GATHER IT ALL UP AND PUT IT IN WITH THE OVERSIZED TRASH...
NOW THAT YOU MENTION IT, WE DON'T USE ANY OF THE STUFF HERE ANYMORE, DO WE?
PACKING PITFALLS, #2:
FINDING THINGS YOU DON'T NEED.
AH...
CAUGHT IN THE ACT.
OH MAN, WHEN DID WE EVEN GET ALL THIS JUNK?
WE'VE GOT EVEN MORE TRASH, NOW...
ち——ん
DING
WE JUST NEED TO BE MINDFUL FROM NOW ON.

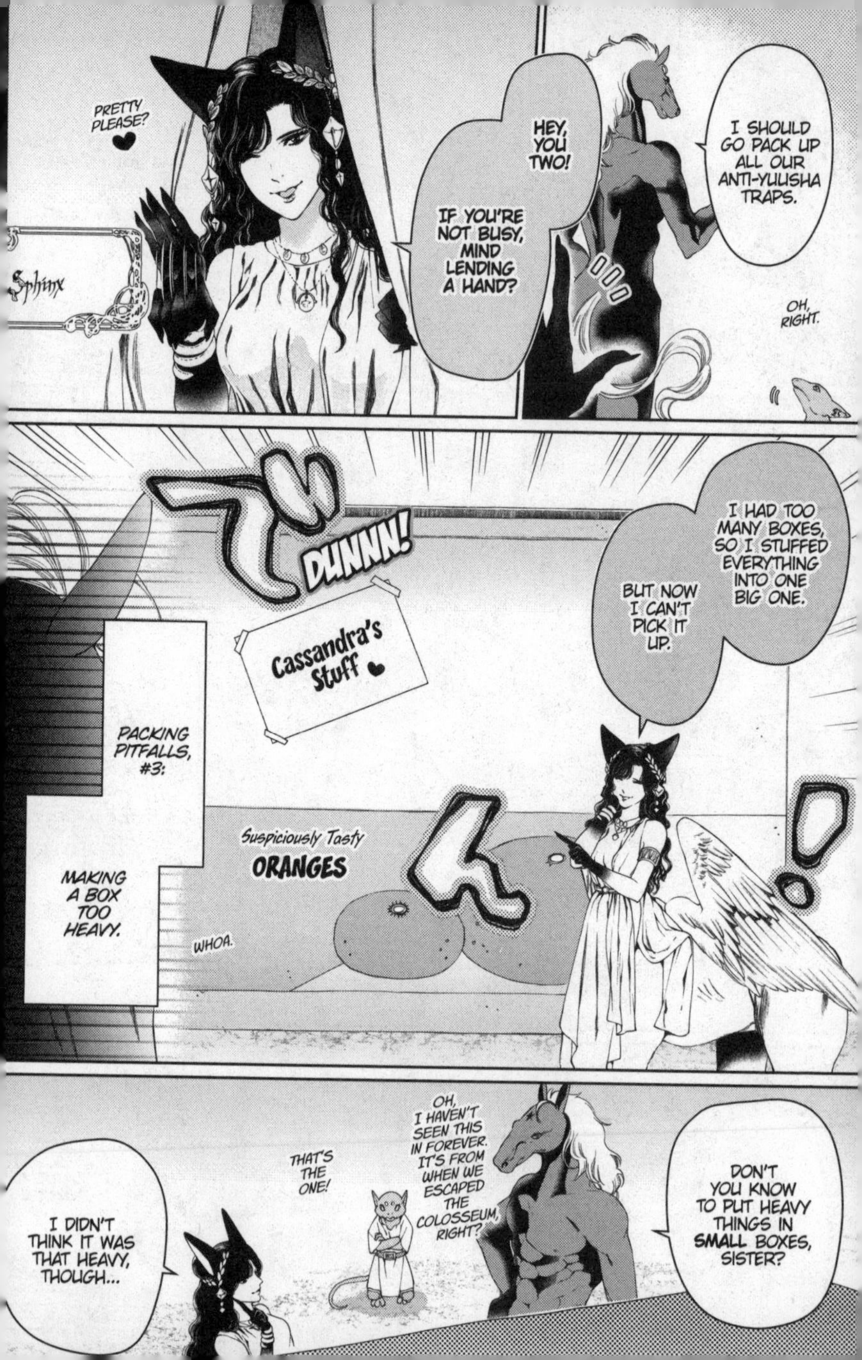
I SHOULD GO PACK UP ALL OUR ANTI-YUUSHA TRAPS.
OH, RIGHT.
HEY, YOU TWO!
IF YOU'RE NOT BUSY, MIND LENDING A HAND?
PRETTY PLEASE?
Sphinx
I HAD TOO MANY BOXES, SO I STUFFED EVERYTHING INTO ONE BIG ONE.
BUT NOW I CAN'T PICK IT UP.
DUNNN!
Cassandra's Stuff
Suspiciously Tasty ORANGES
WHOA.
PACKING PITFALLS, #3:
MAKING A BOX TOO HEAVY.
DON'T YOU KNOW TO PUT HEAVY THINGS IN SMALL BOXES, SISTER?
OH, I HAVEN'T SEEN THIS IN FOREVER. IT'S FROM WHEN WE ESCAPED THE COLOSSEUM, RIGHT?
THAT'S THE ONE!
I DIDN'T THINK IT WAS THAT HEAVY, THOUGH...

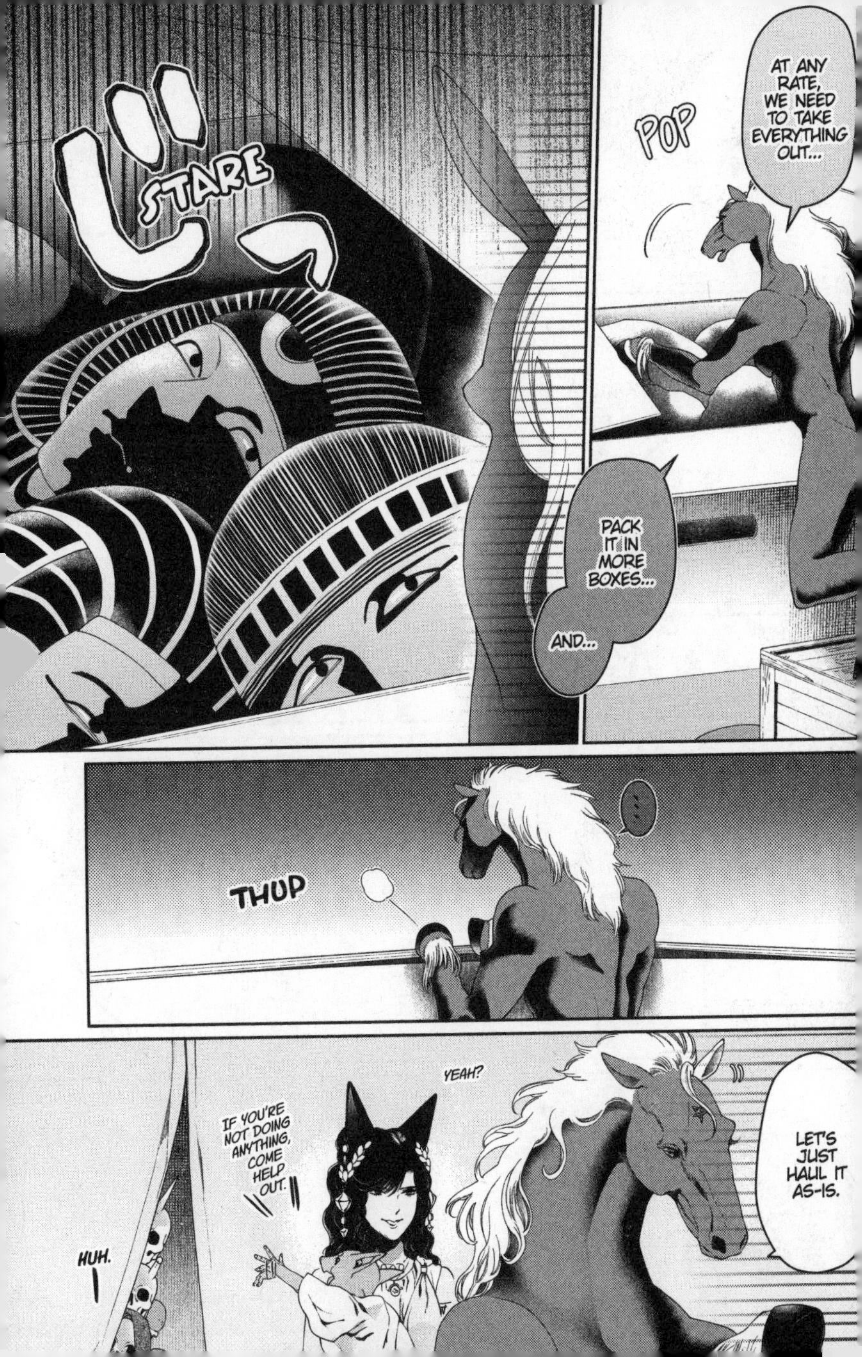
POP
AT ANY RATE, WE NEED TO TAKE EVERYTHING OUT...
PACK IT IN MORE BOXES...
AND...
STARE
...
THUP
LET'S JUST HAUL IT AS-IS.
YEAH?
IF YOU'RE NOT DOING ANYTHING, COME HELP OUT.
HUH.

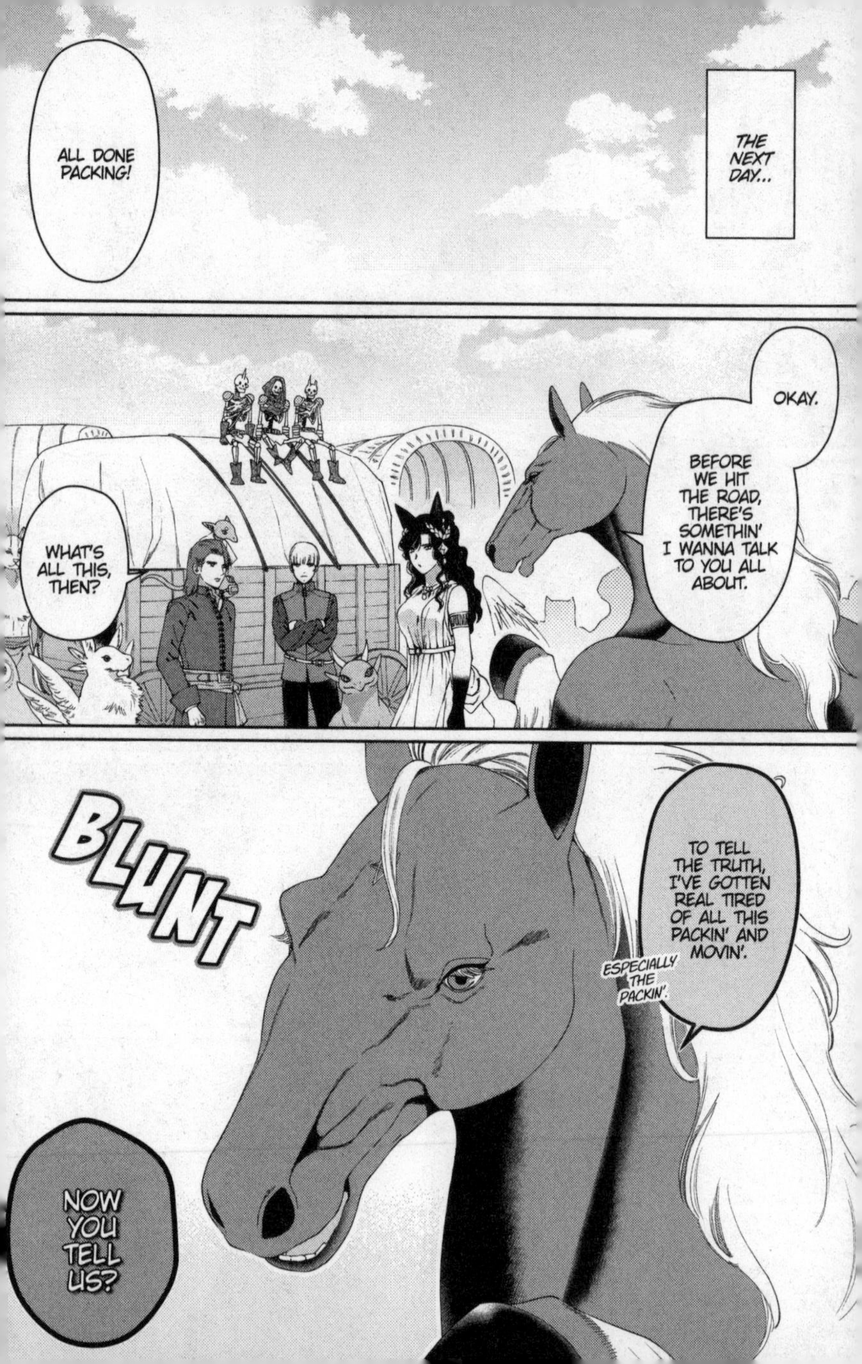
THE NEXT DAY...
ALL DONE PACKING!
OKAY.
BEFORE WE HIT THE ROAD, THERE'S SOMETHIN' I WANNA TALK TO YOU ALL ABOUT.
WHAT'S ALL THIS, THEN?
TO TELL THE TRUTH, I'VE GOTTEN REAL TIRED OF ALL THIS PACKIN' AND MOVIN'.
ESPECIALLY THE PACKIN'.
BLUNT
NOW YOU TELL US?

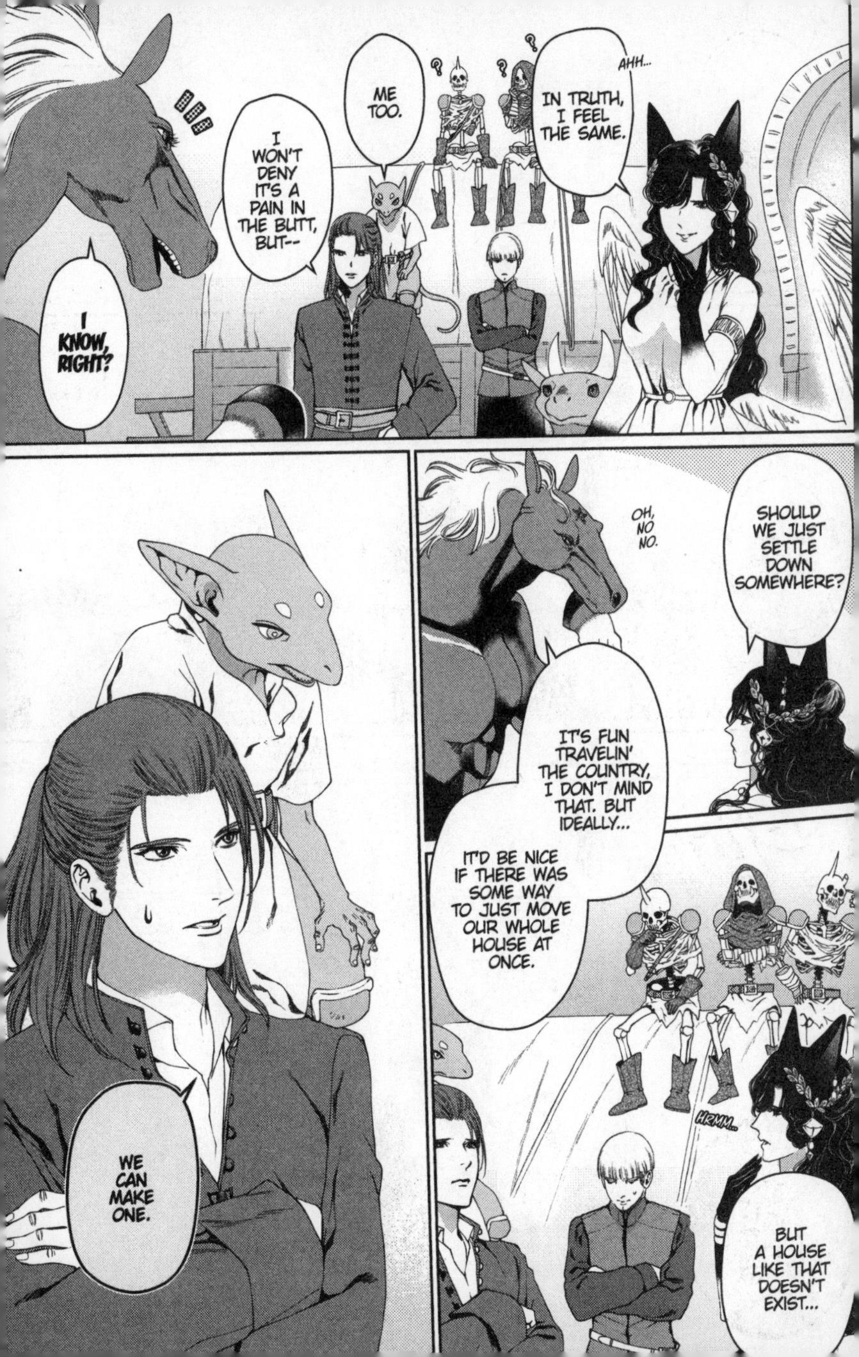
AHH...
IN TRUTH, I FEEL THE SAME.
ME TOO.
I WON'T DENY IT'S A PAIN IN THE BUTT, BUT--
I KNOW, RIGHT?
SHOULD WE JUST SETTLE DOWN SOMEWHERE?
OH, NO NO.
IT'S FUN TRAVELIN' THE COUNTRY, I DON'T MIND THAT. BUT IDEALLY...
IT'D BE NICE IF THERE WAS SOME WAY TO JUST MOVE OUR WHOLE HOUSE AT ONCE.
HRMM...
BUT A HOUSE LIKE THAT DOESN'T EXIST...
WE CAN MAKE ONE.

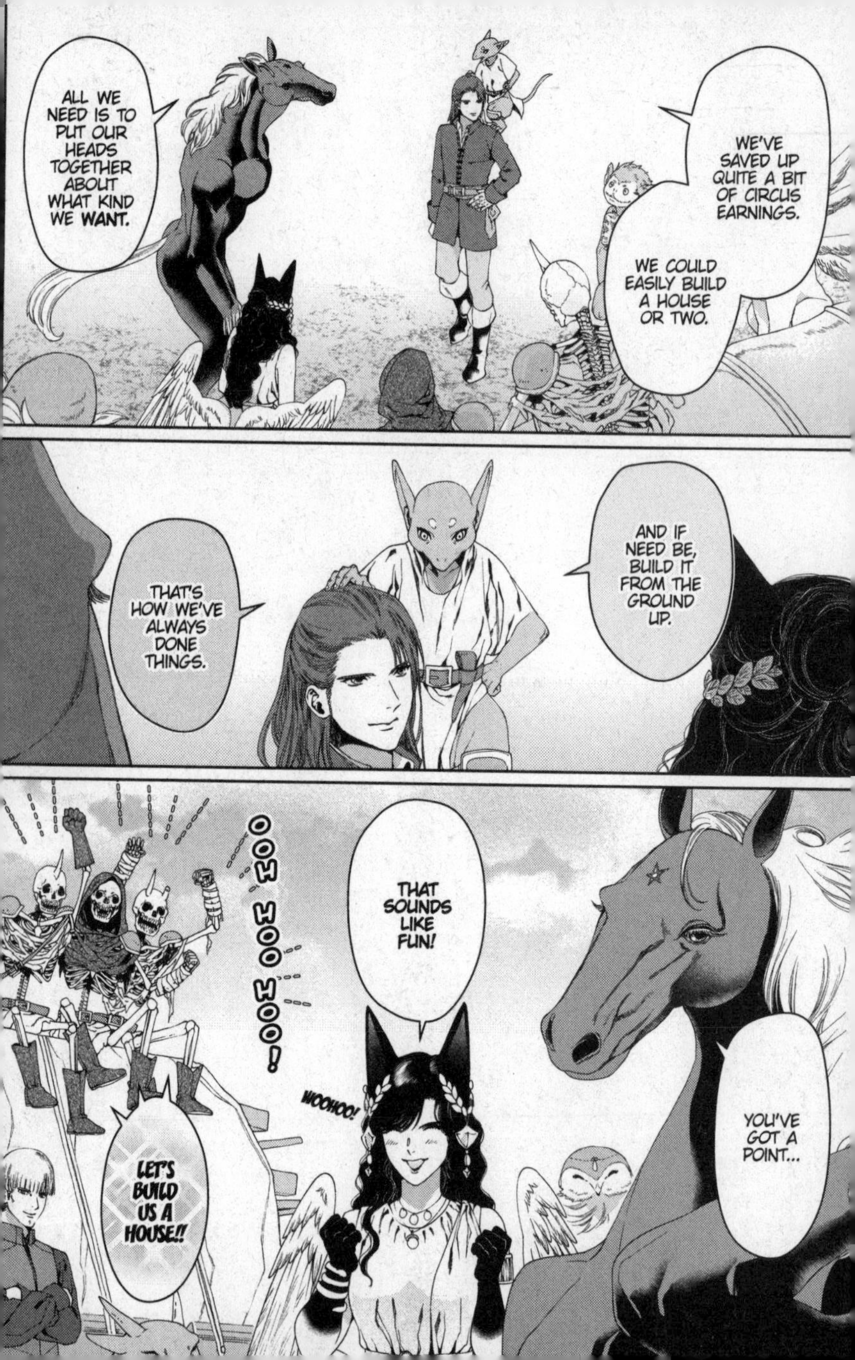
WE'VE SAVED UP QUITE A BIT OF CIRCUS EARNINGS.
WE COULD EASILY BUILD A HOUSE OR TWO.
ALL WE NEED IS TO PUT OUR HEADS TOGETHER ABOUT WHAT KIND WE WANT.
AND IF NEED BE, BUILD IT FROM THE GROUND UP.
THAT'S HOW WE'VE ALWAYS DONE THINGS.
YOU'VE GOT A POINT...
THAT SOUNDS LIKE FUN!
OOOH HOO HOO HOOO!
WOOHOO!
LET'S BUILD US A HOUSE!!

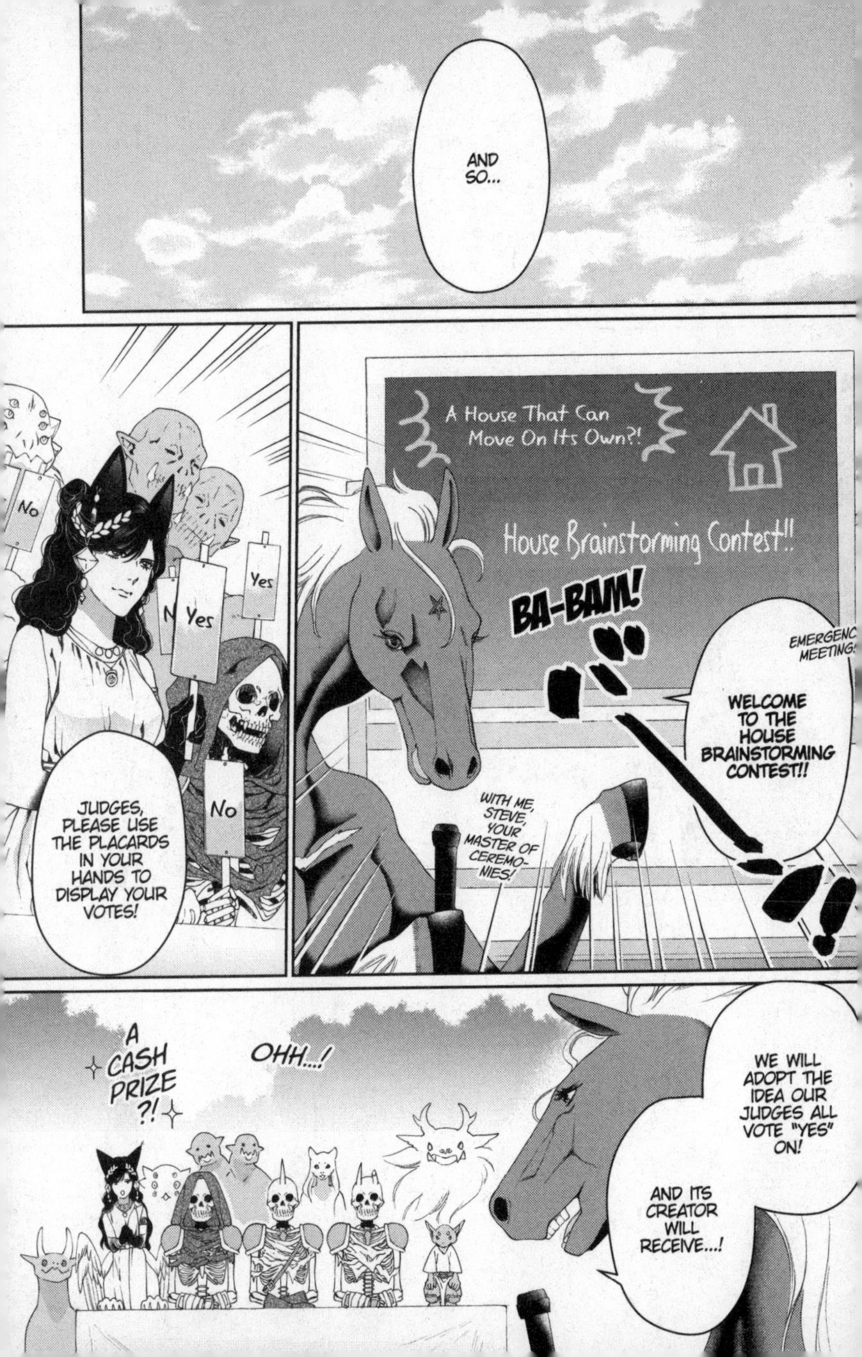
AND SO...
A House That Can Move On Its Own?!
House Brainstorming Contest!!
BA-BAM!
EMERGENC MEETING!
WELCOME TO THE HOUSE BRAINSTORMING CONTEST!!
WITH ME, STEVE, YOUR MASTER OF CEREMO-NIES!
Yes
No
Yes
No
JUDGES, PLEASE USE THE PLACARDS IN YOUR HANDS TO DISPLAY YOUR VOTES!
WE WILL ADOPT THE IDEA OUR JUDGES ALL VOTE "YES" ON!
AND ITS CREATOR WILL RECEIVE...!
OHH...!
A CASH PRIZE?!

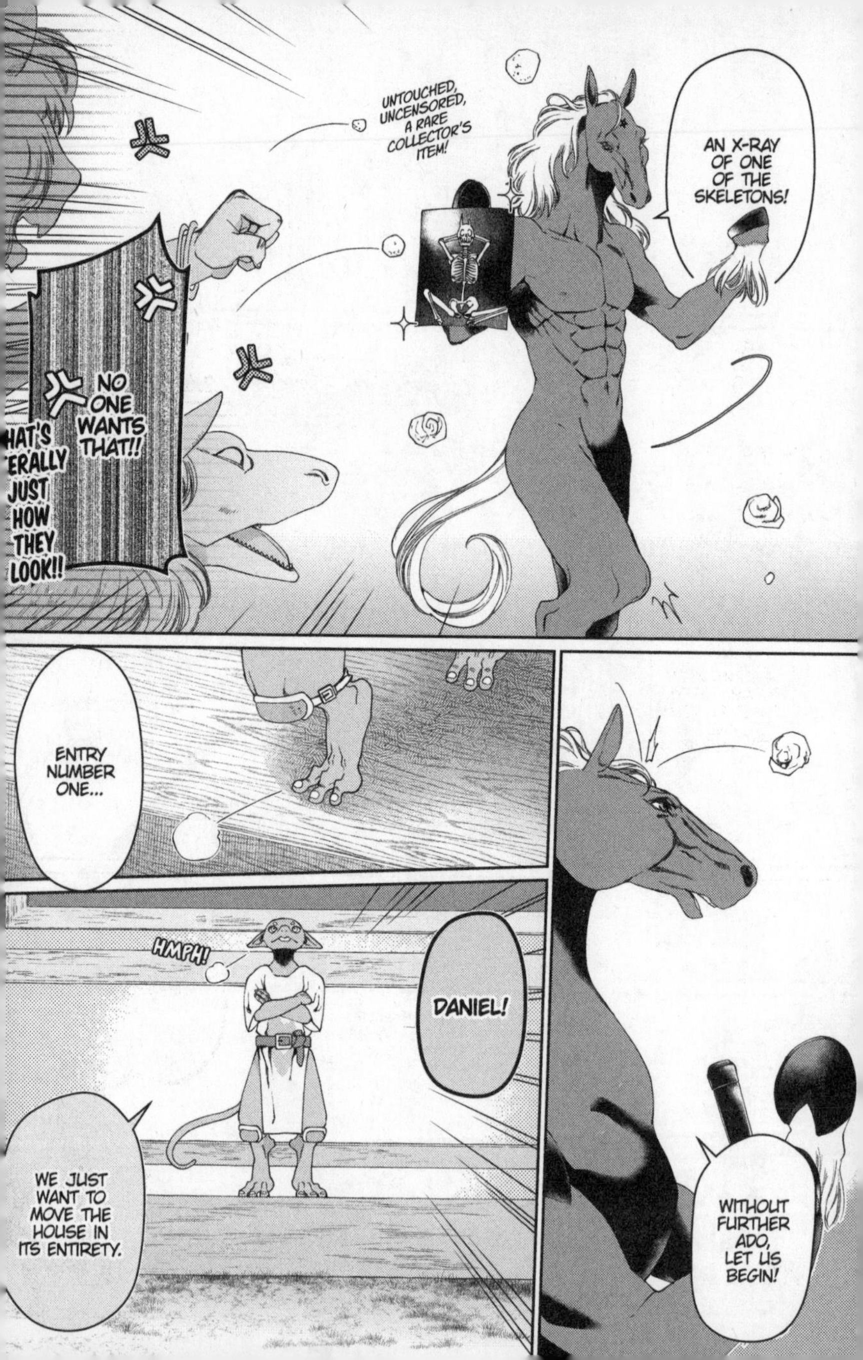
AN X-RAY OF ONE OF THE SKELETONS!
UNTOUCHED, UNCENSORED, A RARE COLLECTOR'S ITEM!
NO ONE WANTS THAT!!
HAT'S ERALLY JUST HOW THEY LOOK!!
WITHOUT FURTHER ADO, LET US BEGIN!
ENTRY NUMBER ONE...
DANIEL!
HMPH!
WE JUST WANT TO MOVE THE HOUSE IN ITS ENTIRETY.

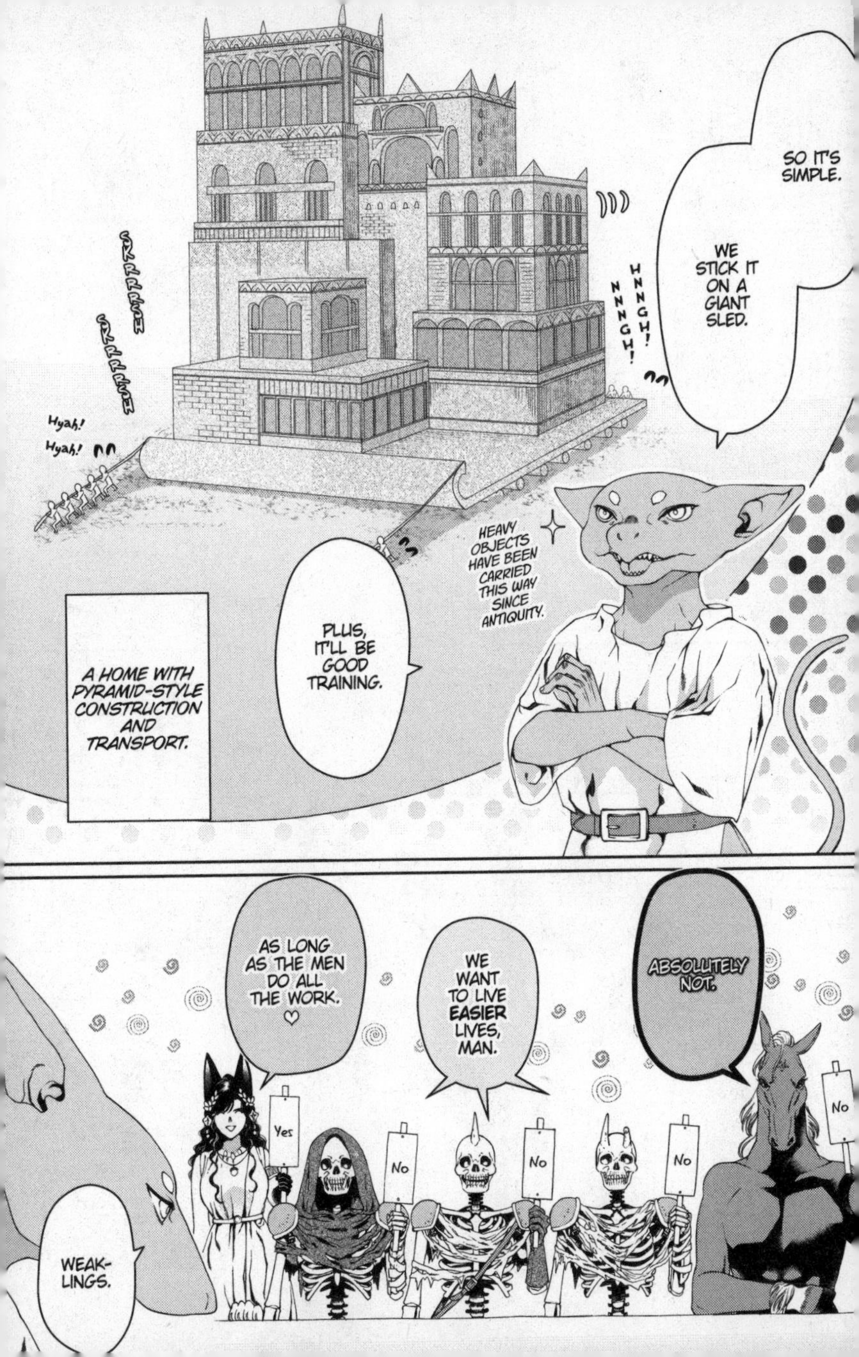
SO IT'S SIMPLE.
WE STICK IT ON A GIANT SLED.
HNNGH!
NNNGH!
HEAVY OBJECTS HAVE BEEN CARRIED THIS WAY SINCE ANTIQUITY.
SKRRRSH
SKRRRSH
Hyah!
Hyah!
PLUS, IT'LL BE GOOD TRAINING.
A HOME WITH PYRAMID-STYLE CONSTRUCTION AND TRANSPORT.
ABSOLUTELY NOT.
No
WE WANT TO LIVE EASIER LIVES, MAN.
No
No
No
AS LONG AS THE MEN DO ALL THE WORK. ♡
Yes
WEAK-LINGS.

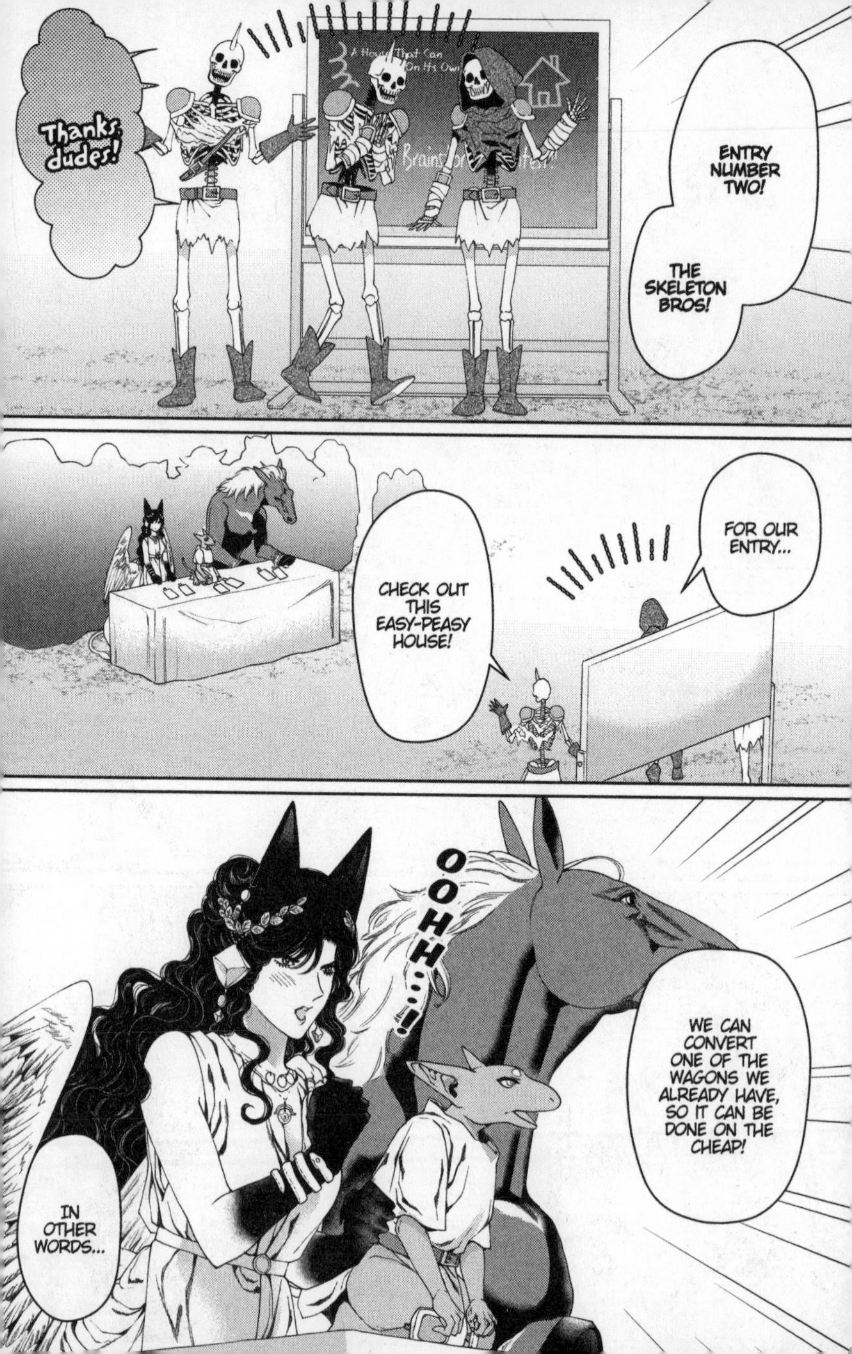
ENTRY NUMBER TWO!
THE SKELETON BROS!
Thanks, dudes!
FOR OUR ENTRY...
CHECK OUT THIS EASY-PEASY HOUSE!
WE CAN CONVERT ONE OF THE WAGONS WE ALREADY HAVE, SO IT CAN BE DONE ON THE CHEAP!
OOHH...!
IN OTHER WORDS...

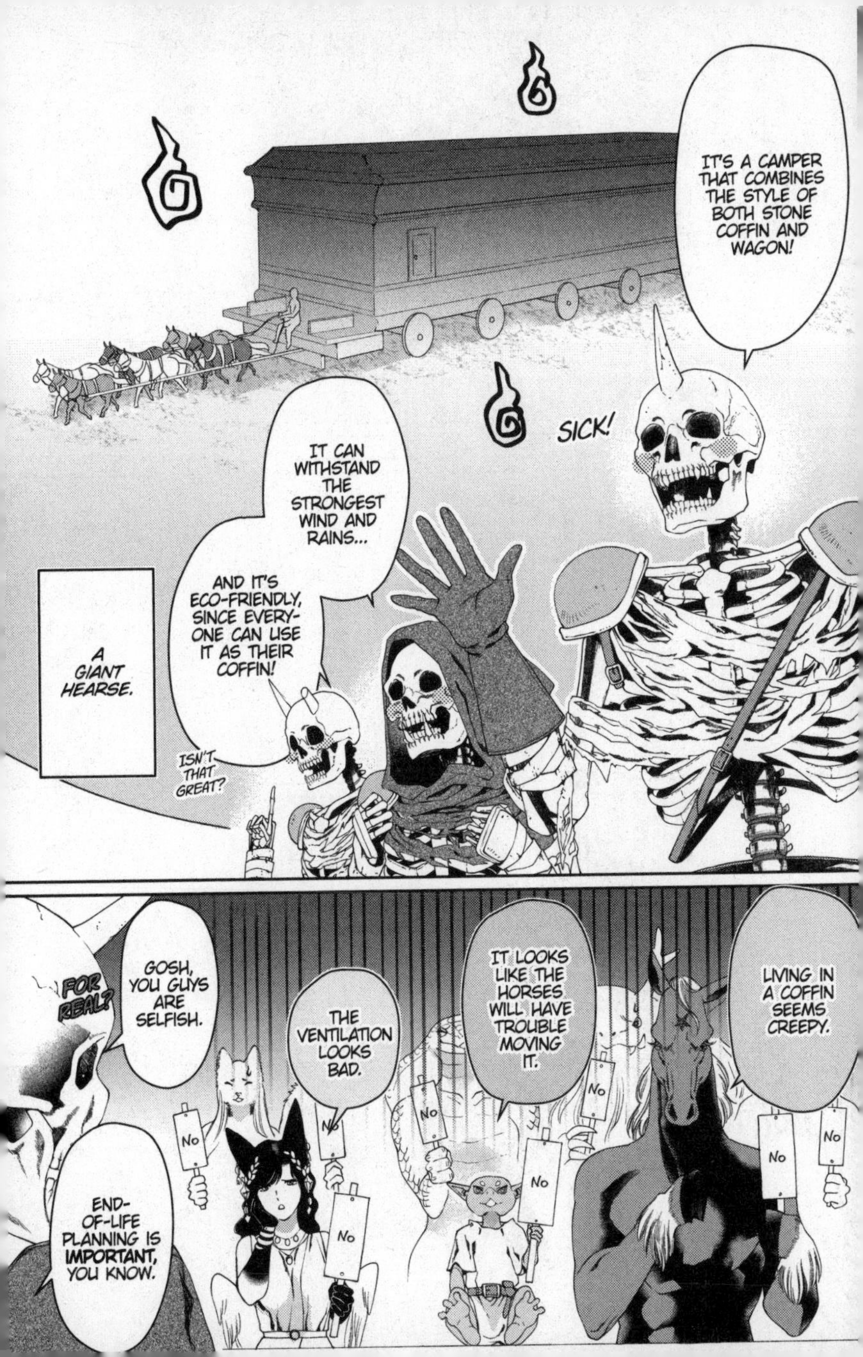
IT'S A CAMPER THAT COMBINES THE STYLE OF BOTH STONE COFFIN AND WAGON!
SICK!
IT CAN WITHSTAND THE STRONGEST WIND AND RAINS...
AND IT'S ECO-FRIENDLY, SINCE EVERY-ONE CAN USE IT AS THEIR COFFIN!
ISN'T THAT GREAT?
A GIANT HEARSE.
LIVING IN A COFFIN SEEMS CREEPY.
No
No
No
IT LOOKS LIKE THE HORSES WILL HAVE TROUBLE MOVING IT.
No
No
THE VENTILATION LOOKS BAD.
No
No
No
GOSH, YOU GUYS ARE SELFISH.
FOR REAL?
END-OF-LIFE PLANNING IS IMPORTANT, YOU KNOW.

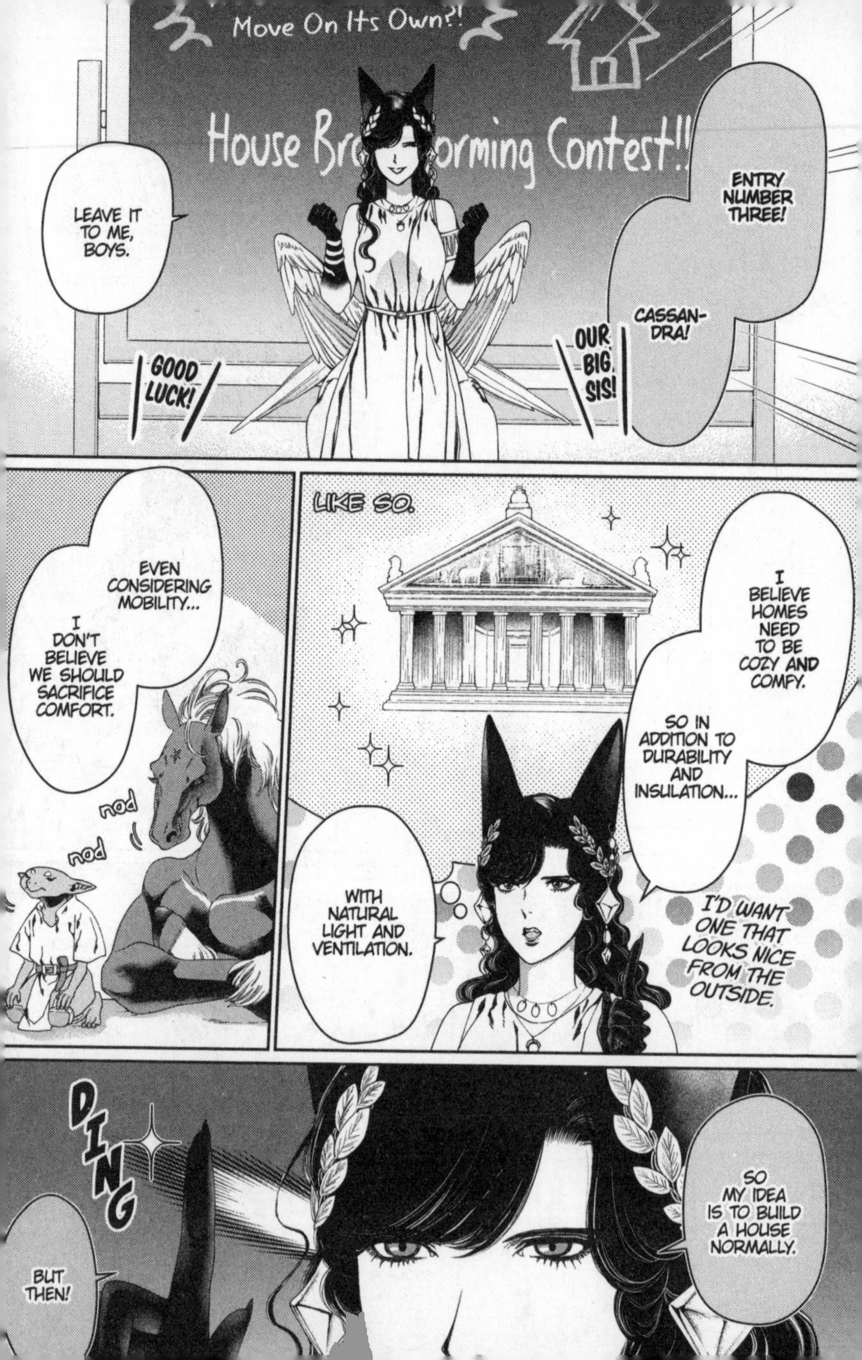
Move On Its Own?!
House Br orming Contest!!
ENTRY NUMBER THREE!
CASSAN-DRA!
OUR BIG SIS!
LEAVE IT TO ME, BOYS.
GOOD LUCK!
I BELIEVE HOMES NEED TO BE COZY AND COMFY.
SO IN ADDITION TO DURABILITY AND INSULATION...
LIKE SO.
I'D WANT ONE THAT LOOKS NICE FROM THE OUTSIDE.
WITH NATURAL LIGHT AND VENTILATION.
EVEN CONSIDERING MOBILITY...
I DON'T BELIEVE WE SHOULD SACRIFICE COMFORT.
nod
nod
SO MY IDEA IS TO BUILD A HOUSE NORMALLY.
DING
BUT THEN!

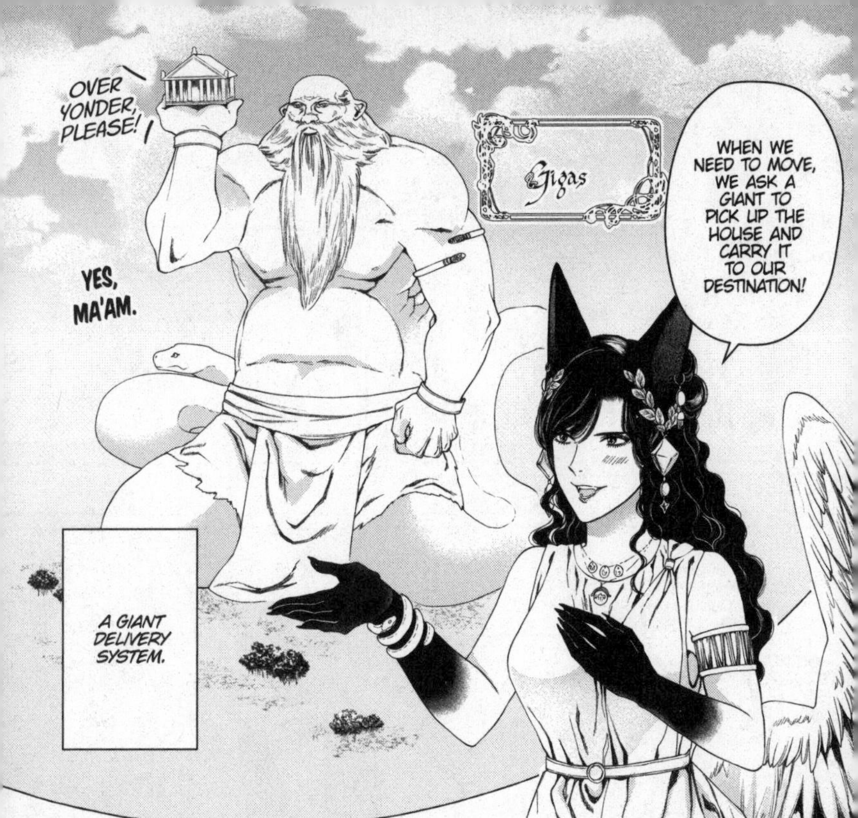
WHEN WE NEED TO MOVE, WE ASK A GIANT TO PICK UP THE HOUSE AND CARRY IT TO OUR DESTINATION!
Gigas
OVER YONDER, PLEASE!
YES, MA'AM.
A GIANT DELIVERY SYSTEM.

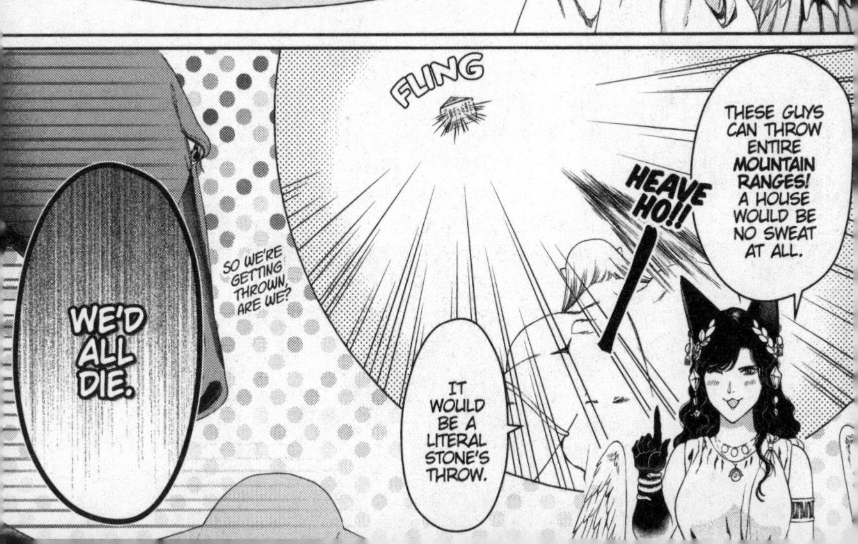
FLING
THESE GUYS CAN THROW ENTIRE MOUNTAIN RANGES! A HOUSE WOULD BE NO SWEAT AT ALL.
HEAVE HO!!
SO WE'RE GETTING THROWN, ARE WE?
IT WOULD BE A LITERAL STONE'S THROW.
WE'D ALL DIE.

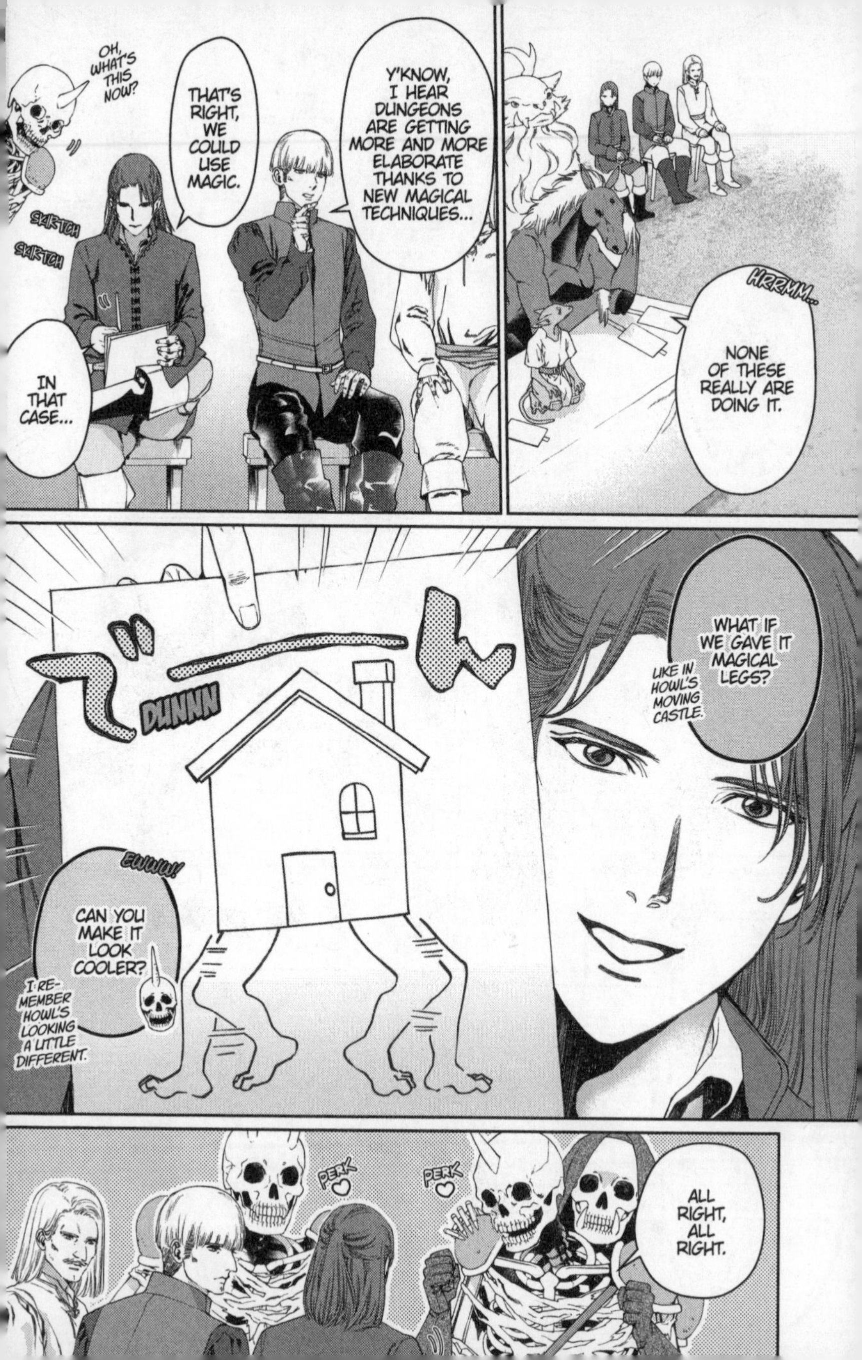
HRRMM...
NONE OF THESE REALLY ARE DOING IT.
Y'KNOW, I HEAR DUNGEONS ARE GETTING MORE AND MORE ELABORATE THANKS TO NEW MAGICAL TECHNIQUES...
THAT'S RIGHT, WE COULD USE MAGIC.
OH, WHAT'S THIS NOW?
SKRTCH
SKRTCH
IN THAT CASE...
WHAT IF WE GAVE IT MAGICAL LEGS?
LIKE IN HOWL'S MOVING CASTLE.
DUNNN
EWWW!
CAN YOU MAKE IT LOOK COOLER?
I RE-MEMBER HOWL'S LOOKING A LITTLE DIFFERENT.
ALL RIGHT, ALL RIGHT.
PERK
PERK

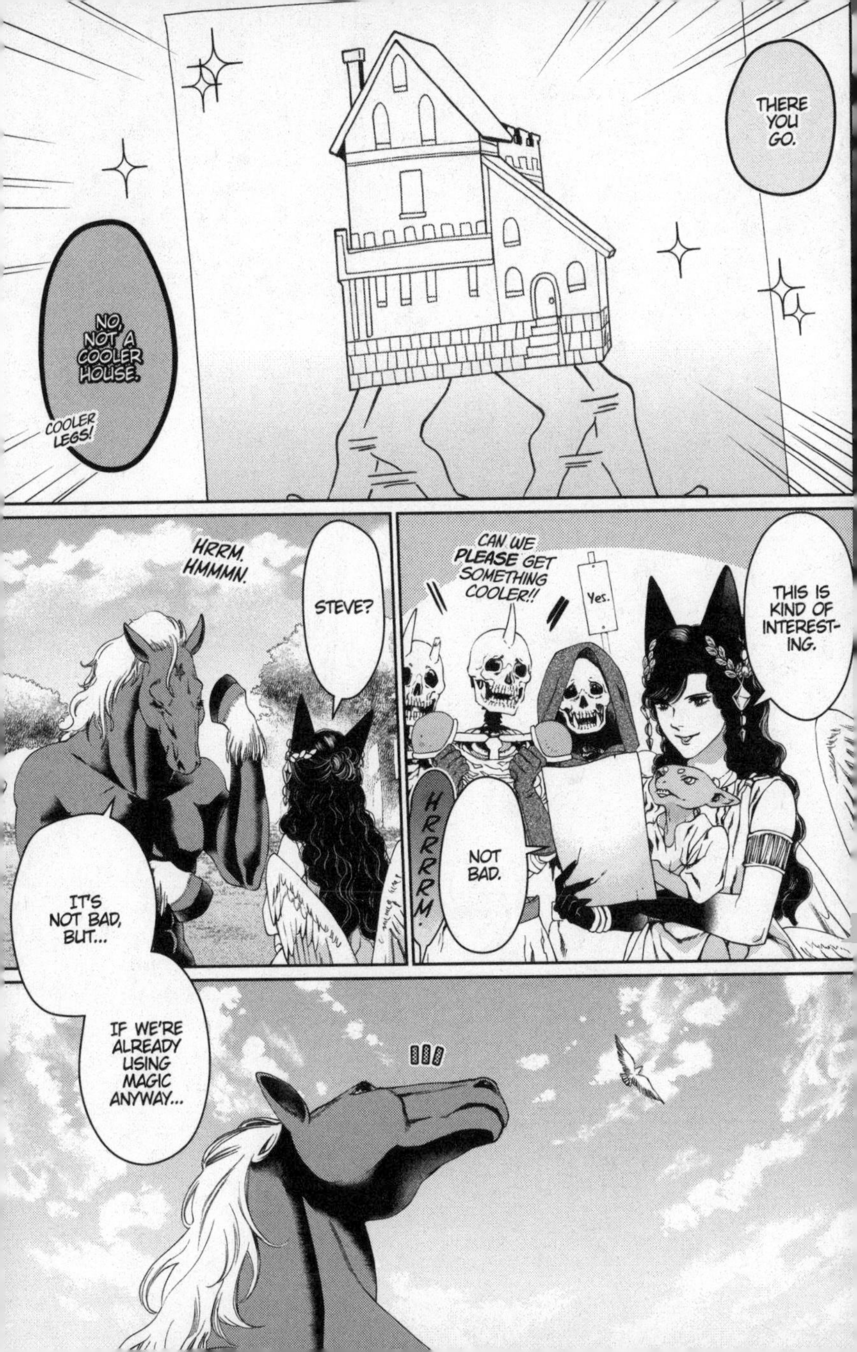
THERE YOU GO.
NO, NOT A COOLER HOUSE.
COOLER LEGS!
THIS IS KIND OF INTEREST-ING.
Yes.
CAN WE PLEASE GET SOMETHING COOLER!!
NOT BAD.
HRRRRM.
STEVE?
HRRM. HMMMN.
IT'S NOT BAD, BUT...
IF WE'RE ALREADY USING MAGIC ANYWAY...

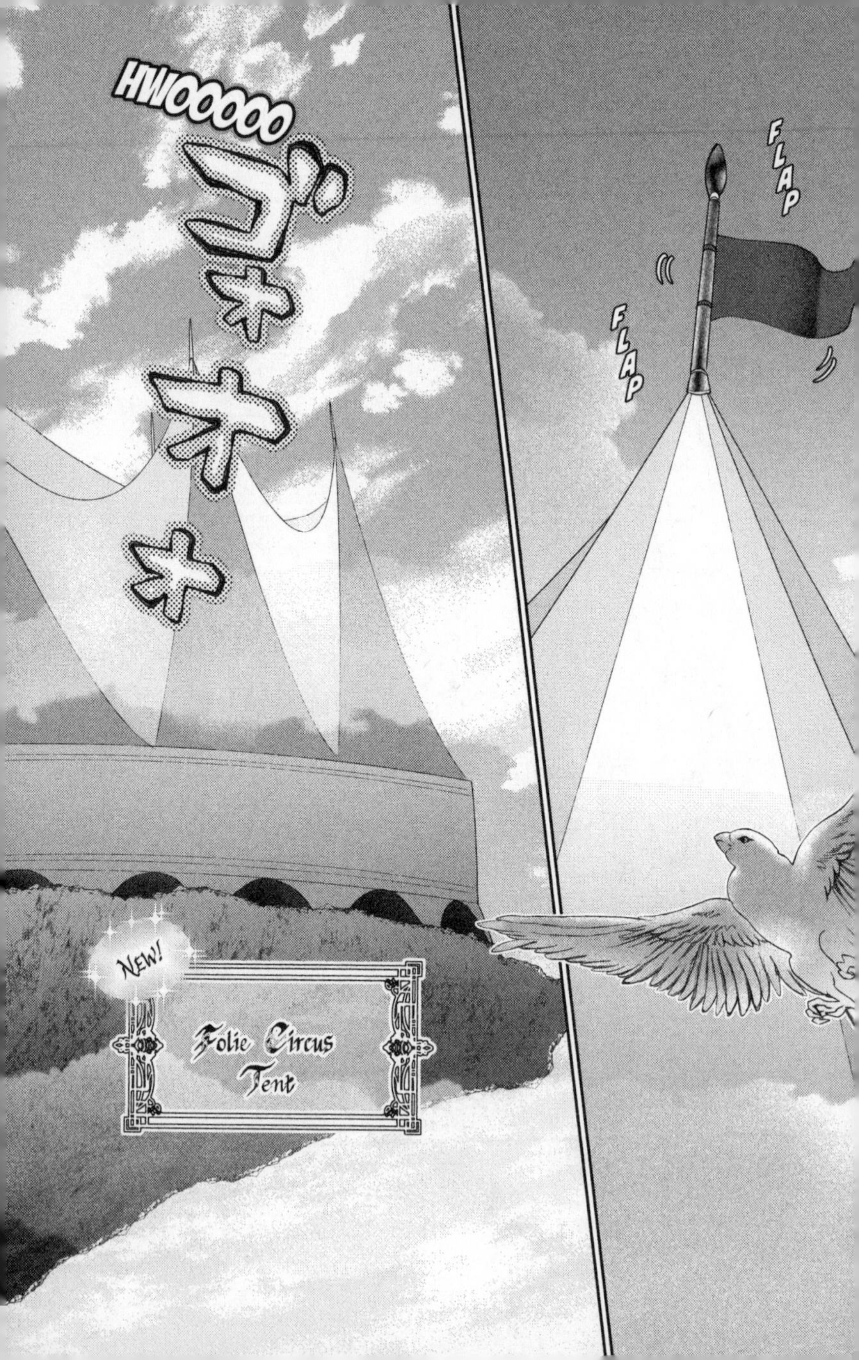
FLAP
FLAP
HWOOOOO
ゴォオオ
NEW!
Folie Circus
Tent

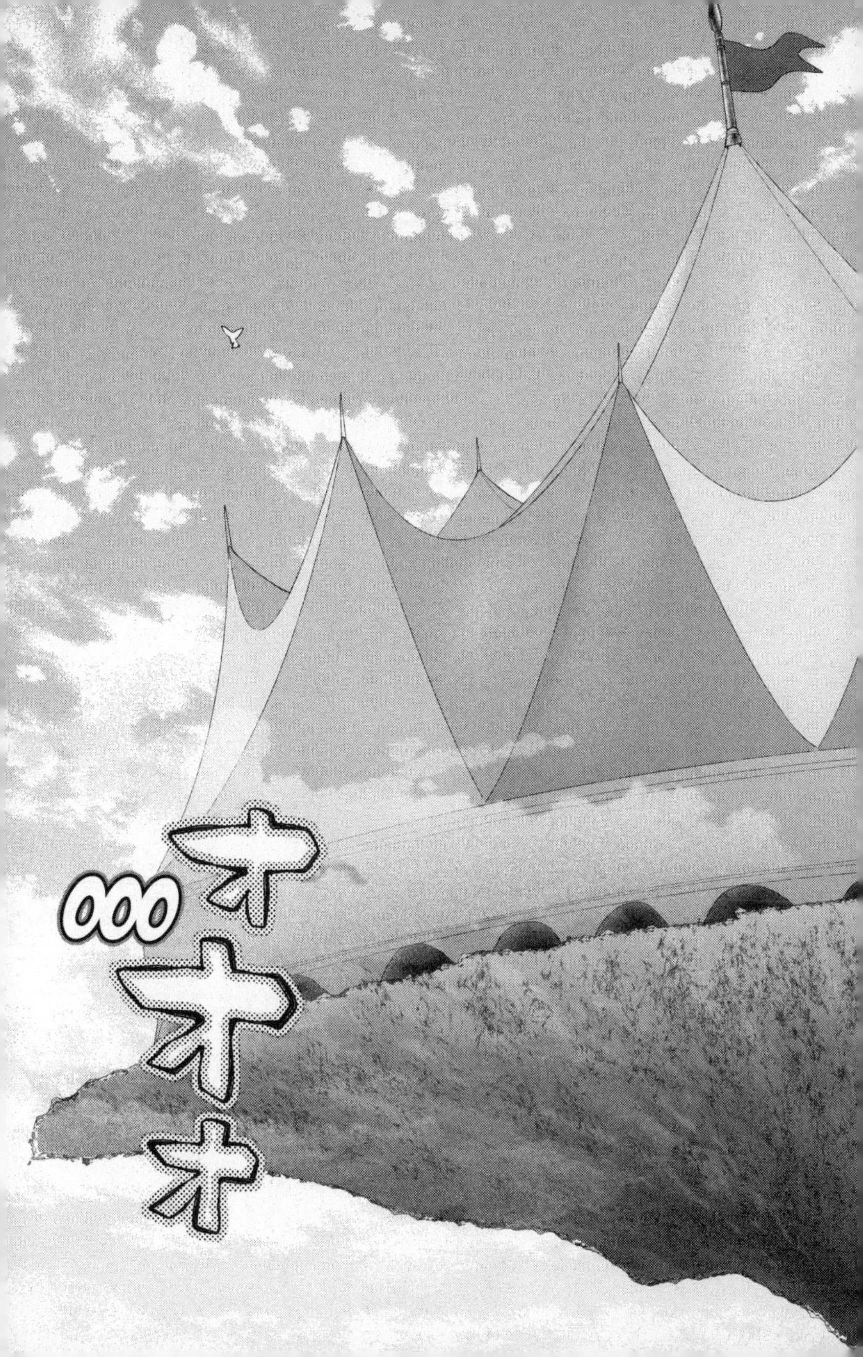
ooo
オオオ

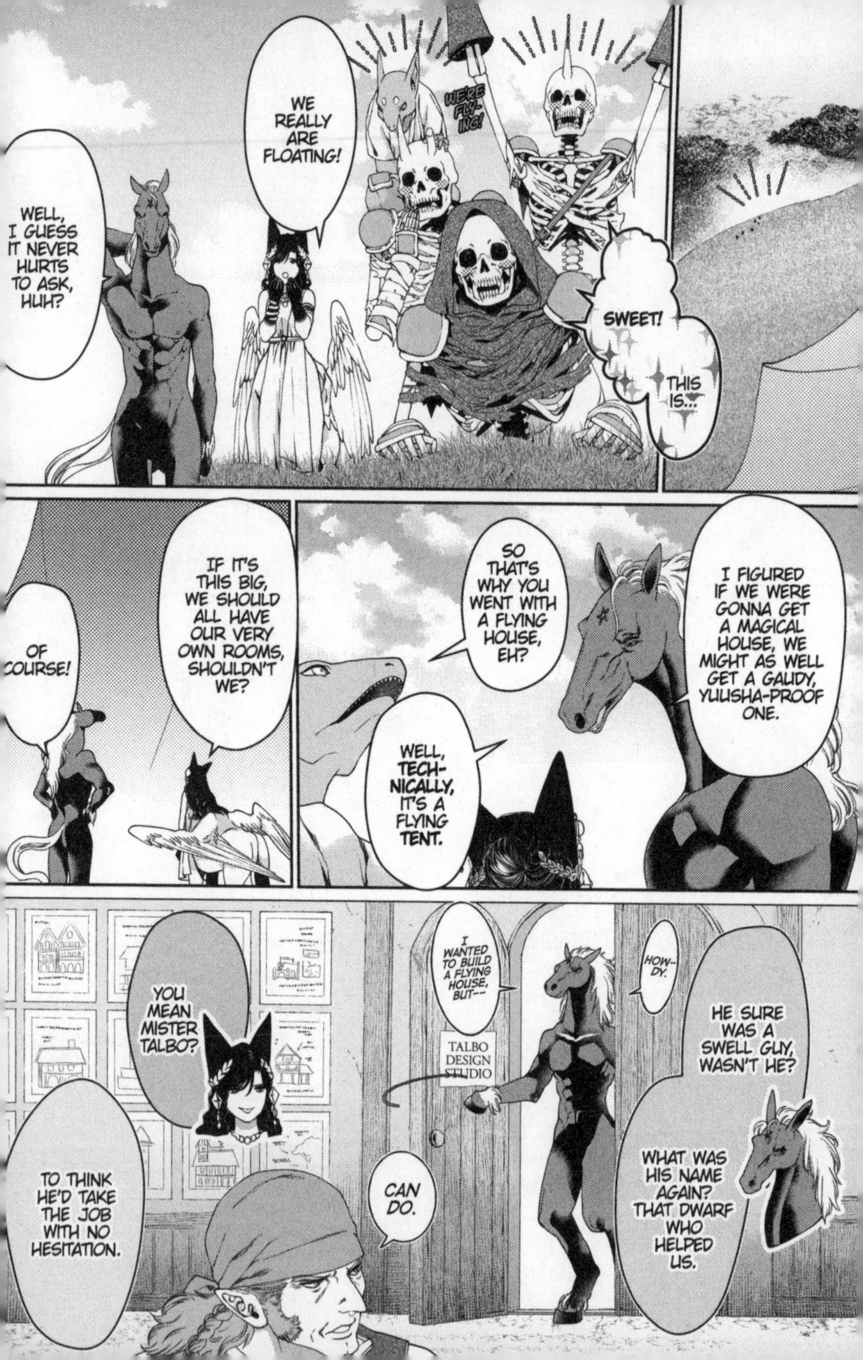
WE'RE FLYING!
WE REALLY ARE FLOATING!
SWEET!
THIS IS...
WELL, I GUESS IT NEVER HURTS TO ASK, HUH?
SO THAT'S WHY YOU WENT WITH A FLYING HOUSE, EH?
I FIGURED IF WE WERE GONNA GET A MAGICAL HOUSE, WE MIGHT AS WELL GET A GAUDY, YUUSHA-PROOF ONE.
WELL, TECHNICALLY, IT'S A FLYING TENT.
IF IT'S THIS BIG, WE SHOULD ALL HAVE OUR VERY OWN ROOMS, SHOULDN'T WE?
OF COURSE!
HE SURE WAS A SWELL GUY, WASN'T HE?
WHAT WAS HIS NAME AGAIN? THAT DWARF WHO HELPED US.
HOWDY.
I WANTED TO BUILD A FLYING HOUSE, BUT--
TALBO DESIGN STUDIO
CAN DO.
YOU MEAN MISTER TALBO?
TO THINK HE'D TAKE THE JOB WITH NO HESITATION.

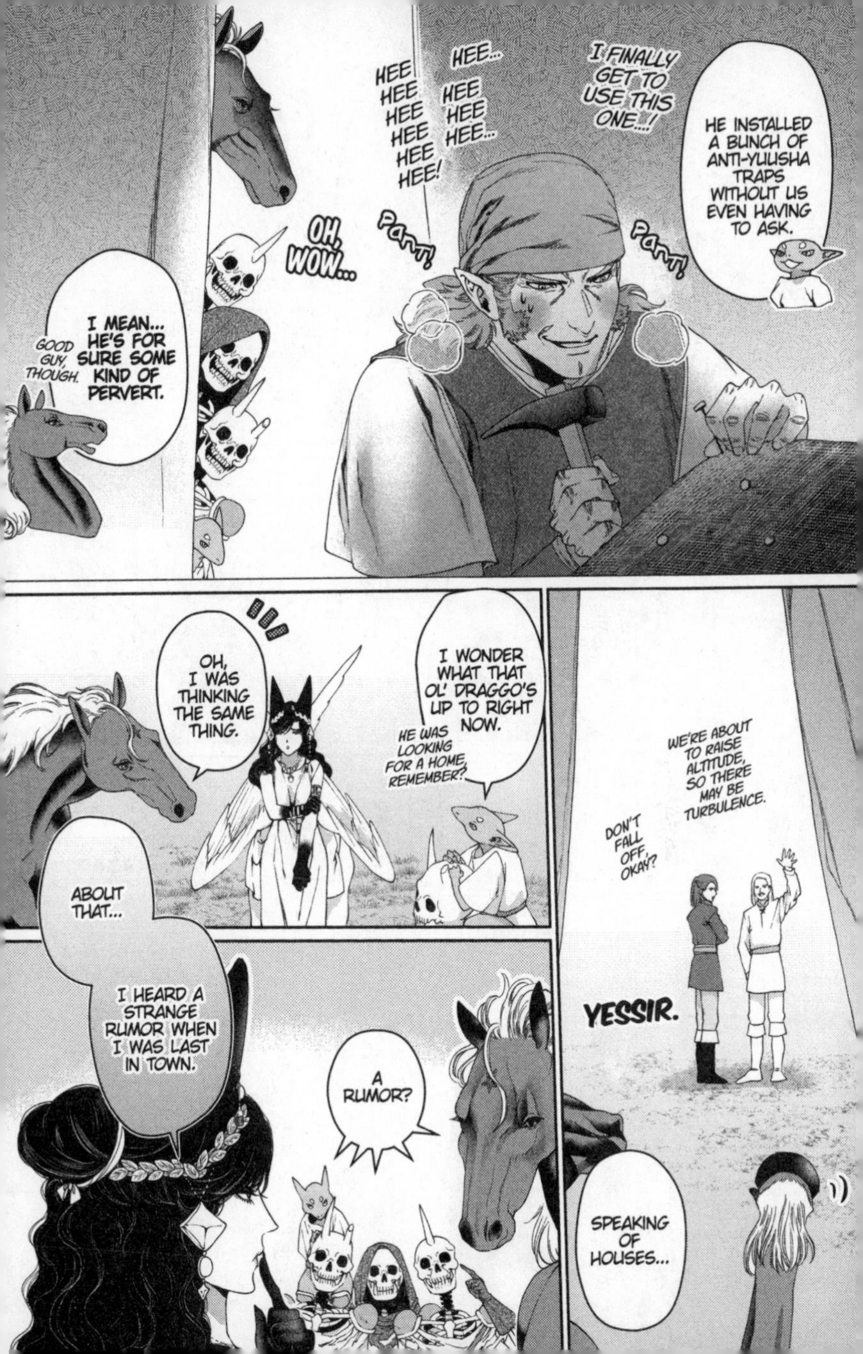
HE INSTALLED A BUNCH OF ANTI-YUUSHA TRAPS WITHOUT US EVEN HAVING TO ASK.
I FINALLY GET TO USE THIS ONE...!
HEE... HEE HEE HEE HEE...
HEE HEE HEE HEE HEE!
Pant!
Pant!
OH, WOW...
I MEAN... HE'S FOR SURE SOME KIND OF PERVERT.
GOOD GUY, THOUGH.
WE'RE ABOUT TO RAISE ALTITUDE, SO THERE MAY BE TURBULENCE.
DON'T FALL OFF, OKAY?
YESSIR.
I WONDER WHAT THAT OL' DRAGGO'S UP TO RIGHT NOW.
HE WAS LOOKING FOR A HOME, REMEMBER?
OH, I WAS THINKING THE SAME THING.
SPEAKING OF HOUSES...
ABOUT THAT...
I HEARD A STRANGE RUMOR WHEN I WAS LAST IN TOWN.
A RUMOR?

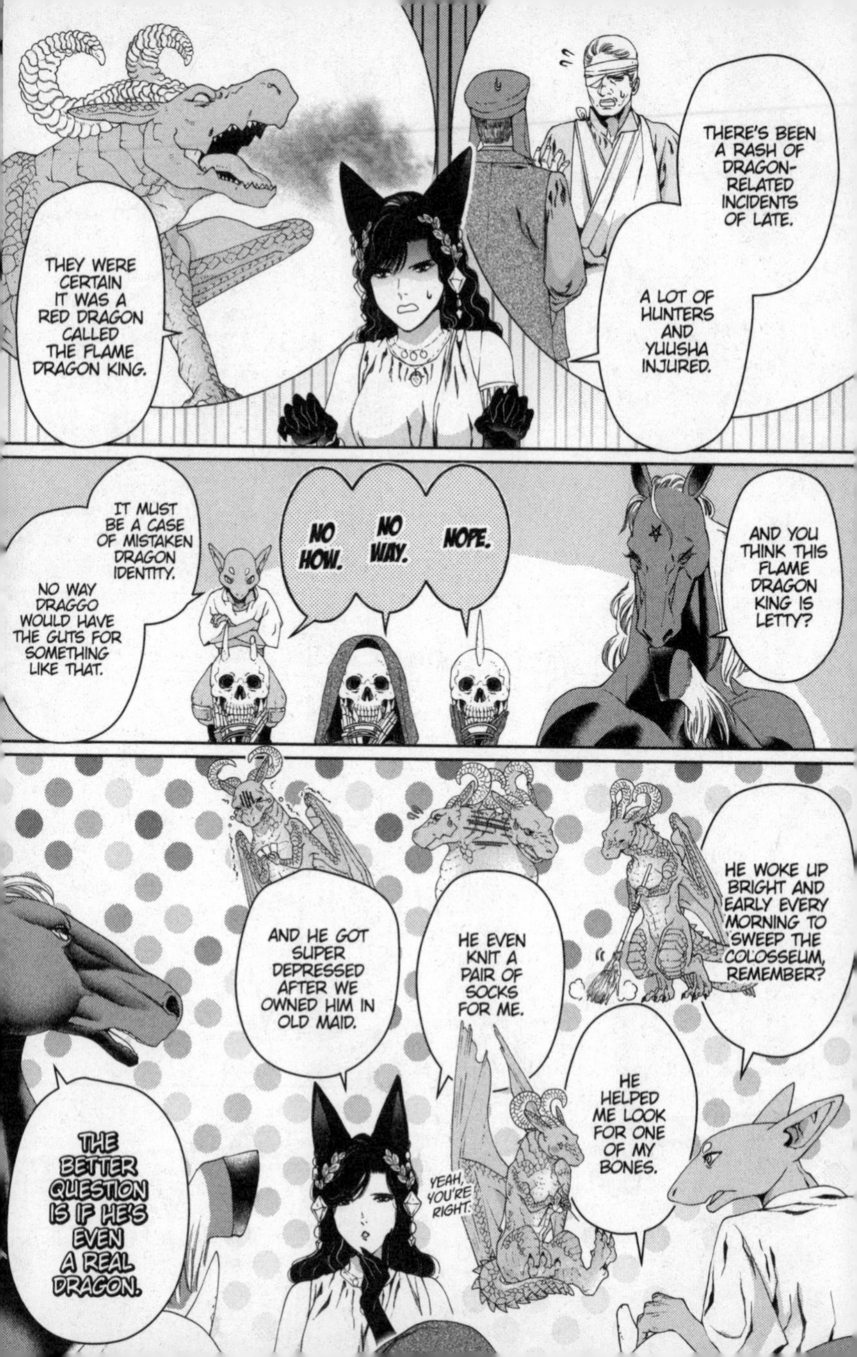
THERE'S BEEN A RASH OF DRAGON-RELATED INCIDENTS OF LATE.
A LOT OF HUNTERS AND YUUSHA INJURED.
THEY WERE CERTAIN IT WAS A RED DRAGON CALLED THE FLAME DRAGON KING.
AND YOU THINK THIS FLAME DRAGON KING IS LETTY?
NOPE.
NO WAY.
NO HOW.
IT MUST BE A CASE OF MISTAKEN DRAGON IDENTITY.
NO WAY DRAGGO WOULD HAVE THE GUTS FOR SOMETHING LIKE THAT.
HE WOKE UP BRIGHT AND EARLY EVERY MORNING TO SWEEP THE COLOSSEUM, REMEMBER?
HE EVEN KNIT A PAIR OF SOCKS FOR ME.
AND HE GOT SUPER DEPRESSED AFTER WE OWNED HIM IN OLD MAID.
HE HELPED ME LOOK FOR ONE OF MY BONES.
YEAH, YOU'RE RIGHT.
THE BETTER QUESTION IS IF HE'S EVEN A REAL DRAGON.

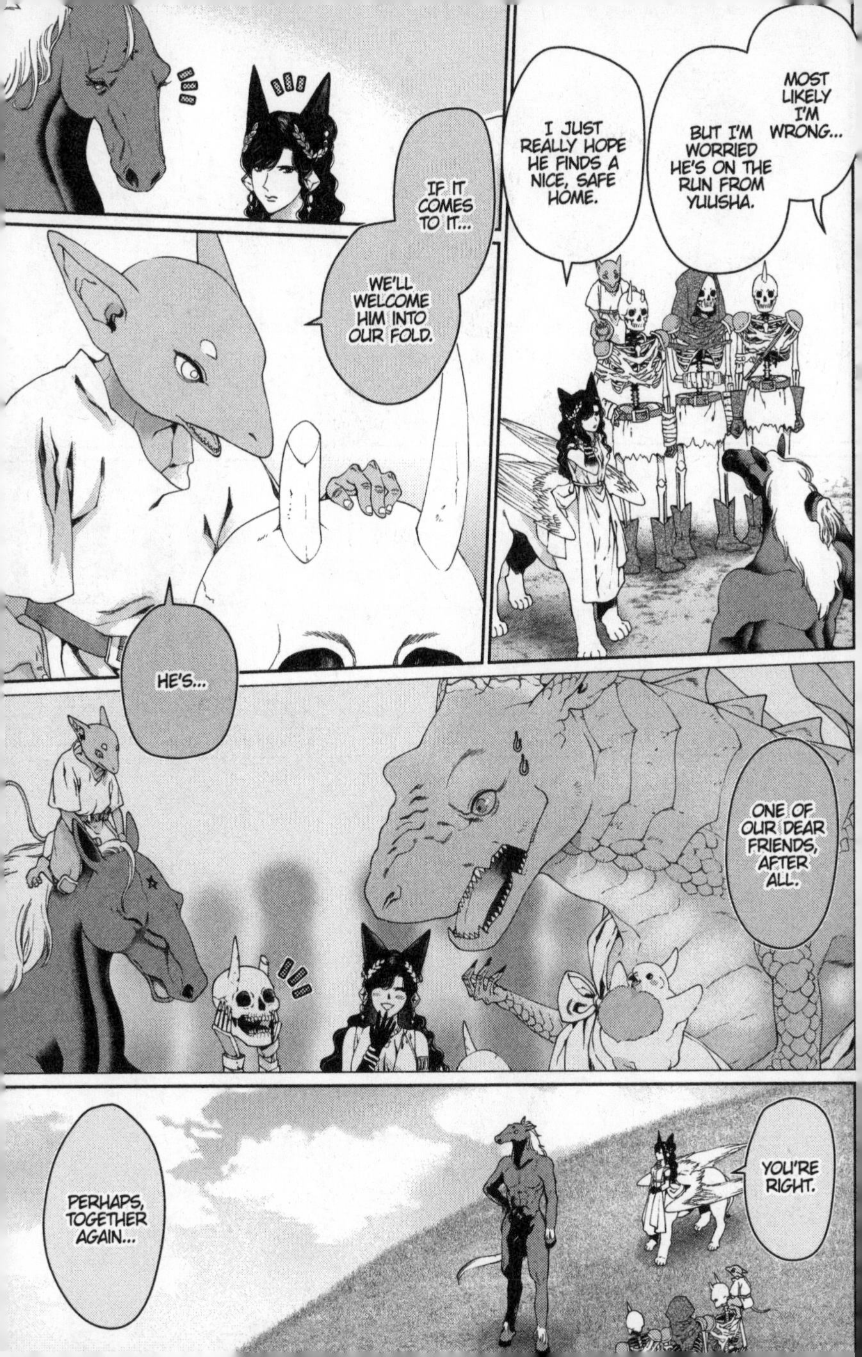
MOST LIKELY I'M WRONG...
BUT I'M WORRIED HE'S ON THE RUN FROM YUUSHA.
I JUST REALLY HOPE HE FINDS A NICE, SAFE HOME.
IF IT COMES TO IT...
WE'LL WELCOME HIM INTO OUR FOLD.
HE'S...
ONE OF OUR DEAR FRIENDS, AFTER ALL.
YOU'RE RIGHT.
PERHAPS, TOGETHER AGAIN...

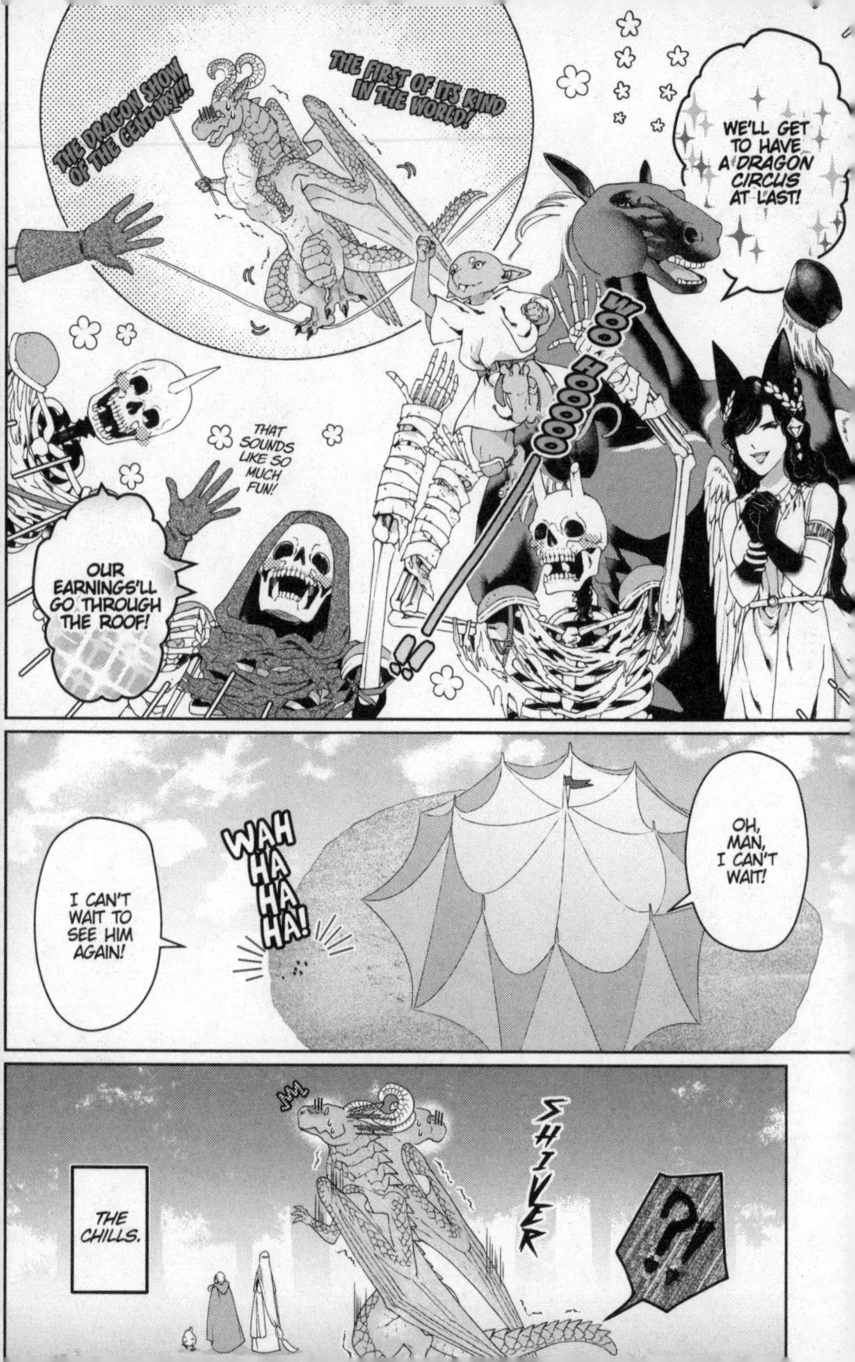
WE'LL GET TO HAVE A DRAGON CIRCUS AT LAST!
THE FIRST OF ITS KIND IN THE WORLD!
THE DRAGON SHOW OF THE CENTURY!!!
WOO HOOOOOO
!!
THAT SOUNDS LIKE SO MUCH FUN!
OUR EARNINGS'LL GO THROUGH THE ROOF!
OH, MAN, I CAN'T WAIT!
WAH HA HA HA!
I CAN'T WAIT TO SEE HIM AGAIN!
SHIVER
?!
THE CHILLS.

A Flying Home

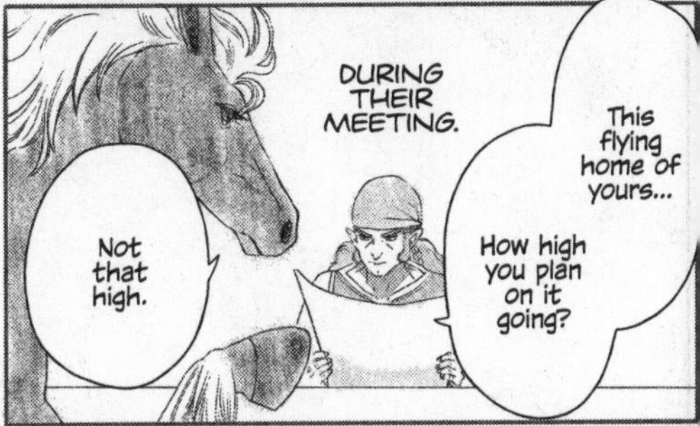
This flying home of yours...
How high you plan on it going?
DURING THEIR MEETING.
Not that high.

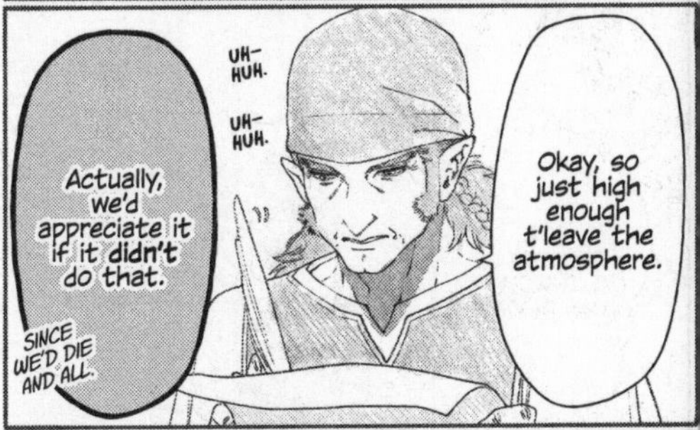
Okay, so just high enough t'leave the atmosphere.
UH-HUH.
UH-HUH.
Actually, we'd appreciate it if it didn't do that.
SINCE WE'D DIE AND ALL.

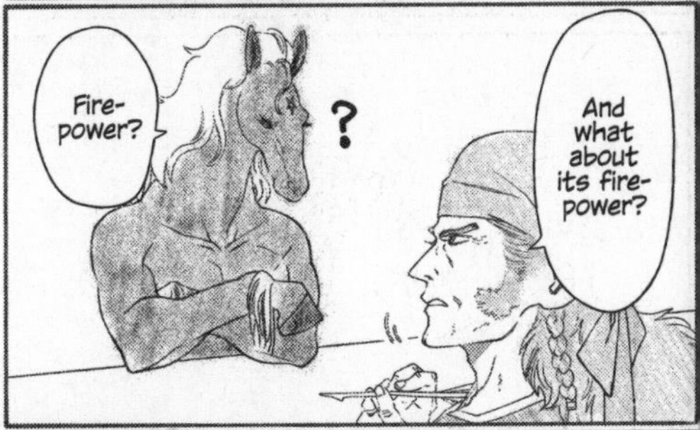
And what about its fire-power?
?
Fire-power?

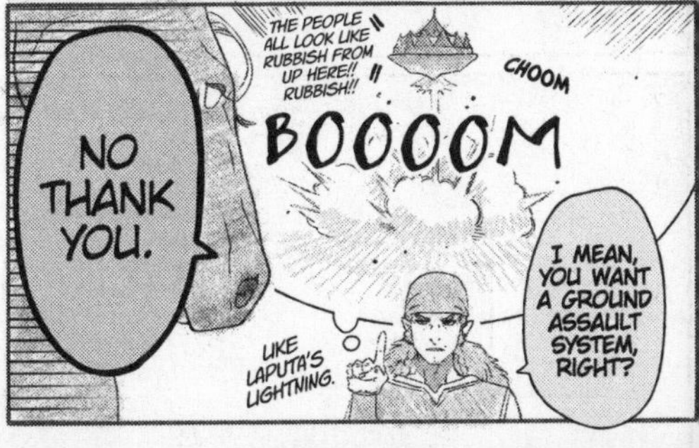
CHOOM
THE PEOPLE ALL LOOK LIKE RUBBISH FROM UP HERE!! RUBBISH!!
BOOOOM
I MEAN, YOU WANT A GROUND ASSAULT SYSTEM, RIGHT?
LIKE LAPUTA'S LIGHTNING.
NO THANK YOU.

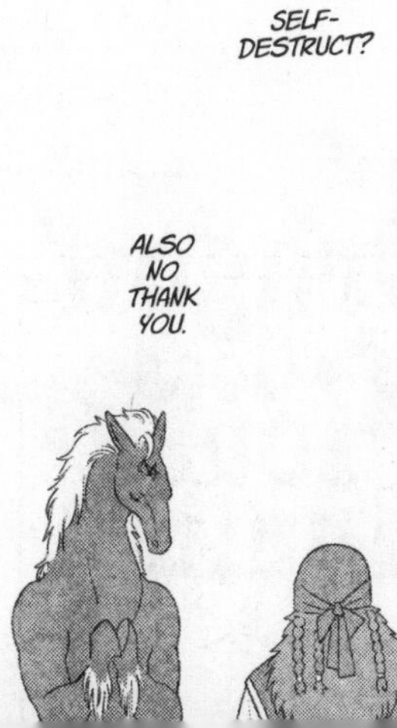
SELF-DESTRUCT?
ALSO NO THANK YOU.

Dragon Goes House-Hunting

House 32: The Underlings Share a Home

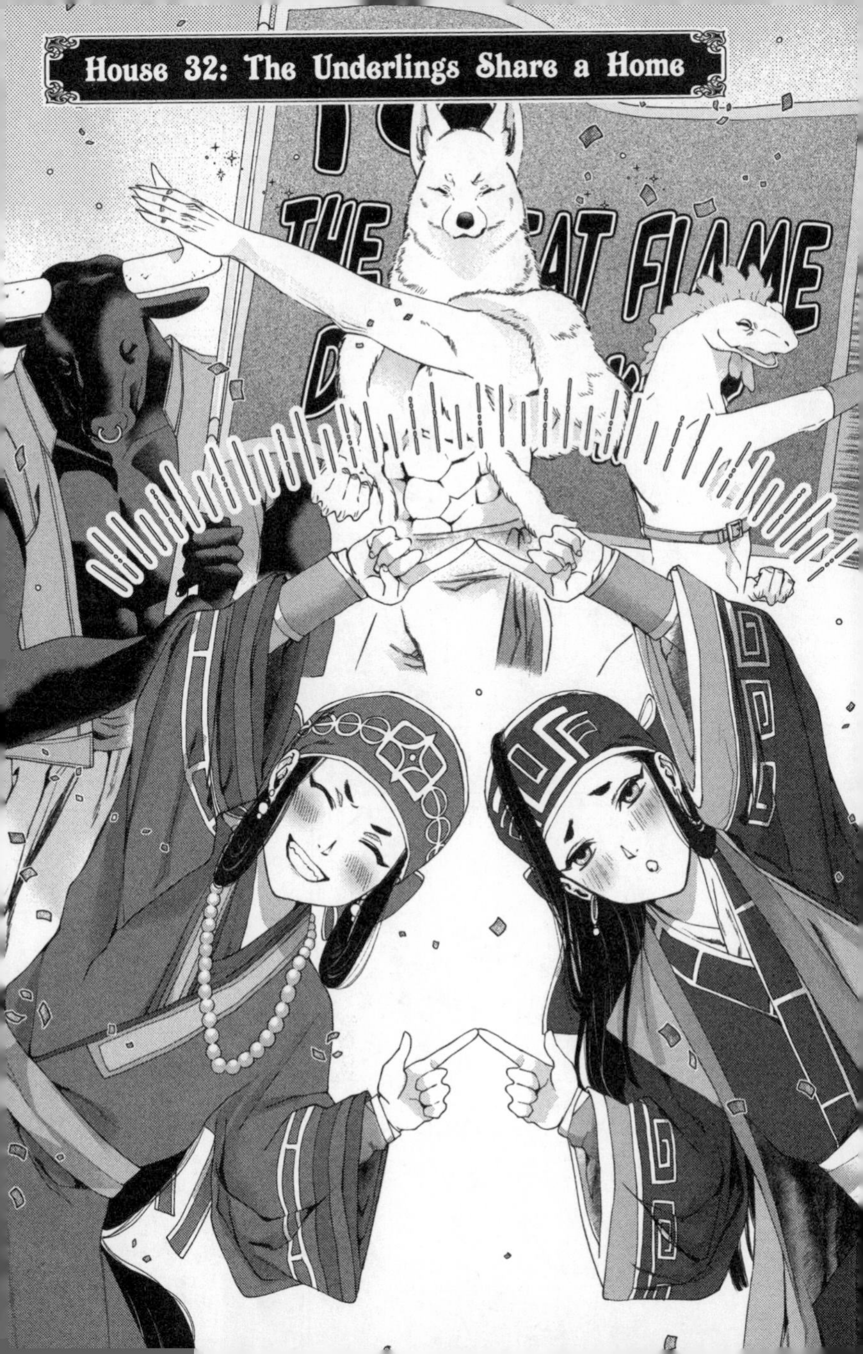

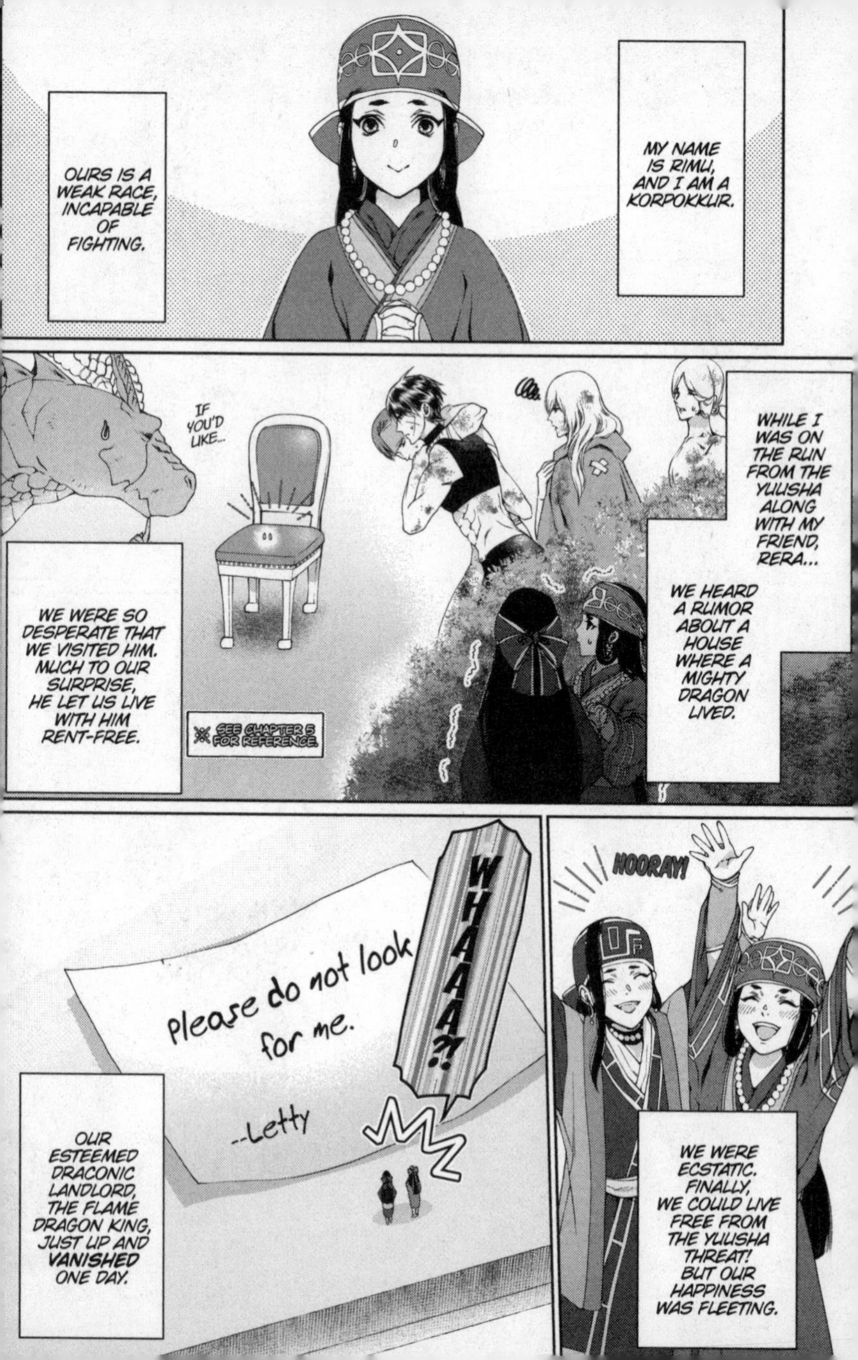
MY NAME IS RIMU, AND I AM A KORPOKKUR.
OURS IS A WEAK RACE, INCAPABLE OF FIGHTING.
WHILE I WAS ON THE RUN FROM THE YUUSHA ALONG WITH MY FRIEND, RERA...
WE HEARD A RUMOR ABOUT A HOUSE WHERE A MIGHTY DRAGON LIVED.
IF YOU'D LIKE...
WE WERE SO DESPERATE THAT WE VISITED HIM. MUCH TO OUR SURPRISE, HE LET US LIVE WITH HIM RENT-FREE.
※ SEE CHAPTER 5 FOR REFERENCE.
HOORAY!
WE WERE ECSTATIC. FINALLY, WE COULD LIVE FREE FROM THE YUUSHA THREAT! BUT OUR HAPPINESS WAS FLEETING.
Please do not look for me.
--Letty
WHAAAA?!
OUR ESTEEMED DRACONIC LANDLORD, THE FLAME DRAGON KING, JUST UP AND VANISHED ONE DAY.

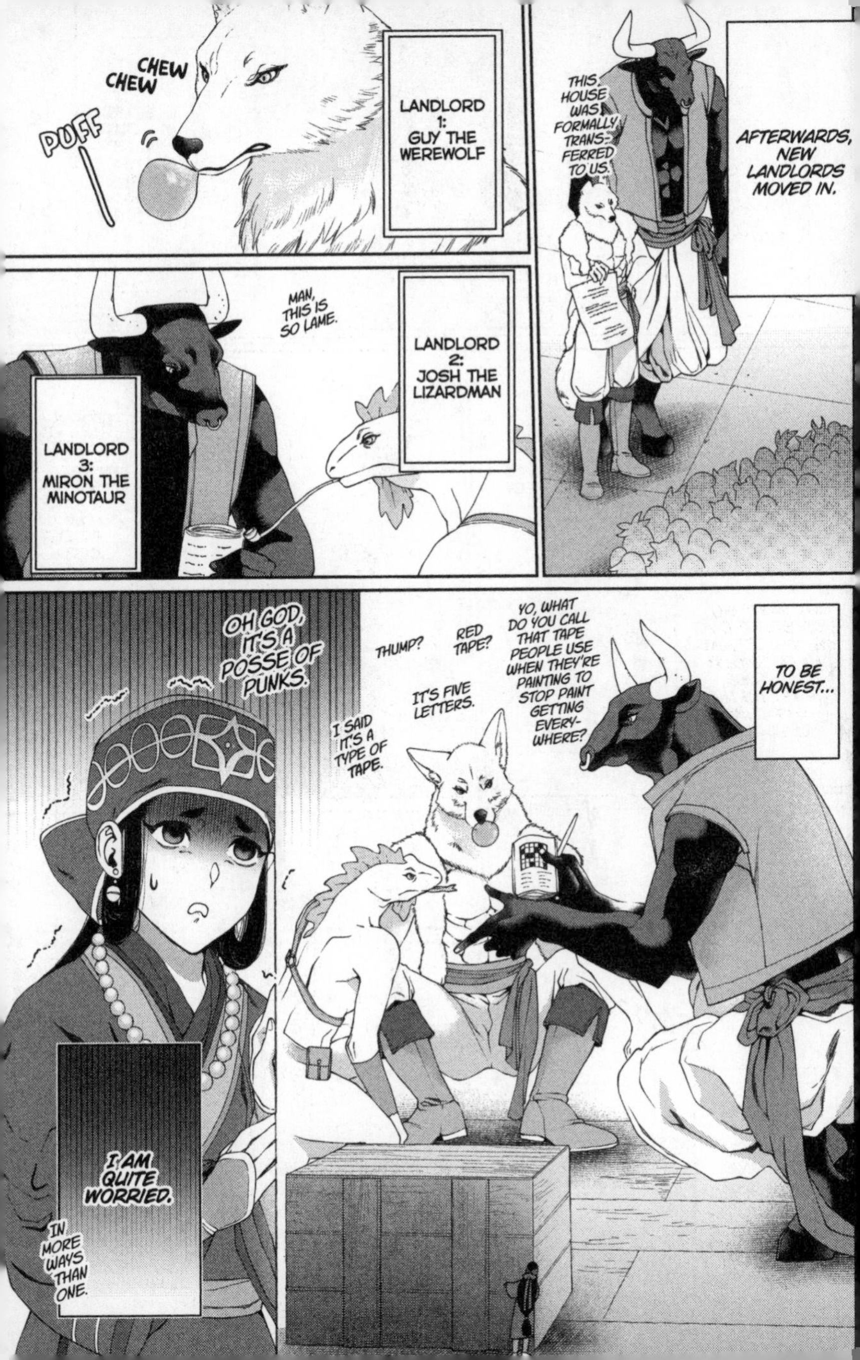
AFTERWARDS, NEW LANDLORDS MOVED IN.
THIS HOUSE WAS FORMALLY TRANSFERRED TO US.
LANDLORD 1: GUY THE WEREWOLF
CHEW CHEW
PUFF
MAN, THIS IS SO LAME.
LANDLORD 2: JOSH THE LIZARDMAN
LANDLORD 3: MIRON THE MINOTAUR
TO BE HONEST...
YO, WHAT DO YOU CALL THAT TAPE PEOPLE USE WHEN THEY'RE PAINTING TO STOP PAINT GETTING EVERYWHERE?
RED TAPE?
THUMP?
IT'S FIVE LETTERS.
I SAID IT'S A TYPE OF TAPE.
OH GOD, IT'S A POSSE OF PUNKS.
I AM QUITE WORRIED.
IN MORE WAYS THAN ONE.

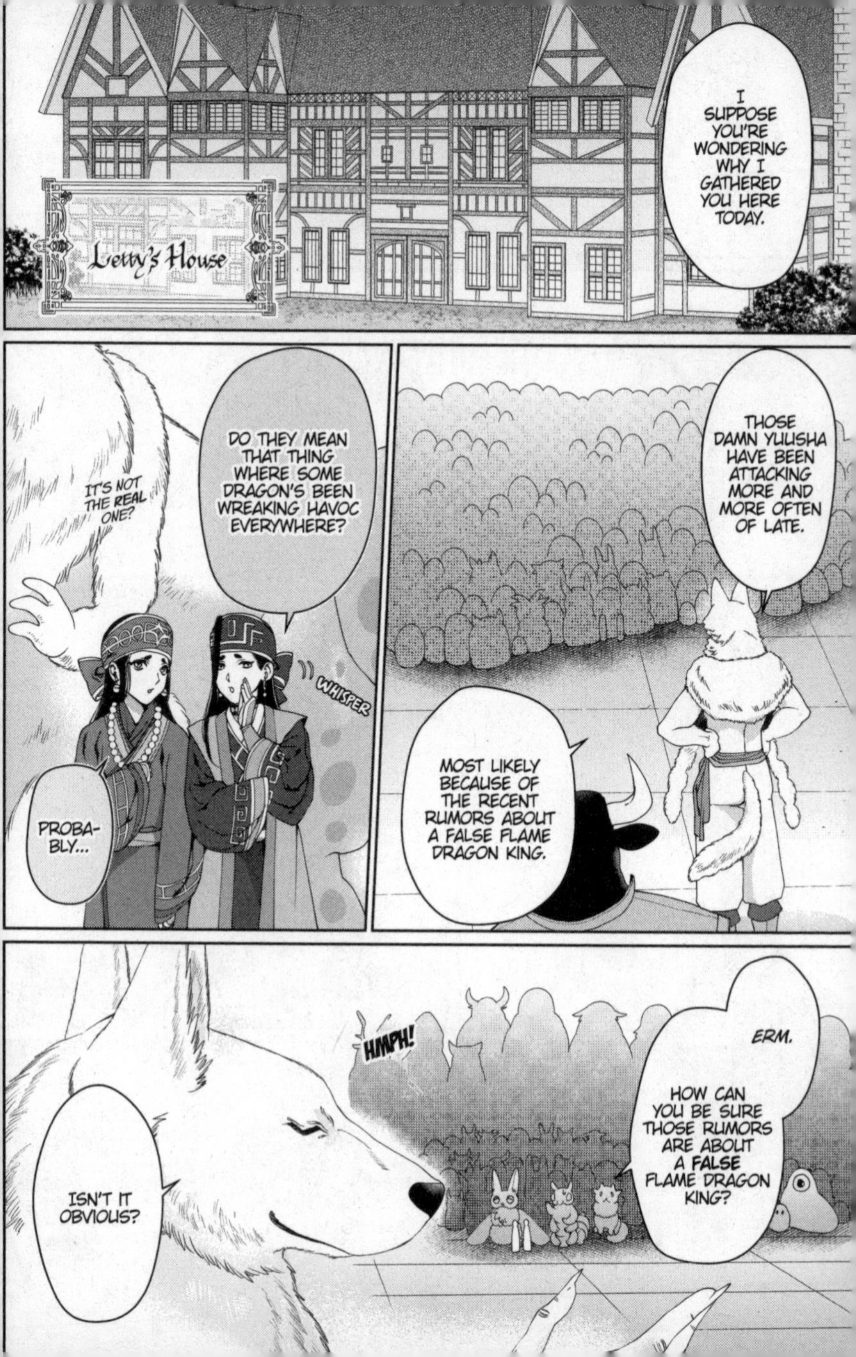
I SUPPOSE YOU'RE WONDERING WHY I GATHERED YOU HERE TODAY.
Letty's House
THOSE DAMN YUUSHA HAVE BEEN ATTACKING MORE AND MORE OFTEN OF LATE.
MOST LIKELY BECAUSE OF THE RECENT RUMORS ABOUT A FALSE FLAME DRAGON KING.
DO THEY MEAN THAT THING WHERE SOME DRAGON'S BEEN WREAKING HAVOC EVERYWHERE?
WHISPER
IT'S NOT THE REAL ONE?
PROBA-BLY...
ERM.
HOW CAN YOU BE SURE THOSE RUMORS ARE ABOUT A FALSE FLAME DRAGON KING?
HMPH!
ISN'T IT OBVIOUS?

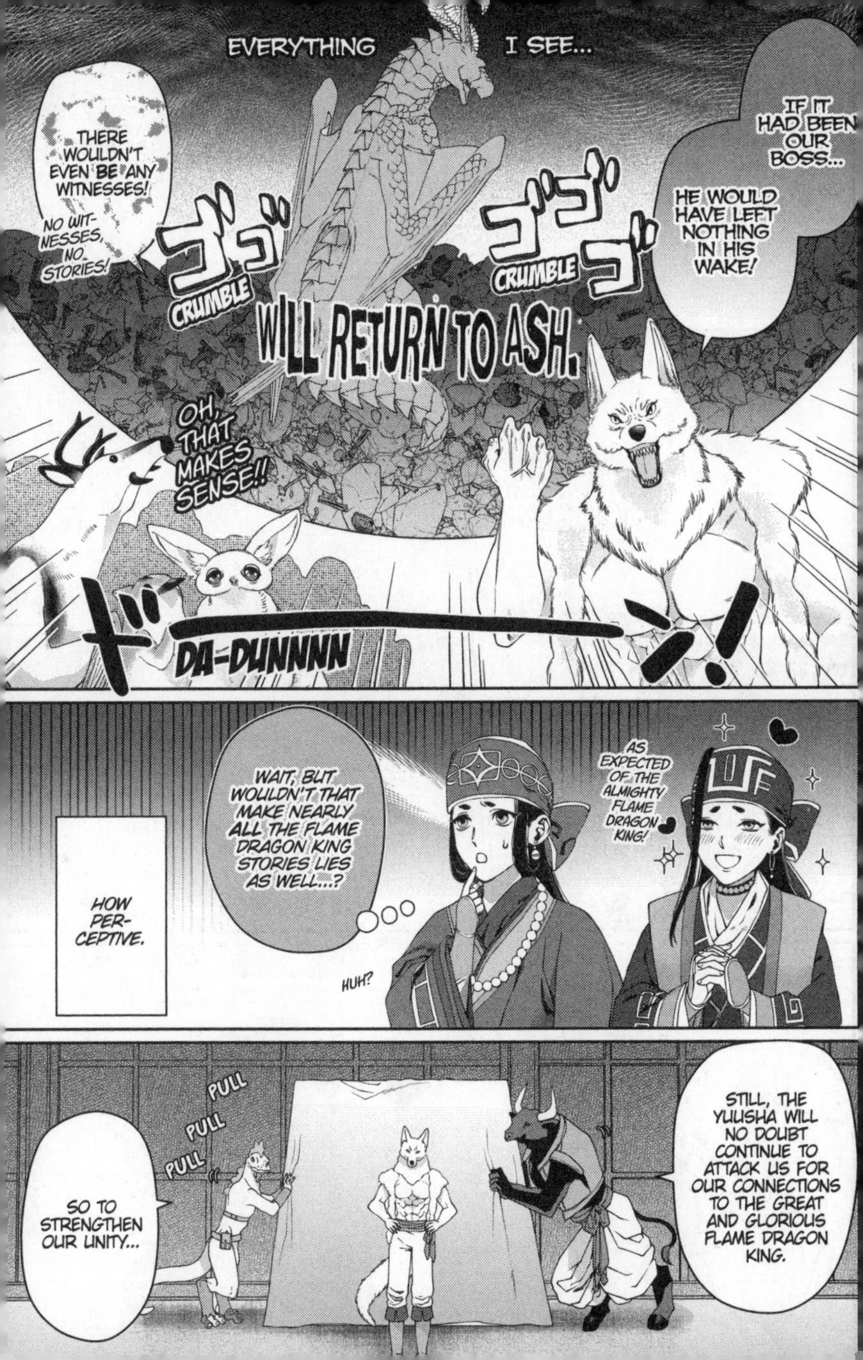
IF IT HAD BEEN OUR BOSS...
HE WOULD HAVE LEFT NOTHING IN HIS WAKE!
EVERYTHING I SEE...
CRUMBLE
CRUMBLE
WILL RETURN TO ASH.
THERE WOULDN'T EVEN BE ANY WITNESSES!
NO WIT-NESSES, NO STORIES!
OH, THAT MAKES SENSE!!
DA-DUNNNN
AS EXPECTED OF THE ALMIGHTY FLAME DRAGON KING!
WAIT, BUT WOULDN'T THAT MAKE NEARLY ALL THE FLAME DRAGON KING STORIES LIES AS WELL...?
HUH?
HOW PER-CEPTIVE.
STILL, THE YUUSHA WILL NO DOUBT CONTINUE TO ATTACK US FOR OUR CONNECTIONS TO THE GREAT AND GLORIOUS FLAME DRAGON KING.
PULL
PULL
PULL
SO TO STRENGTHEN OUR UNITY...

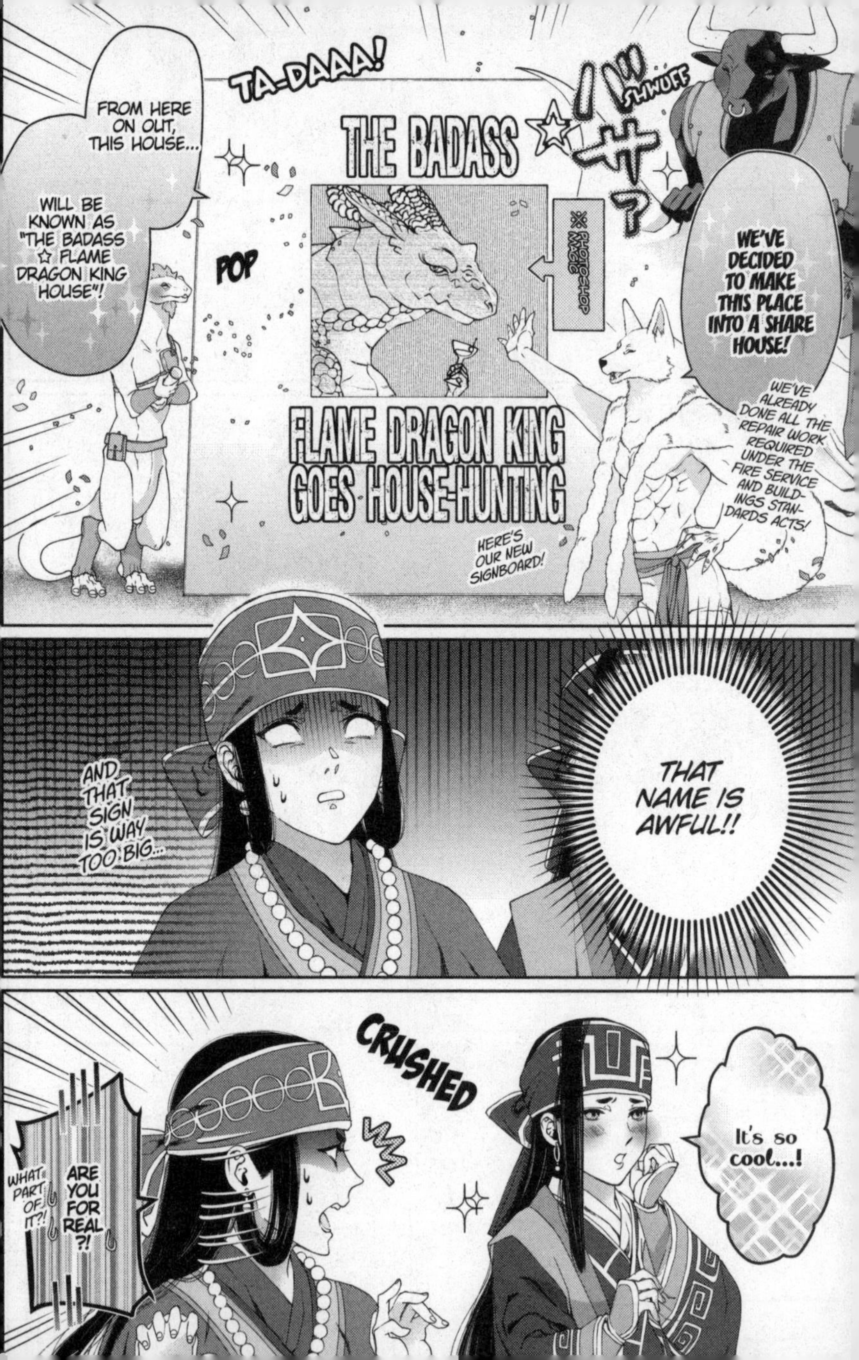
SHWUFF
WE'VE DECIDED TO MAKE THIS PLACE INTO A SHARE HOUSE!
WE'VE ALREADY DONE ALL THE REPAIR WORK REQUIRED UNDER THE FIRE SERVICE AND BUILDINGS STANDARDS ACTS!
TA-DAAA!
THE BADASS ☆ FLAME DRAGON KING GOES HOUSE-HUNTING
※ PHOTOSHOP MAGIC
HERE'S OUR NEW SIGNBOARD!
POP
FROM HERE ON OUT, THIS HOUSE...
WILL BE KNOWN AS "THE BADASS ☆ FLAME DRAGON KING HOUSE"!
THAT NAME IS AWFUL!!
AND THAT SIGN IS WAY TOO BIG...
It's so cool...!
CRUSHED
ARE YOU FOR REAL?!
WHAT PART OF IT?!

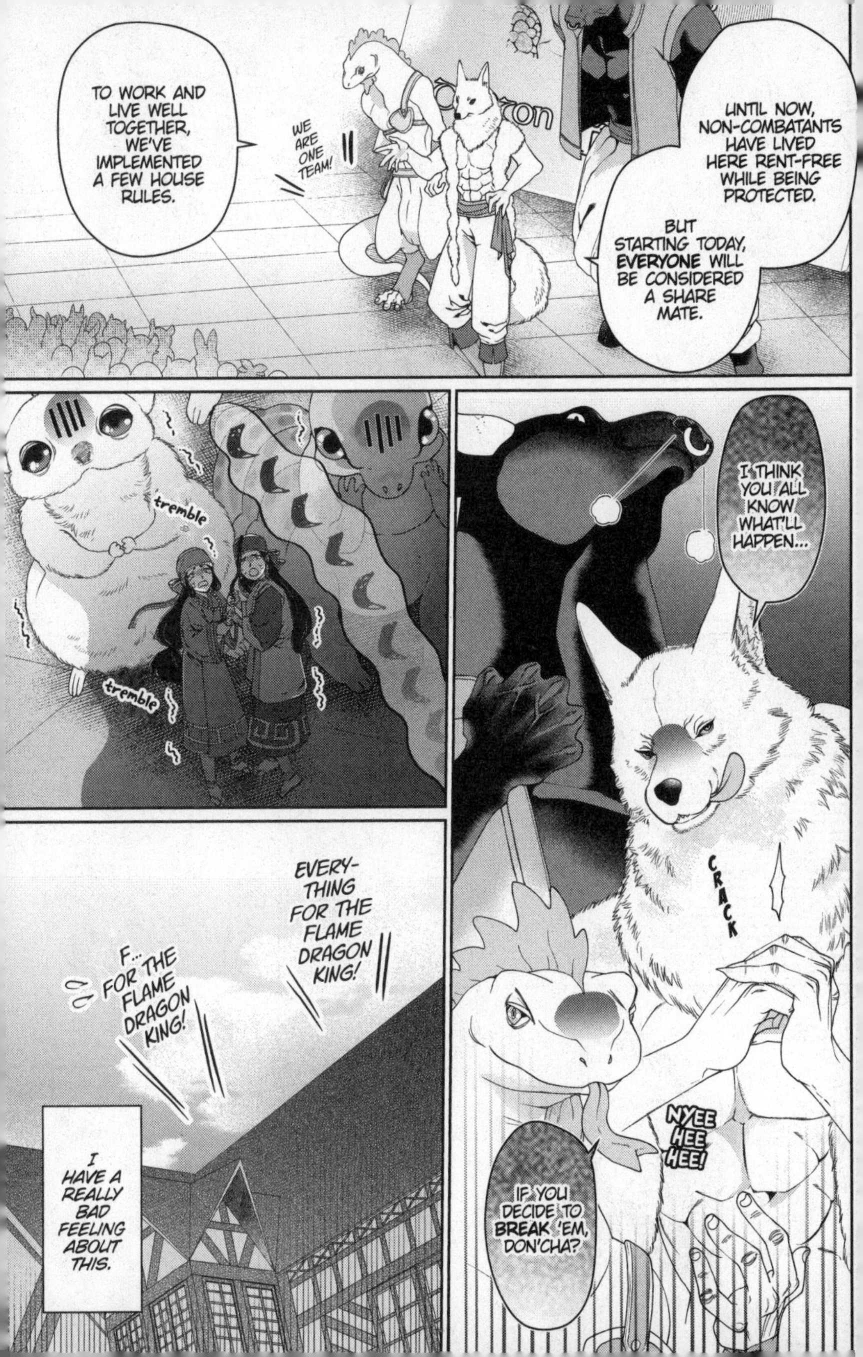
UNTIL NOW, NON-COMBATANTS HAVE LIVED HERE RENT-FREE WHILE BEING PROTECTED.
BUT STARTING TODAY, EVERYONE WILL BE CONSIDERED A SHARE MATE.
WE ARE ONE TEAM!
TO WORK AND LIVE WELL TOGETHER, WE'VE IMPLEMENTED A FEW HOUSE RULES.
I THINK YOU ALL KNOW WHAT'LL HAPPEN...
CRACK
NYEE HEE HEE!
IF YOU DECIDE TO BREAK 'EM, DON'CHA?
tremble
tremble
EVERY-THING FOR THE FLAME DRAGON KING!
F... FOR THE FLAME DRAGON KING!
I HAVE A REALLY BAD FEELING ABOUT THIS.

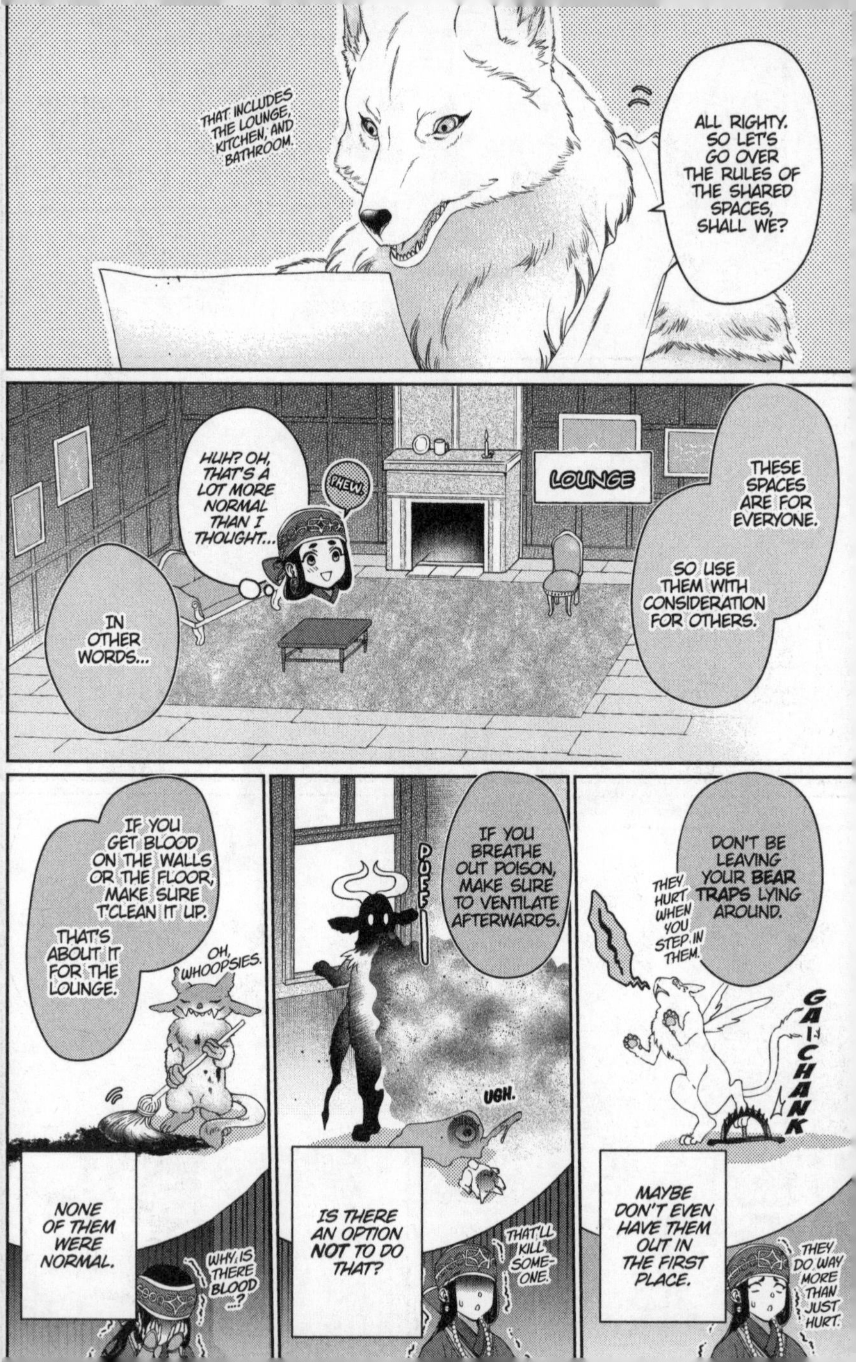
ALL RIGHTY. SO LET'S GO OVER THE RULES OF THE SHARED SPACES, SHALL WE?
THAT INCLUDES THE LOUNGE, KITCHEN, AND BATHROOM.
THESE SPACES ARE FOR EVERYONE.
SO USE THEM WITH CONSIDERATION FOR OTHERS.
LOUNGE
PHEW.
HUH? OH, THAT'S A LOT MORE NORMAL THAN I THOUGHT...
IN OTHER WORDS...
DON'T BE LEAVING YOUR BEAR TRAPS LYING AROUND.
THEY HURT WHEN YOU STEP IN THEM.
GAICHANK
MAYBE DON'T EVEN HAVE THEM OUT IN THE FIRST PLACE.
THEY DO WAY MORE THAN JUST HURT.
IF YOU BREATHE OUT POISON, MAKE SURE TO VENTILATE AFTERWARDS.
PUFF
UGH.
IS THERE AN OPTION NOT TO DO THAT?
THAT'LL KILL SOME-ONE.
IF YOU GET BLOOD ON THE WALLS OR THE FLOOR, MAKE SURE T'CLEAN IT UP.
THAT'S ABOUT IT FOR THE LOUNGE.
OH, WHOOPSIES.
NONE OF THEM WERE NORMAL.
WHY IS THERE BLOOD...?

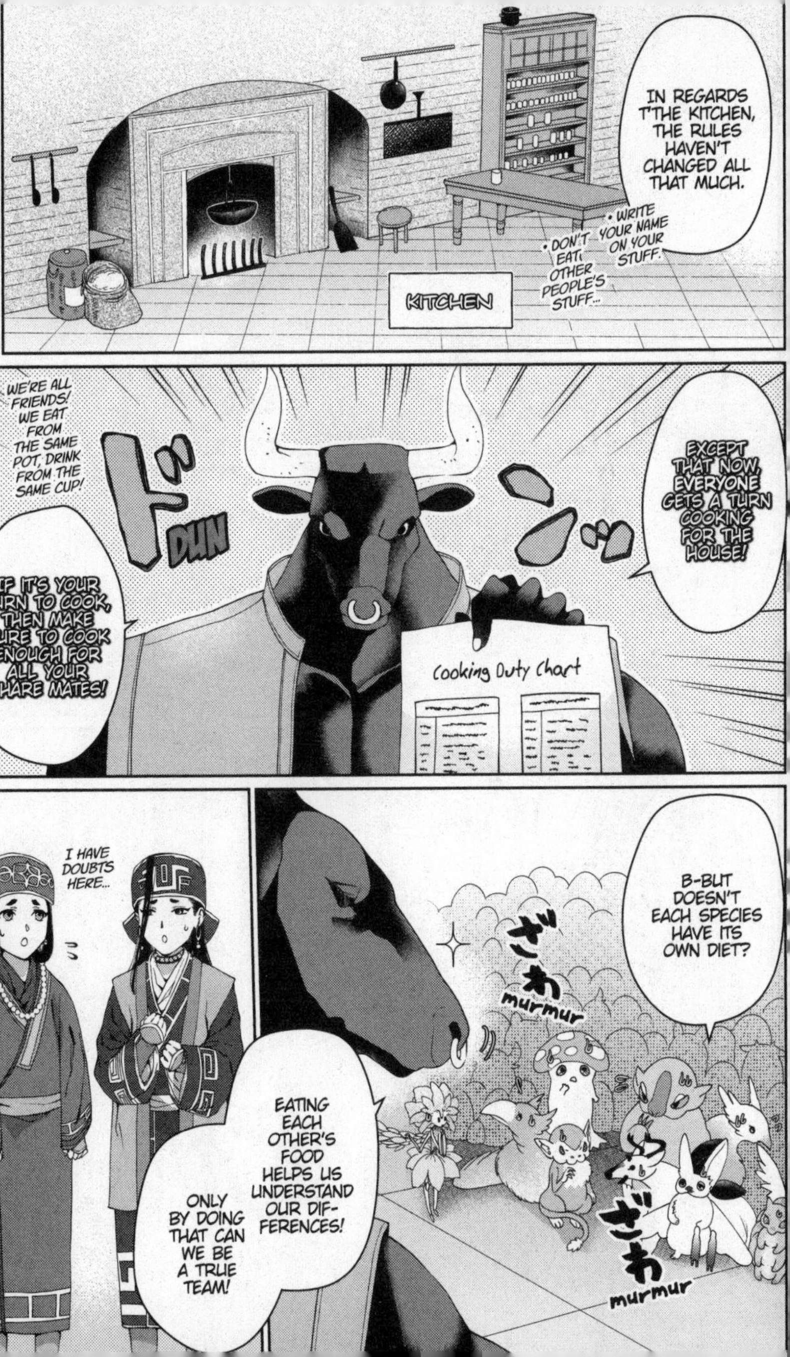
IN REGARDS T'THE KITCHEN, THE RULES HAVEN'T CHANGED ALL THAT MUCH.
• WRITE YOUR NAME ON YOUR STUFF.
• DON'T EAT OTHER PEOPLE'S STUFF...
KITCHEN
EXCEPT THAT NOW, EVERYONE GETS A TURN COOKING FOR THE HOUSE!
Cooking Duty Chart
IF IT'S YOUR TURN TO COOK, THEN MAKE SURE TO COOK ENOUGH FOR ALL YOUR SHARE MATES!
DUN
WE'RE ALL FRIENDS! WE EAT FROM THE SAME POT, DRINK FROM THE SAME CUP!
B-BUT DOESN'T EACH SPECIES HAVE ITS OWN DIET?
murmur
murmur
EATING EACH OTHER'S FOOD HELPS US UNDERSTAND OUR DIF-FERENCES!
ONLY BY DOING THAT CAN WE BE A TRUE TEAM!
I HAVE DOUBTS HERE...

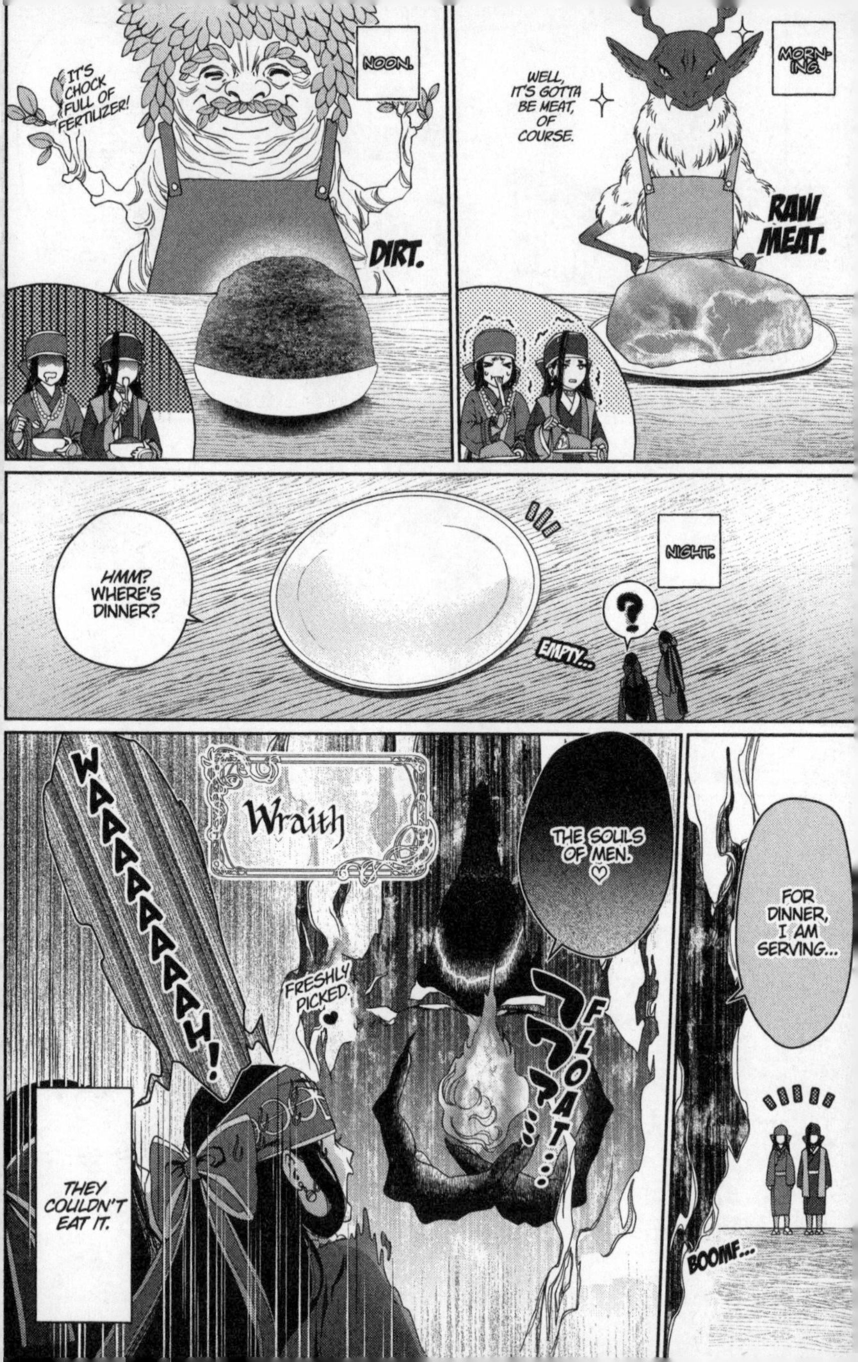
MORN-ING.
WELL, IT'S GOTTA BE MEAT, OF COURSE.
RAW MEAT.
NOON.
IT'S CHOCK FULL OF FERTILIZER!
DIRT.
NIGHT.
HMM? WHERE'S DINNER?
EMPTY...
FOR DINNER, I AM SERVING...
BOOMF...
THE SOULS OF MEN. ♡
Wraith
FLOAT...
FRESHLY PICKED. ♥
WAAAAAAAAH!
THEY COULDN'T EAT IT.

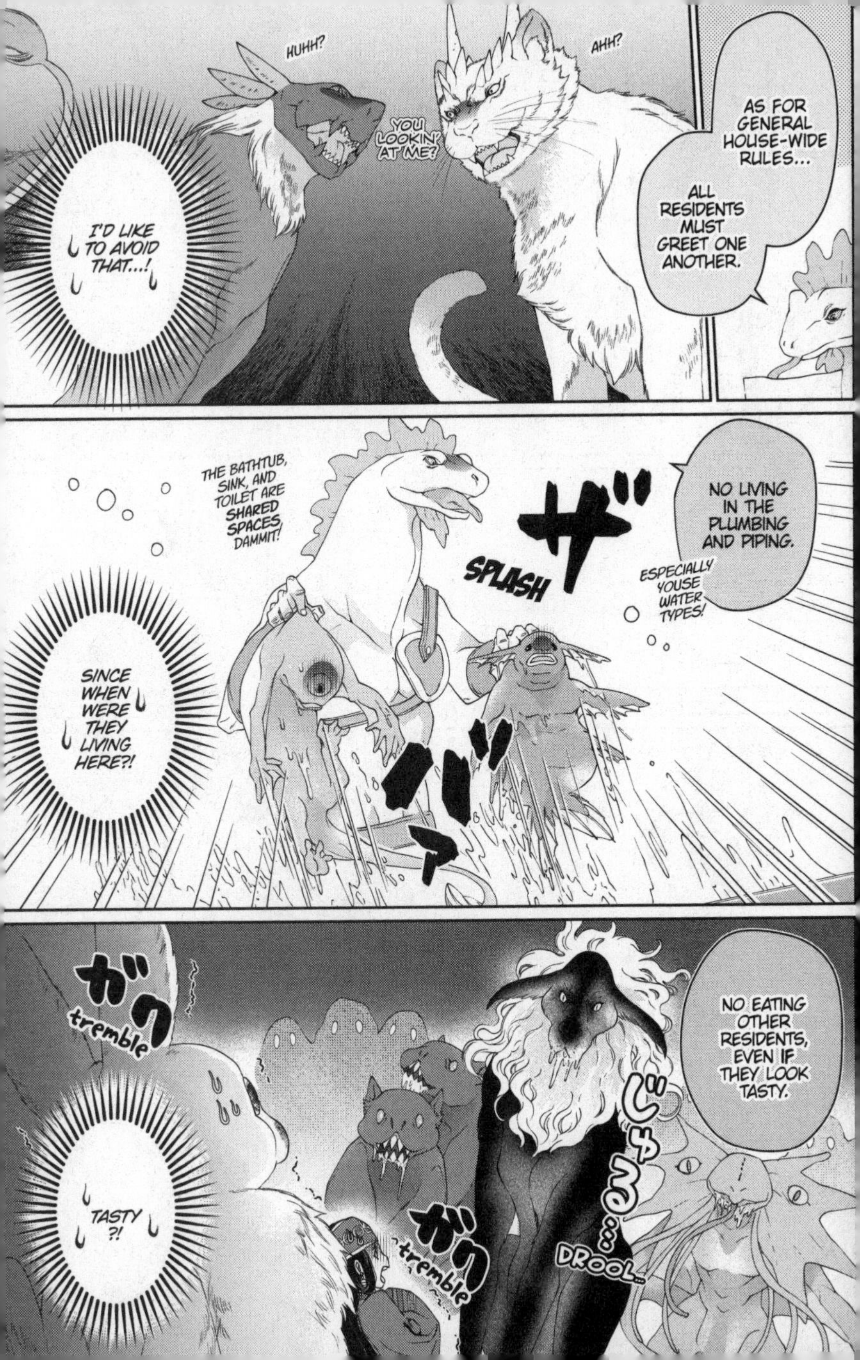
AS FOR GENERAL HOUSE-WIDE RULES...
ALL RESIDENTS MUST GREET ONE ANOTHER.
AHH?
YOU LOOKIN' AT ME?
HUHH?
I'D LIKE TO AVOID THAT...!
NO LIVING IN THE PLUMBING AND PIPING.
ESPECIALLY YOUSE WATER TYPES!
SPLASH
THE BATHTUB, SINK, AND TOILET ARE SHARED SPACES, DAMMIT!
SINCE WHEN WERE THEY LIVING HERE?!
NO EATING OTHER RESIDENTS, EVEN IF THEY LOOK TASTY.
DROOL...
tremble
tremble
TASTY?!

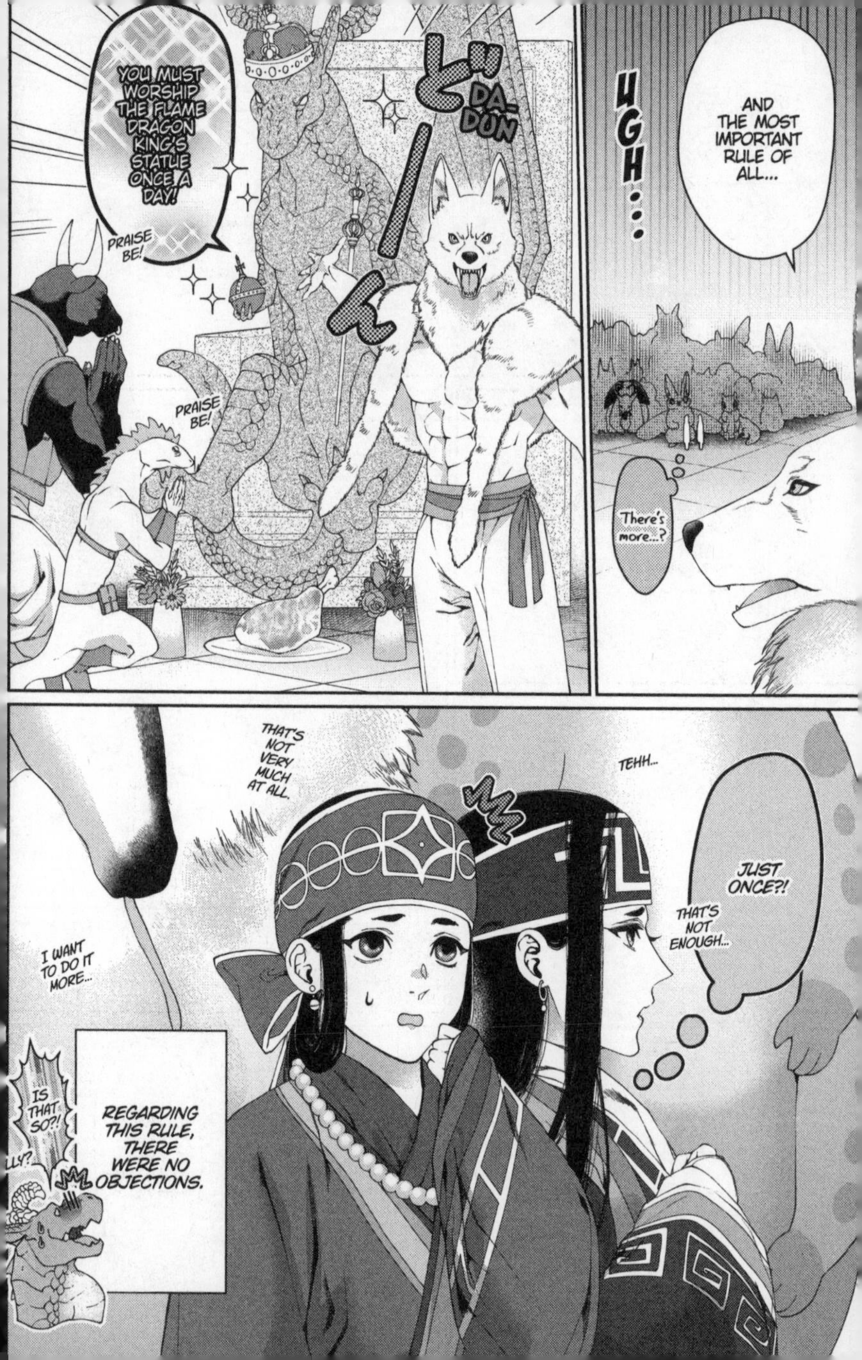
AND THE MOST IMPORTANT RULE OF ALL...
UGH...
There's more...?
どーん
DA-DUN
YOU MUST WORSHIP THE FLAME DRAGON KING'S STATUE ONCE A DAY!
PRAISE BE!
PRAISE BE!
JUST ONCE?!
TEHH...
THAT'S NOT ENOUGH...
THAT'S NOT VERY MUCH AT ALL.
I WANT TO DO IT MORE...
IS THAT SO?!
REGARDING THIS RULE, THERE WERE NO OBJECTIONS.

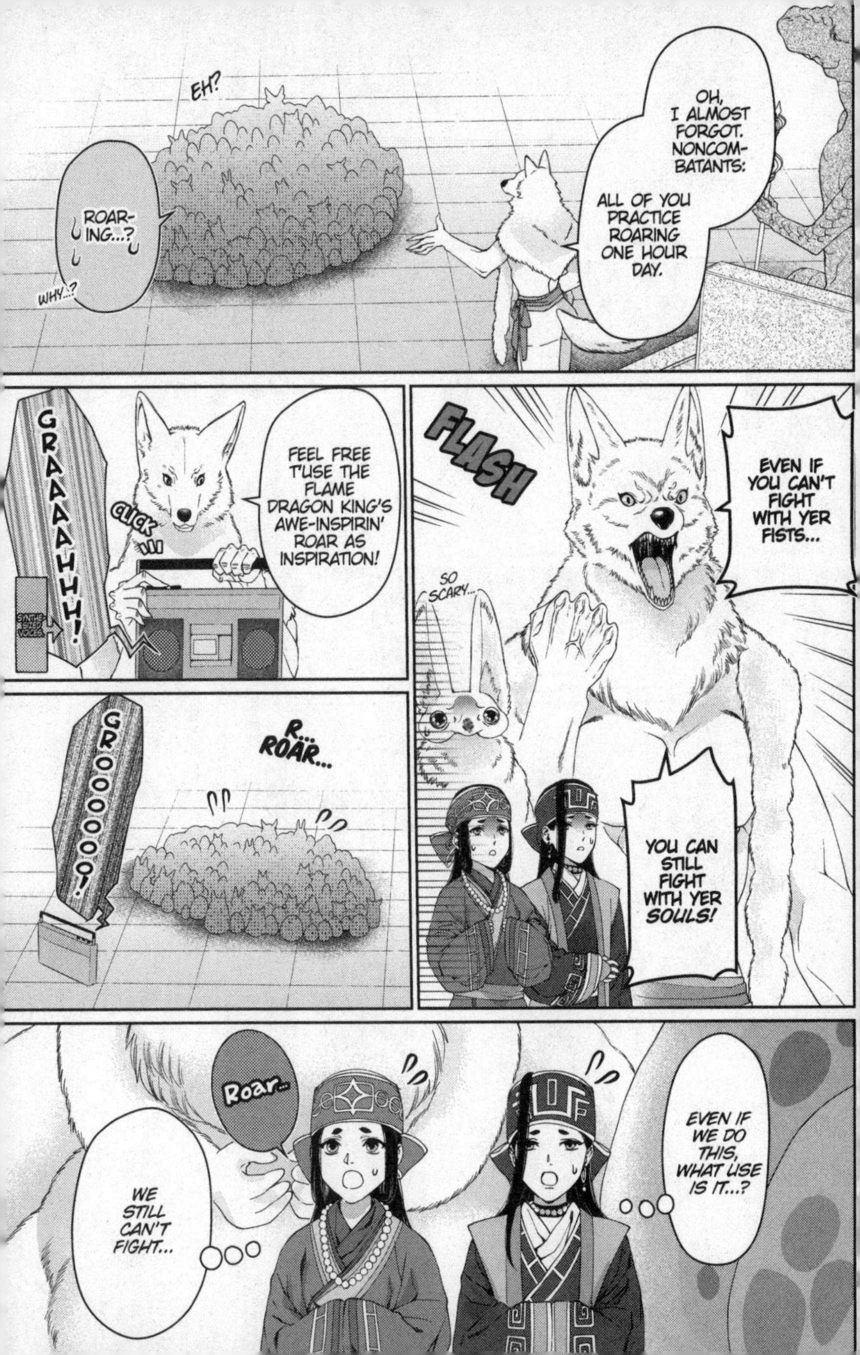
OH, I ALMOST FORGOT. NONCOMBATANTS:
ALL OF YOU PRACTICE ROARING ONE HOUR DAY.
EH?
ROARING...?
WHY...?
FLASH
EVEN IF YOU CAN'T FIGHT WITH YER FISTS...
SO SCARY...
YOU CAN STILL FIGHT WITH YER SOULS!
CLICK
FEEL FREE T'USE THE FLAME DRAGON KING'S AWE-INSPIRIN' ROAR AS INSPIRATION!
GRAAAAAHHH!
SYNTHESIZED VOICES.
GROOOOOOO!
R... ROAR...
EVEN IF WE DO THIS, WHAT USE IS IT...?
Roar...
WE STILL CAN'T FIGHT...

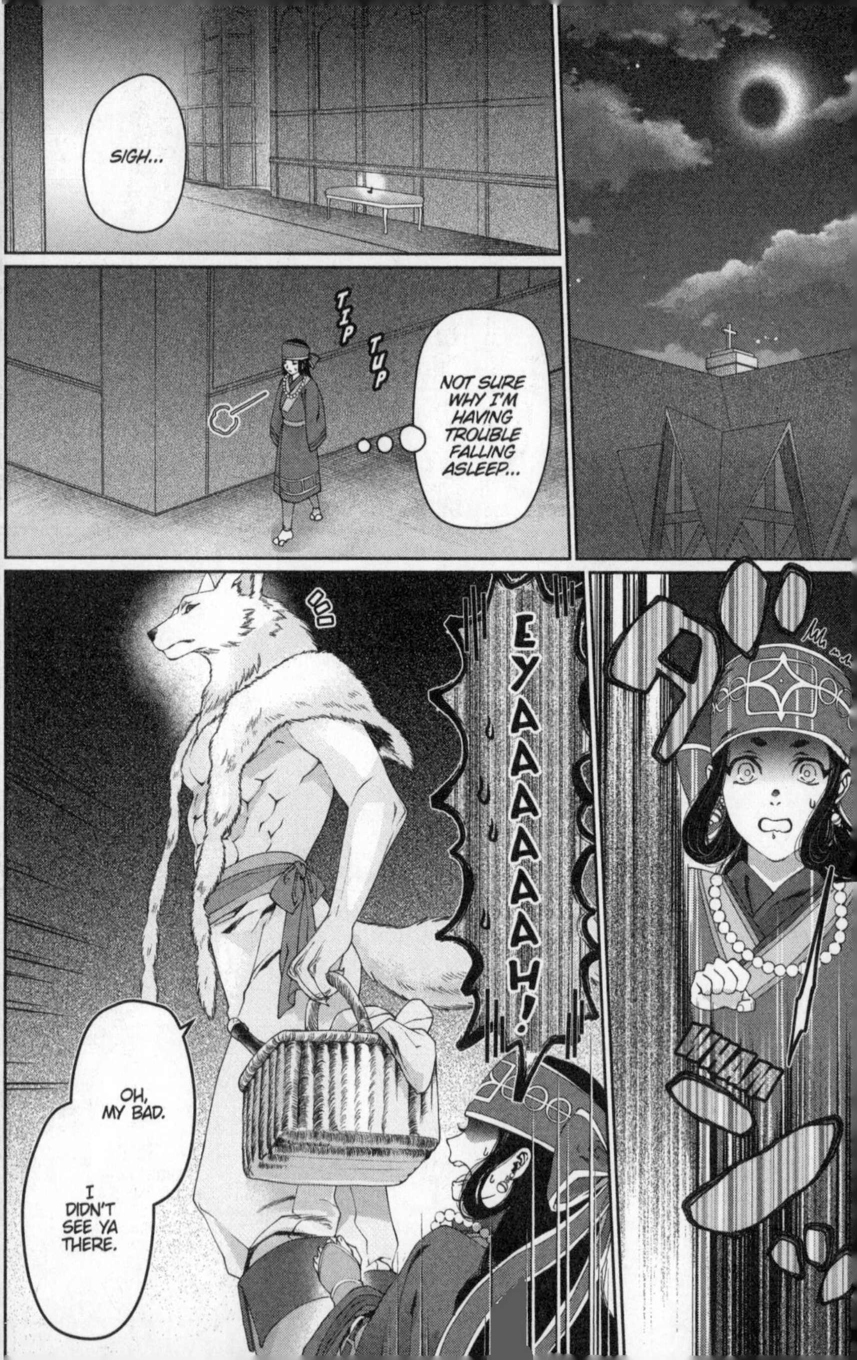
SIGH...
TIP
TUP
NOT SURE WHY I'M HAVING TROUBLE FALLING ASLEEP...
!!
EYAAAAAAH!
OH, MY BAD.
I DIDN'T SEE YA THERE.

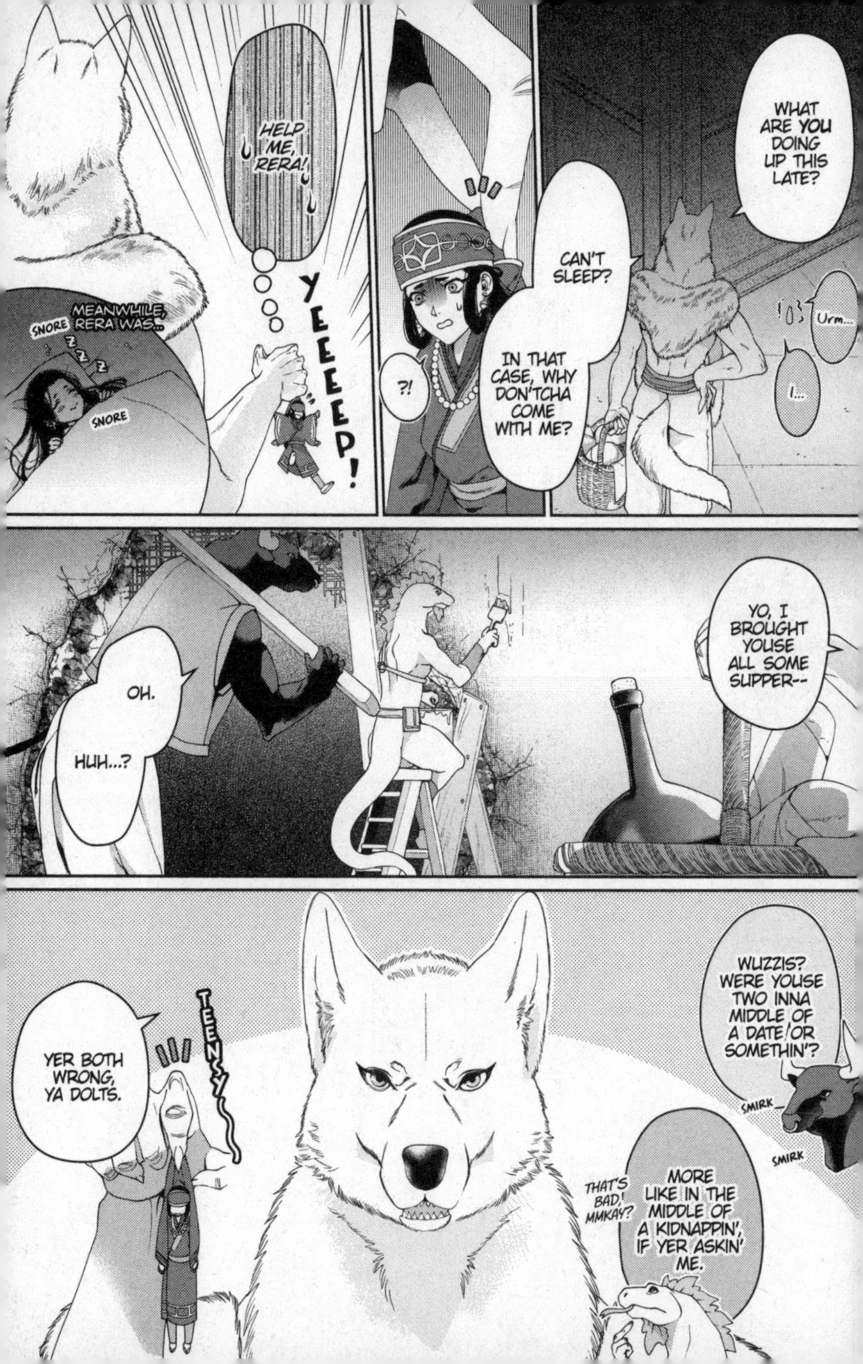
WHAT ARE YOU DOING UP THIS LATE?
Urm...
I...
CAN'T SLEEP?
IN THAT CASE, WHY DON'TCHA COME WITH ME?
?!
HELP ME, RERA!
YEEEEP!
MEANWHILE, RERA WAS...
SNORE
Z Z Z
SNORE
YO, I BROUGHT YOUSE ALL SOME SUPPER--
OH.
HUH...?
WUZZIS? WERE YOUSE TWO INNA MIDDLE OF A DATE OR SOMETHIN'?
SMIRK
SMIRK
MORE LIKE IN THE MIDDLE OF A KIDNAPPIN', IF YER ASKIN' ME.
THAT'S BAD! MMKAY?
TEENSY
YER BOTH WRONG, YA DOLTS.

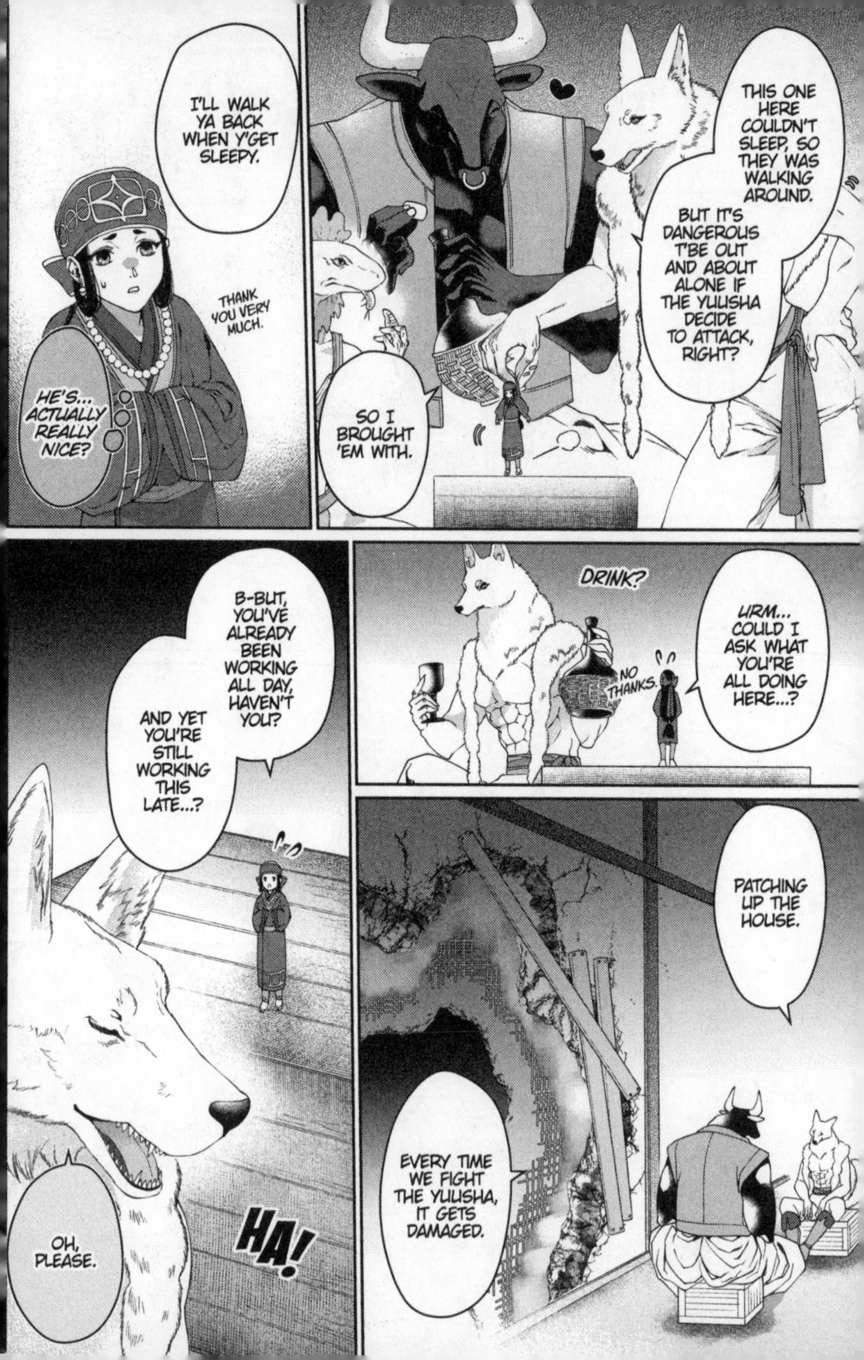

THIS ONE HERE COULDN'T SLEEP, SO THEY WAS WALKING AROUND.
BUT IT'S DANGEROUS T'BE OUT AND ABOUT ALONE IF THE YUUSHA DECIDE TO ATTACK, RIGHT?
SO I BROUGHT 'EM WITH.
I'LL WALK YA BACK WHEN Y'GET SLEEPY.
THANK YOU VERY MUCH.
HE'S... ACTUALLY REALLY NICE?
URM... COULD I ASK WHAT YOU'RE ALL DOING HERE...?
DRINK?
NO THANKS.
PATCHING UP THE HOUSE.
EVERY TIME WE FIGHT THE YUUSHA, IT GETS DAMAGED.
B-BUT, YOU'VE ALREADY BEEN WORKING ALL DAY, HAVEN'T YOU?
AND YET YOU'RE STILL WORKING THIS LATE...?
HA!
OH, PLEASE.

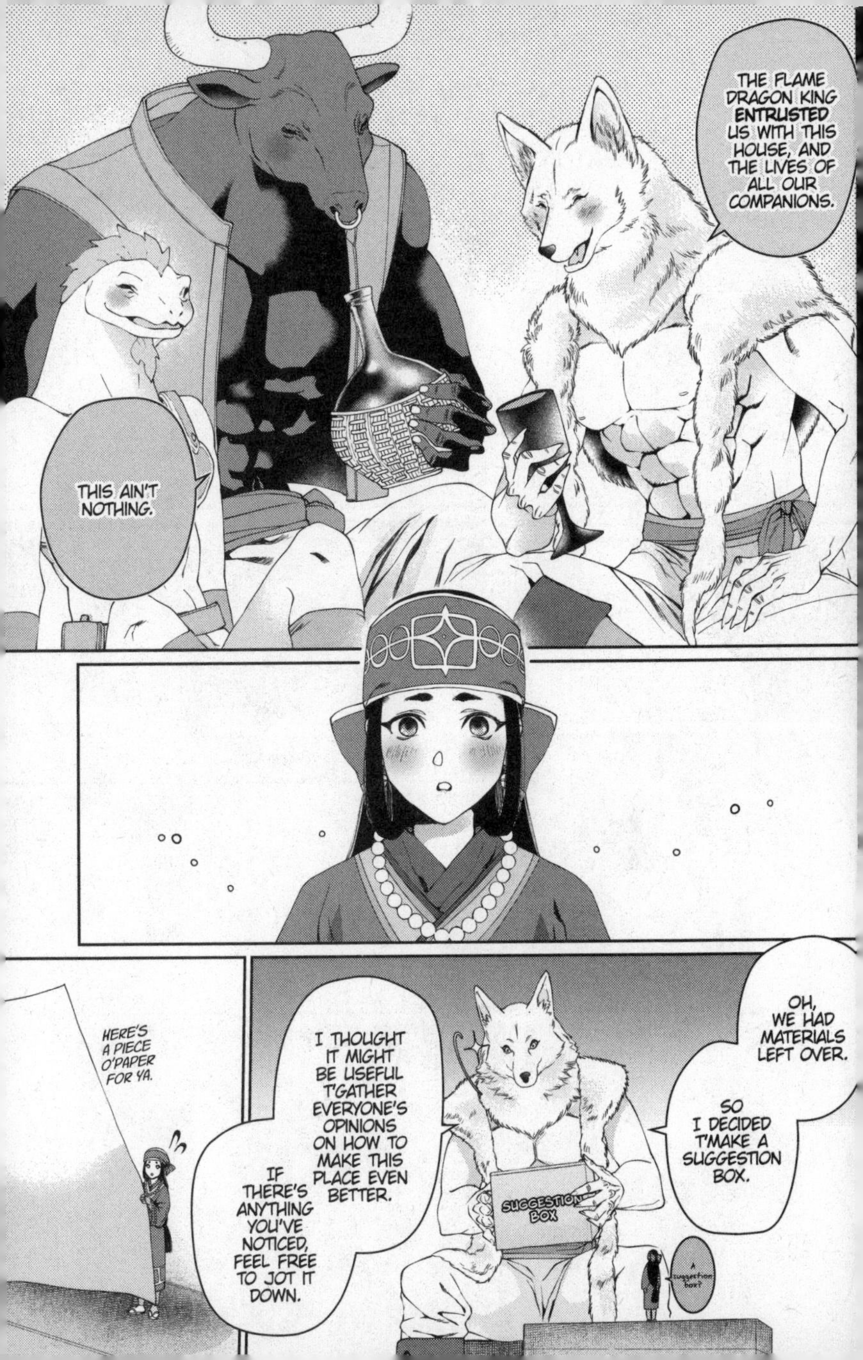
THE FLAME DRAGON KING ENTRUSTED US WITH THIS HOUSE, AND THE LIVES OF ALL OUR COMPANIONS.
THIS AIN'T NOTHING.
OH, WE HAD MATERIALS LEFT OVER.
SO I DECIDED T'MAKE A SUGGESTION BOX.
SUGGESTION BOX
A suggestion box?
I THOUGHT IT MIGHT BE USEFUL T'GATHER EVERYONE'S OPINIONS ON HOW TO MAKE THIS PLACE EVEN BETTER.
IF THERE'S ANYTHING YOU'VE NOTICED, FEEL FREE TO JOT IT DOWN.
HERE'S A PIECE O'PAPER FOR YA.

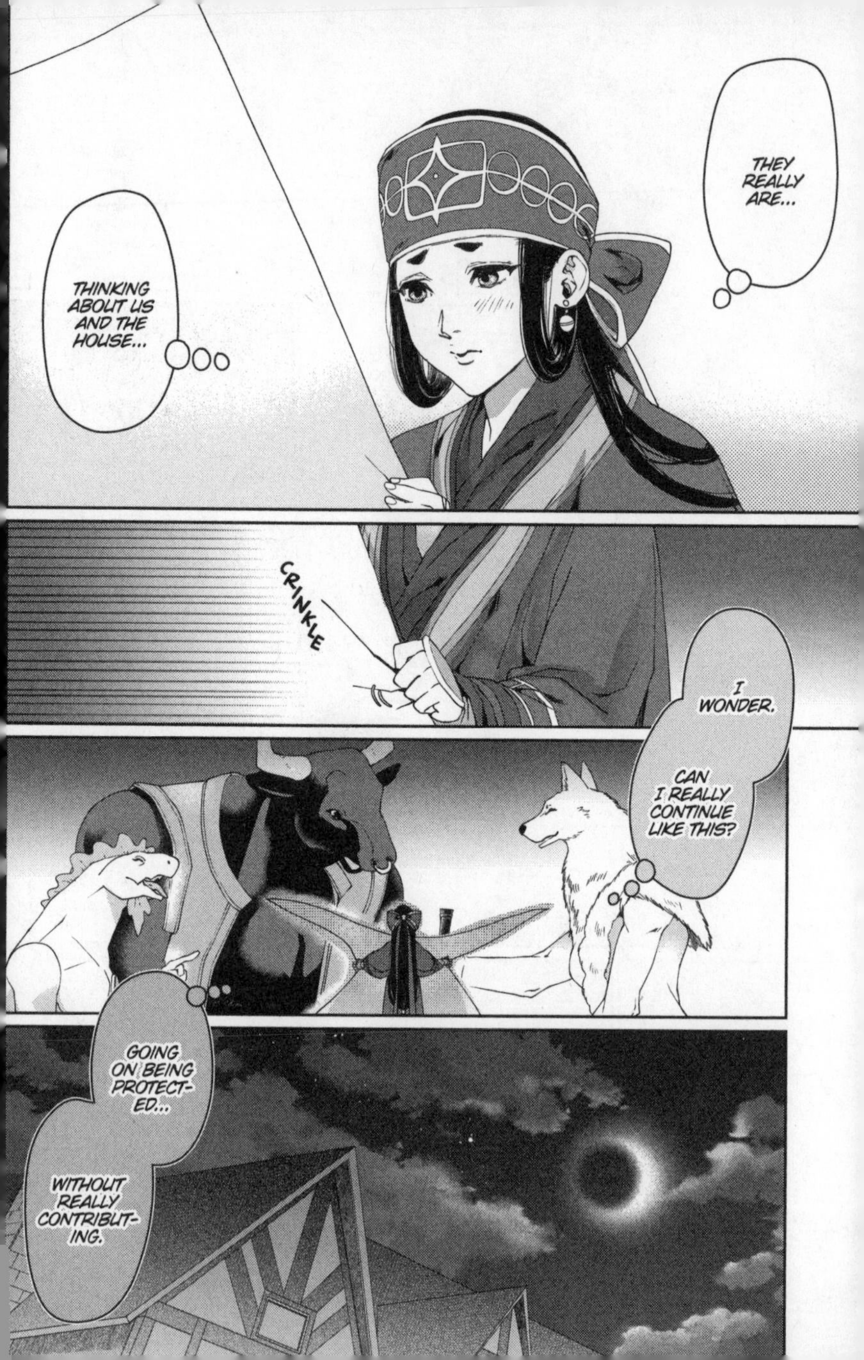
THEY REALLY ARE...
THINKING ABOUT US AND THE HOUSE...
CRINKLE
I WONDER.
CAN I REALLY CONTINUE LIKE THIS?
GOING ON BEING PROTECT-ED...
WITHOUT REALLY CONTRIBUT-ING.

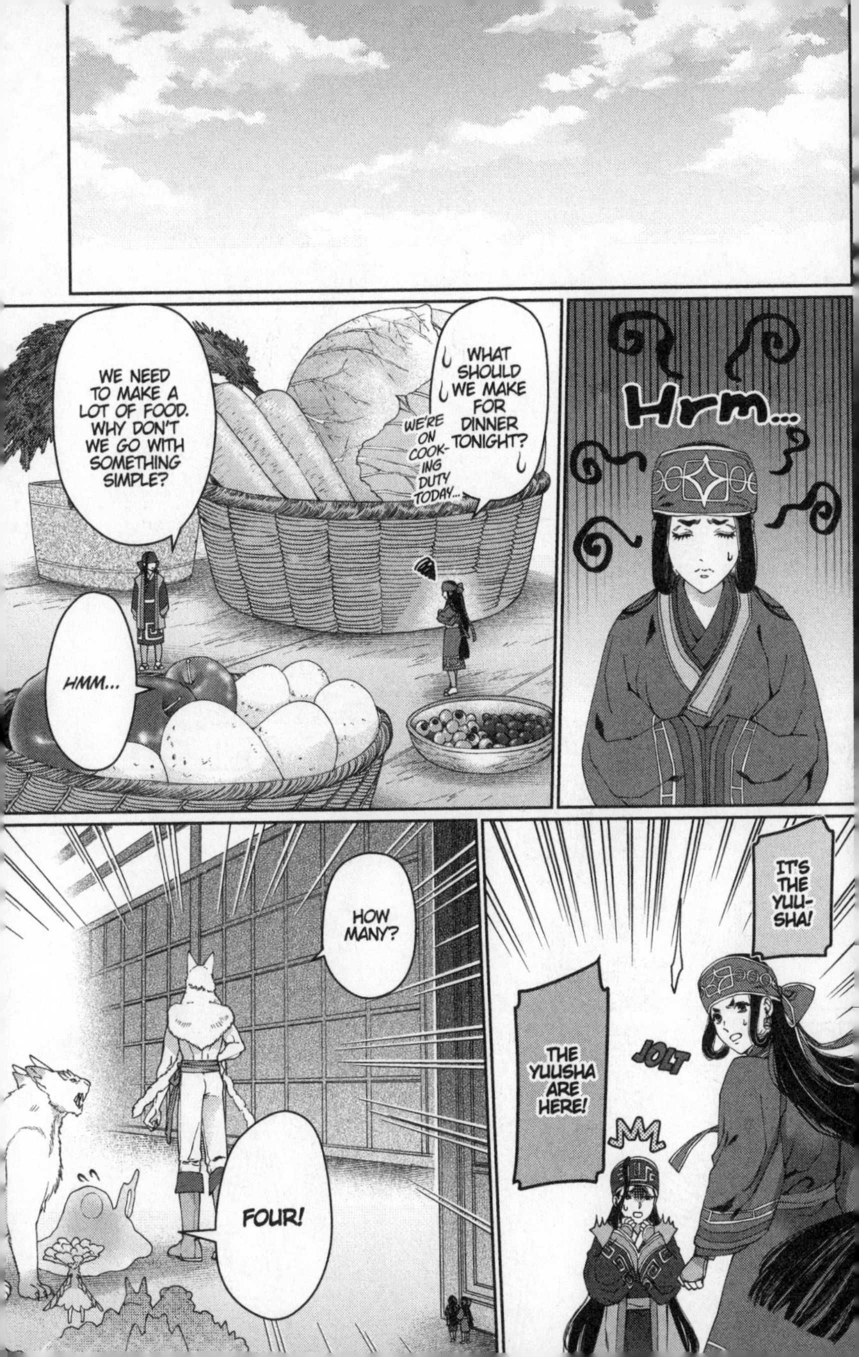
Hrm...
WHAT SHOULD WE MAKE FOR DINNER TONIGHT?
WE'RE ON COOK-ING DUTY TODAY...
WE NEED TO MAKE A LOT OF FOOD. WHY DON'T WE GO WITH SOMETHING SIMPLE?
HMM...
IT'S THE YUU-SHA!
JOLT
THE YUUSHA ARE HERE!
HOW MANY?
FOUR!

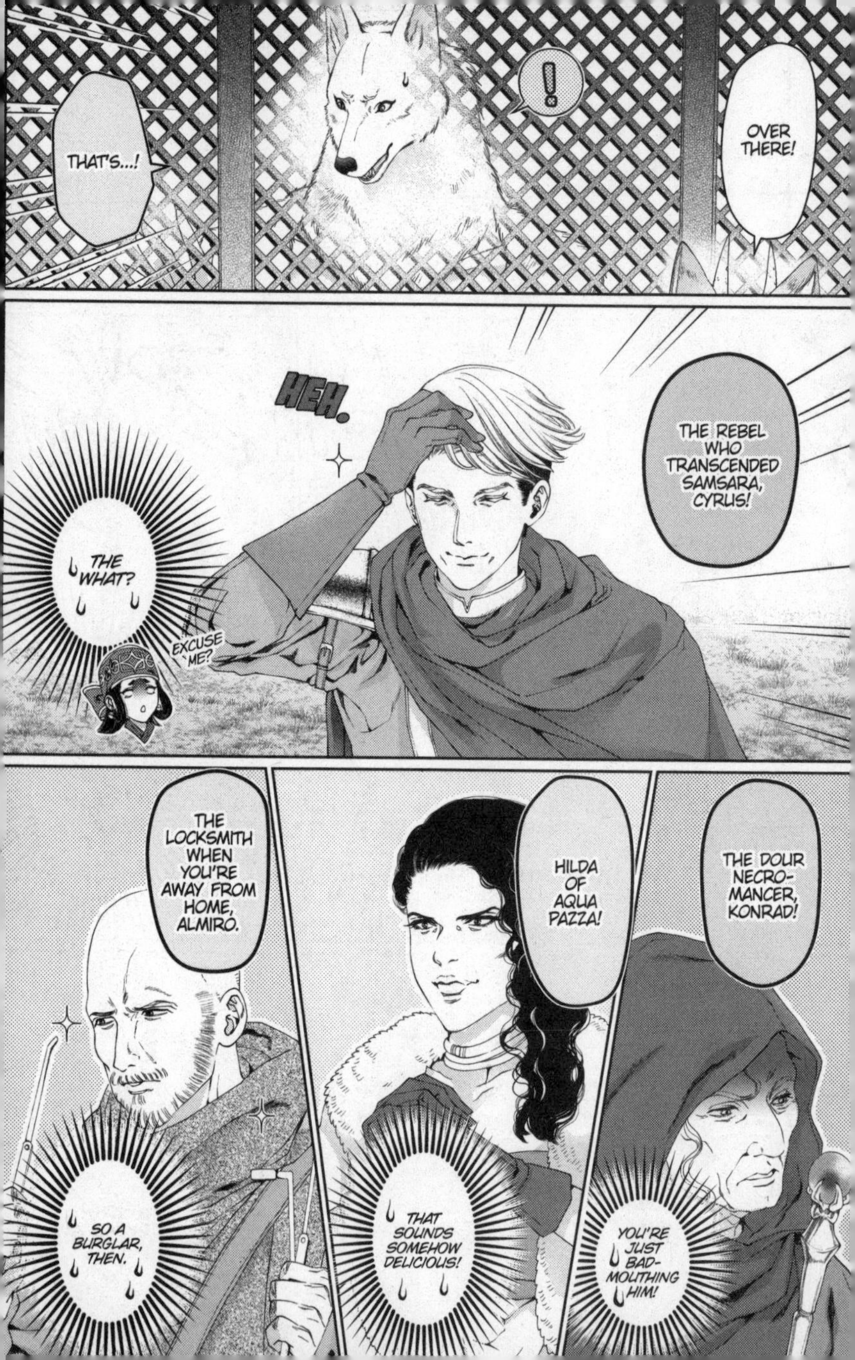
OVER THERE!
!
THAT'S...!
THE REBEL WHO TRANSCENDED SAMSARA, CYRUS!
HEH.
THE WHAT?
EXCUSE ME?
THE DOUR NECRO-MANCER, KONRAD!
YOU'RE JUST BAD-MOUTHING HIM!
HILDA OF AQUA PAZZA!
THAT SOUNDS SOMEHOW DELICIOUS!
THE LOCKSMITH WHEN YOU'RE AWAY FROM HOME, ALMIRO.
SO A BURGLAR, THEN.

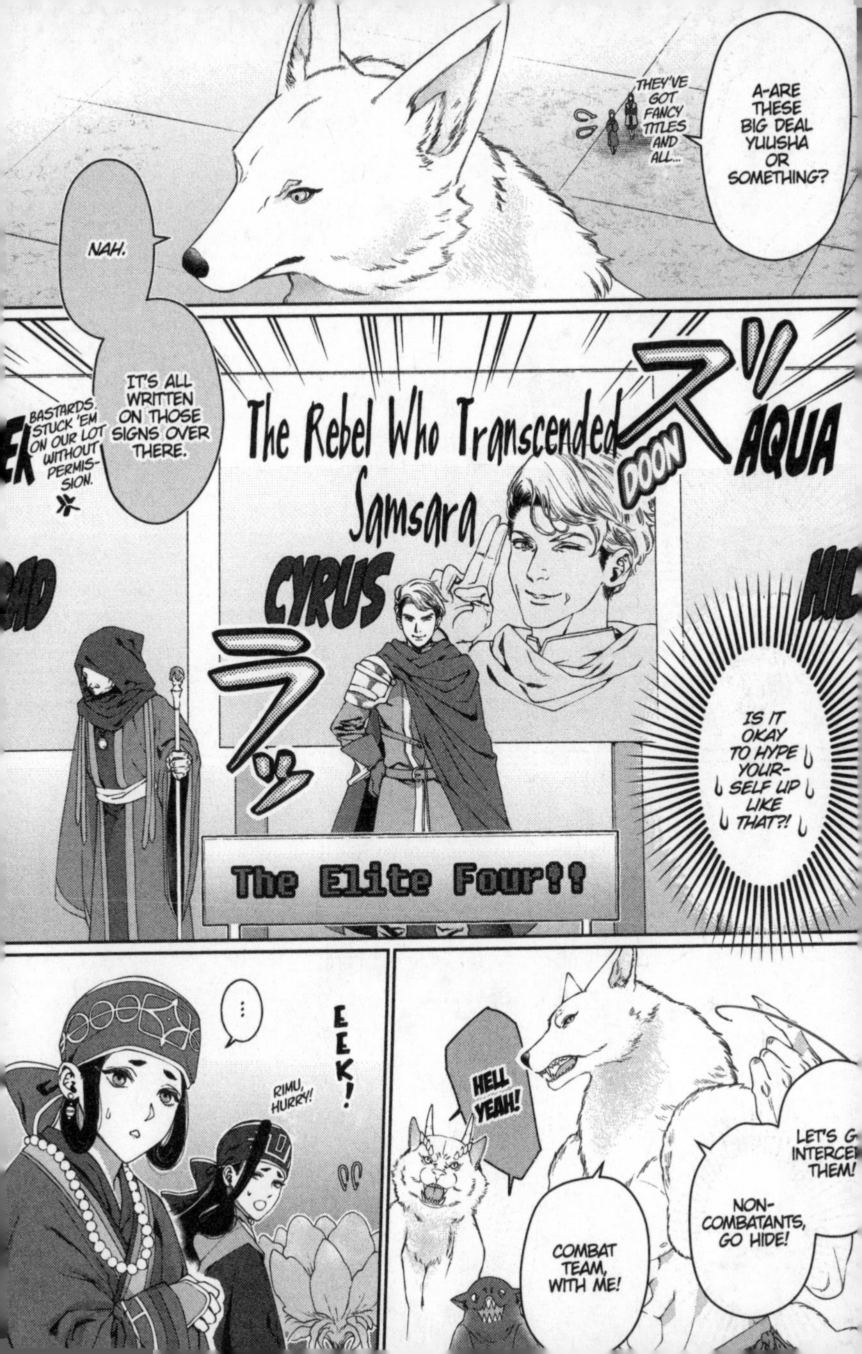
A-ARE THESE BIG DEAL YUUSHA OR SOMETHING?
THEY'VE GOT FANCY TITLES AND ALL...
NAH.
IT'S ALL WRITTEN ON THOSE SIGNS OVER THERE.
BASTARDS. STUCK 'EM ON OUR LOT WITHOUT PERMISSION.
AQUA
DOON
The Rebel Who Transcended Samsara
CYRUS
IS IT OKAY TO HYPE YOURSELF UP LIKE THAT?!
The Elite Four!!
NON-COMBATANTS, GO HIDE!
COMBAT TEAM, WITH ME!
HELL YEAH!
...
EEK!
RIMU, HURRY!

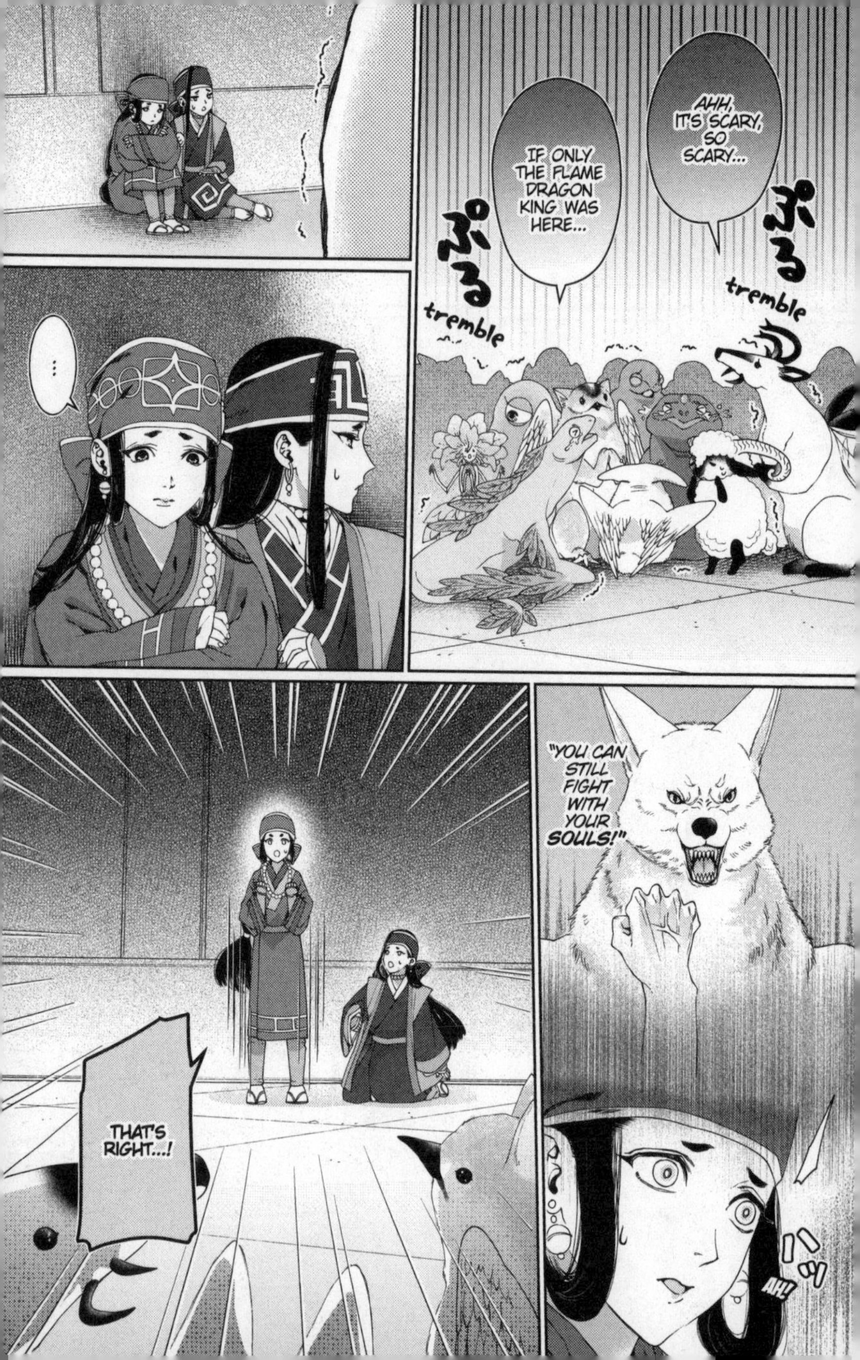
AHH, IT'S SCARY, SO SCARY...
ぷる
tremble
IF ONLY THE FLAME DRAGON KING WAS HERE...
ぷる
tremble
...
"YOU CAN STILL FIGHT WITH YOUR SOULS!"
ハッ
AH!
THAT'S RIGHT...!

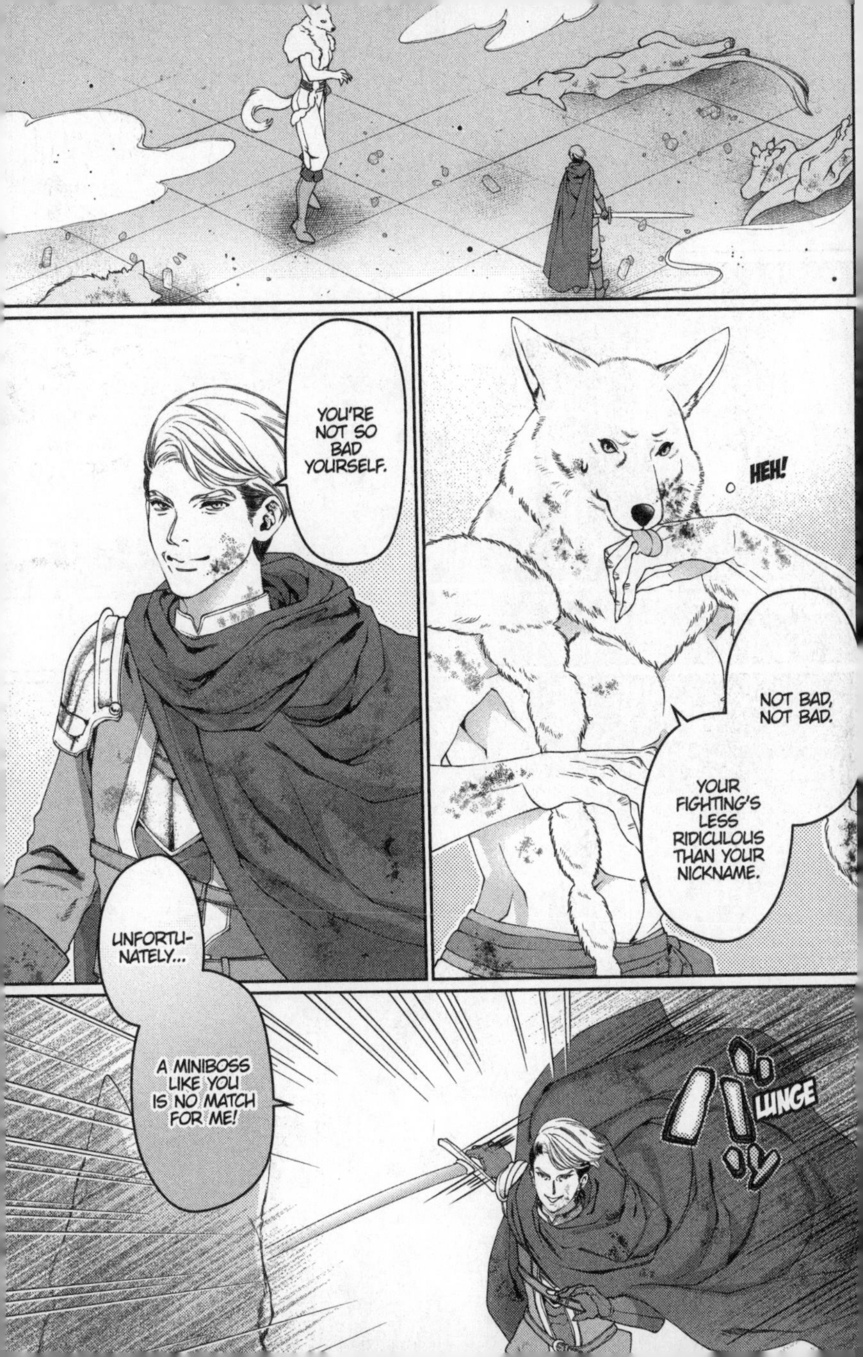
HEH!
NOT BAD, NOT BAD.
YOUR FIGHTING'S LESS RIDICULOUS THAN YOUR NICKNAME.
YOU'RE NOT SO BAD YOURSELF.
UNFORTU-NATELY...
A MINIBOSS LIKE YOU IS NO MATCH FOR ME!
LUNGE

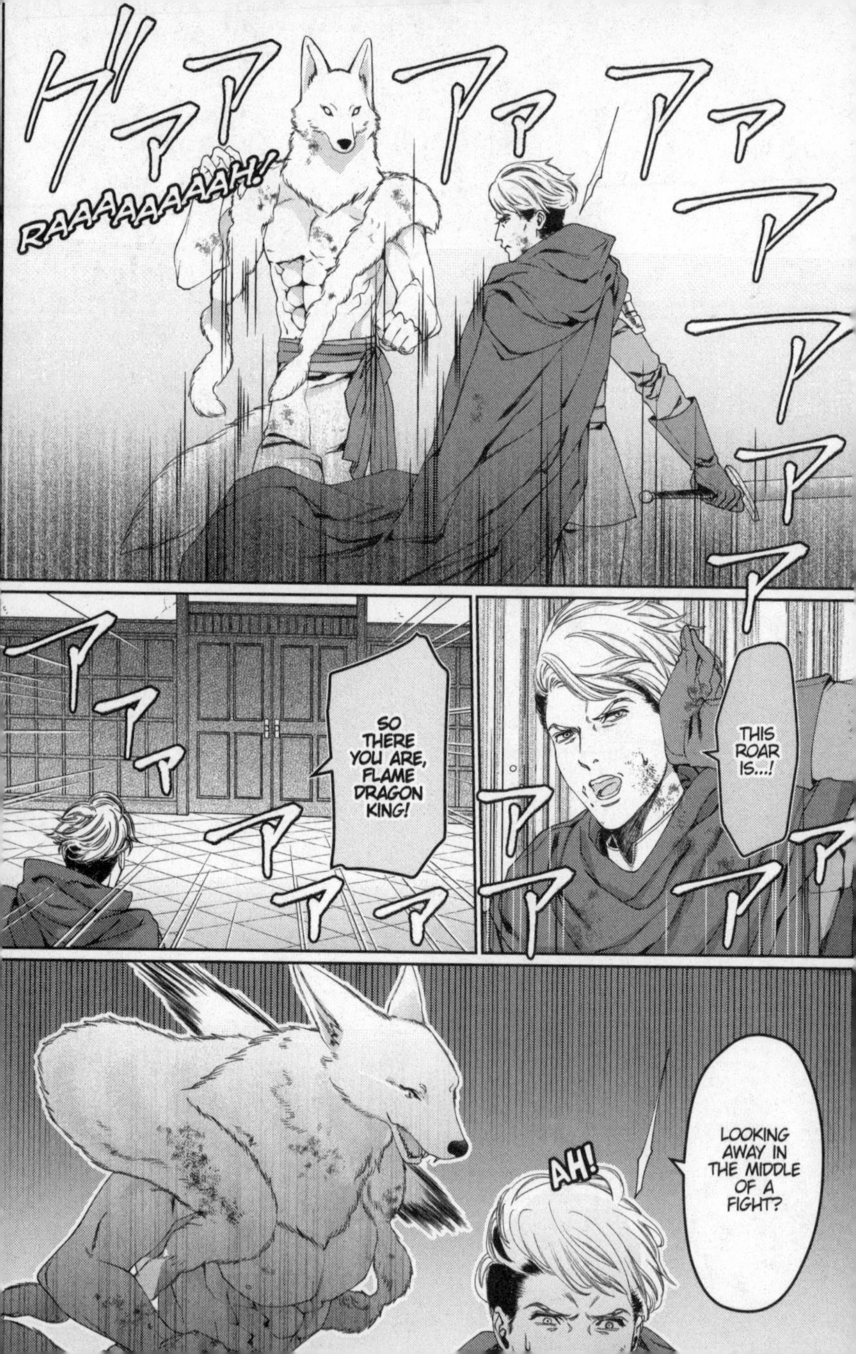
ヴァアアアアアアアアア
RAAAAAAAAAH!
THIS ROAR IS...!
アアアアア
SO THERE YOU ARE, FLAME DRAGON KING!
LOOKING AWAY IN THE MIDDLE OF A FIGHT?
AH!

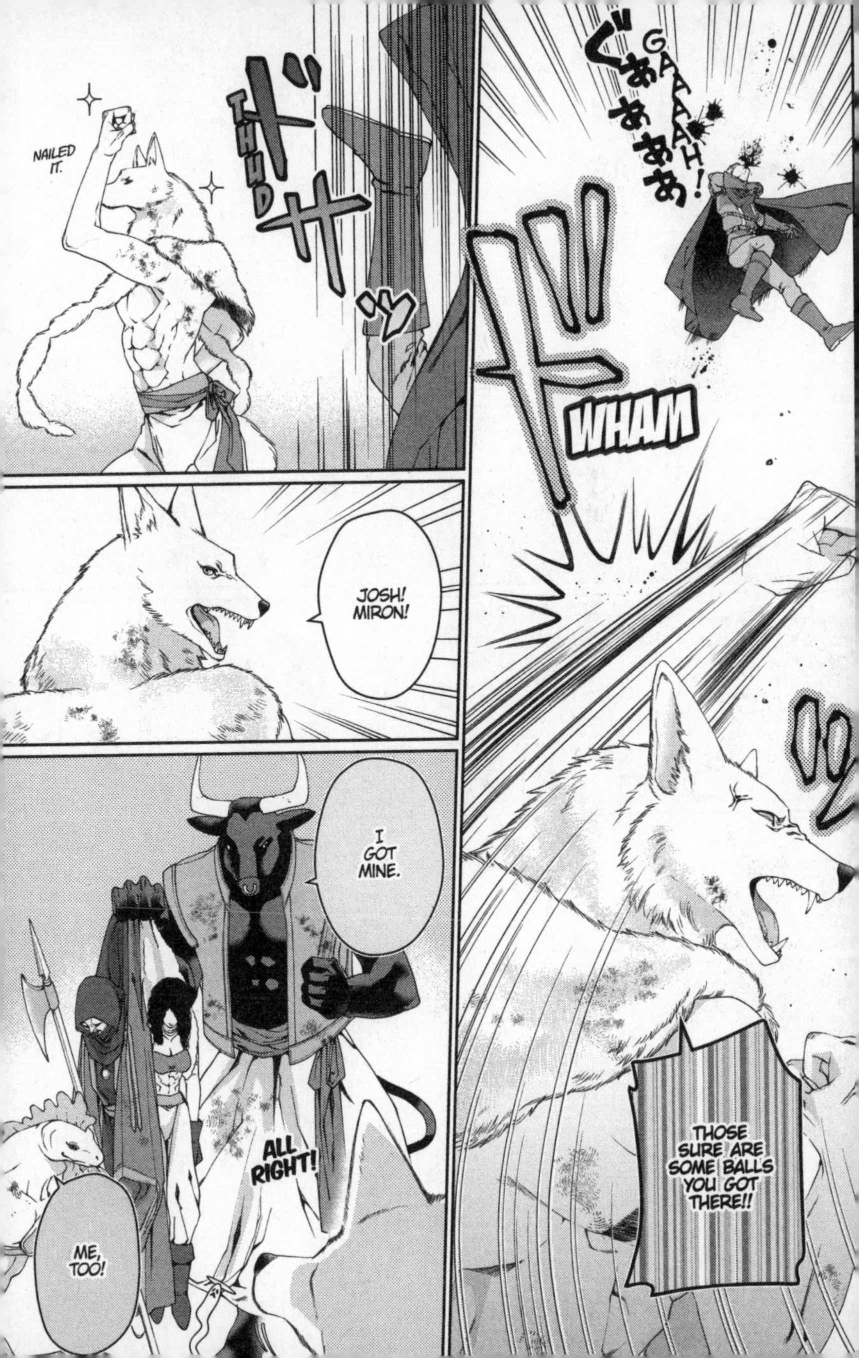
GAAAAH!
WHAM
THOSE SURE ARE SOME BALLS YOU GOT THERE!!
THUD
NAILED IT.
JOSH! MIRON!
I GOT MINE.
ALL RIGHT!
ME, TOO!

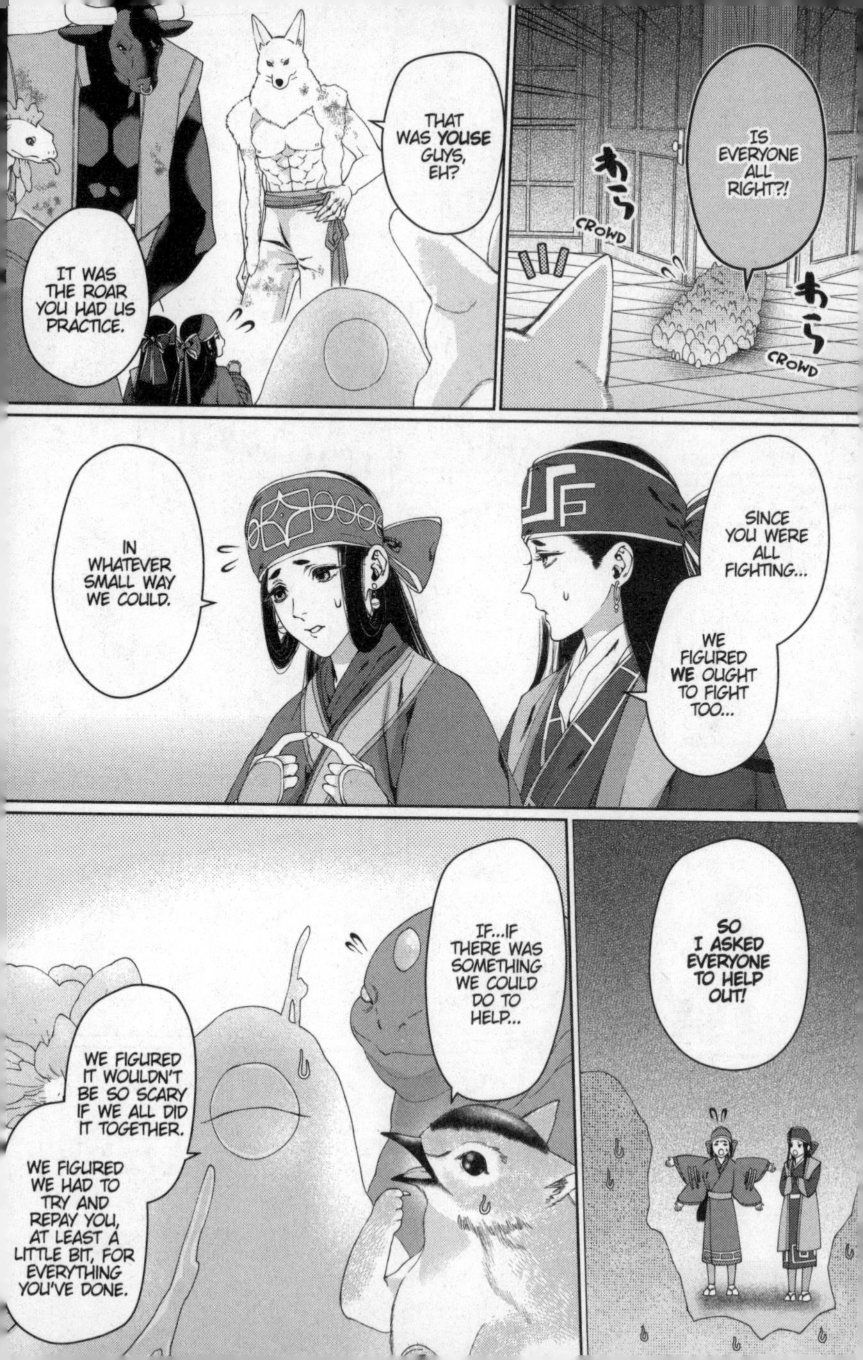

IS EVERYONE ALL RIGHT?!
わら
CROWD
わら
CROWD
THAT WAS YOUSE GUYS, EH?
IT WAS THE ROAR YOU HAD US PRACTICE.
SINCE YOU WERE ALL FIGHTING...
WE FIGURED WE OUGHT TO FIGHT TOO...
IN WHATEVER SMALL WAY WE COULD.
SO I ASKED EVERYONE TO HELP OUT!
IF...IF THERE WAS SOMETHING WE COULD DO TO HELP...
WE FIGURED IT WOULDN'T BE SO SCARY IF WE ALL DID IT TOGETHER.
WE FIGURED WE HAD TO TRY AND REPAY YOU, AT LEAST A LITTLE BIT, FOR EVERYTHING YOU'VE DONE.

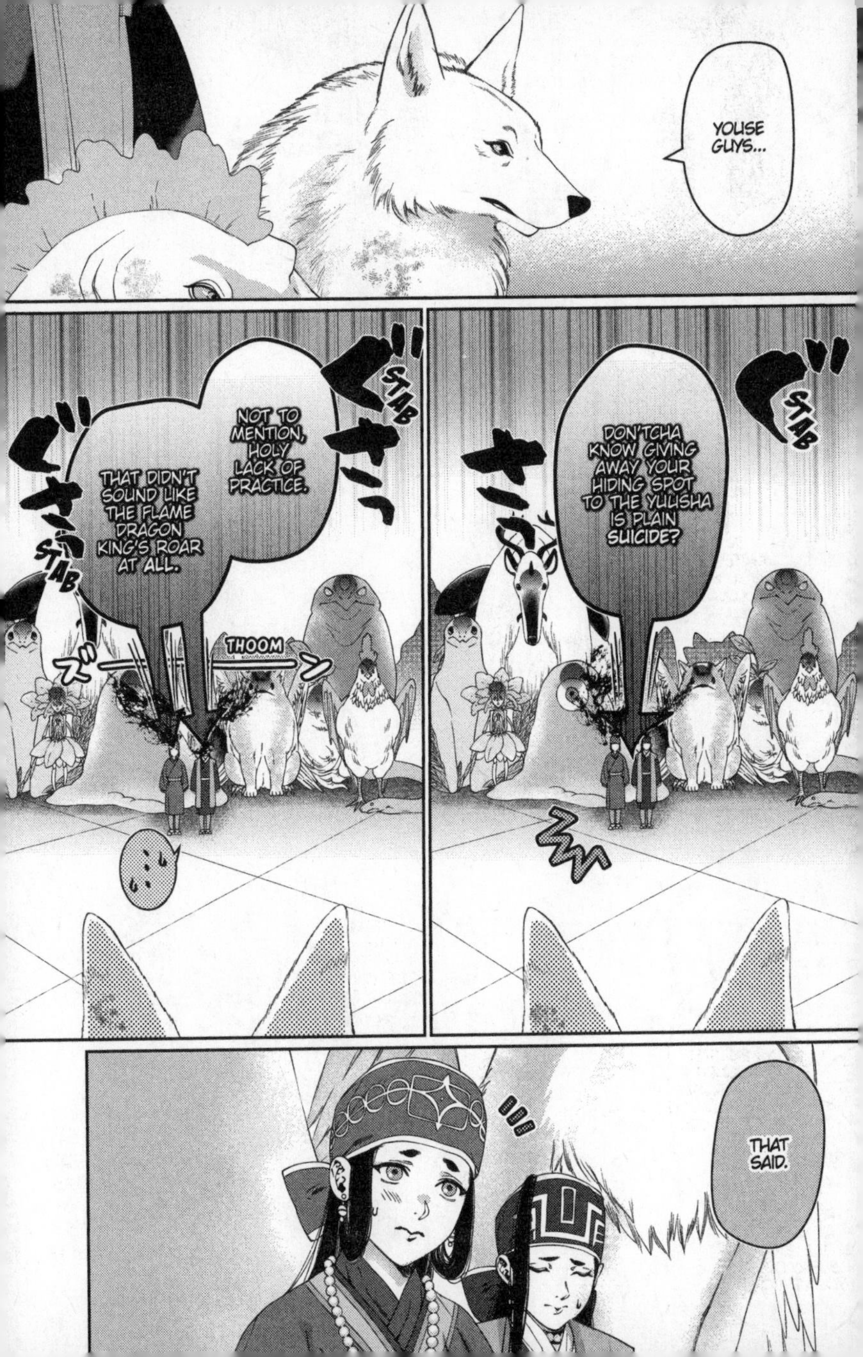
YOUSE GUYS...
STAB
DON'TCHA KNOW GIVING AWAY YOUR HIDING SPOT TO THE YUUSHA IS PLAIN SUICIDE?
STAB
NOT TO MENTION, HOLY LACK OF PRACTICE.
THAT DIDN'T SOUND LIKE THE FLAME DRAGON KING'S ROAR AT ALL.
STAB
THOOM
THAT SAID.

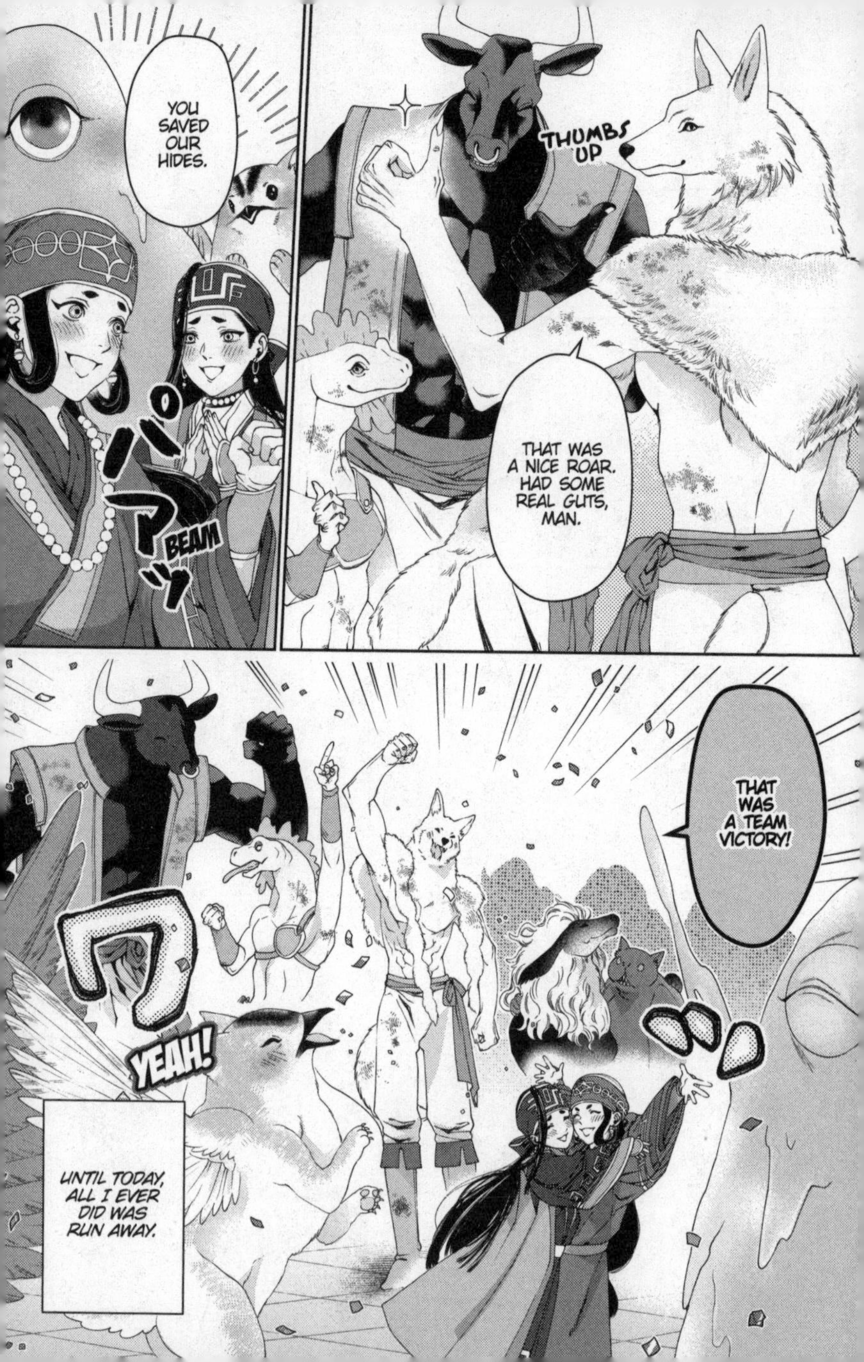
THUMBS UP
THAT WAS A NICE ROAR. HAD SOME REAL GUTS, MAN.
YOU SAVED OUR HIDES.
BEAM
THAT WAS A TEAM VICTORY!
YEAH!
UNTIL TODAY, ALL I EVER DID WAS RUN AWAY.

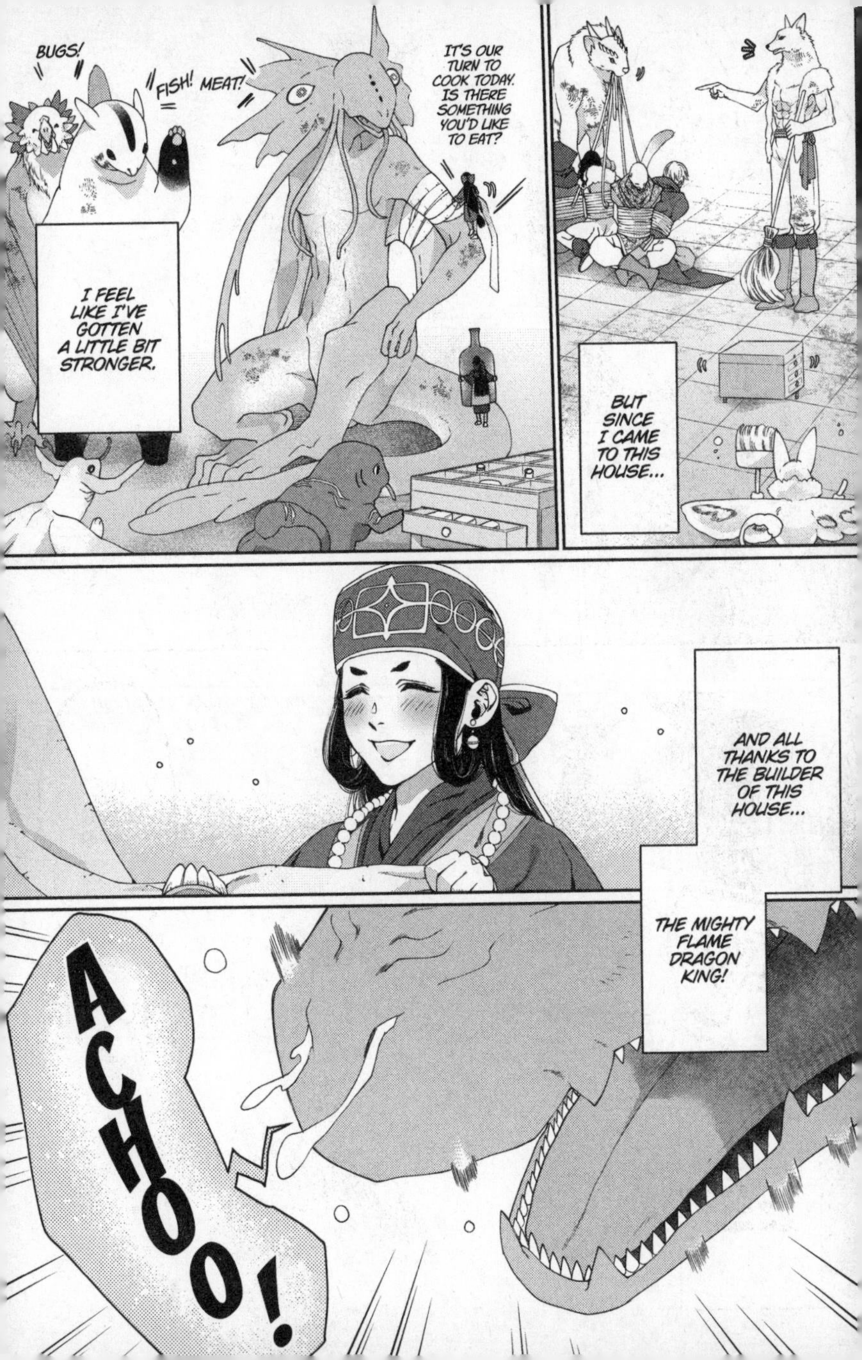
BUT SINCE I CAME TO THIS HOUSE...
IT'S OUR TURN TO COOK TODAY. IS THERE SOMETHING YOU'D LIKE TO EAT?
MEAT!
FISH!
BUGS!
I FEEL LIKE I'VE GOTTEN A LITTLE BIT STRONGER.
AND ALL THANKS TO THE BUILDER OF THIS HOUSE...
THE MIGHTY FLAME DRAGON KING!
ACHOO!

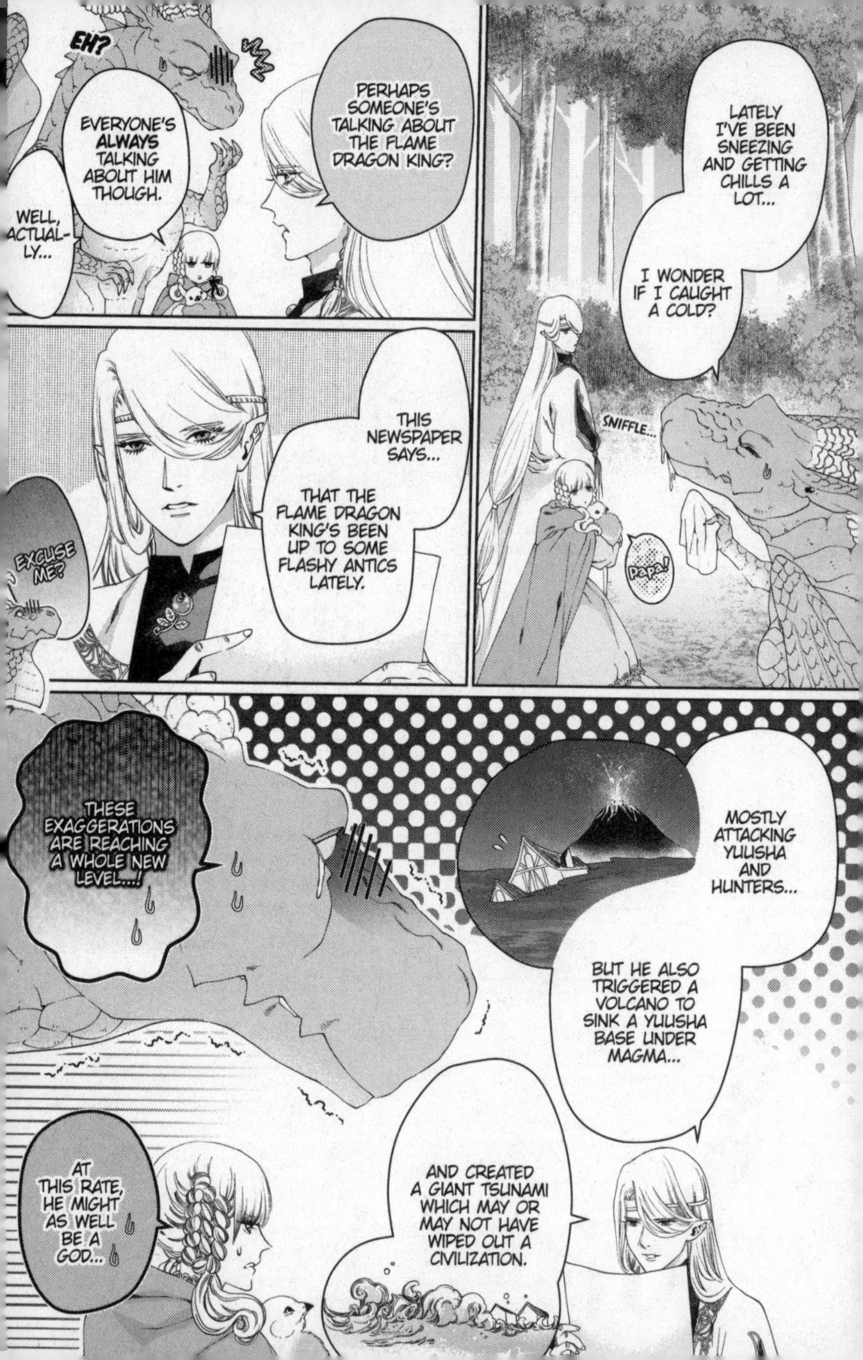

LATELY I'VE BEEN SNEEZING AND GETTING CHILLS A LOT...
I WONDER IF I CAUGHT A COLD?
SNIFFLE...
Papa!
PERHAPS SOMEONE'S TALKING ABOUT THE FLAME DRAGON KING?
EH?
EVERYONE'S **ALWAYS** TALKING ABOUT HIM THOUGH.
WELL, ACTUAL-LY...
THIS NEWSPAPER SAYS...
THAT THE FLAME DRAGON KING'S BEEN UP TO SOME FLASHY ANTICS LATELY.
EXCUSE ME?
MOSTLY ATTACKING YUUSHA AND HUNTERS...
BUT HE ALSO TRIGGERED A VOLCANO TO SINK A YUUSHA BASE UNDER MAGMA...
THESE EXAGGERATIONS ARE REACHING A WHOLE NEW LEVEL...!
AND CREATED A GIANT TSUNAMI WHICH MAY OR MAY NOT HAVE WIPED OUT A CIVILIZATION.
AT THIS RATE, HE MIGHT AS WELL BE A GOD...

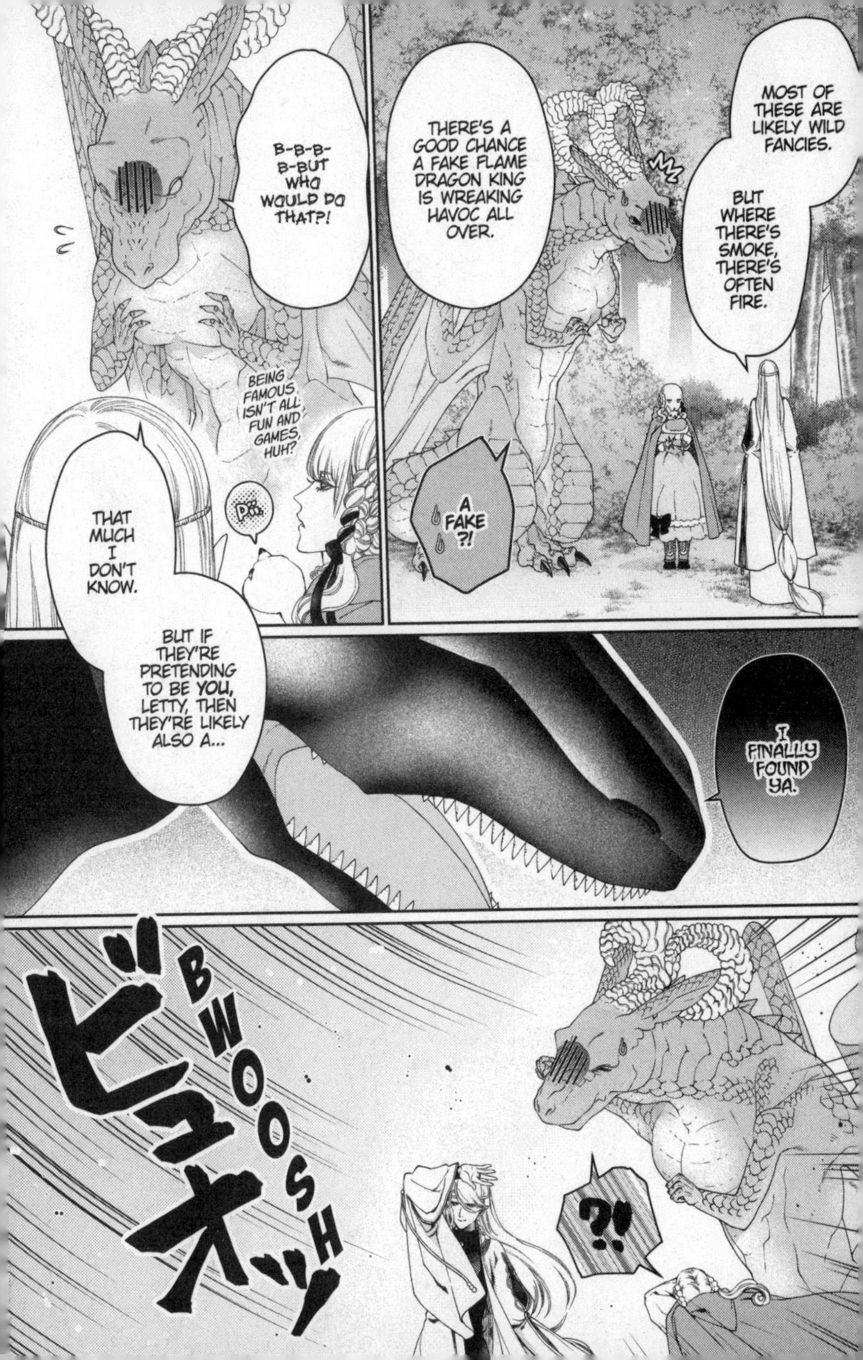
MOST OF THESE ARE LIKELY WILD FANCIES.
BUT WHERE THERE'S SMOKE, THERE'S OFTEN FIRE.
THERE'S A GOOD CHANCE A FAKE FLAME DRAGON KING IS WREAKING HAVOC ALL OVER.
A FAKE?!
B-B-B-B-BUT WHO WOULD DO THAT?!
BEING FAMOUS ISN'T ALL FUN AND GAMES, HUH?
Pi...
THAT MUCH I DON'T KNOW.
BUT IF THEY'RE PRETENDING TO BE YOU, LETTY, THEN THEY'RE LIKELY ALSO A...
I FINALLY FOUND YA.
BWOOSH
?!

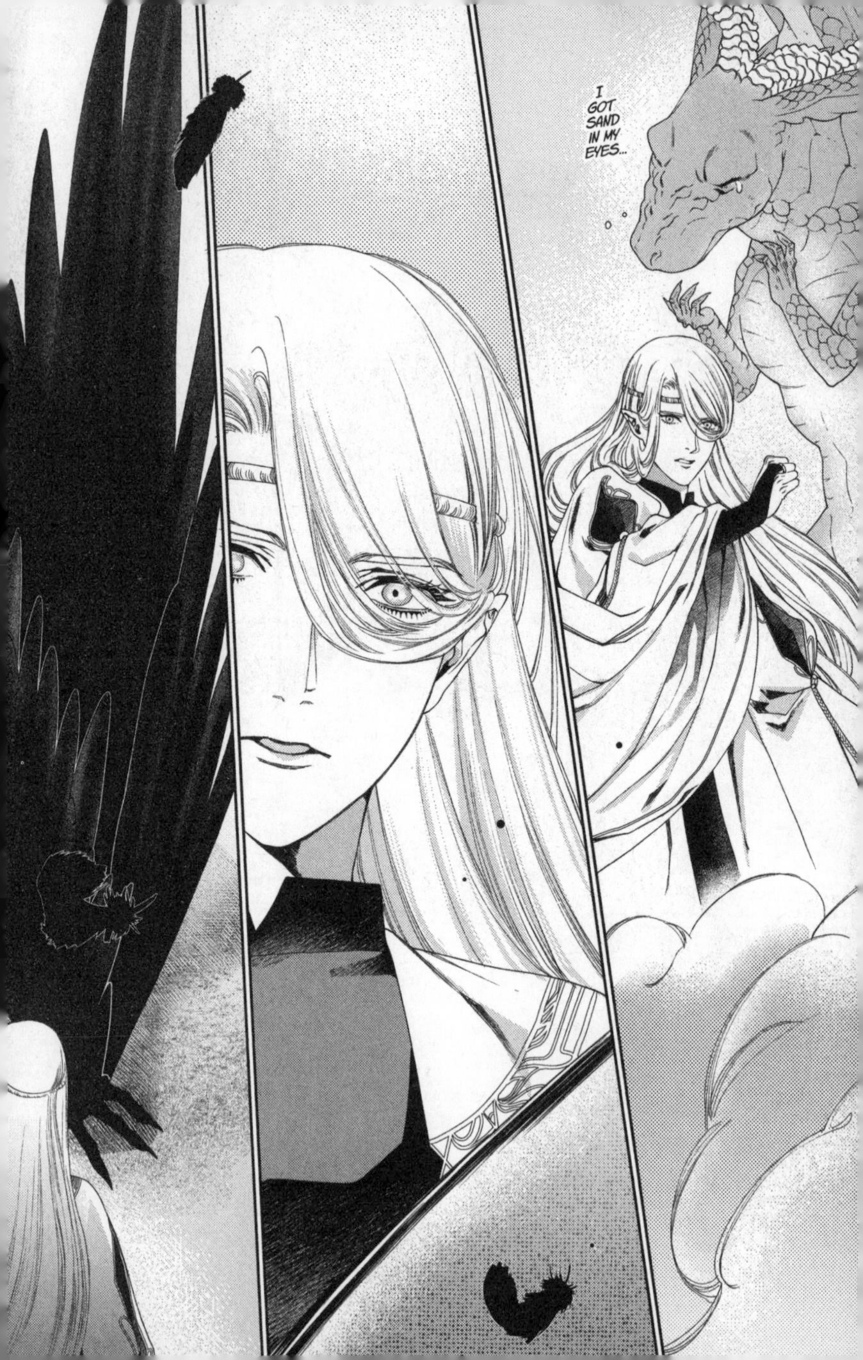
I GOT SAND IN MY EYES...

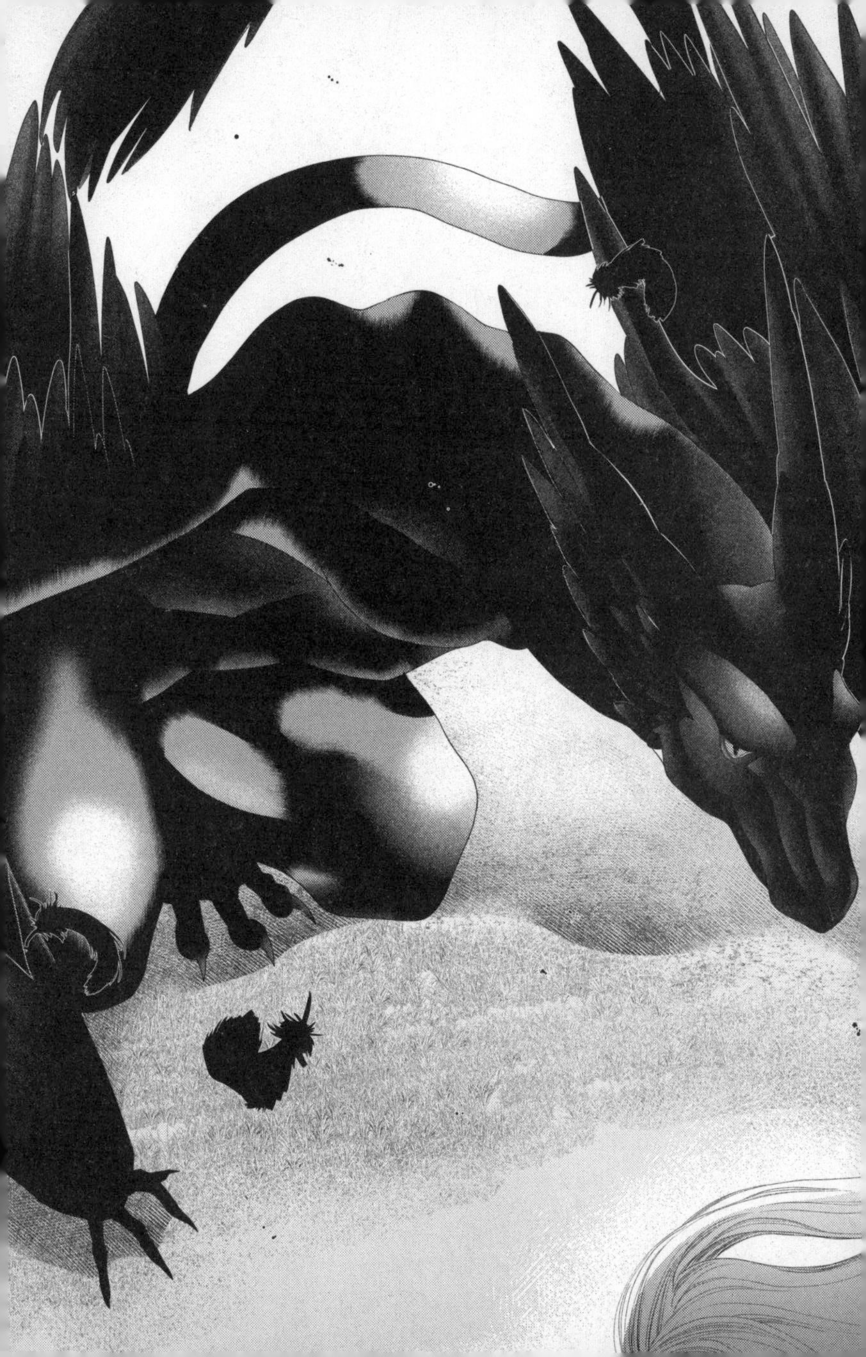

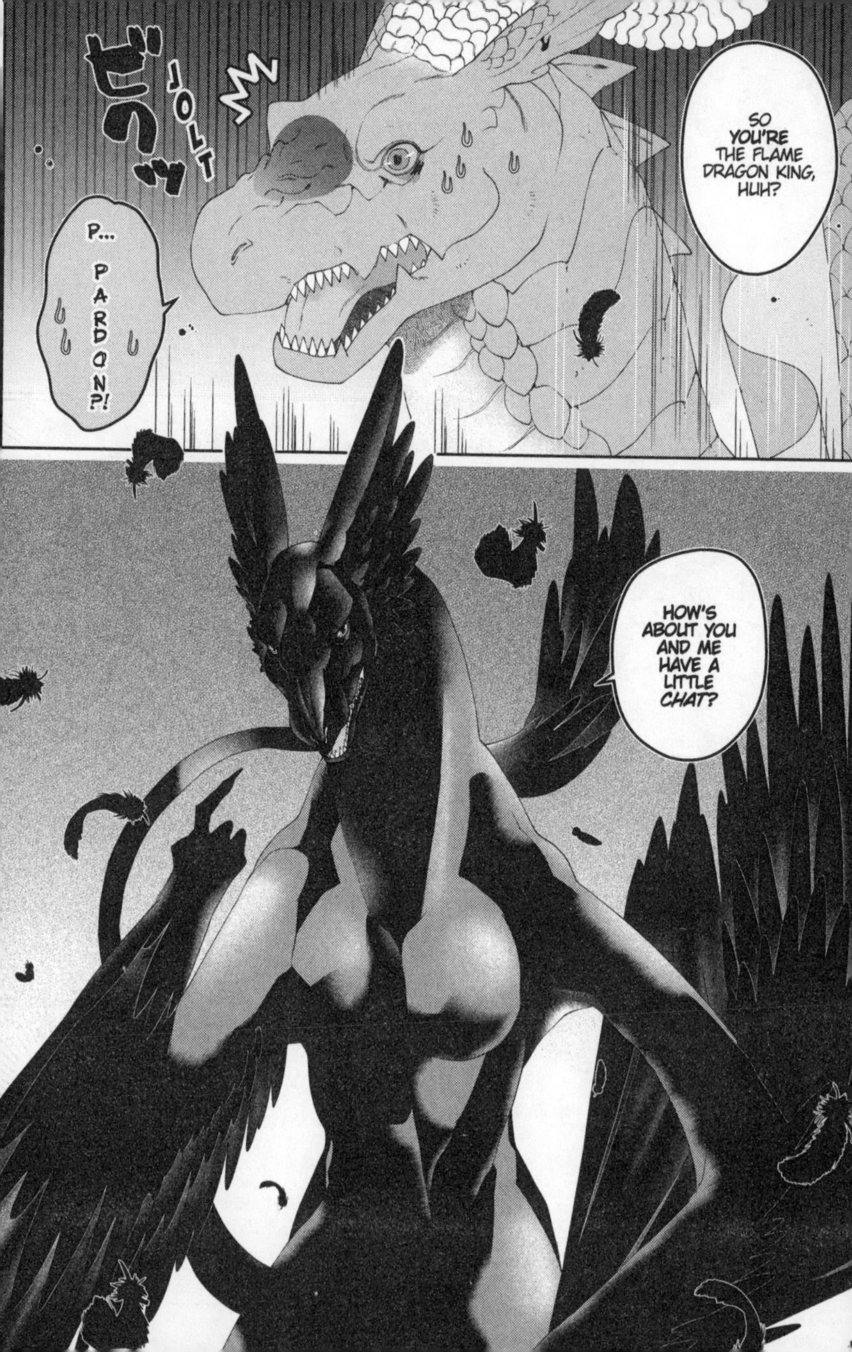
SO YOU'RE THE FLAME DRAGON KING, HUH?
JOLT
P... PARDON?!
HOW'S ABOUT YOU AND ME HAVE A LITTLE CHAT?

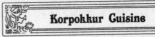

Korpokkur Cuisine

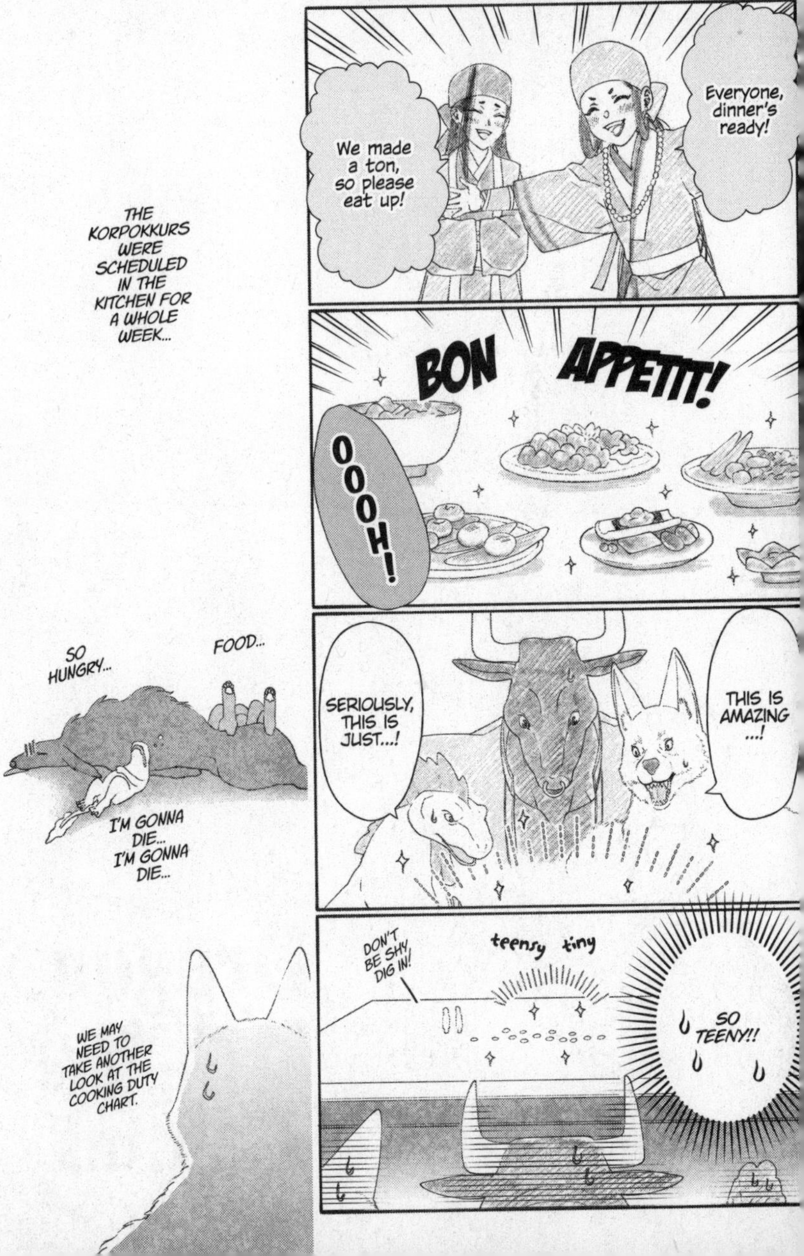
Everyone, dinner's ready!
We made a ton, so please eat up!
BON APPETIT!
OOOH!
THIS IS AMAZING ...!
SERIOUSLY, THIS IS JUST...!
teensy tiny
DON'T BE SHY DIG IN!
SO TEENY!!
THE KORPOKKURS WERE SCHEDULED IN THE KITCHEN FOR A WHOLE WEEK...
FOOD...
SO HUNGRY...
I'M GONNA DIE... I'M GONNA DIE...
WE MAY NEED TO TAKE ANOTHER LOOK AT THE COOKING DUTY CHART.

Dragon Goes House-Hunting

House 33: An Enterprising Home (Part 1)

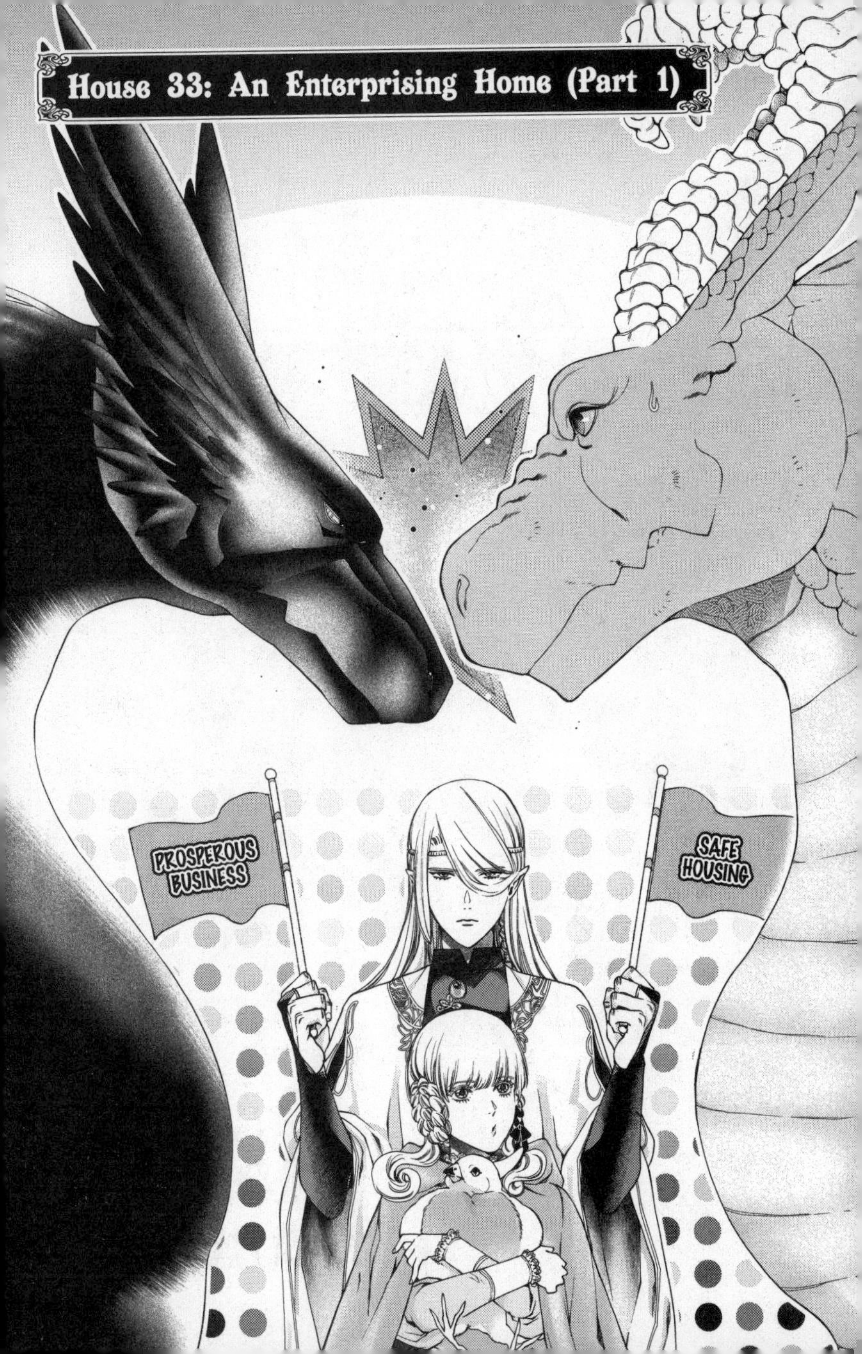
PROSPEROUS BUSINESS
SAFE HOUSING

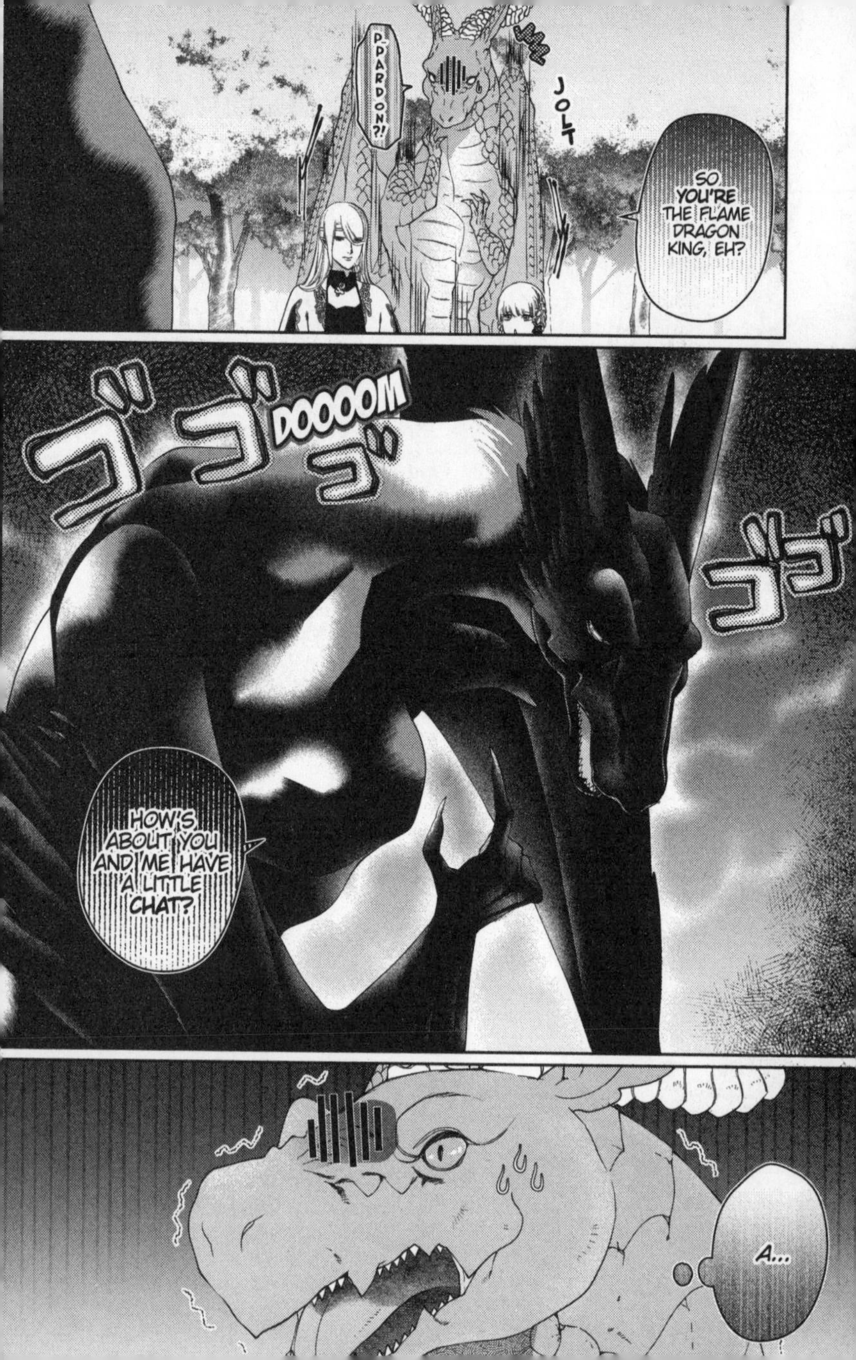
SO YOU'RE THE FLAME DRAGON KING, EH?
JOLT
P-PARDON?!
ゴゴゴ
DOOOOM
ゴゴゴ
HOW'S ABOUT YOU AND ME HAVE A LITTLE CHAT?
A...

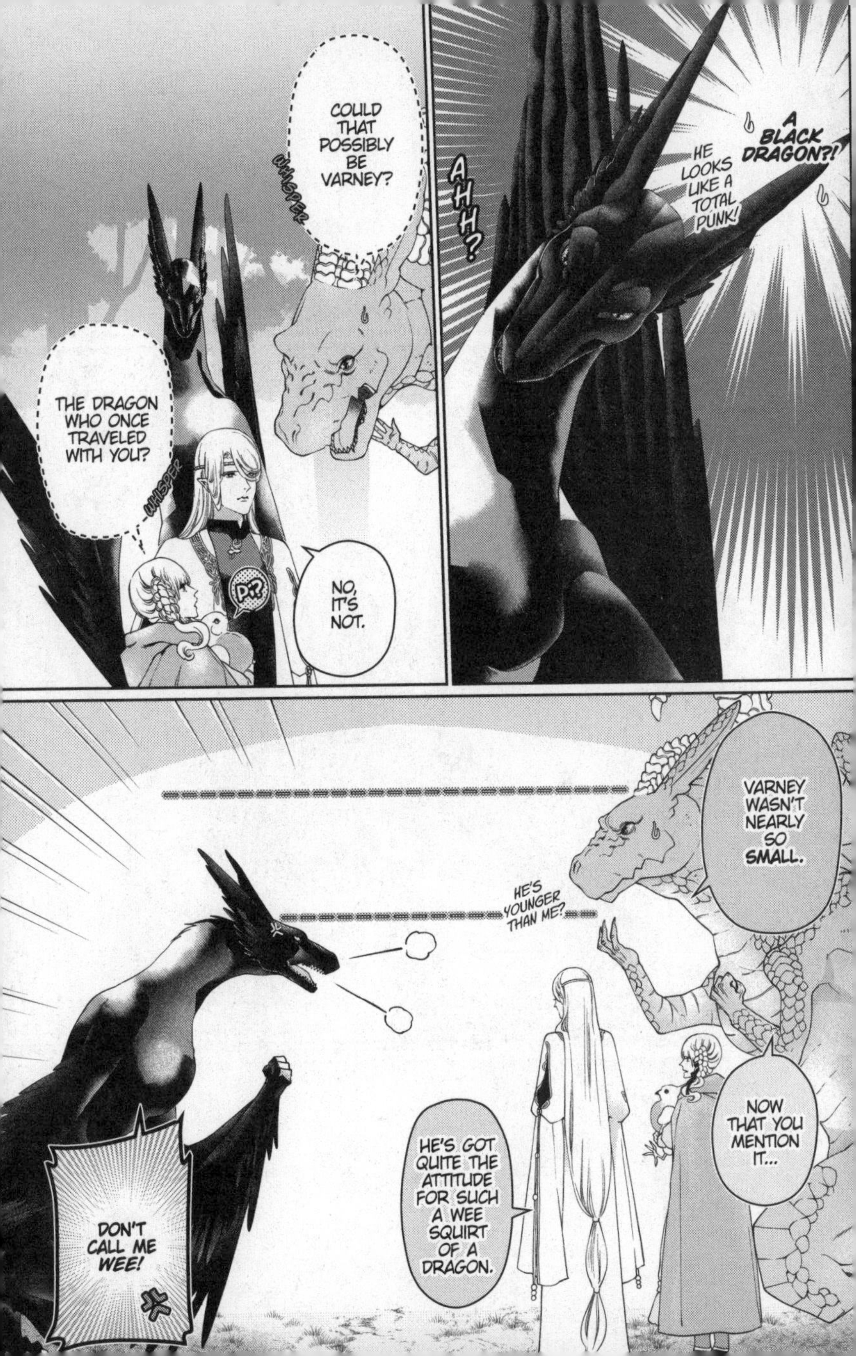
A BLACK DRAGON?!
HE LOOKS LIKE A TOTAL PUNK!
AHH?
COULD THAT POSSIBLY BE VARNEY?
WHISPER
THE DRAGON WHO ONCE TRAVELED WITH YOU?
WHISPER
P?
NO, IT'S NOT.
VARNEY WASN'T NEARLY SO SMALL.
HE'S YOUNGER THAN ME?
NOW THAT YOU MENTION IT...
HE'S GOT QUITE THE ATTITUDE FOR SUCH A WEE SQUIRT OF A DRAGON.
DON'T CALL ME WEE!

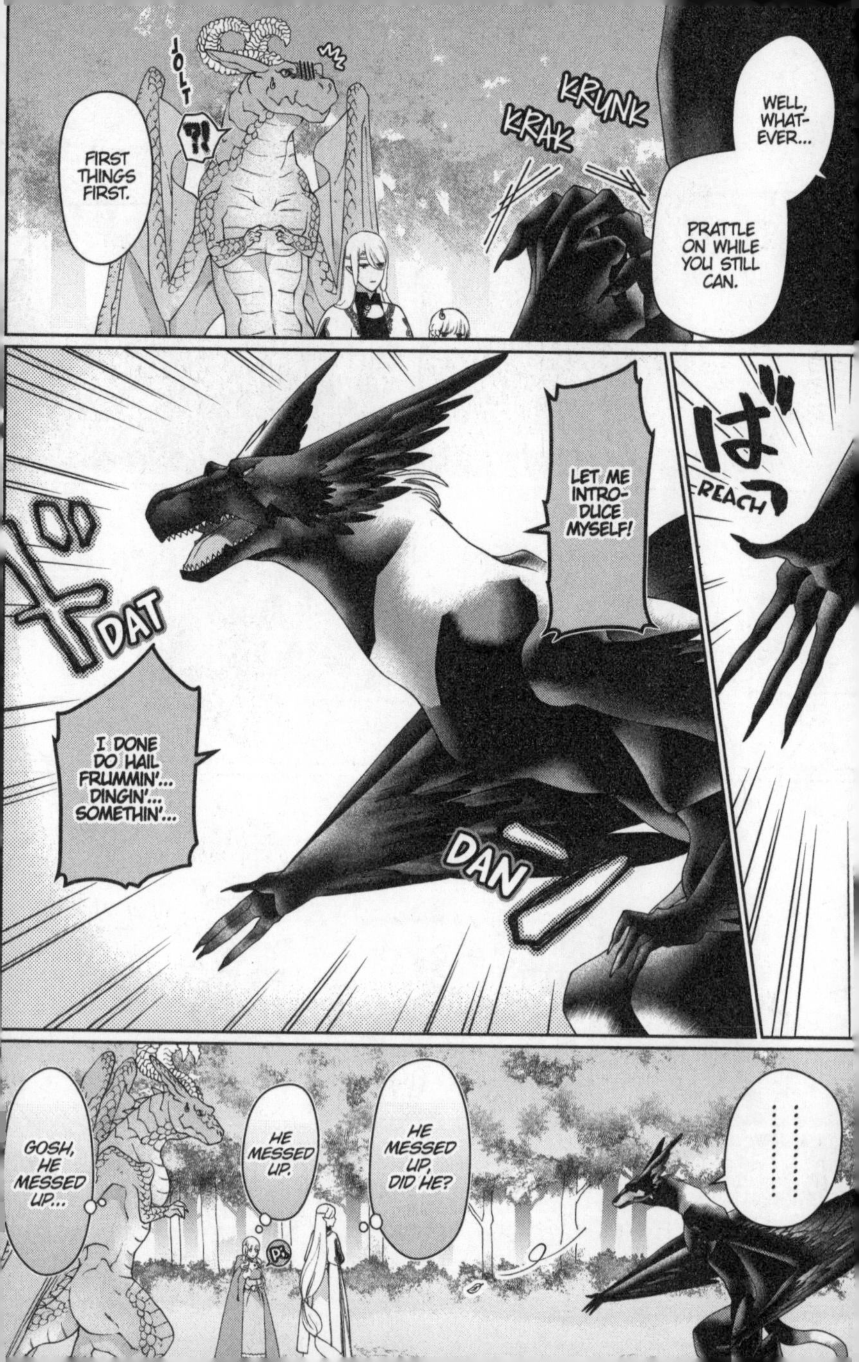
WELL, WHAT-EVER...
PRATTLE ON WHILE YOU STILL CAN.
KRUNK
KRAK
JOLT
?!
FIRST THINGS FIRST.
ばっ
REACH
LET ME INTRO-DUCE MYSELF!
DAT
I DONE DO HAIL FRUMMIN'... DINGIN'... SOMETHIN'...
DAN
......
HE MESSED UP, DID HE?
HE MESSED UP.
GOSH, HE MESSED UP...

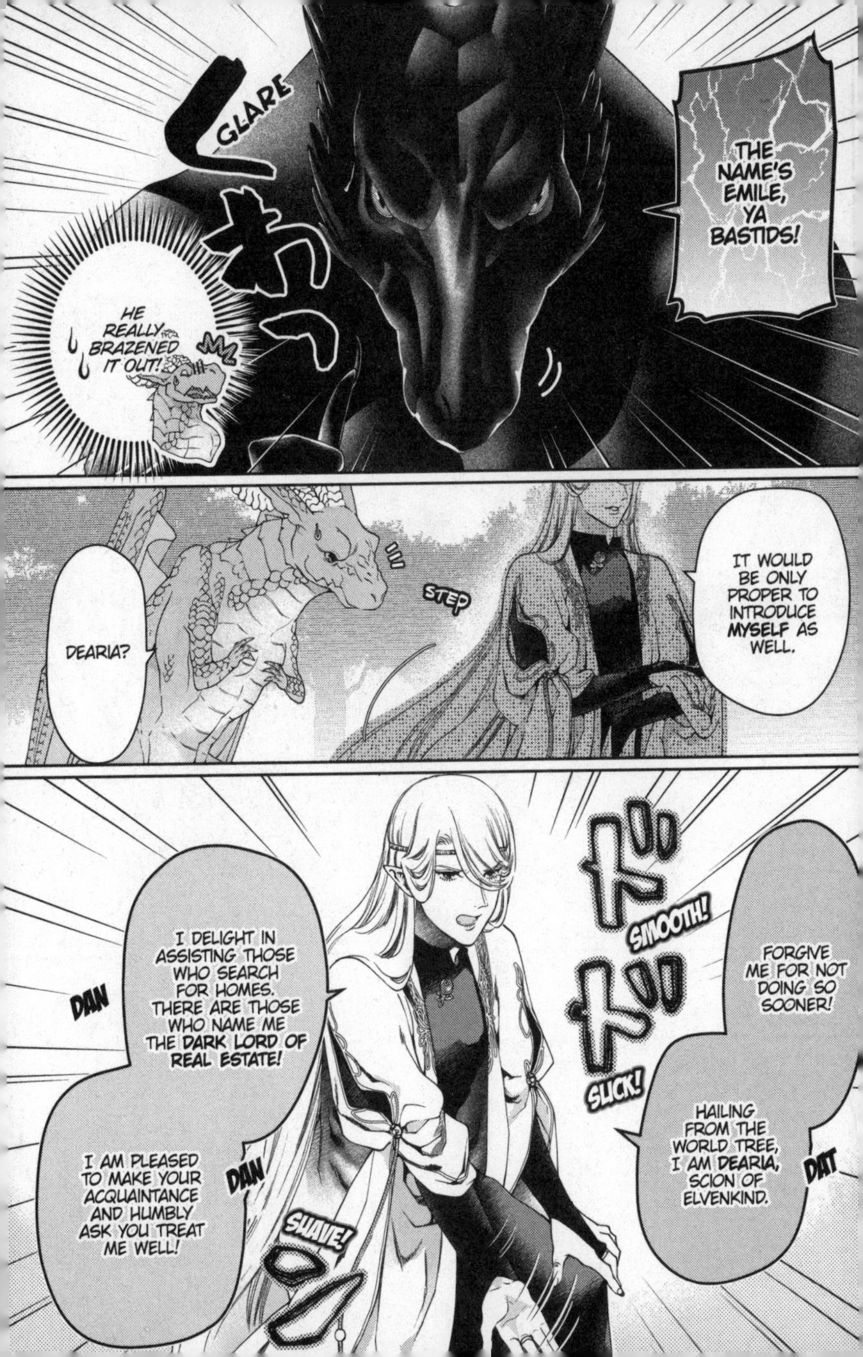
THE NAME'S EMILE, YA BASTIDS!
GLARE
HE REALLY BRAZENED IT OUT!
IT WOULD BE ONLY PROPER TO INTRODUCE **MYSELF** AS WELL.
STEP
DEARIA?
FORGIVE ME FOR NOT DOING SO SOONER!
SMOOTH!
SLICK!
HAILING FROM THE WORLD TREE, I AM **DEARIA**, SCION OF ELVENKIND.
DAT
DAN
I DELIGHT IN ASSISTING THOSE WHO SEARCH FOR HOMES. THERE ARE THOSE WHO NAME ME THE **DARK LORD** OF **REAL ESTATE**!
DAN
I AM PLEASED TO MAKE YOUR ACQUAINTANCE AND HUMBLY ASK YOU TREAT ME WELL!
SHAVE!

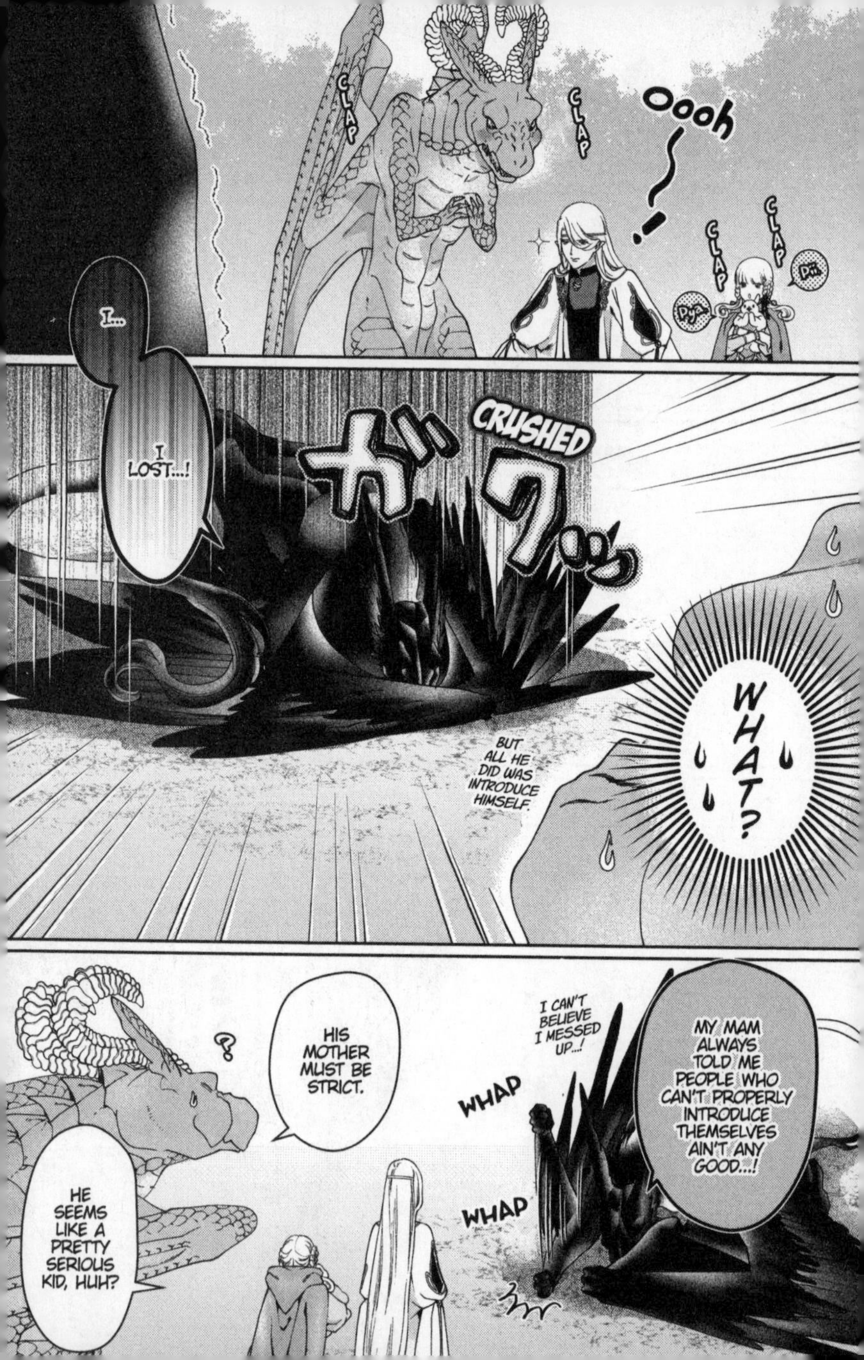
Oooh ~~~!
CLAP
CLAP
CLAP
CLAP
Pii
Pya
I...
WHAT?
BUT ALL HE DID WAS INTRODUCE HIMSELF.
CRUSHED
ガクッ
I LOST...!
MY MAM ALWAYS TOLD ME PEOPLE WHO CAN'T PROPERLY INTRODUCE THEMSELVES AIN'T ANY GOOD...!
I CAN'T BELIEVE I MESSED UP...!
WHAP
WHAP
HIS MOTHER MUST BE STRICT.
?
HE SEEMS LIKE A PRETTY SERIOUS KID, HUH?

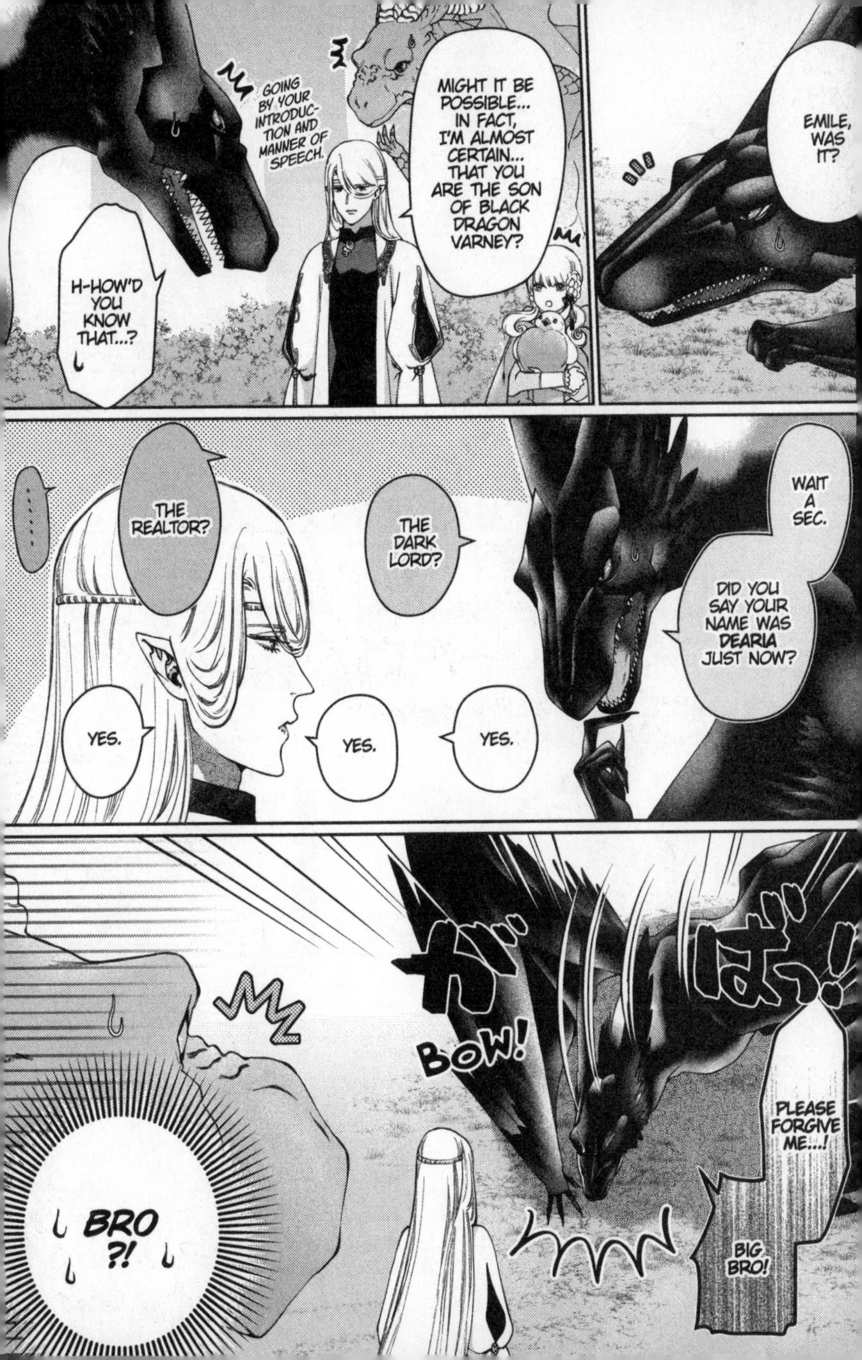

EMILE, WAS IT?
MIGHT IT BE POSSIBLE... IN FACT, I'M ALMOST CERTAIN... THAT YOU ARE THE SON OF BLACK DRAGON VARNEY?
GOING BY YOUR INTRODUCTION AND MANNER OF SPEECH.
H-HOW'D YOU KNOW THAT...?
WAIT A SEC.
DID YOU SAY YOUR NAME WAS DEARIA JUST NOW?
YES.
THE DARK LORD?
YES.
THE REALTOR?
YES.
......
がばっ!!
BOW!
PLEASE FORGIVE ME...!
BIG BRO!
BRO?!

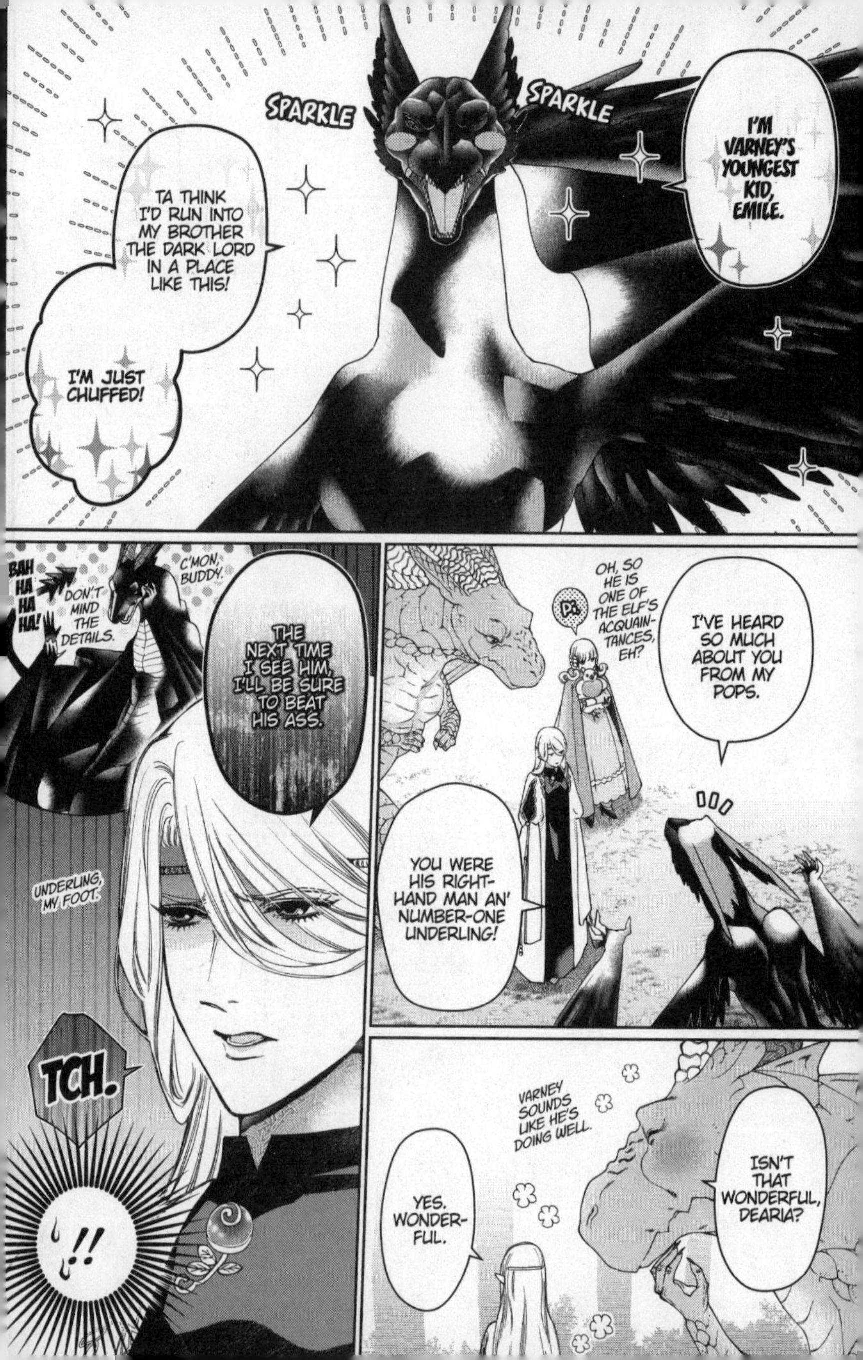
I'M VARNEY'S YOUNGEST KID, EMILE.
SPARKLE
SPARKLE
TA THINK I'D RUN INTO MY BROTHER THE DARK LORD IN A PLACE LIKE THIS!
I'M JUST CHUFFED!
I'VE HEARD SO MUCH ABOUT YOU FROM MY POPS.
OH, SO HE IS ONE OF THE ELF'S ACQUAIN-TANCES, EH?
YOU WERE HIS RIGHT-HAND MAN AN' NUMBER-ONE UNDERLING!
ISN'T THAT WONDERFUL, DEARIA?
VARNEY SOUNDS LIKE HE'S DOING WELL.
YES. WONDER-FUL.
THE NEXT TIME I SEE HIM, I'LL BE SURE TO BEAT HIS ASS.
C'MON, BUDDY. DON'T MIND THE DETAILS.
BAH HA HA HA!
UNDERLING, MY FOOT.
TCH.
!!

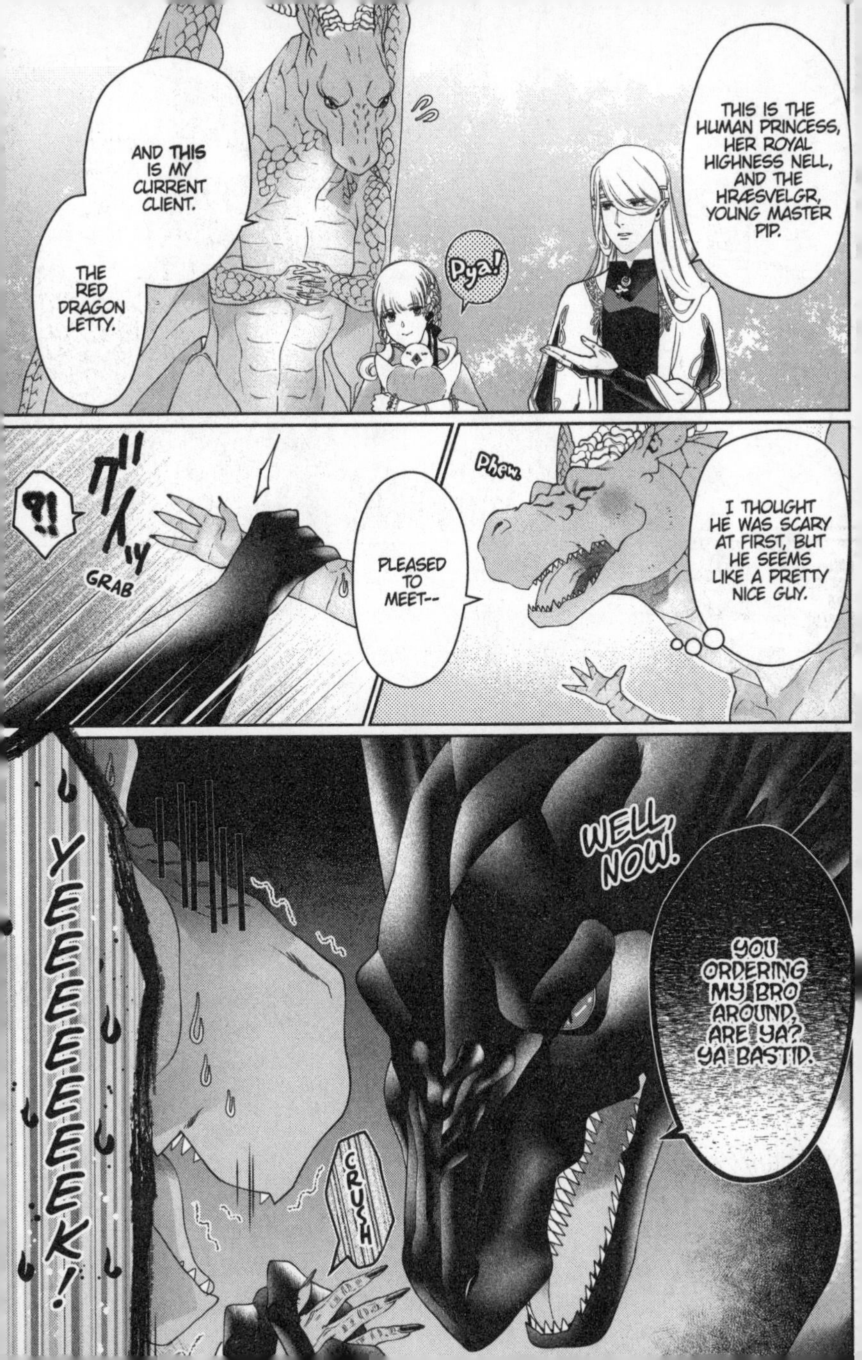
THIS IS THE HUMAN PRINCESS, HER ROYAL HIGHNESS NELL, AND THE HRÆSVELGR, YOUNG MASTER PIP.
Pya!
AND THIS IS MY CURRENT CLIENT.
THE RED DRAGON LETTY.
Phew.
I THOUGHT HE WAS SCARY AT FIRST, BUT HE SEEMS LIKE A PRETTY NICE GUY.
PLEASED TO MEET--
?!
GRAB
WELL, NOW.
YOU ORDERING MY BRO AROUND, ARE YA? YA BASTID.
CRUSH
YEEEEEEEEEK!

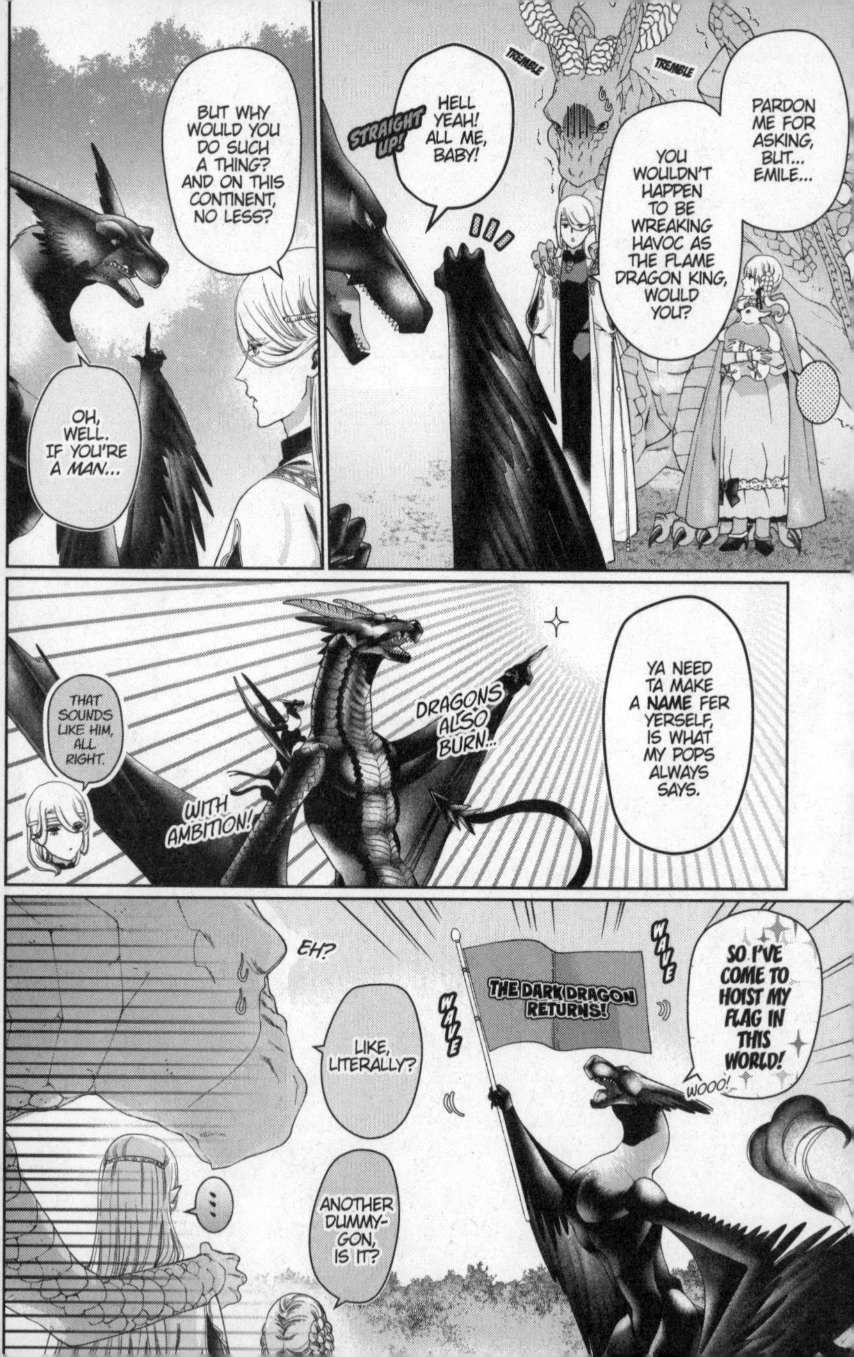
TREMBLE
TREMBLE
PARDON ME FOR ASKING, BUT... EMILE...
YOU WOULDN'T HAPPEN TO BE WREAKING HAVOC AS THE FLAME DRAGON KING, WOULD YOU?
HELL YEAH! ALL ME, BABY!
STRAIGHT UP!
BUT WHY WOULD YOU DO SUCH A THING? AND ON THIS CONTINENT, NO LESS?
OH, WELL. IF YOU'RE A MAN...
YA NEED TA MAKE A NAME FER YERSELF, IS WHAT MY POPS ALWAYS SAYS.
DRAGONS ALSO BURN...
WITH AMBITION!
THAT SOUNDS LIKE HIM, ALL RIGHT.
SO I'VE COME TO HOIST MY FLAG IN THIS WORLD!
WOOO!
WAVE
THE DARK DRAGON RETURNS!
WAVE
EH?
LIKE, LITERALLY?
ANOTHER DUMMY-GON, IS IT?
...

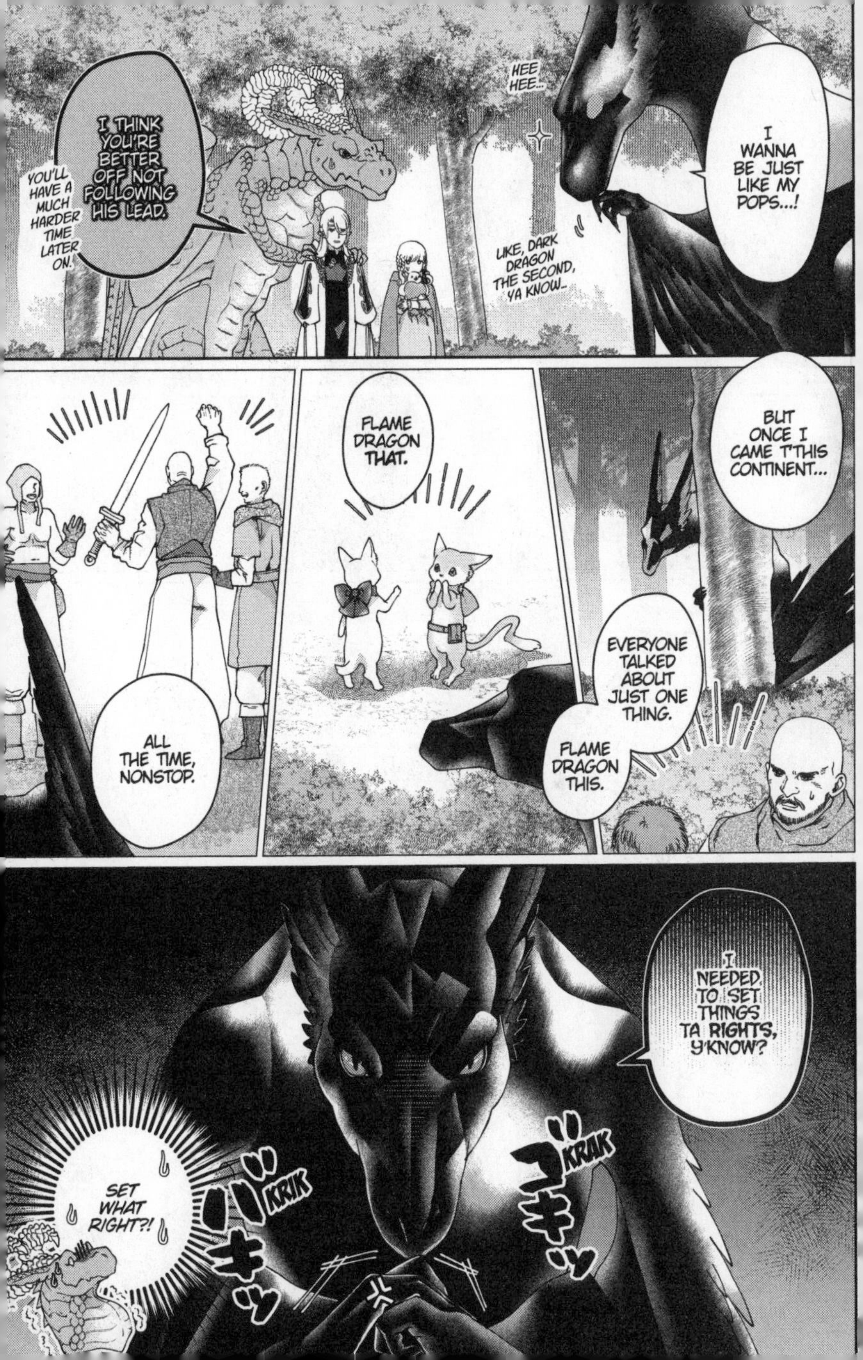

HEE HEE...
I WANNA BE JUST LIKE MY POPS...!
LIKE, DARK DRAGON THE SECOND, YA KNOW...
I THINK YOU'RE BETTER OFF NOT FOLLOWING HIS LEAD.
YOU'LL HAVE A MUCH HARDER TIME LATER ON.
BUT ONCE I CAME T'THIS CONTINENT...
EVERYONE TALKED ABOUT JUST ONE THING.
FLAME DRAGON THIS.
FLAME DRAGON THAT.
ALL THE TIME, NONSTOP.
I NEEDED TO SET THINGS TA RIGHTS, Y'KNOW?
KRAK
KRIK
SET WHAT RIGHT?!

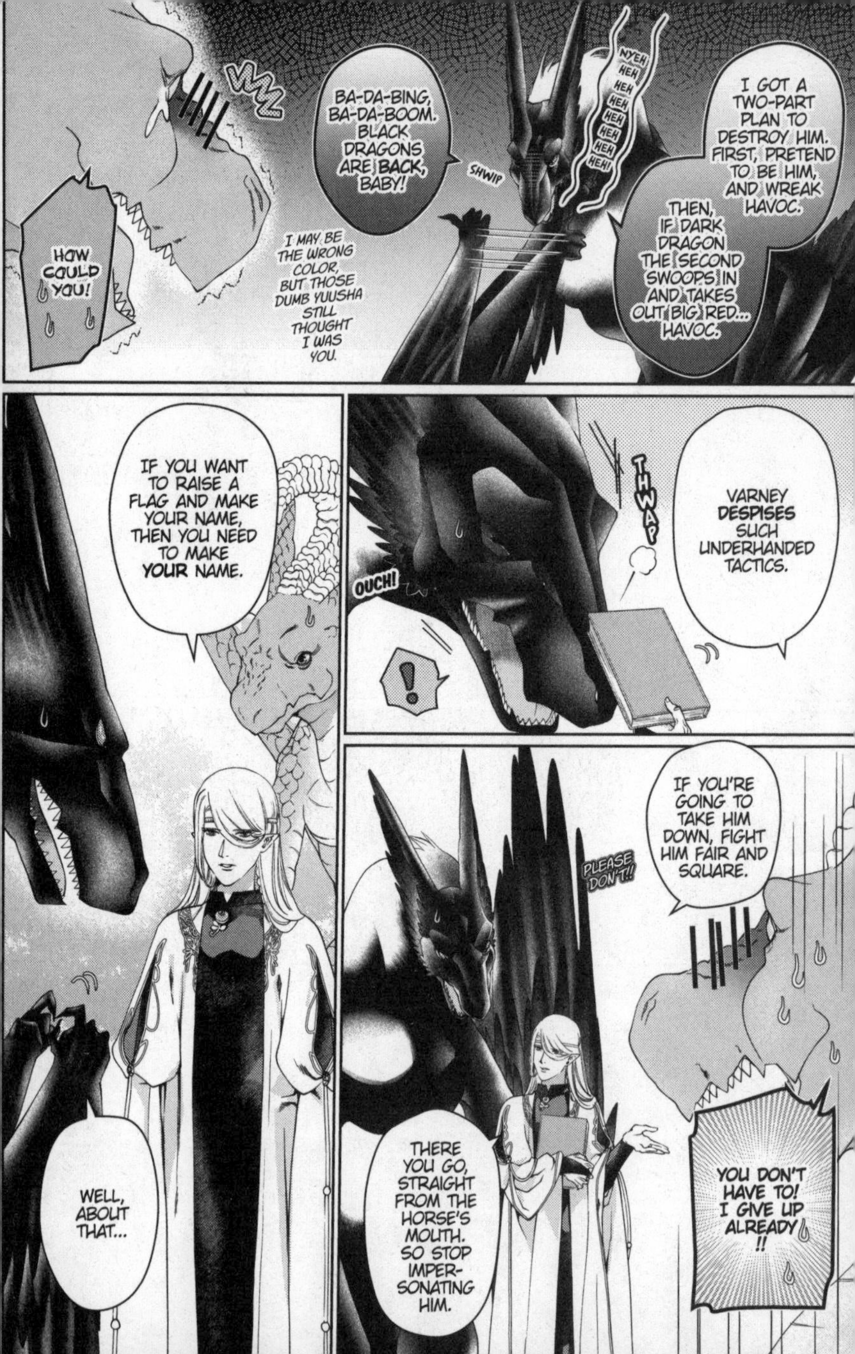
I GOT A TWO-PART PLAN TO DESTROY HIM. FIRST, PRETEND TO BE HIM, AND WREAK HAVOC.
THEN, IF DARK DRAGON THE SECOND SWOOPS IN AND TAKES OUT BIG RED... HAVOC.
NYEH HEH HEH HEH HEH HEH HEH HEH!
SHWIP
BA-DA-BING, BA-DA-BOOM. BLACK DRAGONS ARE BACK, BABY!!
I MAY BE THE WRONG COLOR, BUT THOSE DUMB YUUSHA STILL THOUGHT I WAS YOU.
HOW COULD YOU!
VARNEY DESPISES SUCH UNDERHANDED TACTICS.
THWAP
OUCH!
!
IF YOU'RE GOING TO TAKE HIM DOWN, FIGHT HIM FAIR AND SQUARE.
PLEASE DON'T!!
YOU DON'T HAVE TO! I GIVE UP ALREADY!!
THERE YOU GO, STRAIGHT FROM THE HORSE'S MOUTH. SO STOP IMPER-SONATING HIM.
IF YOU WANT TO RAISE A FLAG AND MAKE YOUR NAME, THEN YOU NEED TO MAKE YOUR NAME.
WELL, ABOUT THAT...

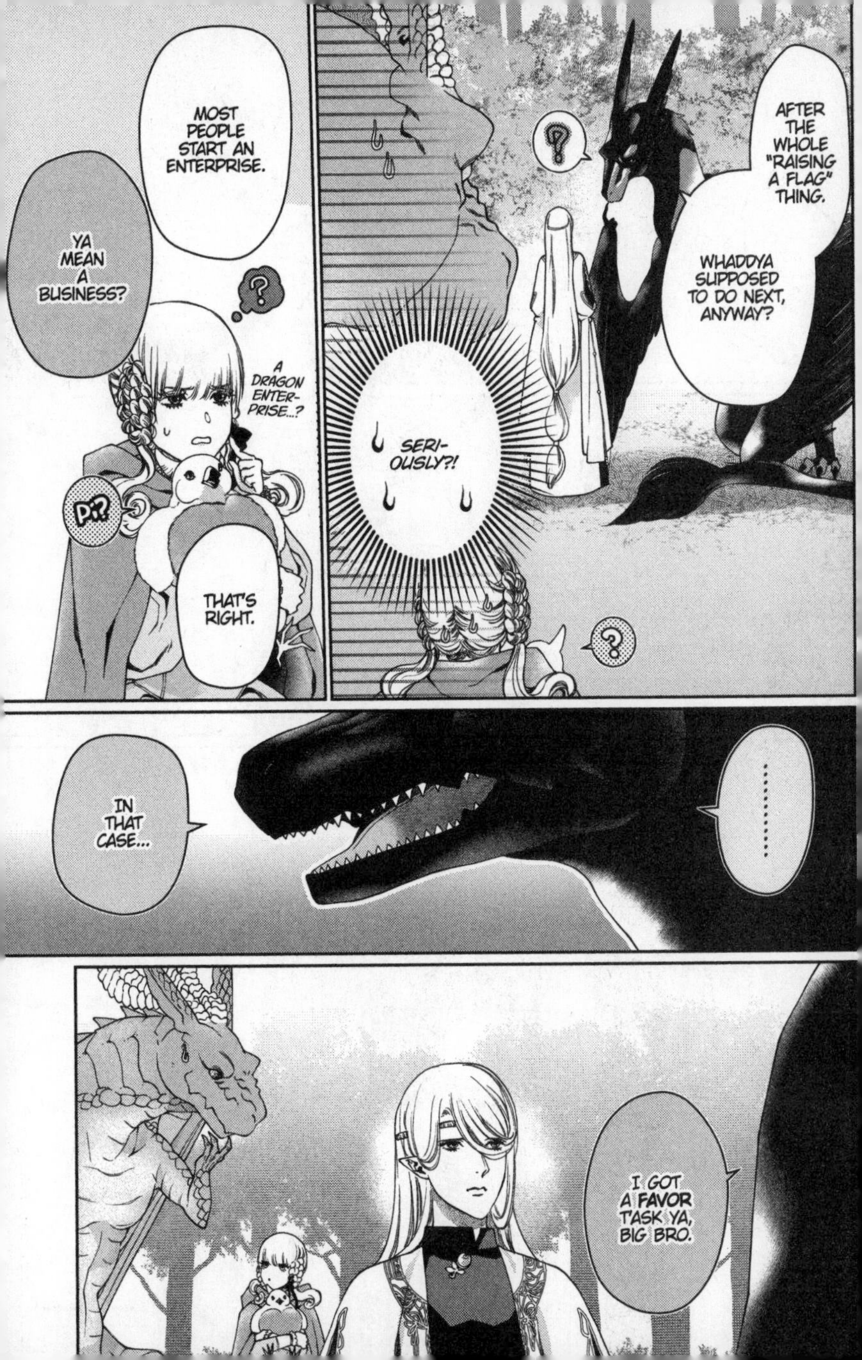
AFTER THE WHOLE "RAISING A FLAG" THING.
WHADDYA SUPPOSED TO DO NEXT, ANYWAY?
?
SERI-OUSLY?!
?
MOST PEOPLE START AN ENTERPRISE.
YA MEAN A BUSINESS?
?
A DRAGON ENTER-PRISE...?
P..?
THAT'S RIGHT.
......
IN THAT CASE...
I GOT A FAVOR T'ASK YA, BIG BRO.

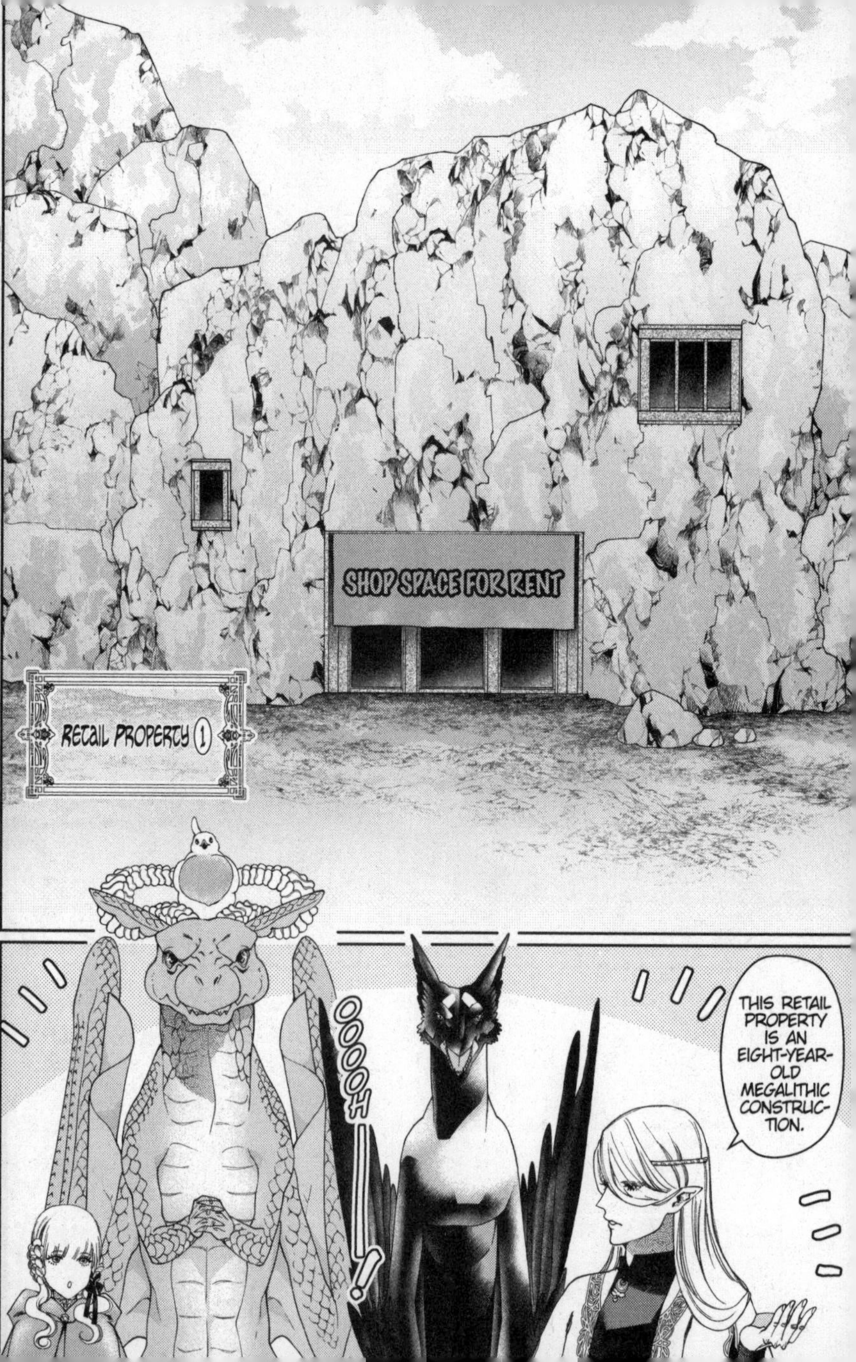
SHOP SPACE FOR RENT
RETAIL PROPERTY 1
THIS RETAIL PROPERTY IS AN EIGHT-YEAR-OLD MEGALITHIC CONSTRUCTION.
OOOOH!

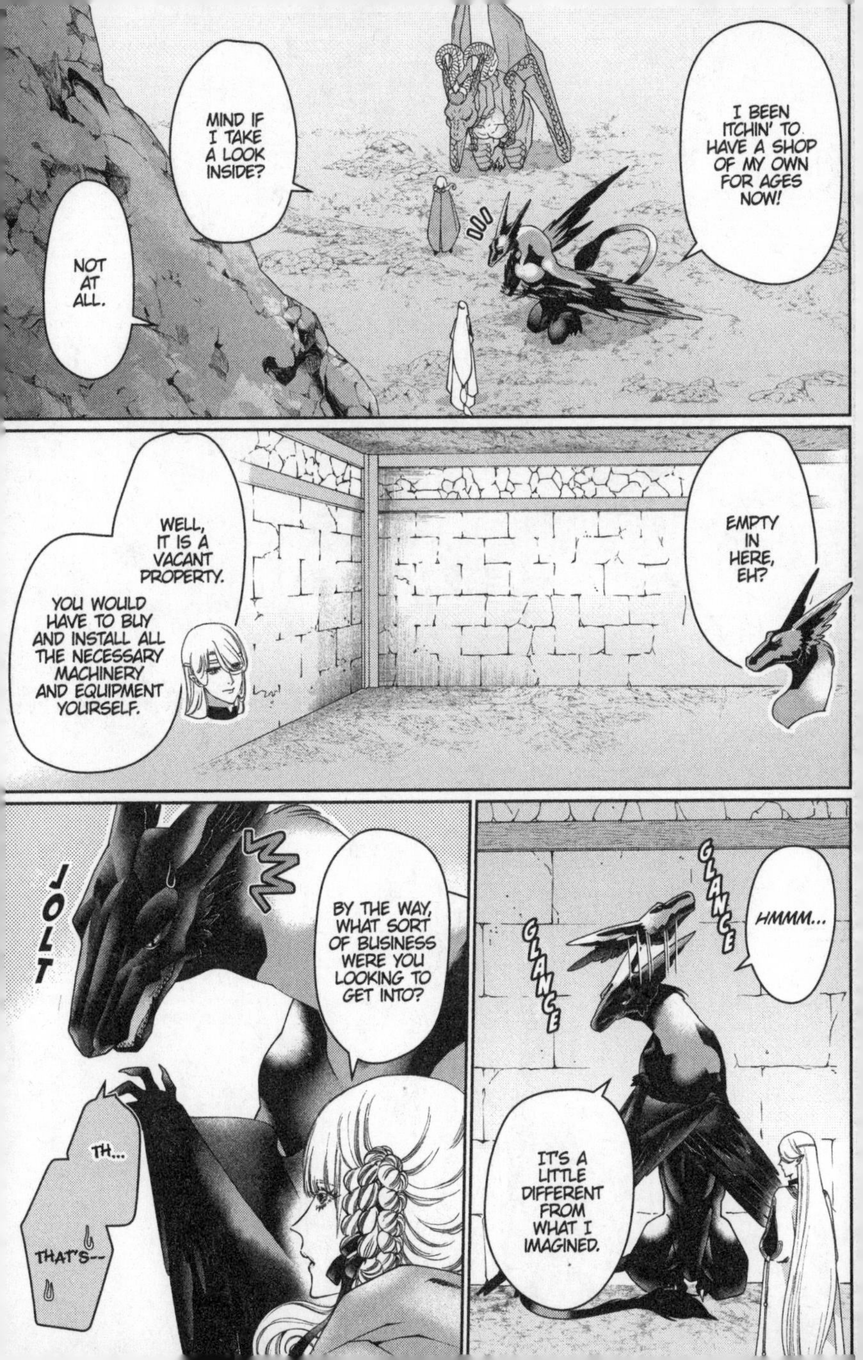
I BEEN ITCHIN' TO HAVE A SHOP OF MY OWN FOR AGES NOW!
MIND IF I TAKE A LOOK INSIDE?
NOT AT ALL.
EMPTY IN HERE, EH?
WELL, IT IS A VACANT PROPERTY.
YOU WOULD HAVE TO BUY AND INSTALL ALL THE NECESSARY MACHINERY AND EQUIPMENT YOURSELF.
GLANCE
HMMM...
GLANCE
IT'S A LITTLE DIFFERENT FROM WHAT I IMAGINED.
BY THE WAY, WHAT SORT OF BUSINESS WERE YOU LOOKING TO GET INTO?
JOLT
TH...
THAT'S--

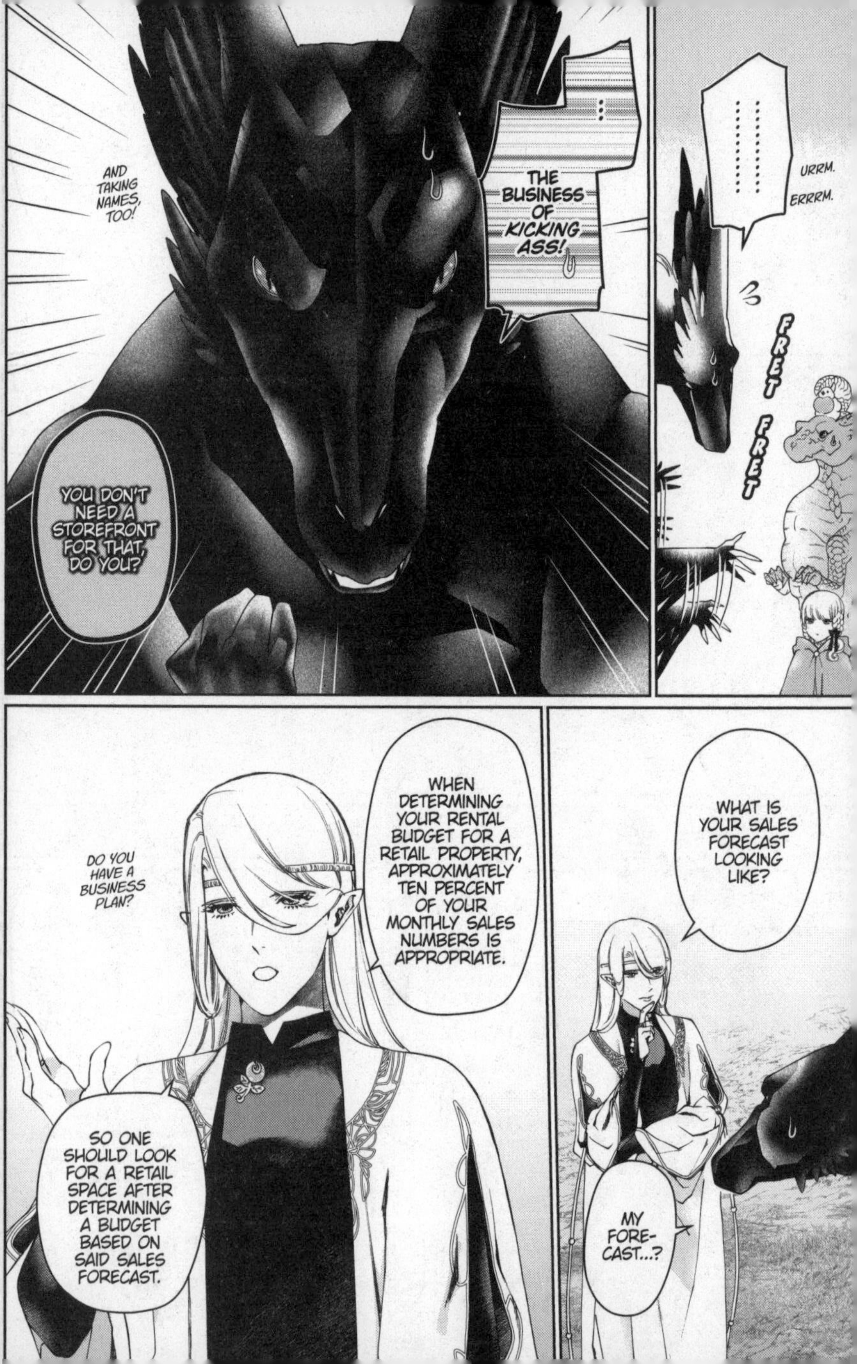
......
URRM.
ERRRM.
FRET FRET
......
THE BUSINESS OF KICKING ASS!
AND TAKING NAMES, TOO!
YOU DON'T NEED A STOREFRONT FOR THAT, DO YOU?
WHAT IS YOUR SALES FORECAST LOOKING LIKE?
MY FORE-CAST...?
WHEN DETERMINING YOUR RENTAL BUDGET FOR A RETAIL PROPERTY, APPROXIMATELY TEN PERCENT OF YOUR MONTHLY SALES NUMBERS IS APPROPRIATE.
DO YOU HAVE A BUSINESS PLAN?
SO ONE SHOULD LOOK FOR A RETAIL SPACE AFTER DETERMINING A BUDGET BASED ON SAID SALES FORECAST.

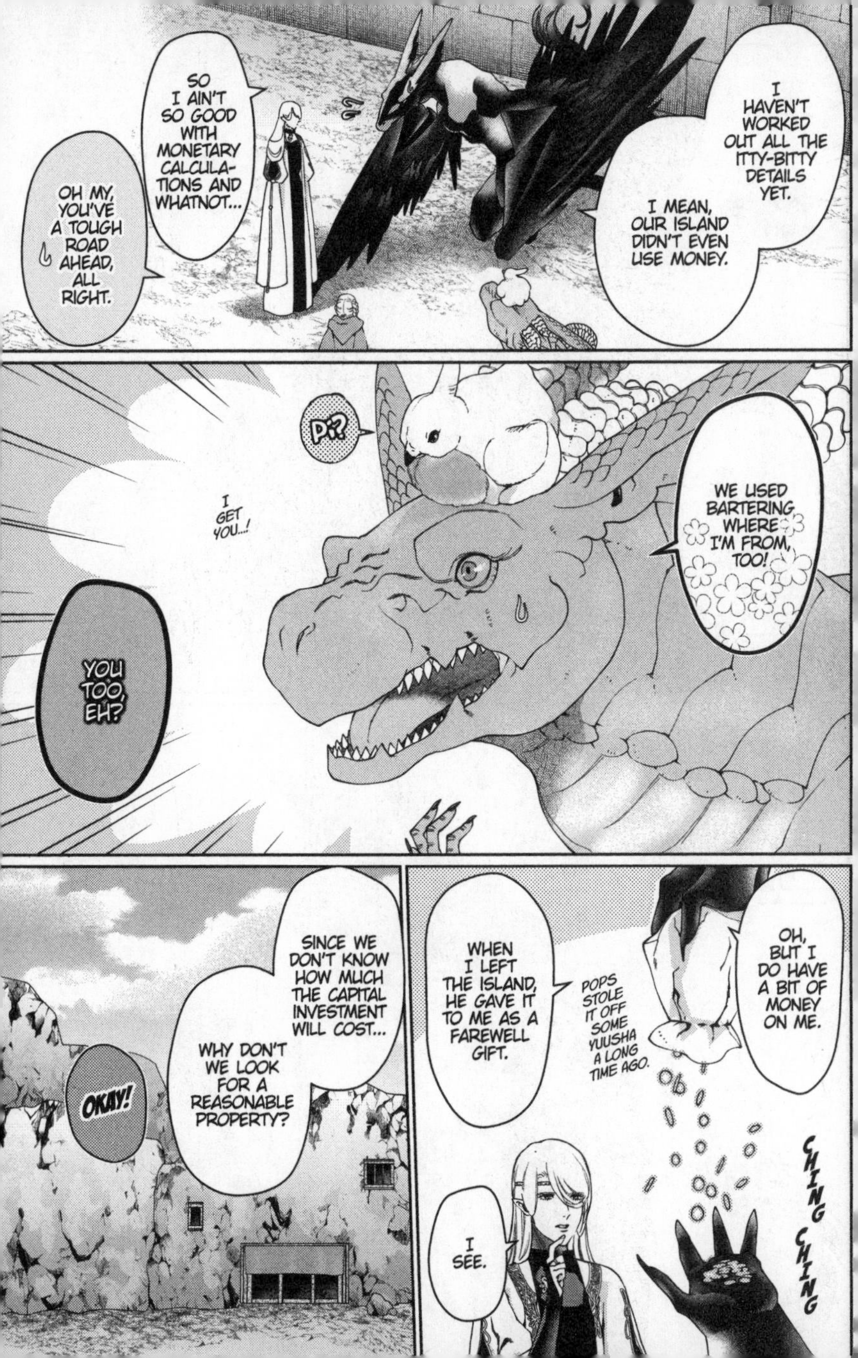
I HAVEN'T WORKED OUT ALL THE ITTY-BITTY DETAILS YET.
I MEAN, OUR ISLAND DIDN'T EVEN USE MONEY.
SO I AIN'T SO GOOD WITH MONETARY CALCULATIONS AND WHATNOT...
OH MY, YOU'VE A TOUGH ROAD AHEAD, ALL RIGHT.
PI?
WE USED BARTERING WHERE I'M FROM, TOO!
I GET YOU...!
YOU TOO, EH?
OH, BUT I DO HAVE A BIT OF MONEY ON ME.
POPS STOLE IT OFF SOME YUUSHA A LONG TIME AGO.
WHEN I LEFT THE ISLAND, HE GAVE IT TO ME AS A FAREWELL GIFT.
CHING CHING
I SEE.
SINCE WE DON'T KNOW HOW MUCH THE CAPITAL INVESTMENT WILL COST...
WHY DON'T WE LOOK FOR A REASONABLE PROPERTY?
OKAY!

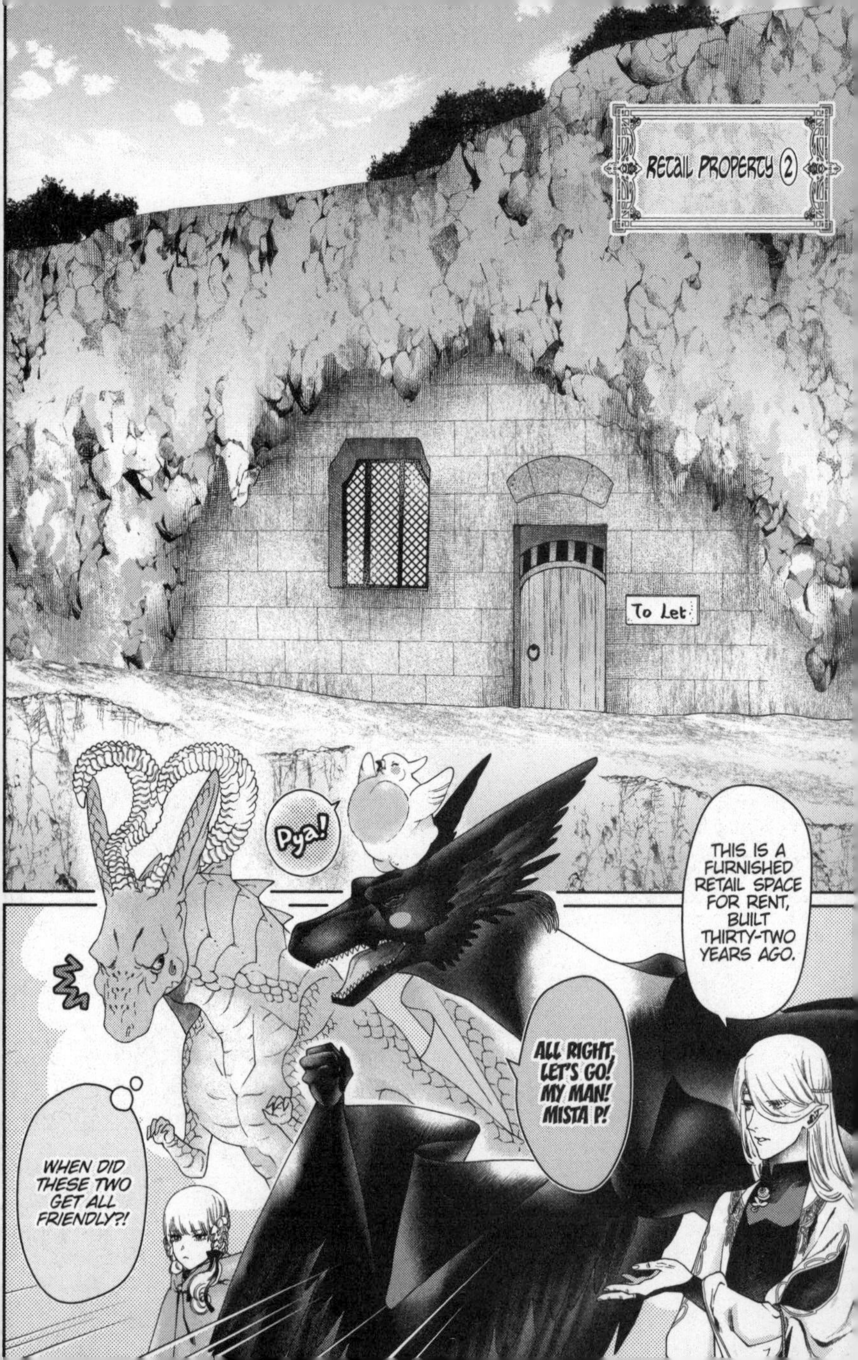
RETAIL PROPERTY 2
To Let
Pya!
THIS IS A FURNISHED RETAIL SPACE FOR RENT, BUILT THIRTY-TWO YEARS AGO.
ALL RIGHT, LET'S GO! MY MAN! MISTA P!
WHEN DID THESE TWO GET ALL FRIENDLY?!

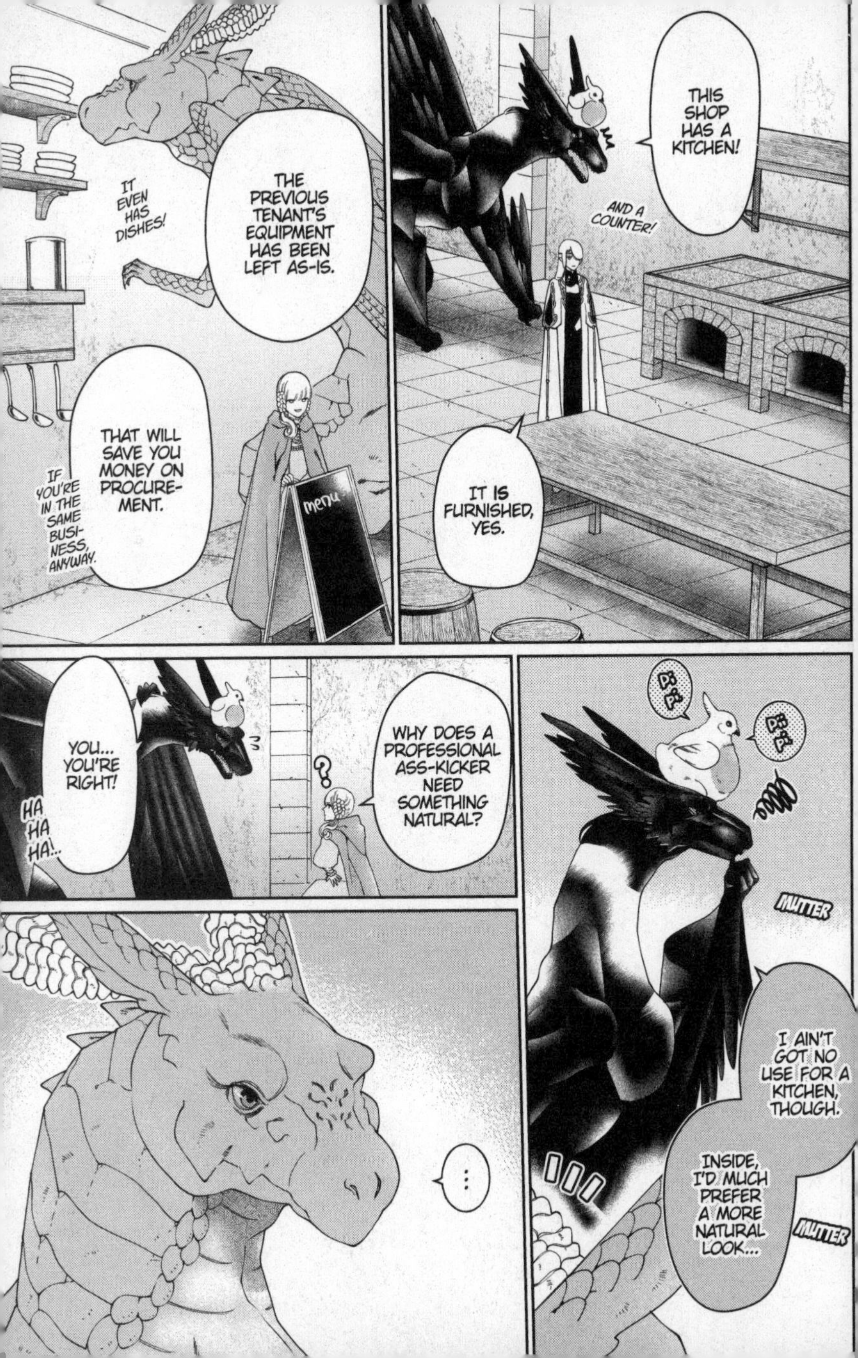
THIS SHOP HAS A KITCHEN!
AND A COUNTER!
IT IS FURNISHED, YES.
THE PREVIOUS TENANT'S EQUIPMENT HAS BEEN LEFT AS-IS.
IT EVEN HAS DISHES!
THAT WILL SAVE YOU MONEY ON PROCURE-MENT.
IF YOU'RE IN THE SAME BUSI-NESS, ANYWAY.
menu
Pi Pi
Pi Pi
MUTTER
I AIN'T GOT NO USE FOR A KITCHEN, THOUGH.
INSIDE, I'D MUCH PREFER A MORE NATURAL LOOK...
MUTTER
WHY DOES A PROFESSIONAL ASS-KICKER NEED SOMETHING NATURAL?
?
YOU... YOU'RE RIGHT!
HA HA HA!...
...

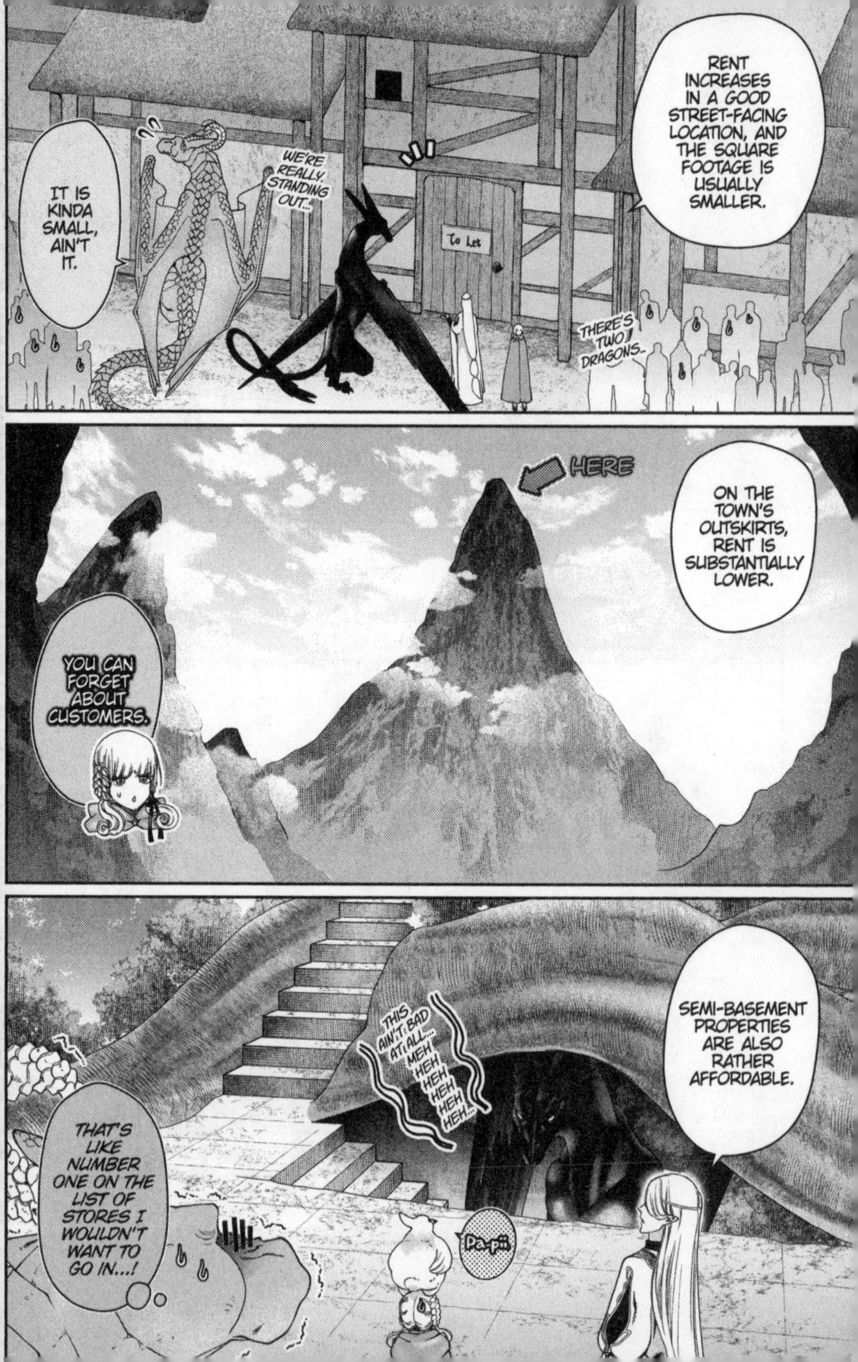
RENT INCREASES IN A GOOD STREET-FACING LOCATION, AND THE SQUARE FOOTAGE IS USUALLY SMALLER.
To Let
WE'RE REALLY STANDING OUT...
IT IS KINDA SMALL, AIN'T IT.
THERE'S TWO DRAGONS...
ON THE TOWN'S OUTSKIRTS, RENT IS SUBSTANTIALLY LOWER.
HERE
YOU CAN FORGET ABOUT CUSTOMERS.
SEMI-BASEMENT PROPERTIES ARE ALSO RATHER AFFORDABLE.
THIS AIN'T BAD AT ALL... MEH HEH HEH HEH HEH...
Da-pii
THAT'S LIKE NUMBER ONE ON THE LIST OF STORES I WOULDN'T WANT TO GO IN...!

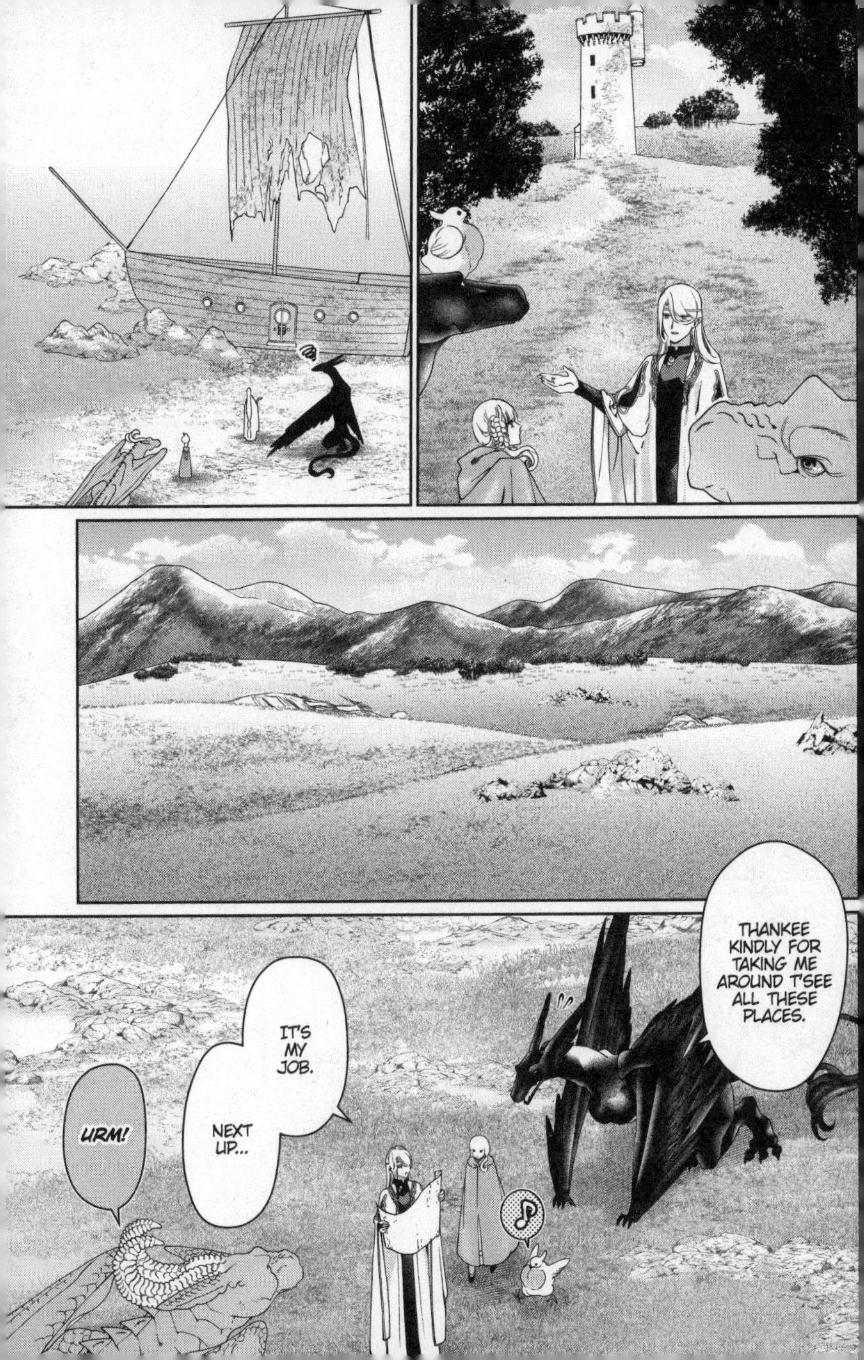
THANKEE KINDLY FOR TAKING ME AROUND T'SEE ALL THESE PLACES.
IT'S MY JOB.
NEXT UP...
URM!

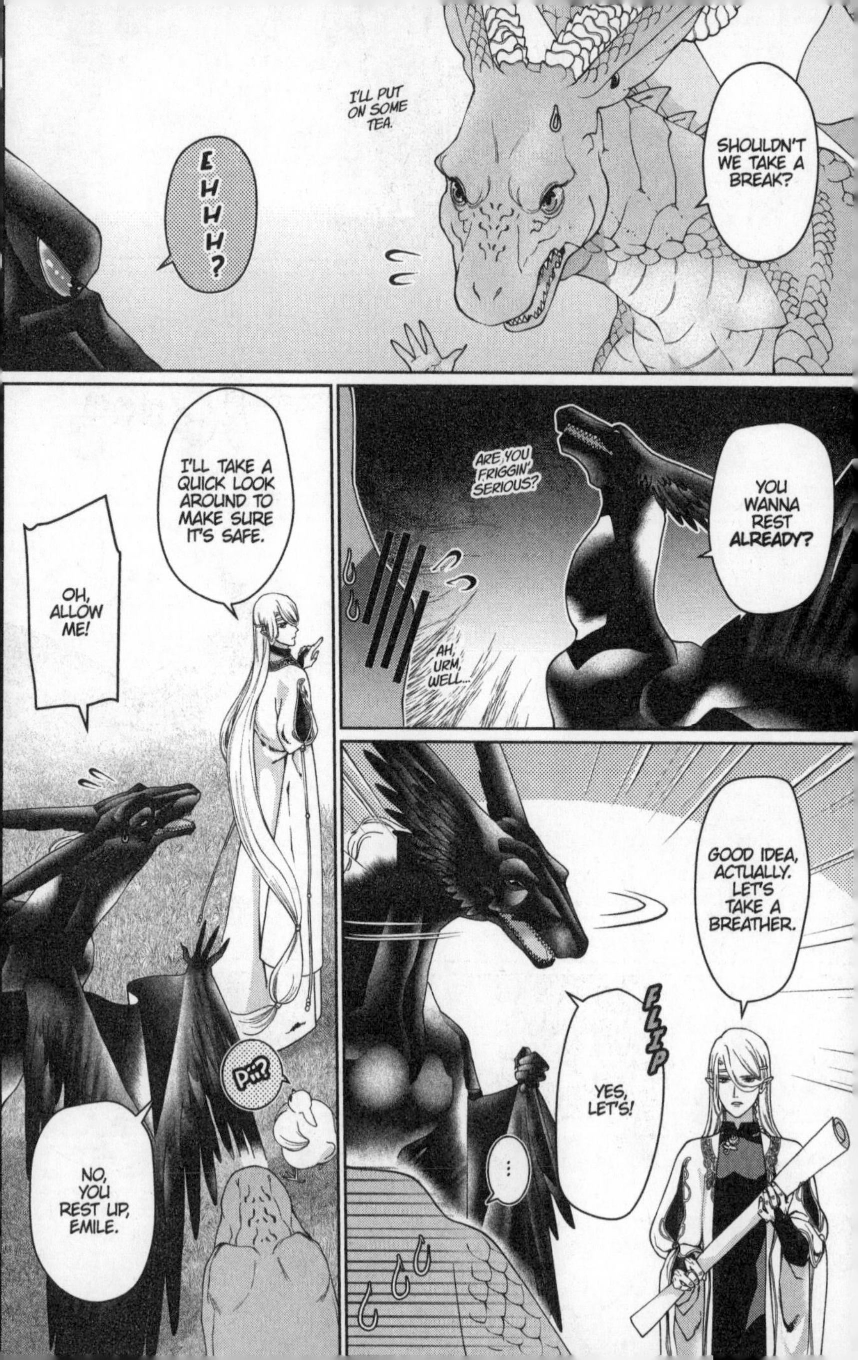
SHOULDN'T WE TAKE A BREAK?
I'LL PUT ON SOME TEA.
EHHH?
YOU WANNA REST ALREADY?
ARE YOU FRIGGIN' SERIOUS?
AH, URM, WELL...
GOOD IDEA, ACTUALLY. LET'S TAKE A BREATHER.
FLIP
YES, LET'S!
...
I'LL TAKE A QUICK LOOK AROUND TO MAKE SURE IT'S SAFE.
OH, ALLOW ME!
Pii?
NO, YOU REST UP, EMILE.

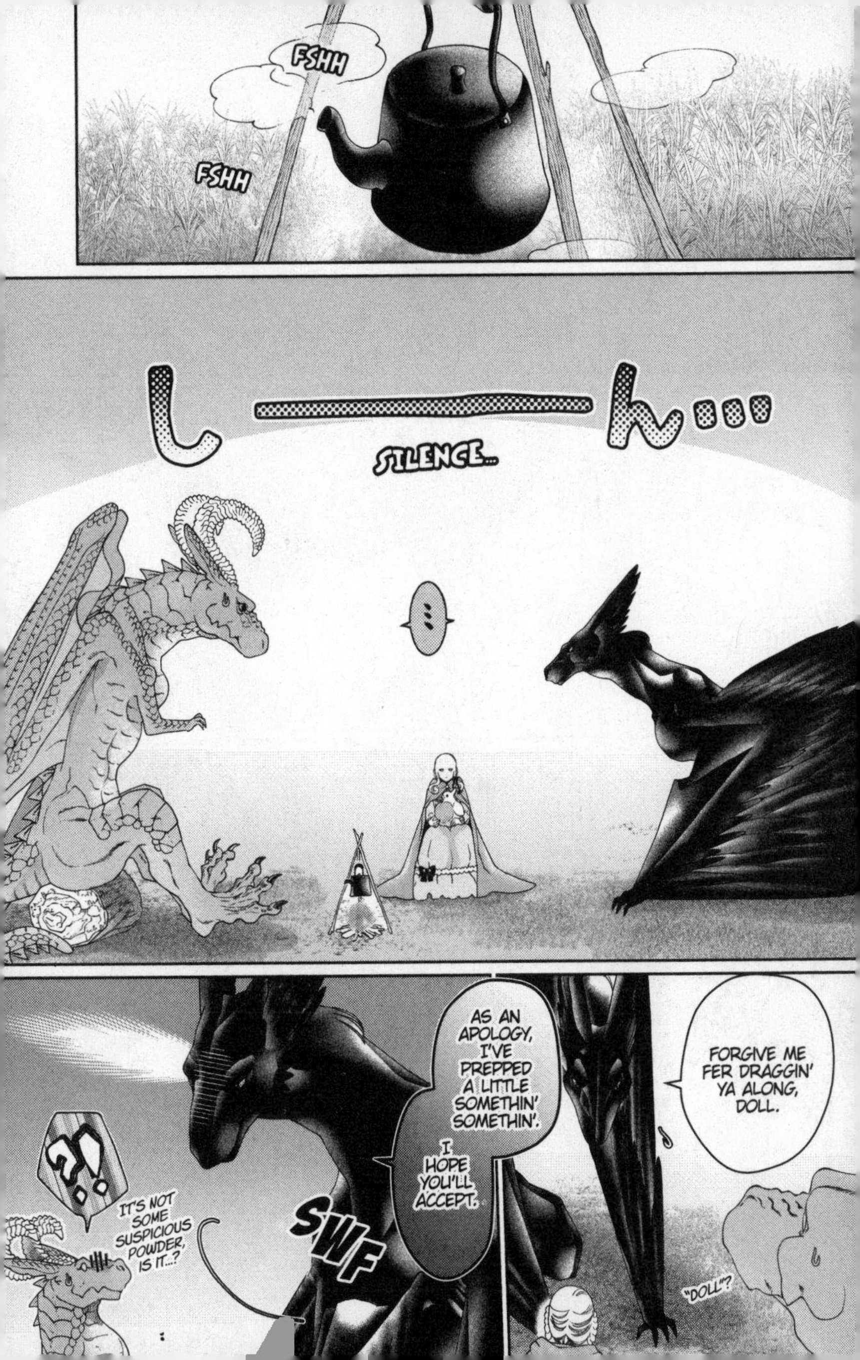
FSHH
FSHH
しーーーーーーん…
SILENCE...
...
FORGIVE ME FER DRAGGIN' YA ALONG, DOLL.
AS AN APOLOGY, I'VE PREPPED A LITTLE SOMETHIN' SOMETHIN'.
I HOPE YOU'LL ACCEPT.
"DOLL"?
SWF
?!
IT'S NOT SOME SUSPICIOUS POWDER, IS IT...?

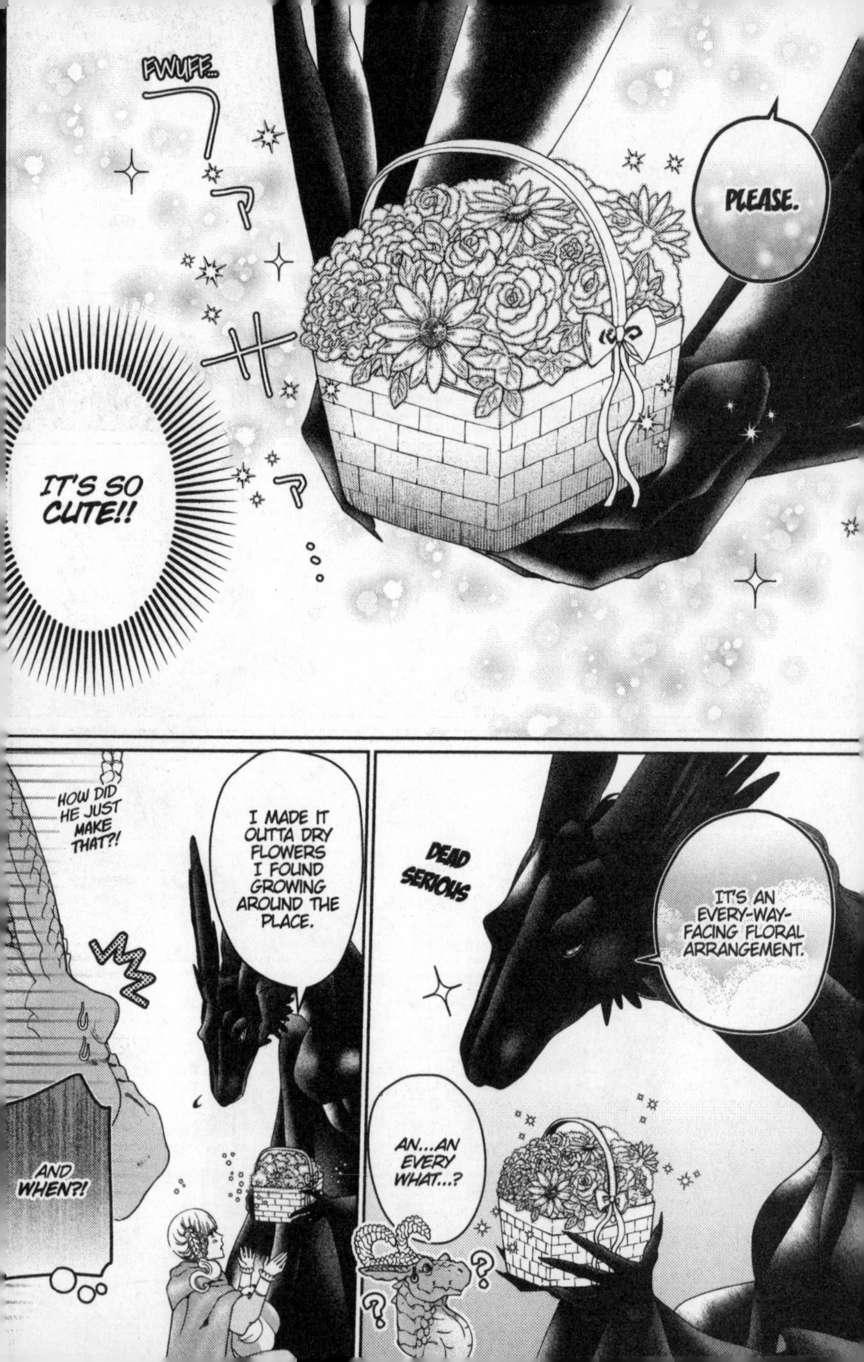
PLEASE.
FWUFF...
IT'S SO CUTE!!
DEAD SERIOUS
IT'S AN EVERY-WAY-FACING FLORAL ARRANGEMENT.
AN...AN EVERY WHAT...?
I MADE IT OUTTA DRY FLOWERS I FOUND GROWING AROUND THE PLACE.
HOW DID HE JUST MAKE THAT?!
AND WHEN?!

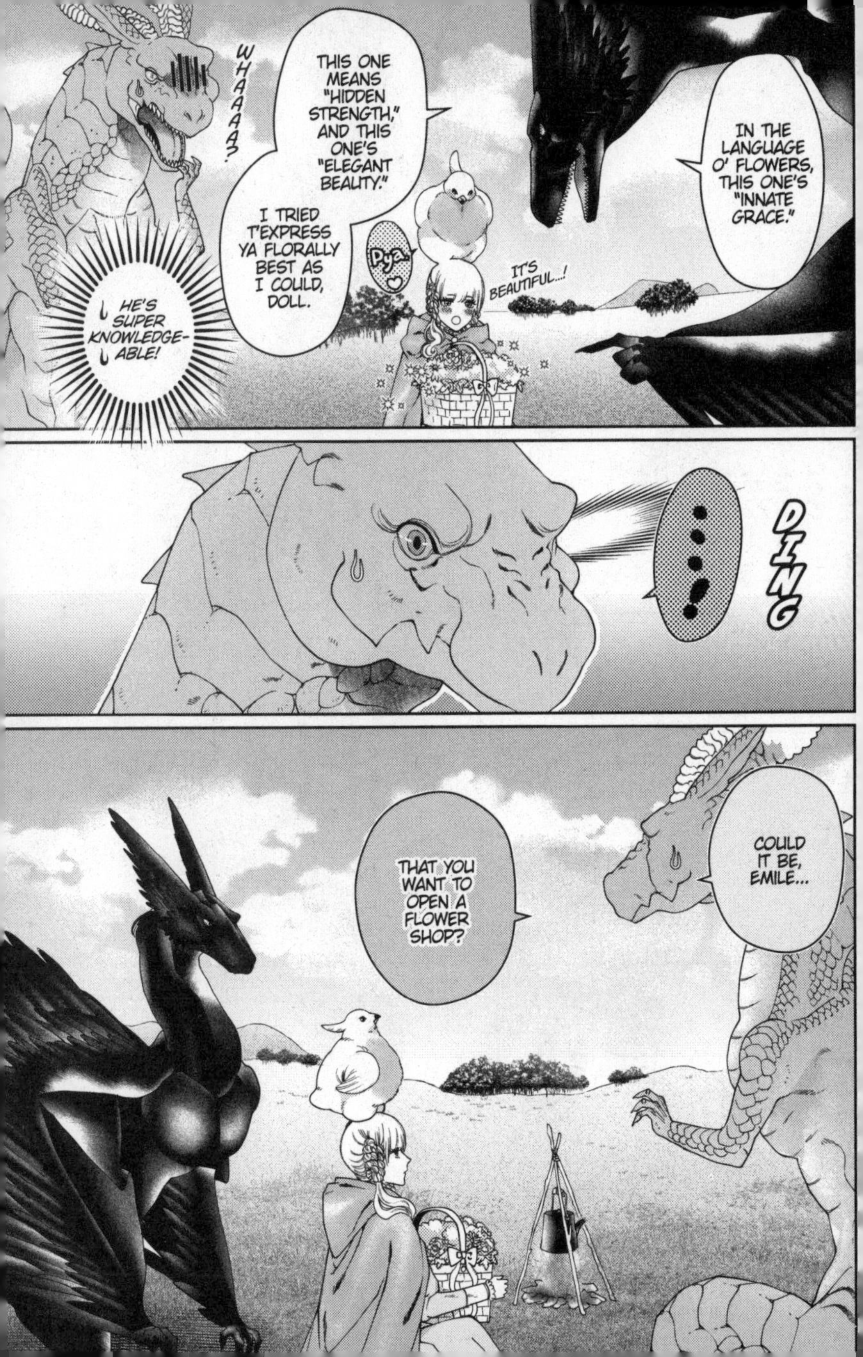
IN THE LANGUAGE O' FLOWERS, THIS ONE'S "INNATE GRACE."
IT'S BEAUTIFUL...!
Pya...
THIS ONE MEANS "HIDDEN STRENGTH," AND THIS ONE'S "ELEGANT BEAUTY."
I TRIED T'EXPRESS YA FLORALLY BEST AS I COULD, DOLL.
WHAAAAA?
HE'S SUPER KNOWLEDGE-ABLE!
DING
....!
COULD IT BE, EMILE...
THAT YOU WANT TO OPEN A FLOWER SHOP?

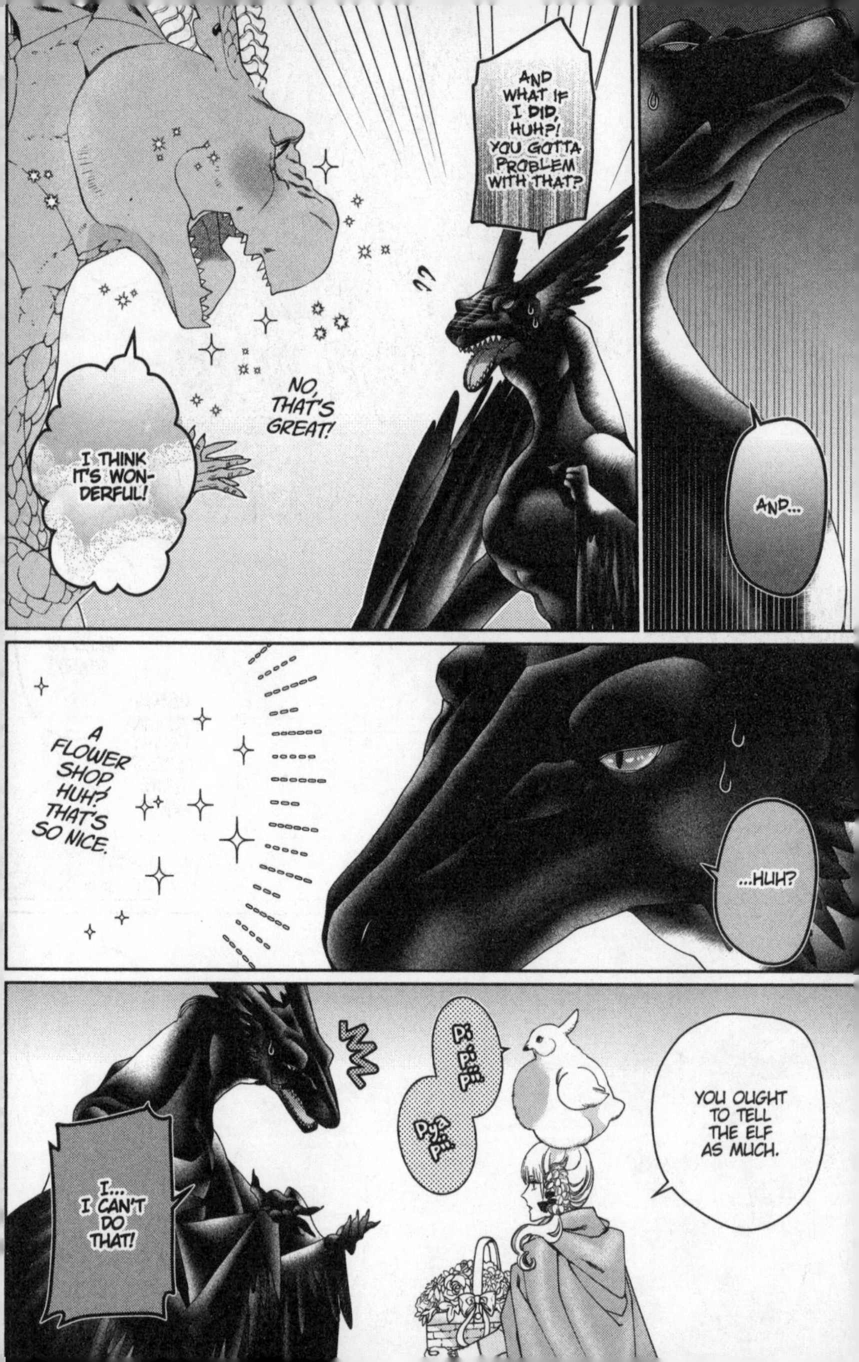
AND...
AND WHAT IF I DID, HUH?! YOU GOTTA PROBLEM WITH THAT?
NO, THAT'S GREAT!
I THINK IT'S WON-DERFUL!
...HUH?
A FLOWER SHOP HUH? THAT'S SO NICE.
YOU OUGHT TO TELL THE ELF AS MUCH.
Pi Pi Pi...
Pya P...
I... I CAN'T DO THAT!

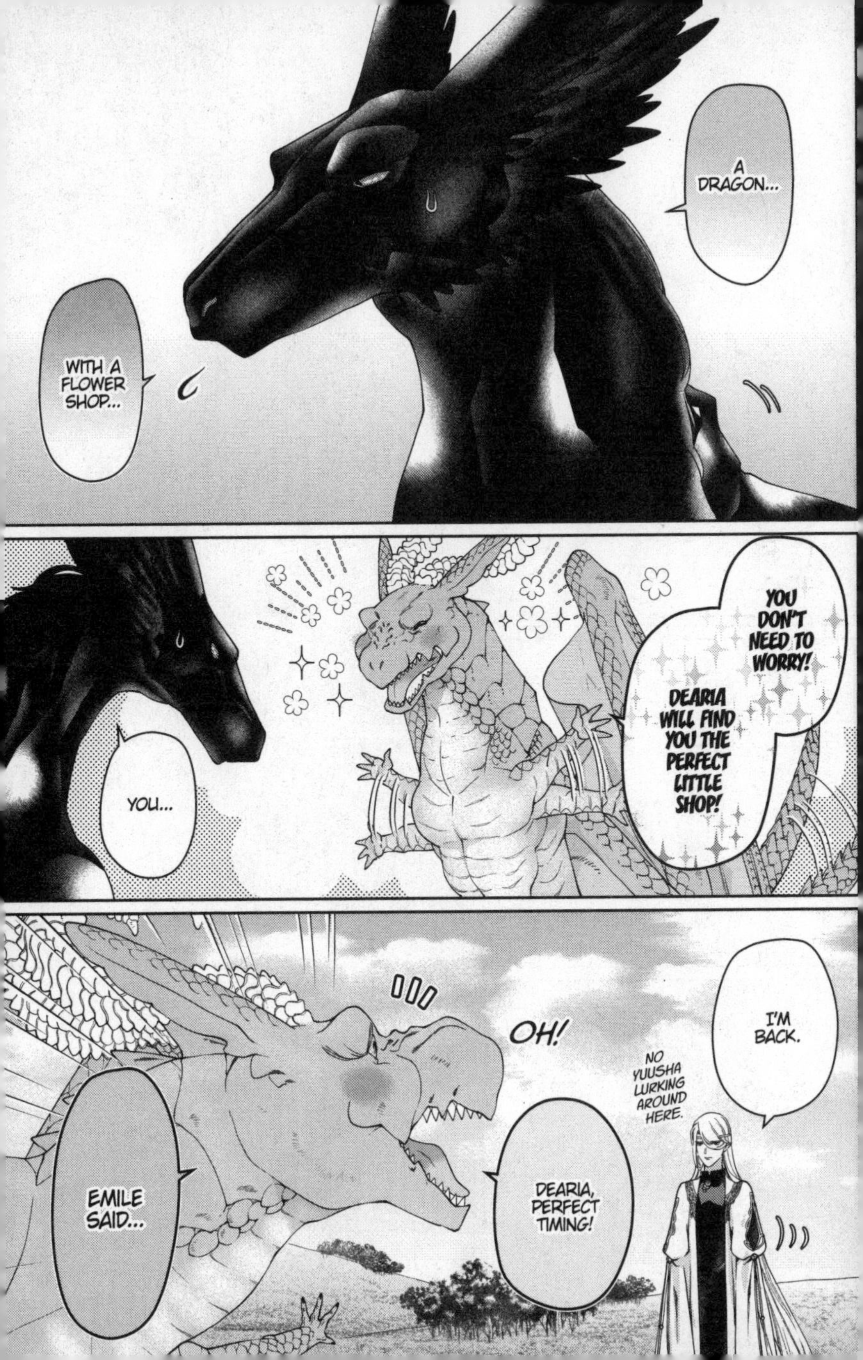
A DRAGON...
WITH A FLOWER SHOP...
YOU DON'T NEED TO WORRY!
DEARIA WILL FIND YOU THE PERFECT LITTLE SHOP!
YOU...
I'M BACK.
NO YUUSHA LURKING AROUND HERE.
OH!
DEARIA, PERFECT TIMING!
EMILE SAID...

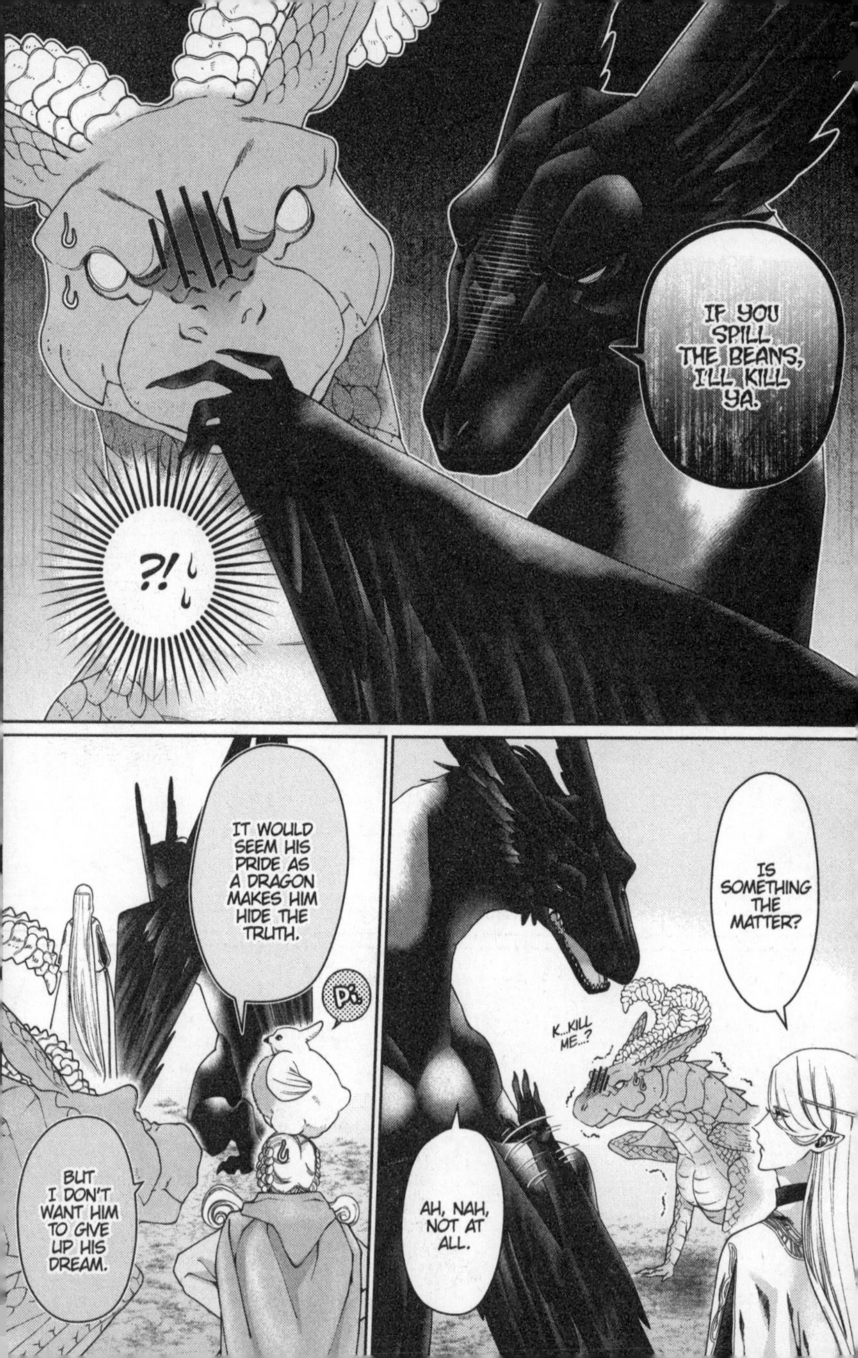
IF YOU SPILL THE BEANS, I'LL KILL YA.
?!
IS SOMETHING THE MATTER?
K...KILL ME...?
AH, NAH, NOT AT ALL.
IT WOULD SEEM HIS PRIDE AS A DRAGON MAKES HIM HIDE THE TRUTH.
Pi
BUT I DON'T WANT HIM TO GIVE UP HIS DREAM.

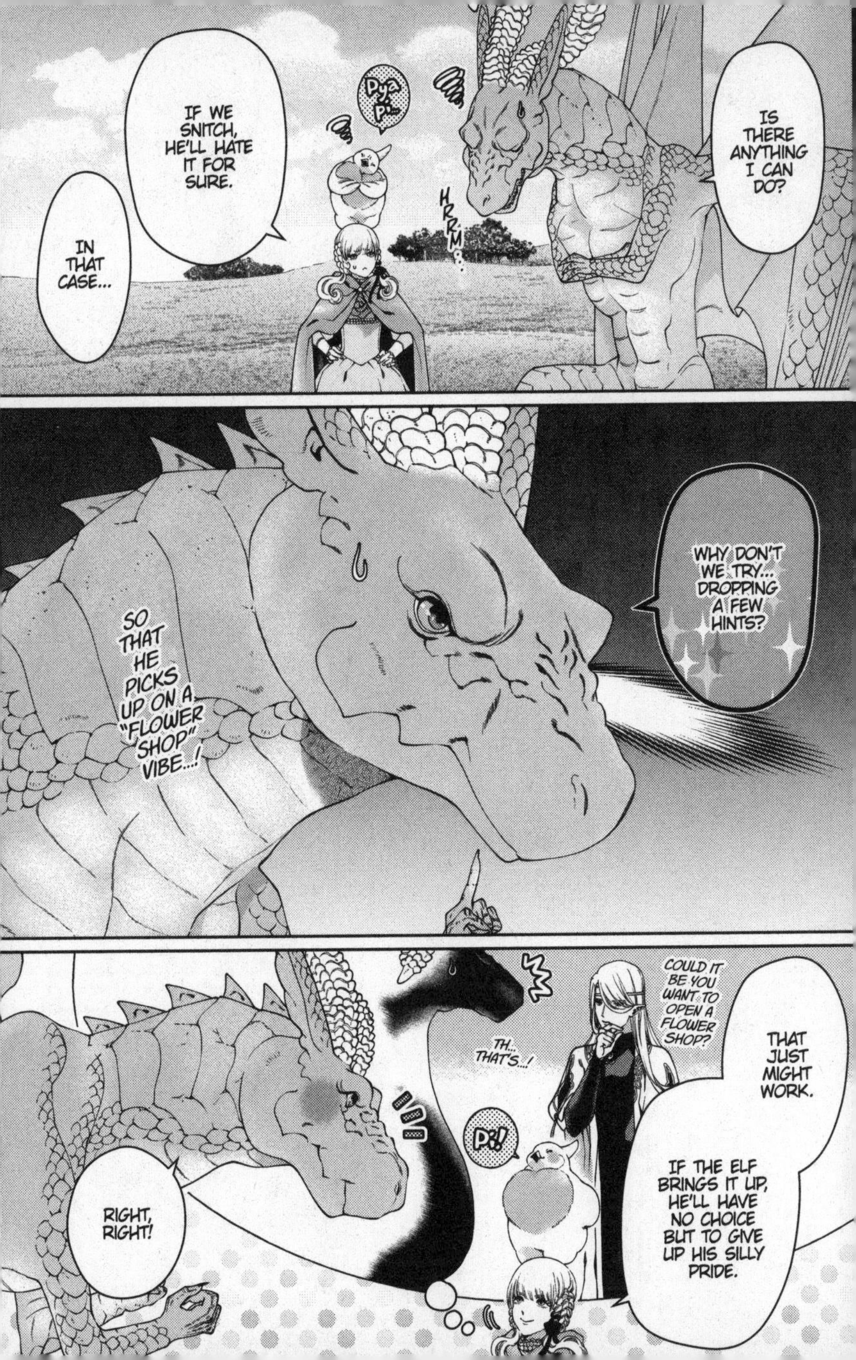
IS THERE ANYTHING I CAN DO?
HRRM..
Pya pi...
IF WE SNITCH, HE'LL HATE IT FOR SURE.
IN THAT CASE...
WHY DON'T WE TRY... DROPPING A FEW HINTS?
SO THAT HE PICKS UP ON A "FLOWER SHOP" VIBE...!
COULD IT BE YOU WANT TO OPEN A FLOWER SHOP?
THAT JUST MIGHT WORK.
IF THE ELF BRINGS IT UP, HE'LL HAVE NO CHOICE BUT TO GIVE UP HIS SILLY PRIDE.
TH... THAT'S...!
Pi!
RIGHT, RIGHT!

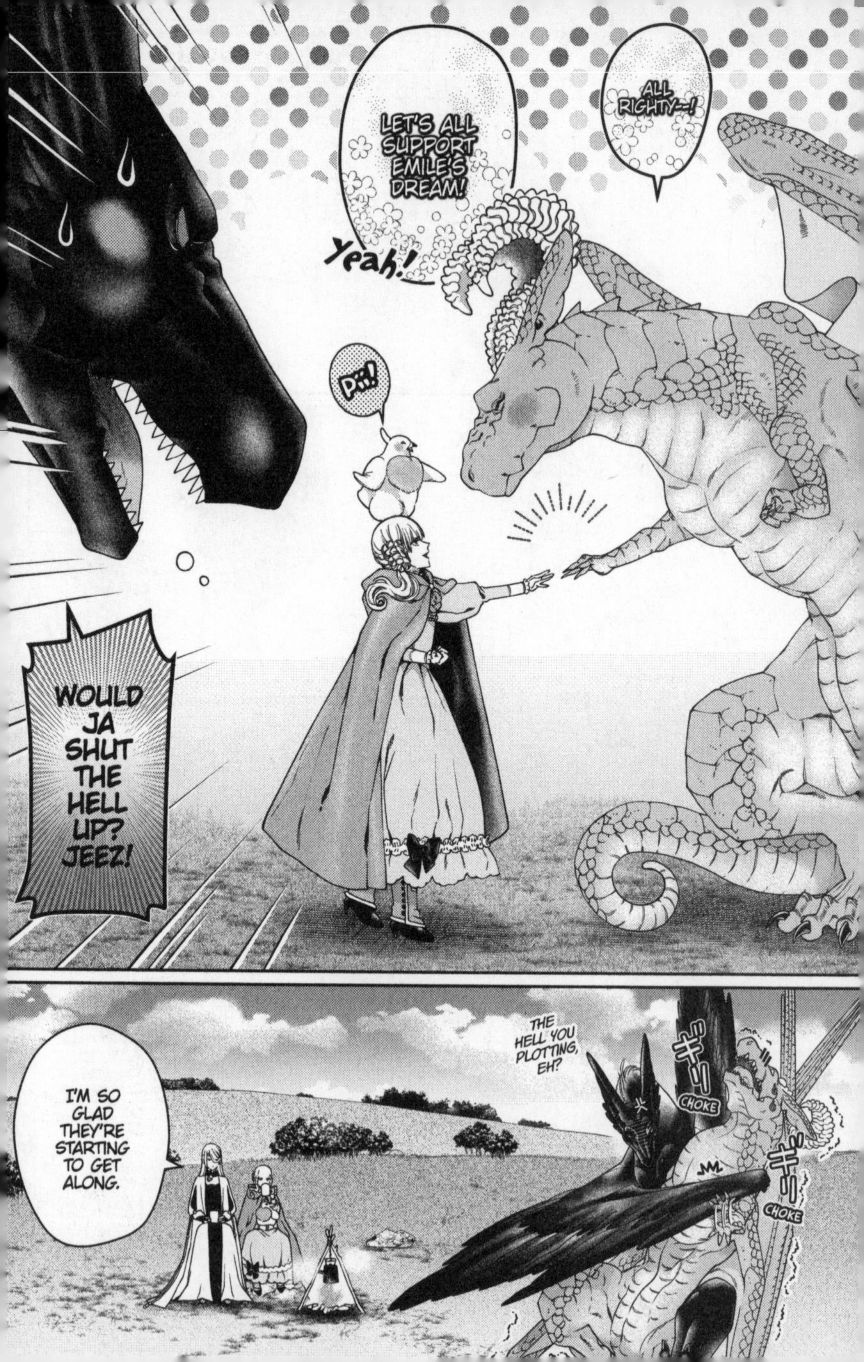
ALL RIGHTY--!
LET'S ALL SUPPORT EMILE'S DREAM!
Yeah!
Pii!
WOULD JA SHUT THE HELL UP? JEEZ!
THE HELL YOU PLOTTING, EH?
ギリ
CHOKE
ギリ
CHOKE
I'M SO GLAD THEY'RE STARTING TO GET ALONG.

Punks Nowadays

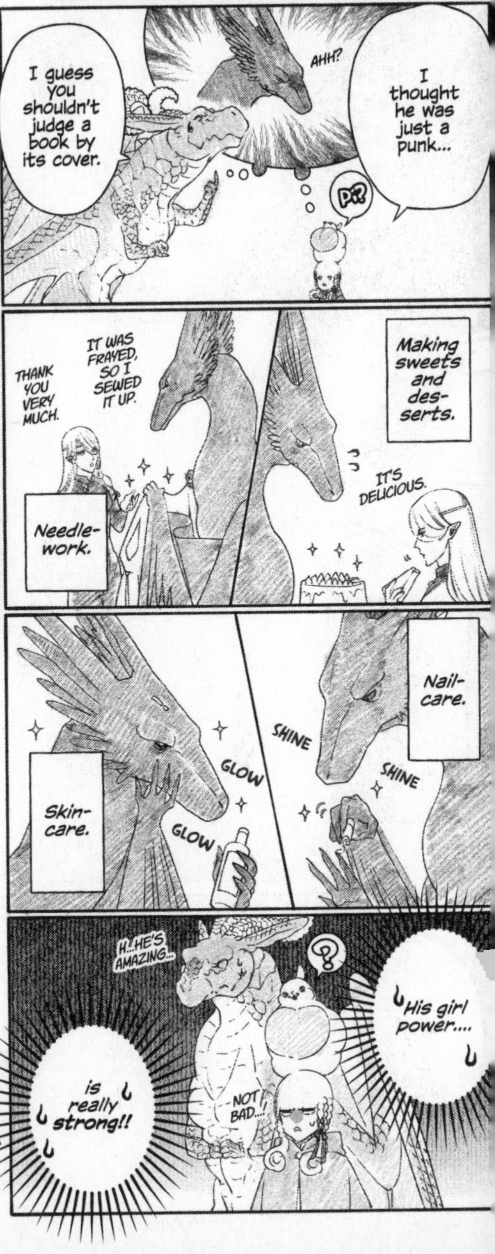
I thought he was just a punk...
AHH?
I guess you shouldn't judge a book by its cover.
Making sweets and des-serts.
IT'S DELICIOUS.
IT WAS FRAYED, SO I SEWED IT UP.
THANK YOU VERY MUCH.
Needle-work.
Nail-care.
SHINE
SHINE
GLOW
Skin-care.
GLOW
His girl power....
is really strong!!
?
H...HE'S AMAZING...
NOT BAD...!

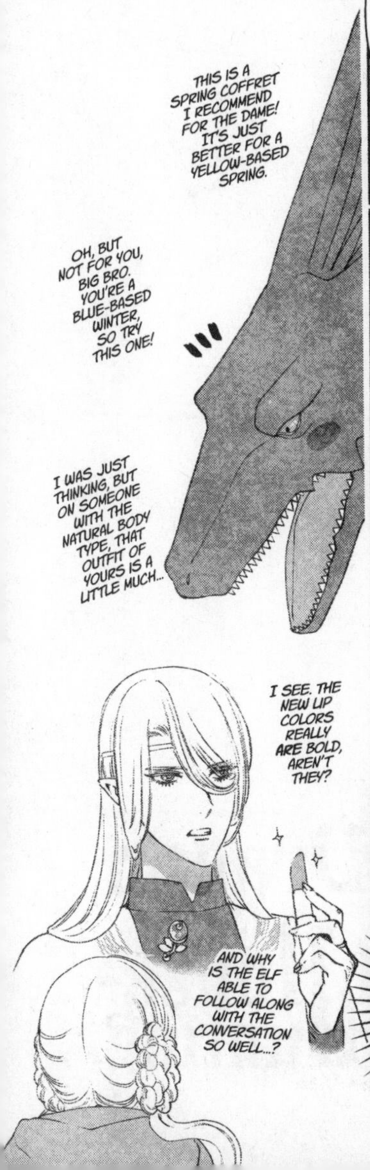
THIS IS A SPRING COFFRET I RECOMMEND FOR THE DAME! IT'S JUST BETTER FOR A YELLOW-BASED SPRING.
OH, BUT NOT FOR YOU, BIG BRO. YOU'RE A BLUE-BASED WINTER, SO TRY THIS ONE!
I WAS JUST THINKING, BUT ON SOMEONE WITH THE NATURAL BODY TYPE, THAT OUTFIT OF YOURS IS A LITTLE MUCH...
I SEE. THE NEW LIP COLORS REALLY ARE BOLD, AREN'T THEY?
AND WHY IS THE ELF ABLE TO FOLLOW ALONG WITH THE CONVERSATION SO WELL...?

Dragon Goes House-Hunting

House 34: An Enterprising Home (Part 2)

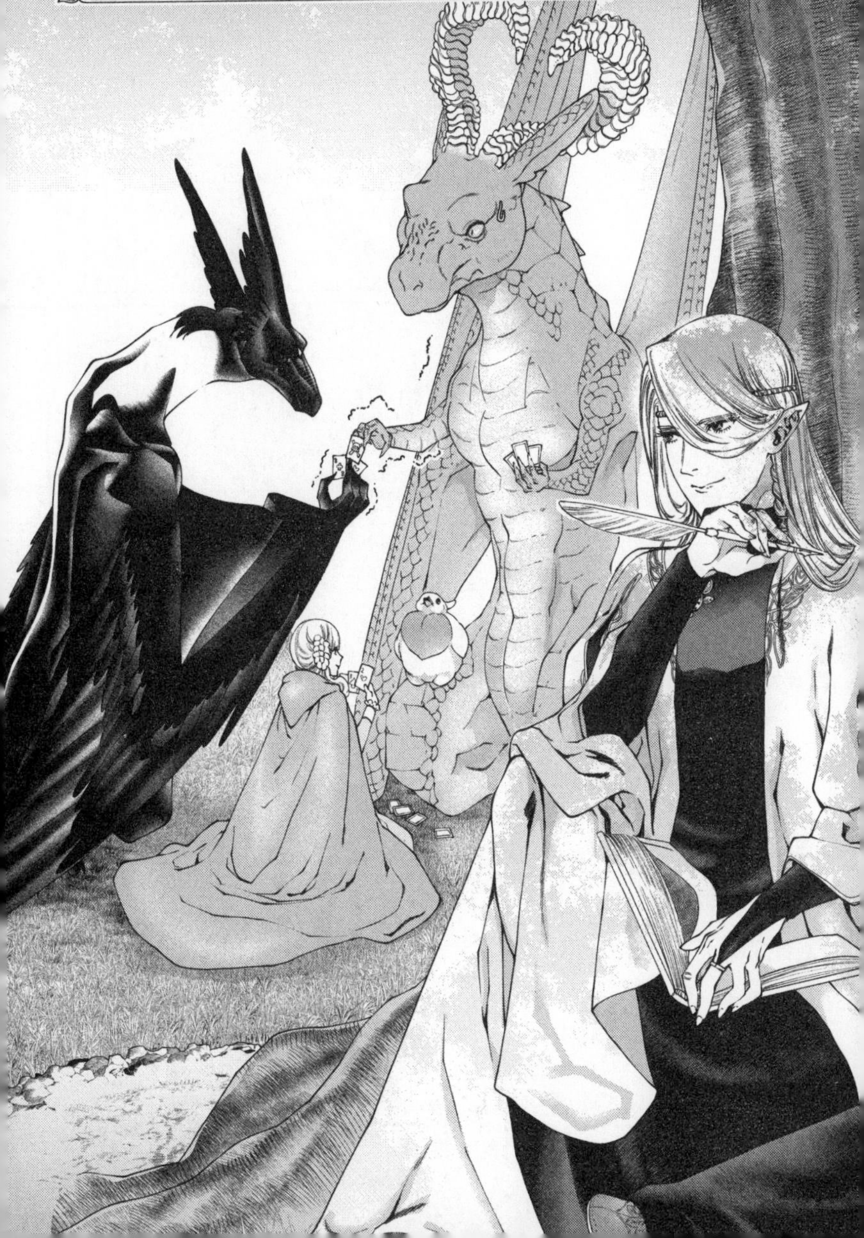

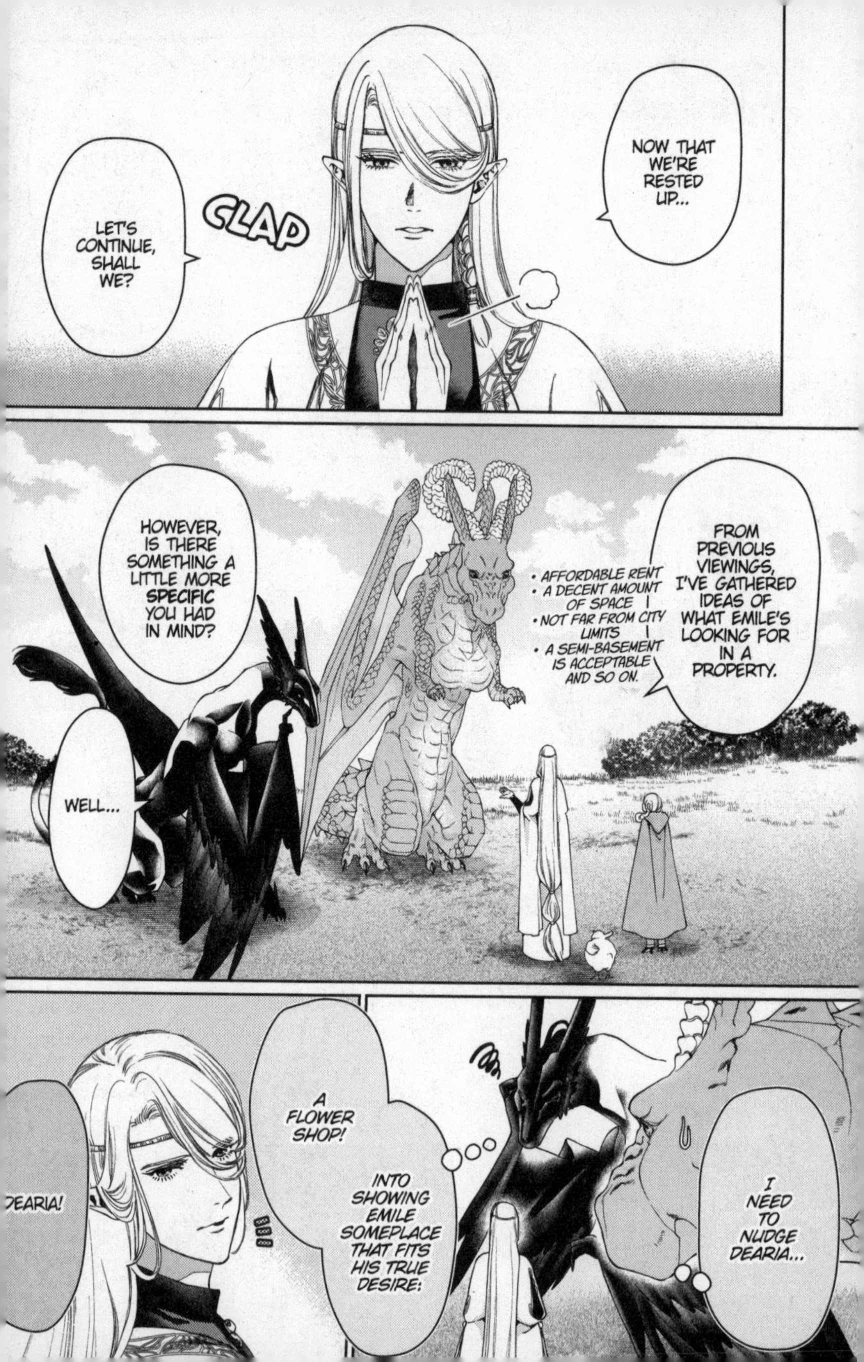
NOW THAT WE'RE RESTED UP...
CLAP
LET'S CONTINUE, SHALL WE?
FROM PREVIOUS VIEWINGS, I'VE GATHERED IDEAS OF WHAT EMILE'S LOOKING FOR IN A PROPERTY.
• AFFORDABLE RENT
• A DECENT AMOUNT OF SPACE
• NOT FAR FROM CITY LIMITS
• A SEMI-BASEMENT IS ACCEPTABLE
AND SO ON.
HOWEVER, IS THERE SOMETHING A LITTLE MORE **SPECIFIC** YOU HAD IN MIND?
WELL...
I NEED TO NUDGE DEARIA...
INTO SHOWING EMILE SOMEPLACE THAT FITS HIS TRUE DESIRE:
A FLOWER SHOP!
DEARIA!

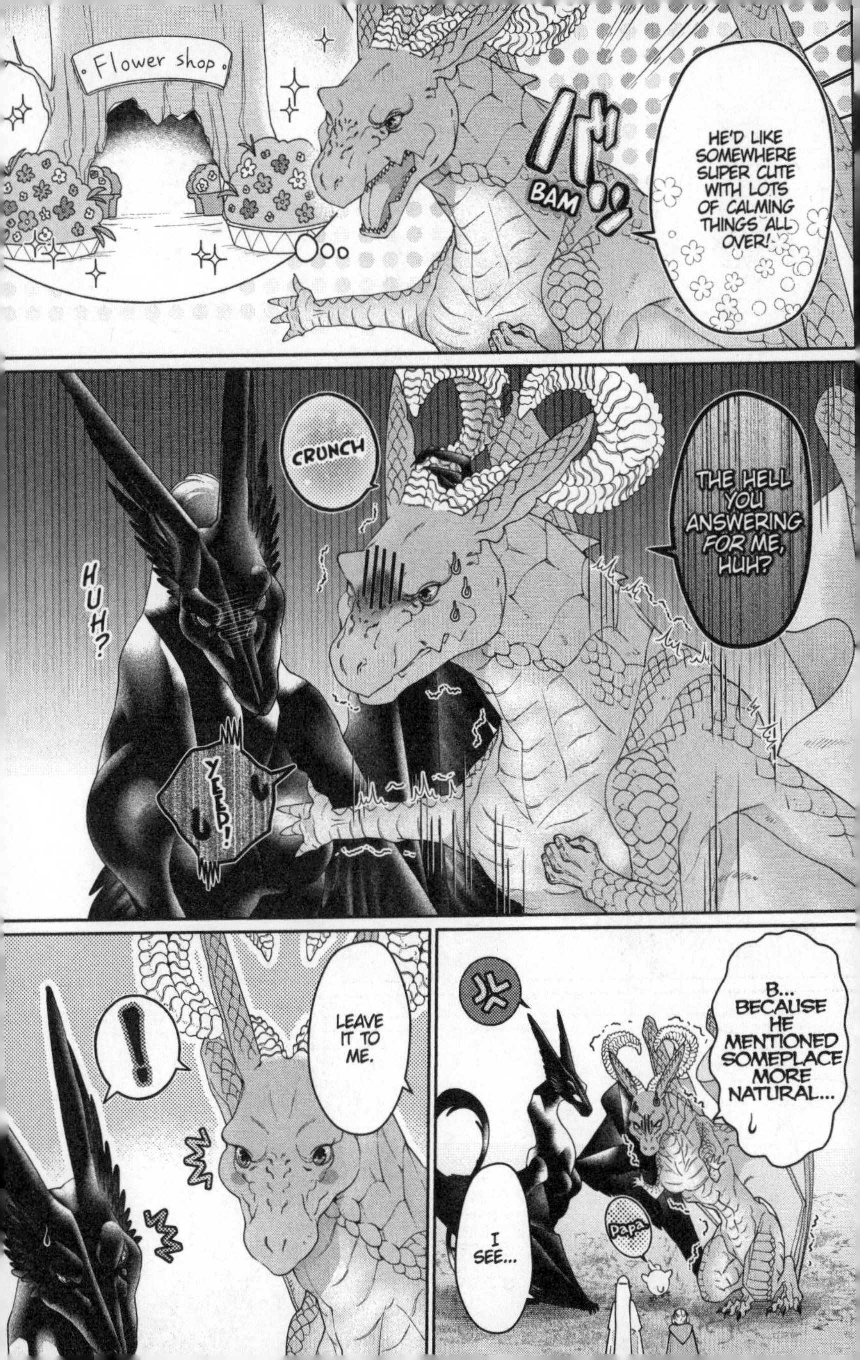
HE'D LIKE SOMEWHERE SUPER CUTE WITH LOTS OF CALMING THINGS ALL OVER!
BAM
Flower shop
THE HELL YOU ANSWERING FOR ME, HUH?
CRUNCH
HUH?
YEEP!
B... BECAUSE HE MENTIONED SOMEPLACE MORE NATURAL...
I SEE...
Papa
LEAVE IT TO ME.
!

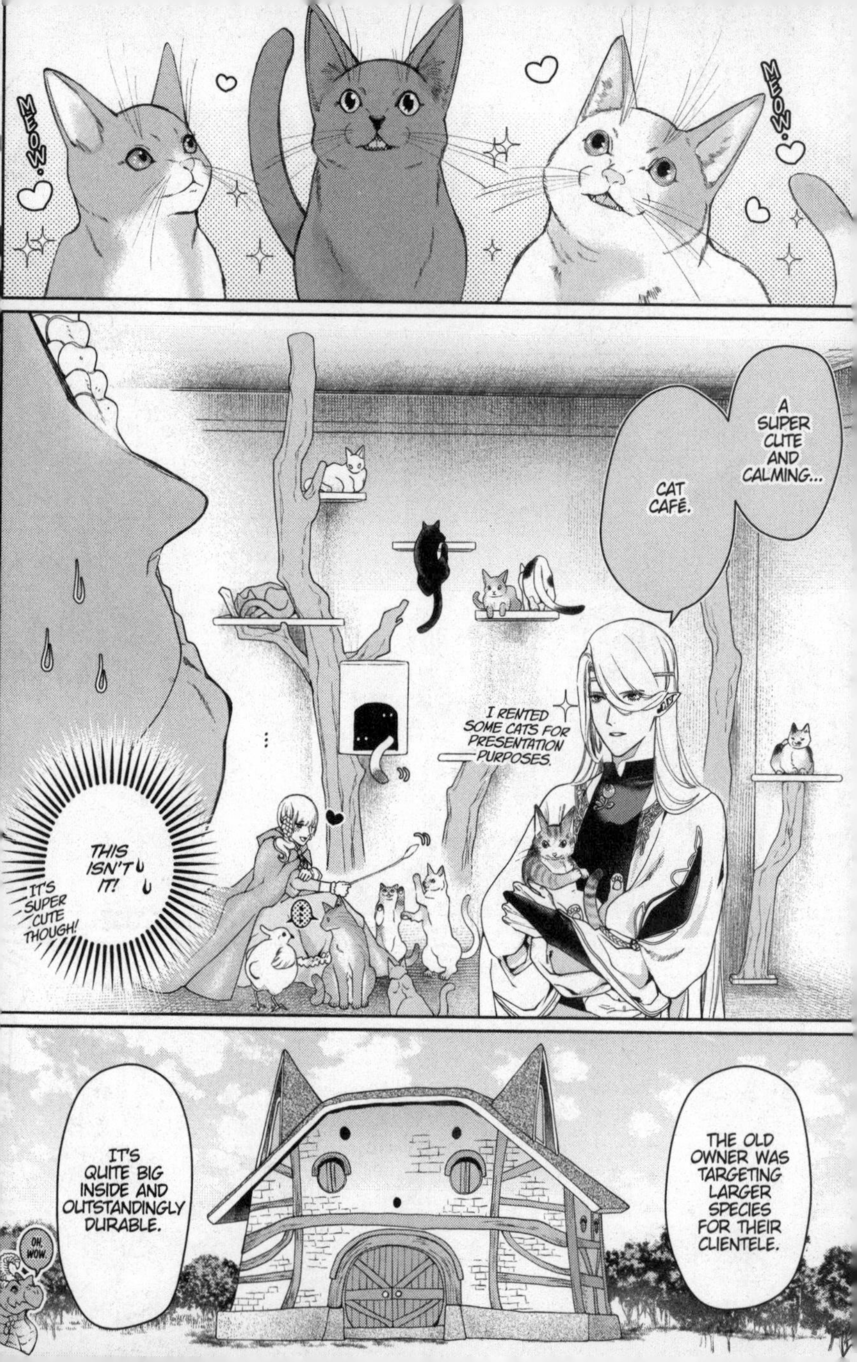
MEOW.
MEOW.
A SUPER CUTE AND CALMING...
CAT CAFÉ.
I RENTED SOME CATS FOR PRESENTATION PURPOSES.
...
THIS ISN'T IT!
IT'S SUPER CUTE THOUGH!
THE OLD OWNER WAS TARGETING LARGER SPECIES FOR THEIR CLIENTELE.
IT'S QUITE BIG INSIDE AND OUTSTANDINGLY DURABLE.
OH, WOW.

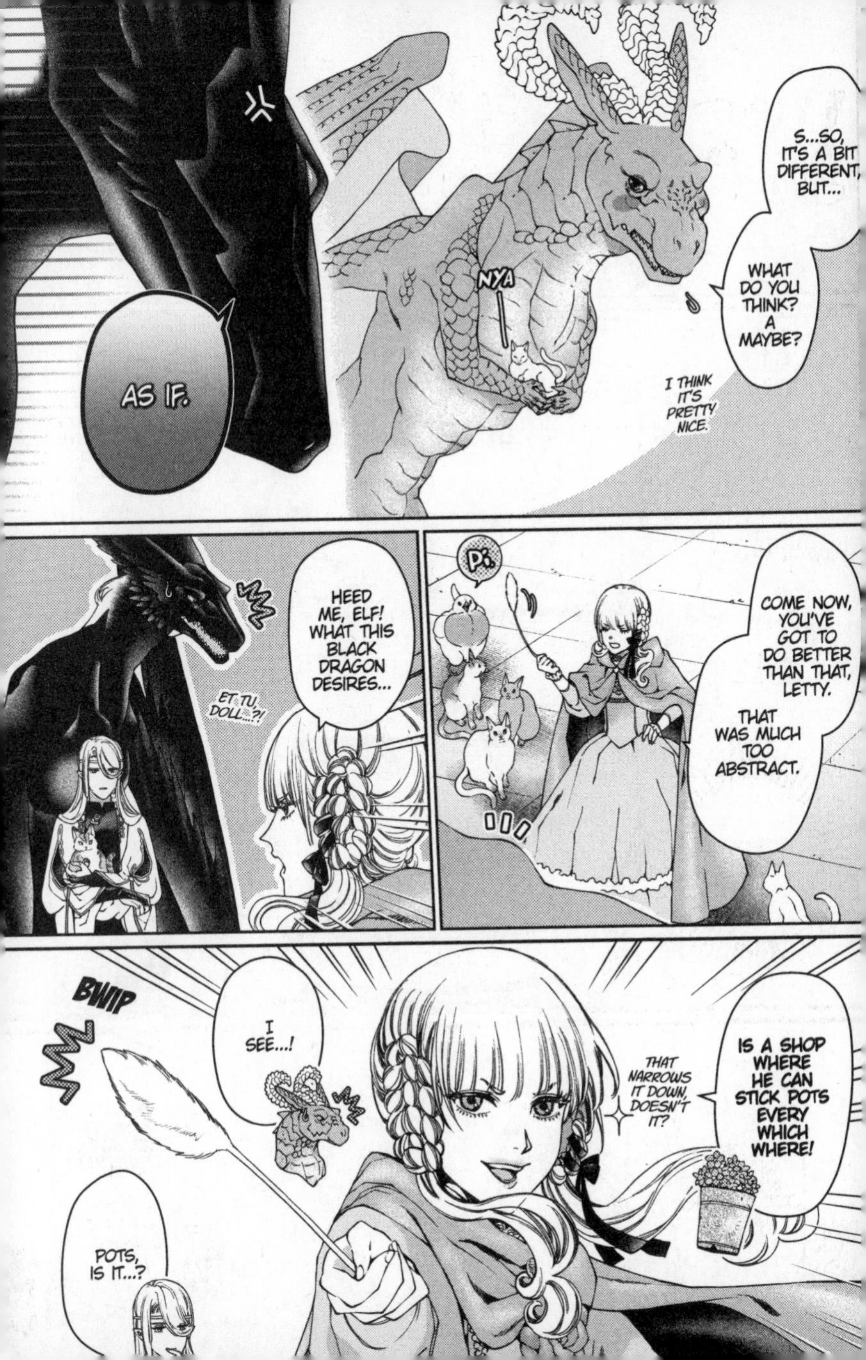
S...SO, IT'S A BIT DIFFERENT, BUT...
WHAT DO YOU THINK? A MAYBE?
I THINK IT'S PRETTY NICE.
NYA
AS IF.
Pi
COME NOW, YOU'VE GOT TO DO BETTER THAN THAT, LETTY.
THAT WAS MUCH TOO ABSTRACT.
HEED ME, ELF! WHAT THIS BLACK DRAGON DESIRES...
ET TU, DOLL...?!
IS A SHOP WHERE HE CAN STICK POTS EVERY WHICH WHERE!
THAT NARROWS IT DOWN, DOESN'T IT?
I SEE...!
BWIP
POTS, IS IT...?

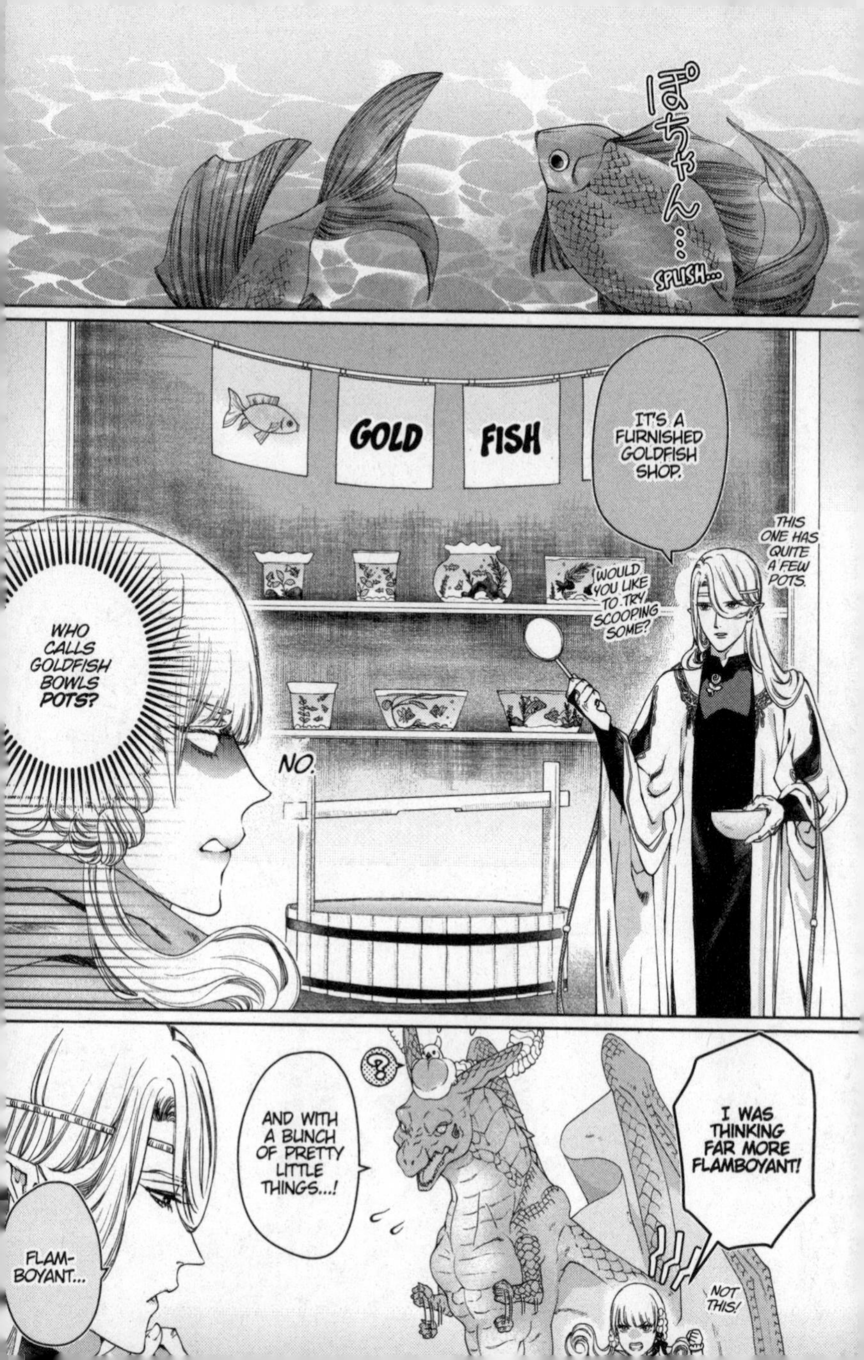
ぽちゃん…
SPLISH...
GOLD
FISH
IT'S A FURNISHED GOLDFISH SHOP.
THIS ONE HAS QUITE A FEW POTS.
WOULD YOU LIKE TO TRY SCOOPING SOME?
WHO CALLS GOLDFISH BOWLS POTS?
NO.
I WAS THINKING FAR MORE FLAMBOYANT!
NOT THIS!
?
AND WITH A BUNCH OF PRETTY LITTLE THINGS...!
FLAM-BOYANT...

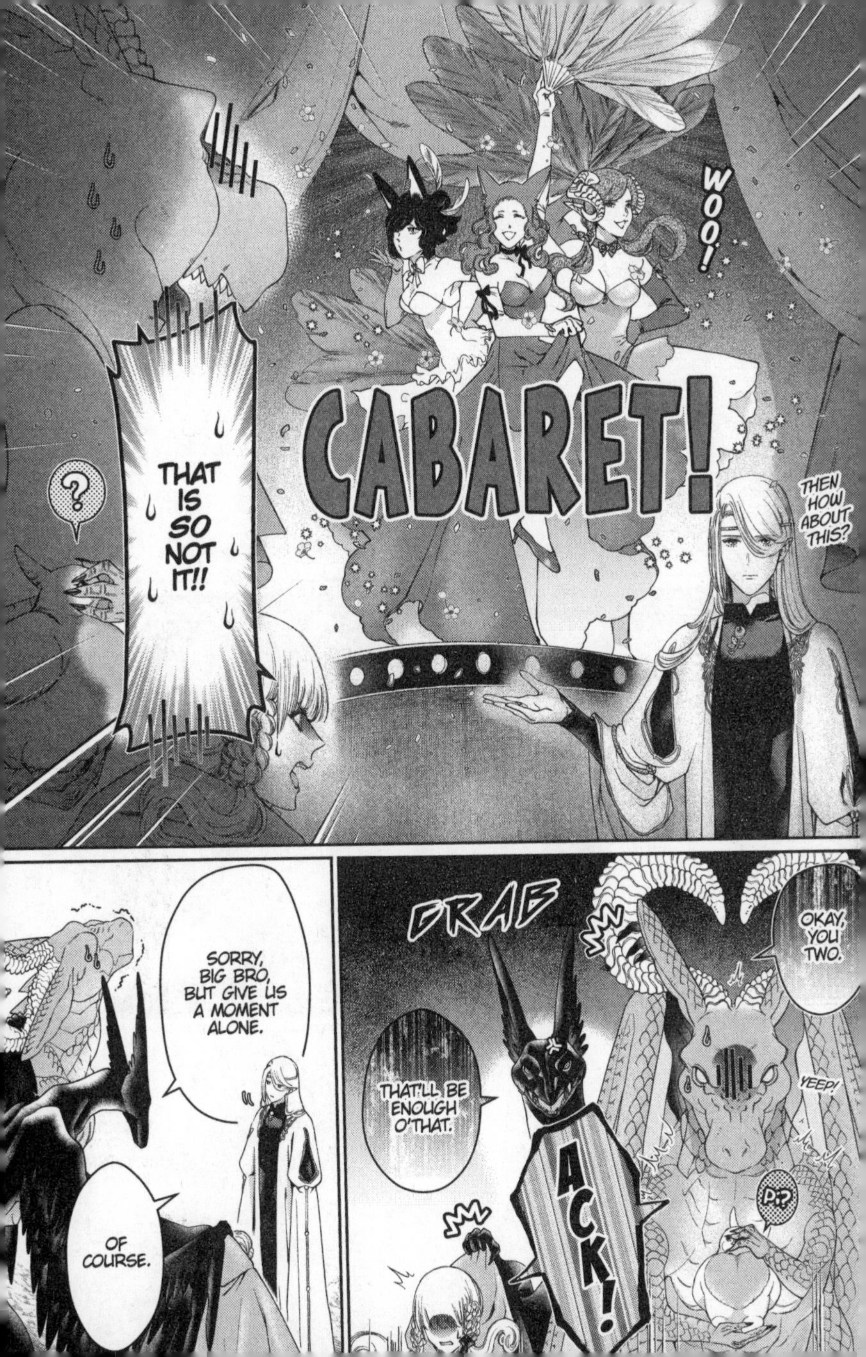
THEN HOW ABOUT THIS?
WOO!
CABARET!
?
THAT IS SO NOT IT!!
OKAY, YOU TWO.
GRAB
YEEP!
THAT'LL BE ENOUGH O'THAT.
ACK!
P?
SORRY, BIG BRO, BUT GIVE US A MOMENT ALONE.
OF COURSE.

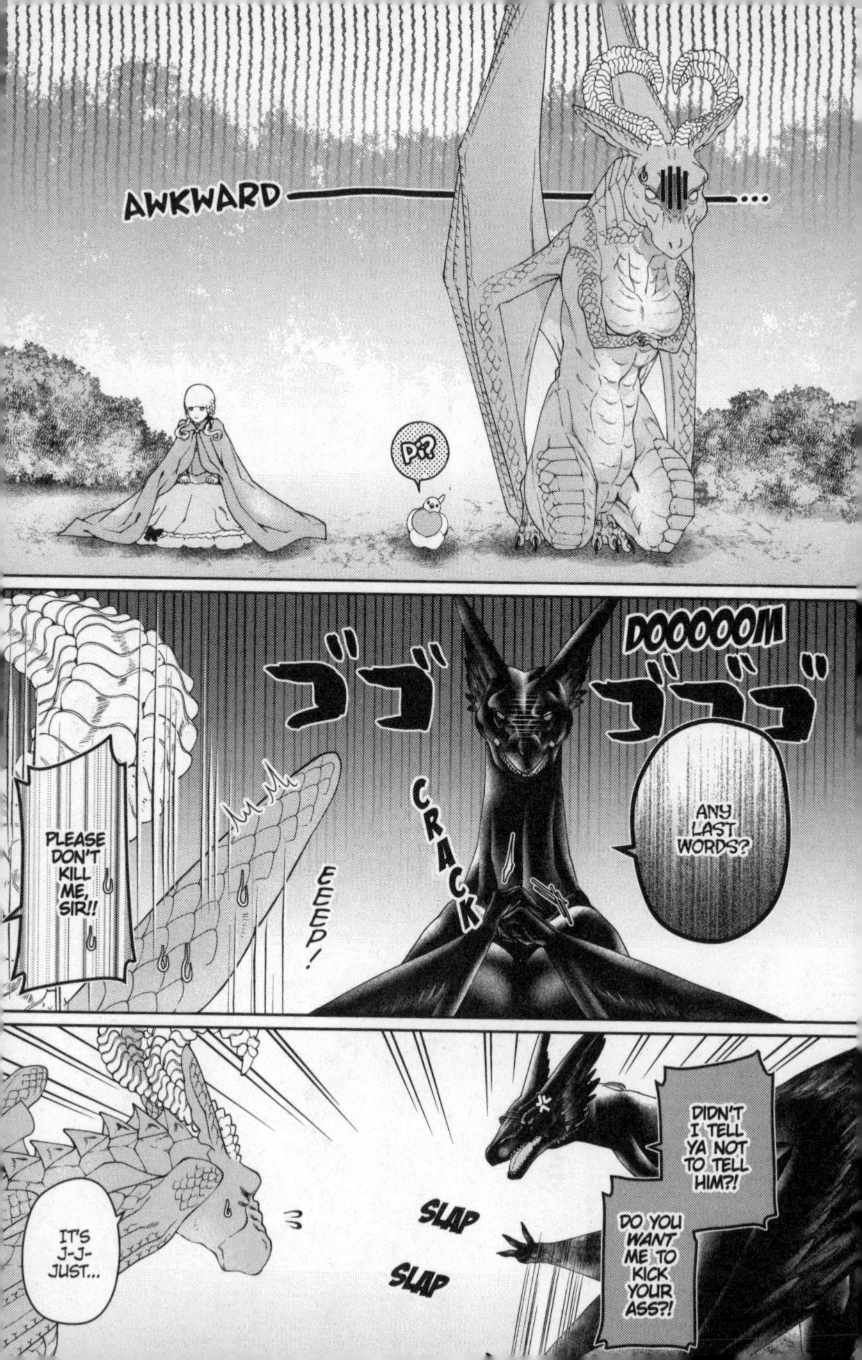
AWKWARD———...
Pi?
DOOOOOM
ゴゴゴ
ゴゴ
ANY LAST WORDS?
CRACK
EEEP!
PLEASE DON'T KILL ME, SIR!!
DIDN'T I TELL YA NOT TO TELL HIM?!
DO YOU WANT ME TO KICK YOUR ASS?!
SLAP
SLAP
IT'S J-J-JUST...

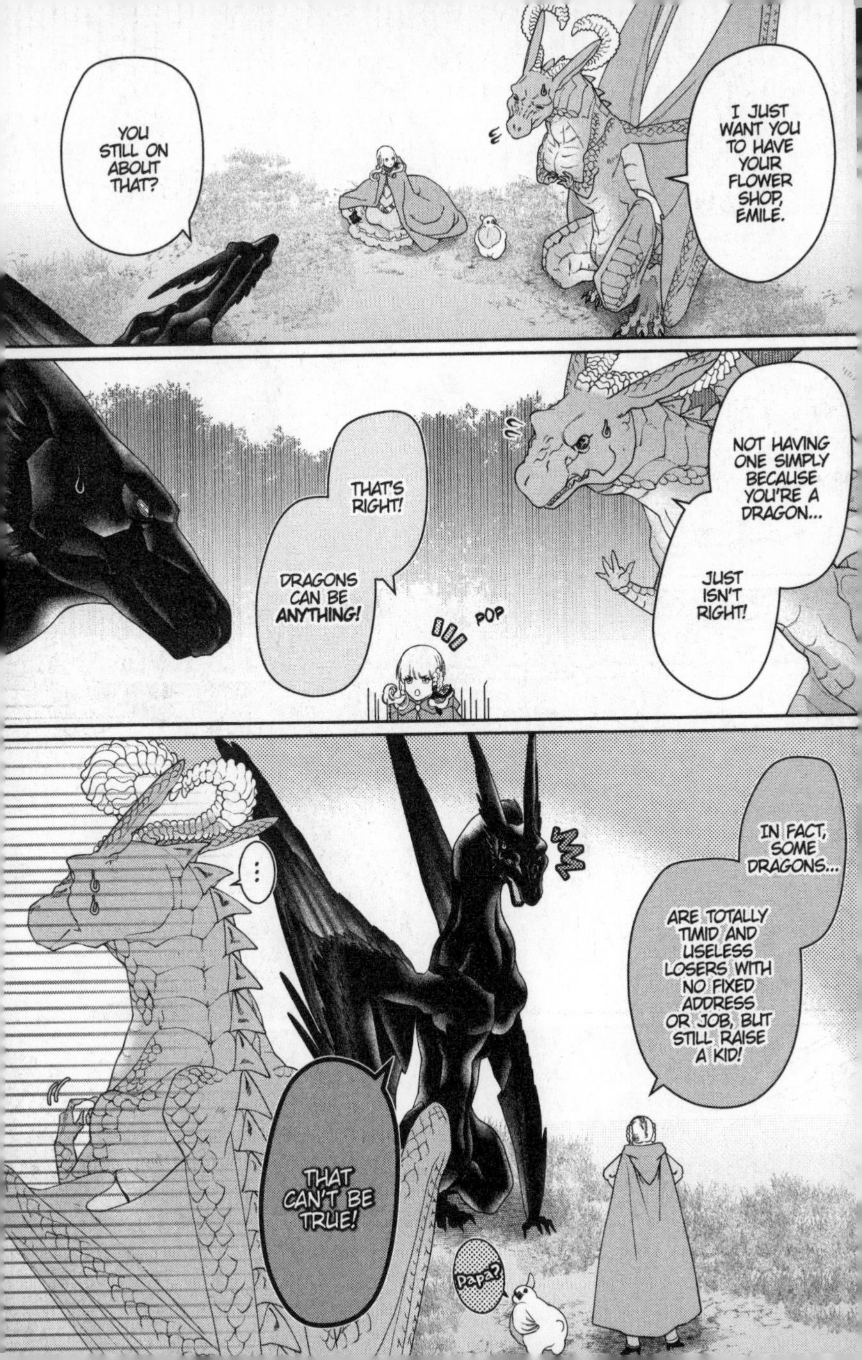
I JUST WANT YOU TO HAVE YOUR FLOWER SHOP, EMILE.
YOU STILL ON ABOUT THAT?
NOT HAVING ONE SIMPLY BECAUSE YOU'RE A DRAGON...
JUST ISN'T RIGHT!
POP
THAT'S RIGHT!
DRAGONS CAN BE ANYTHING!
IN FACT, SOME DRAGONS...
ARE TOTALLY TIMID AND USELESS LOSERS WITH NO FIXED ADDRESS OR JOB, BUT STILL RAISE A KID!
...
THAT CAN'T BE TRUE!
Papa?

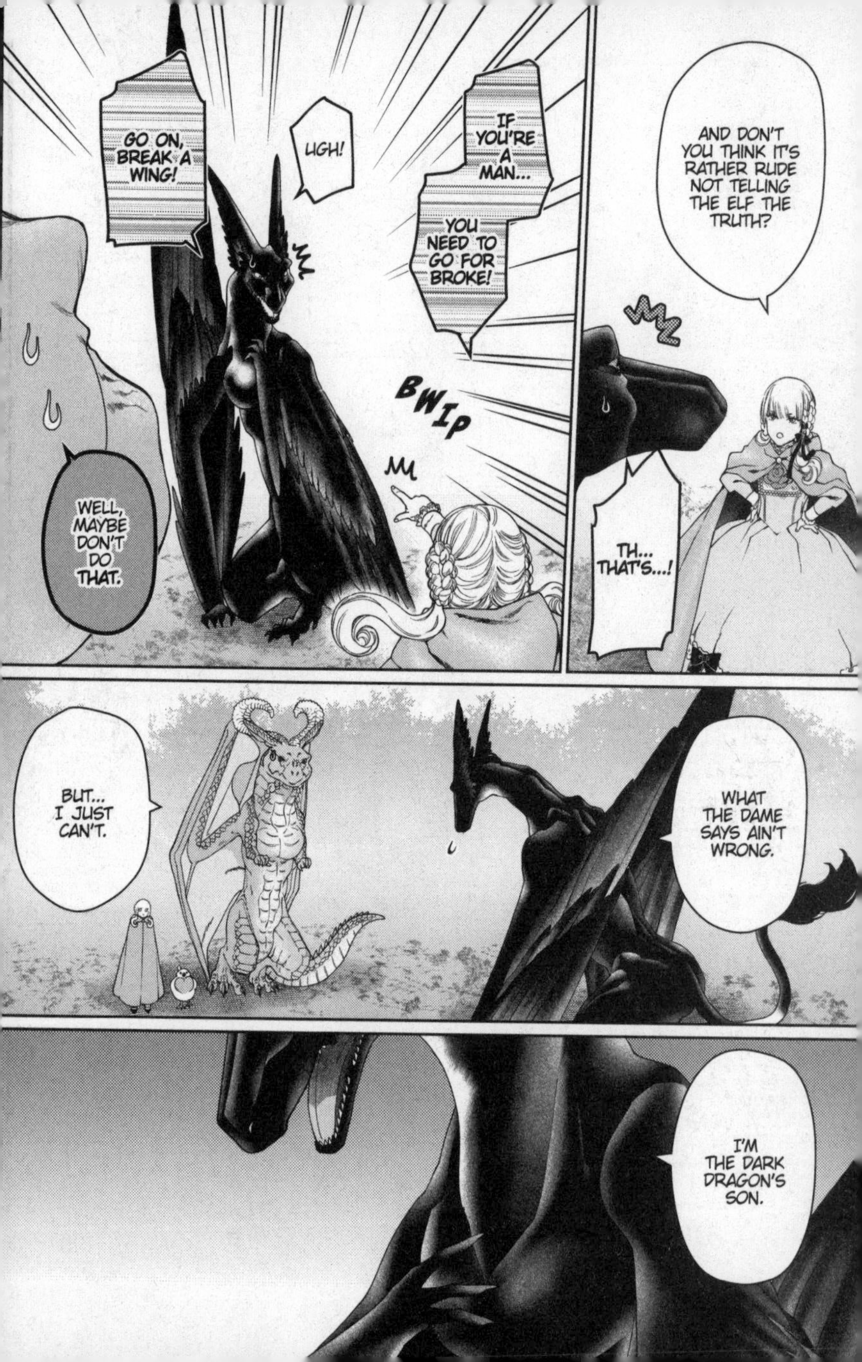
AND DON'T YOU THINK IT'S RATHER RUDE NOT TELLING THE ELF THE TRUTH?
TH... THAT'S...!
IF YOU'RE A MAN...
YOU NEED TO GO FOR BROKE!
BWIP
UGH!
GO ON, BREAK A WING!
WELL, MAYBE DON'T DO THAT.
WHAT THE DAME SAYS AIN'T WRONG.
BUT... I JUST CAN'T.
I'M THE DARK DRAGON'S SON.

HE'S THE STRONGEST, TOUGHEST DRAGON THERE IS.

HE'S A HERO WHO PROTECTS WEAK NON-HUMANS.

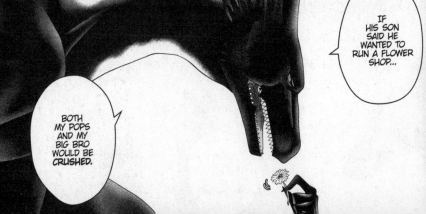

IF HIS SON SAID HE WANTED TO RUN A FLOWER SHOP...

BOTH MY POPS AND MY BIG BRO WOULD BE CRUSHED.

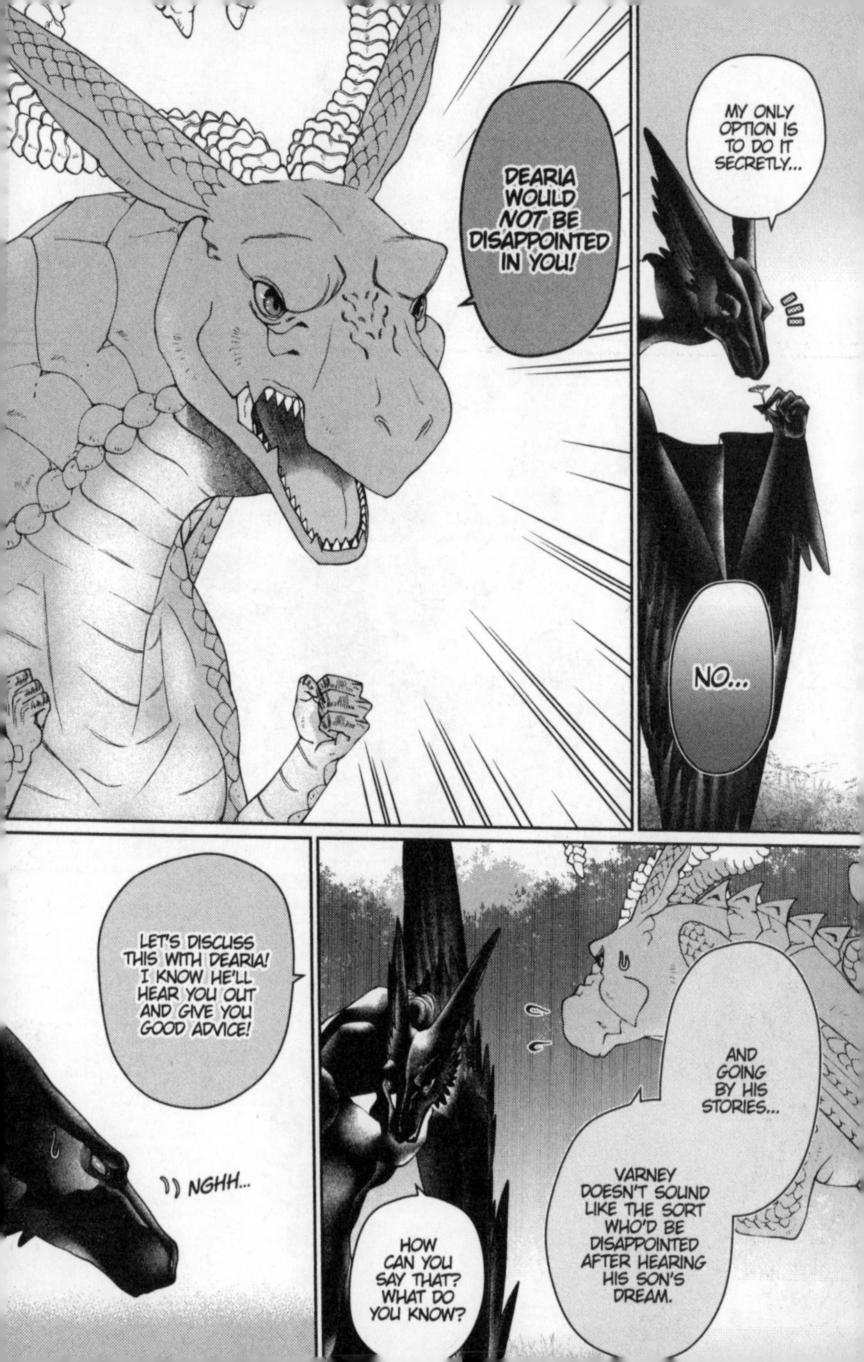
MY ONLY OPTION IS TO DO IT SECRETLY...
NO...
DEARIA WOULD *NOT* BE DISAPPOINTED IN YOU!
AND GOING BY HIS STORIES...
VARNEY DOESN'T SOUND LIKE THE SORT WHO'D BE DISAPPOINTED AFTER HEARING HIS SON'S DREAM.
HOW CAN YOU SAY THAT? WHAT DO YOU KNOW?
LET'S DISCUSS THIS WITH DEARIA! I KNOW HE'LL HEAR YOU OUT AND GIVE YOU GOOD ADVICE!
NGHH...

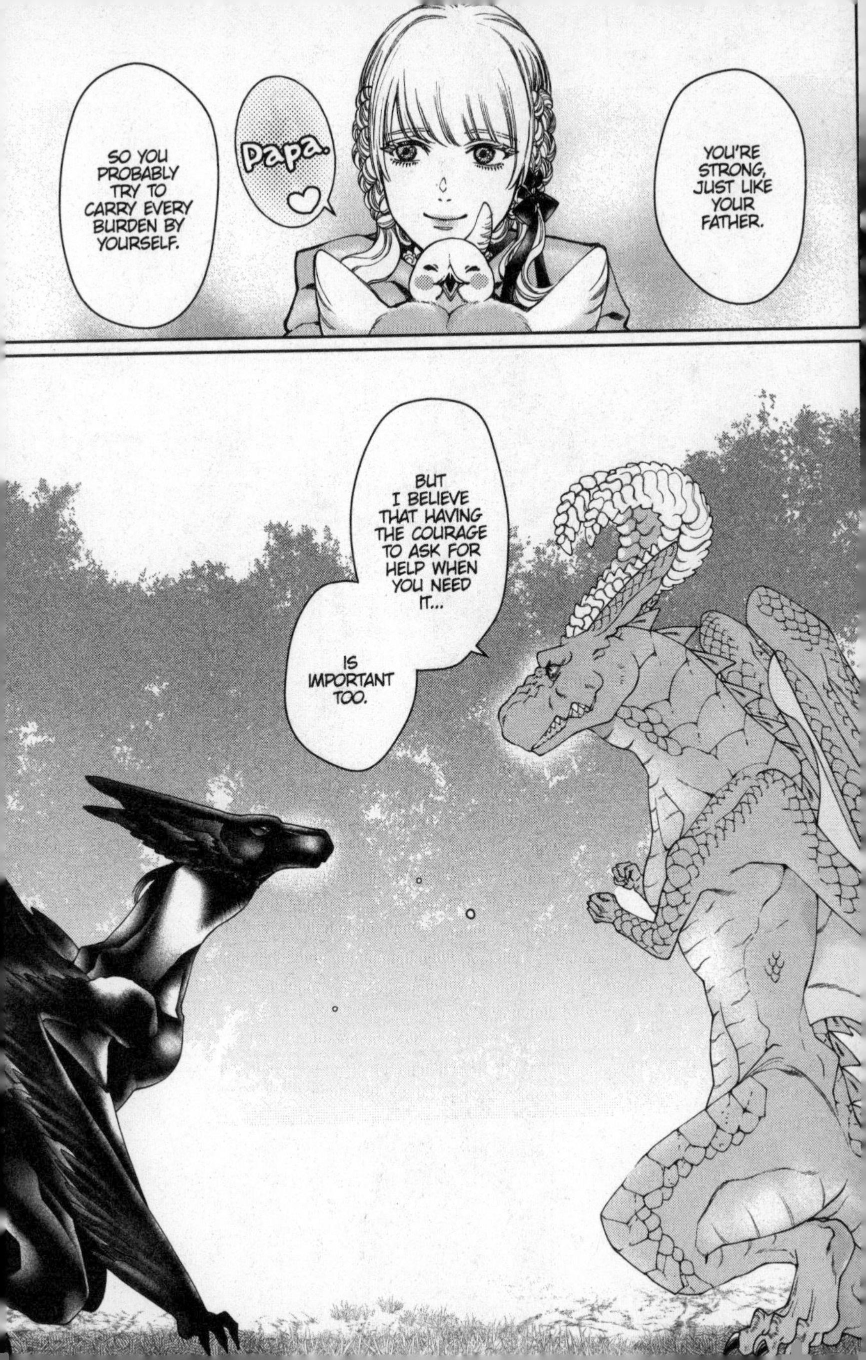
YOU'RE STRONG, JUST LIKE YOUR FATHER.
Papa. ♥
SO YOU PROBABLY TRY TO CARRY EVERY BURDEN BY YOURSELF.
BUT I BELIEVE THAT HAVING THE COURAGE TO ASK FOR HELP WHEN YOU NEED IT...
IS IMPORTANT TOO.

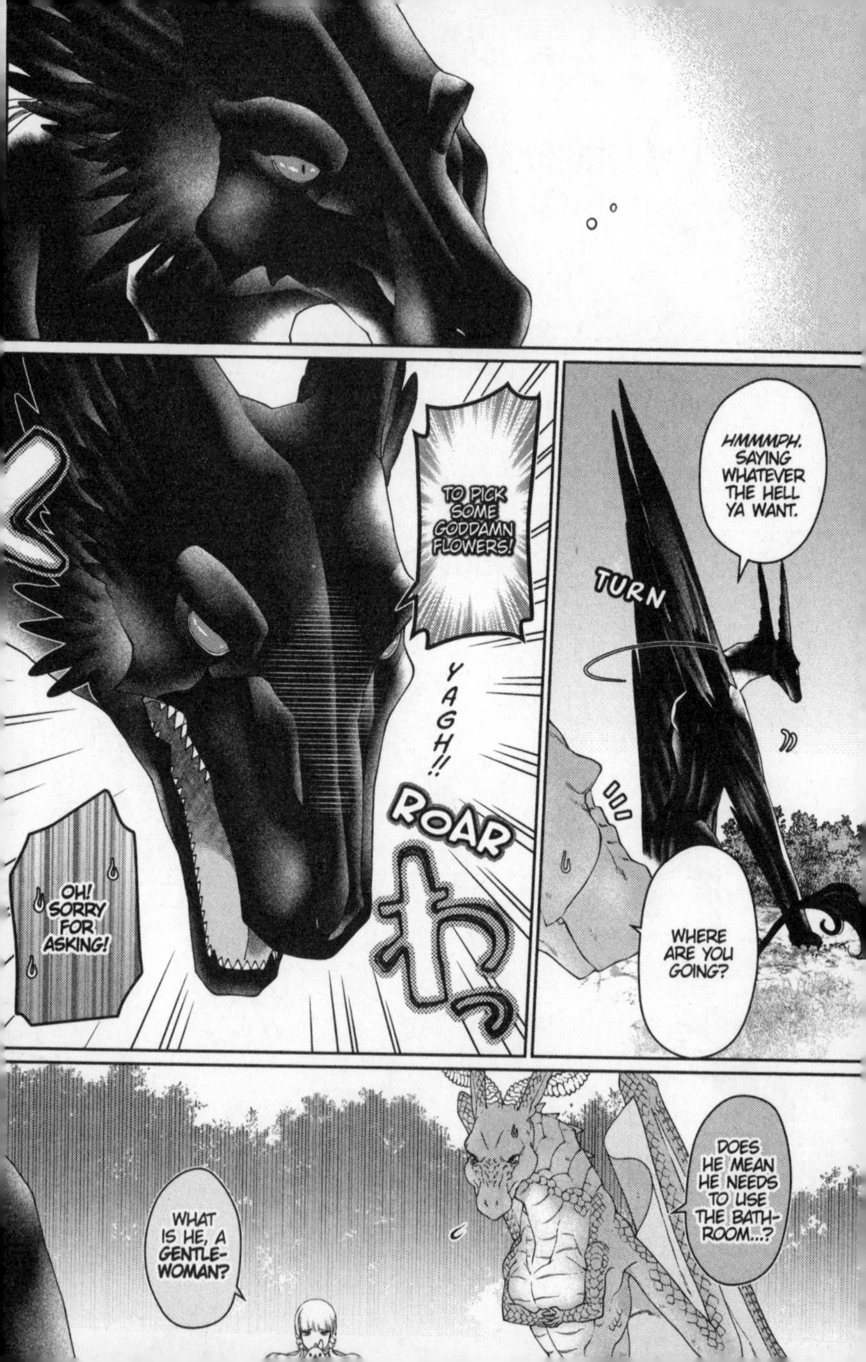
HMMMPH. SAYING WHATEVER THE HELL YA WANT.
TURN
WHERE ARE YOU GOING?
TO PICK SOME GODDAMN FLOWERS!
YAGH!!
ROAR
OH! SORRY FOR ASKING!
DOES HE MEAN HE NEEDS TO USE THE BATH-ROOM...?
WHAT IS HE, A GENTLE-WOMAN?

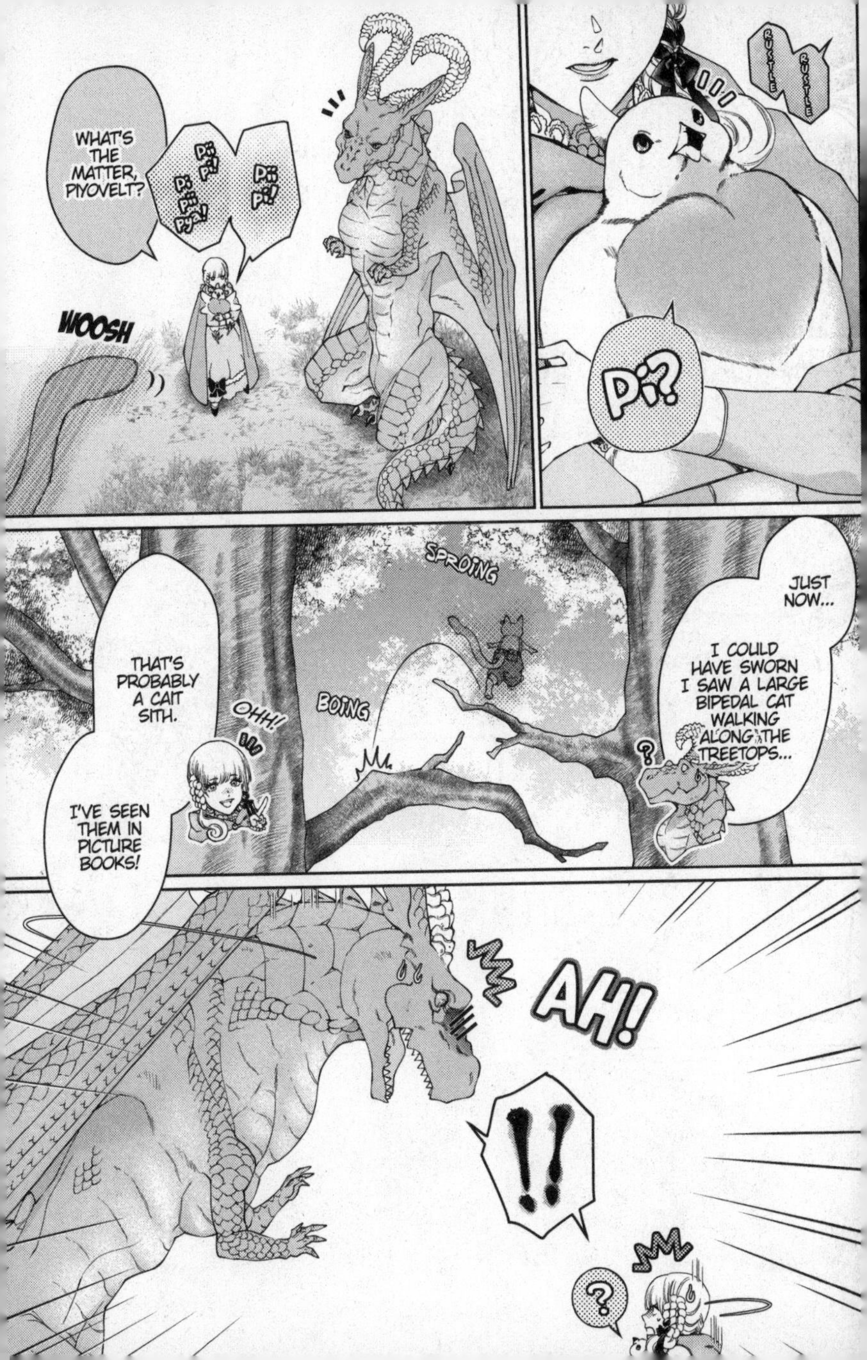
RUSTLE
RUSTLE
Pi?
Pii Pi!
Pi Pii Pya!
Pii Pi!
WHAT'S THE MATTER, PIYOVELT?
WOOSH
JUST NOW...
I COULD HAVE SWORN I SAW A LARGE BIPEDAL CAT WALKING ALONG THE TREETOPS...
?
SPROING
BOING
THAT'S PROBABLY A CAIT SITH.
OHH!
I'VE SEEN THEM IN PICTURE BOOKS!
AH!
!!
?

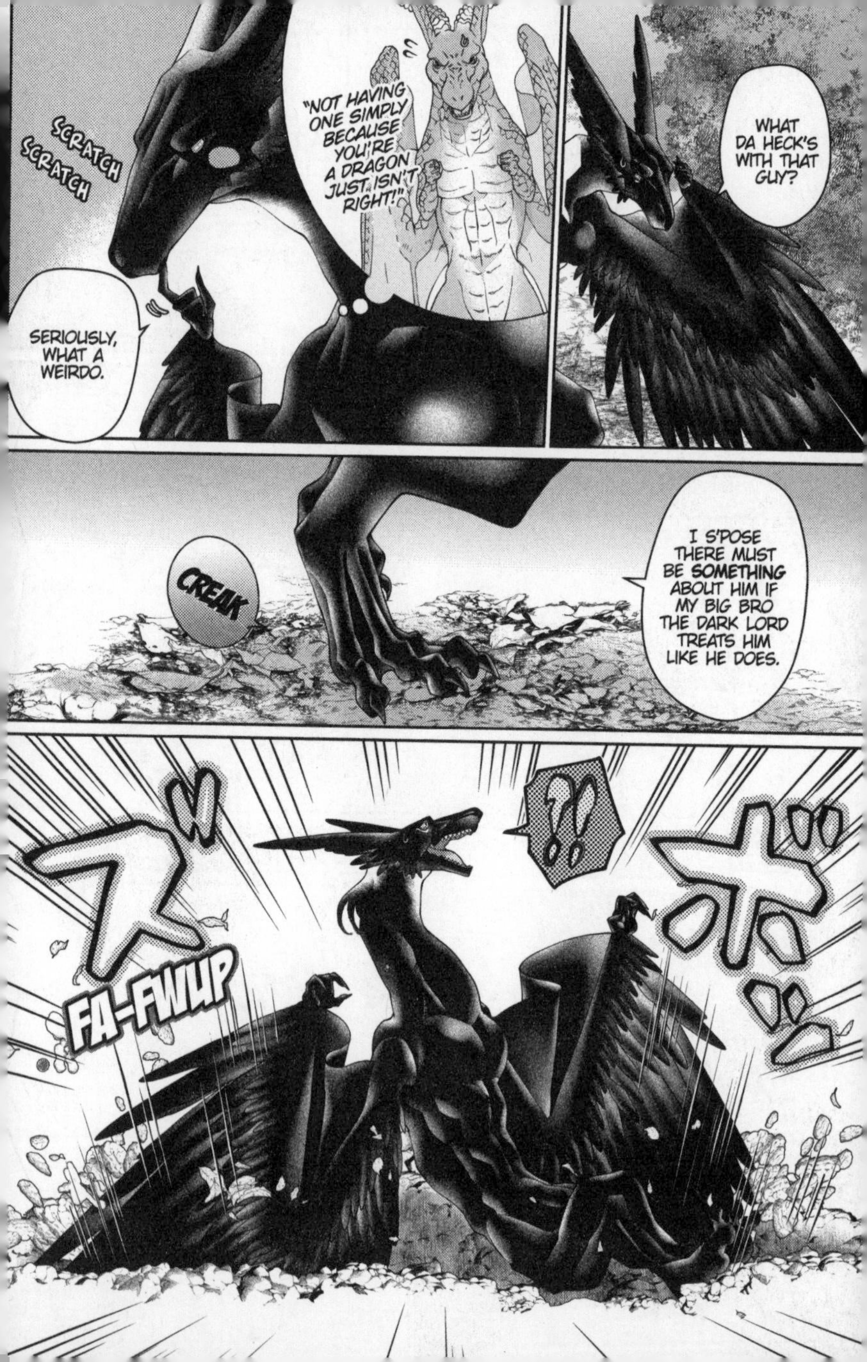
WHAT DA HECK'S WITH THAT GUY?
"NOT HAVING ONE SIMPLY BECAUSE YOU'RE A DRAGON JUST ISN'T RIGHT!"
SCRATCH SCRATCH
SERIOUSLY, WHAT A WEIRDO.
I S'POSE THERE MUST BE **SOMETHING** ABOUT HIM IF MY BIG BRO THE DARK LORD TREATS HIM LIKE HE DOES.
CREAK
?!
FA-FWUP

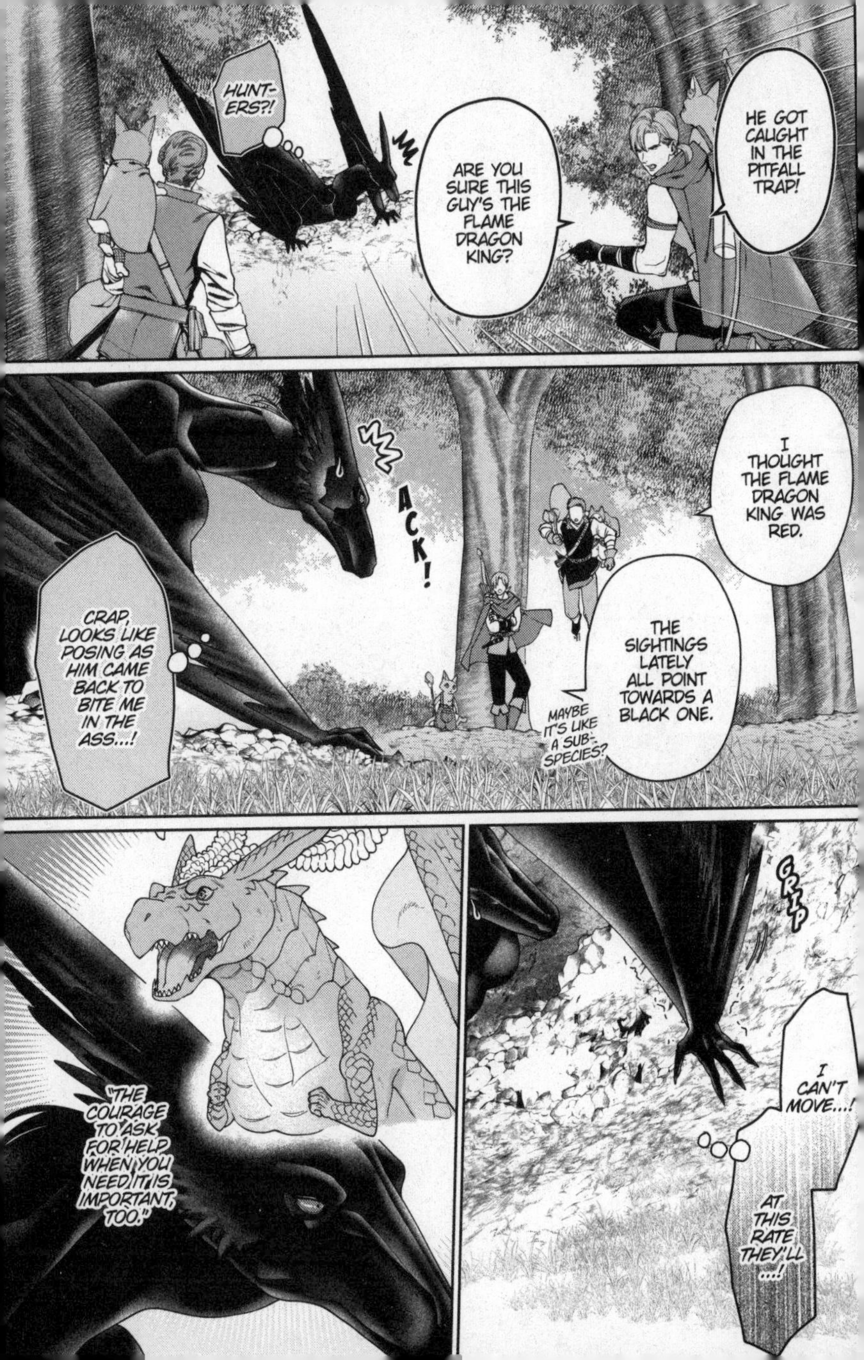
HE GOT CAUGHT IN THE PITFALL TRAP!
ARE YOU SURE THIS GUY'S THE FLAME DRAGON KING?
HUNT-ERS?!
I THOUGHT THE FLAME DRAGON KING WAS RED.
THE SIGHTINGS LATELY ALL POINT TOWARDS A BLACK ONE.
MAYBE IT'S LIKE A SUB-SPECIES?
ACK!
CRAP, LOOKS LIKE POSING AS HIM CAME BACK TO BITE ME IN THE ASS...!
GRIP
I CAN'T MOVE...!
AT THIS RATE THEY'LL ...!
"THE COURAGE TO ASK FOR HELP WHEN YOU NEED IT IS IMPORTANT, TOO."

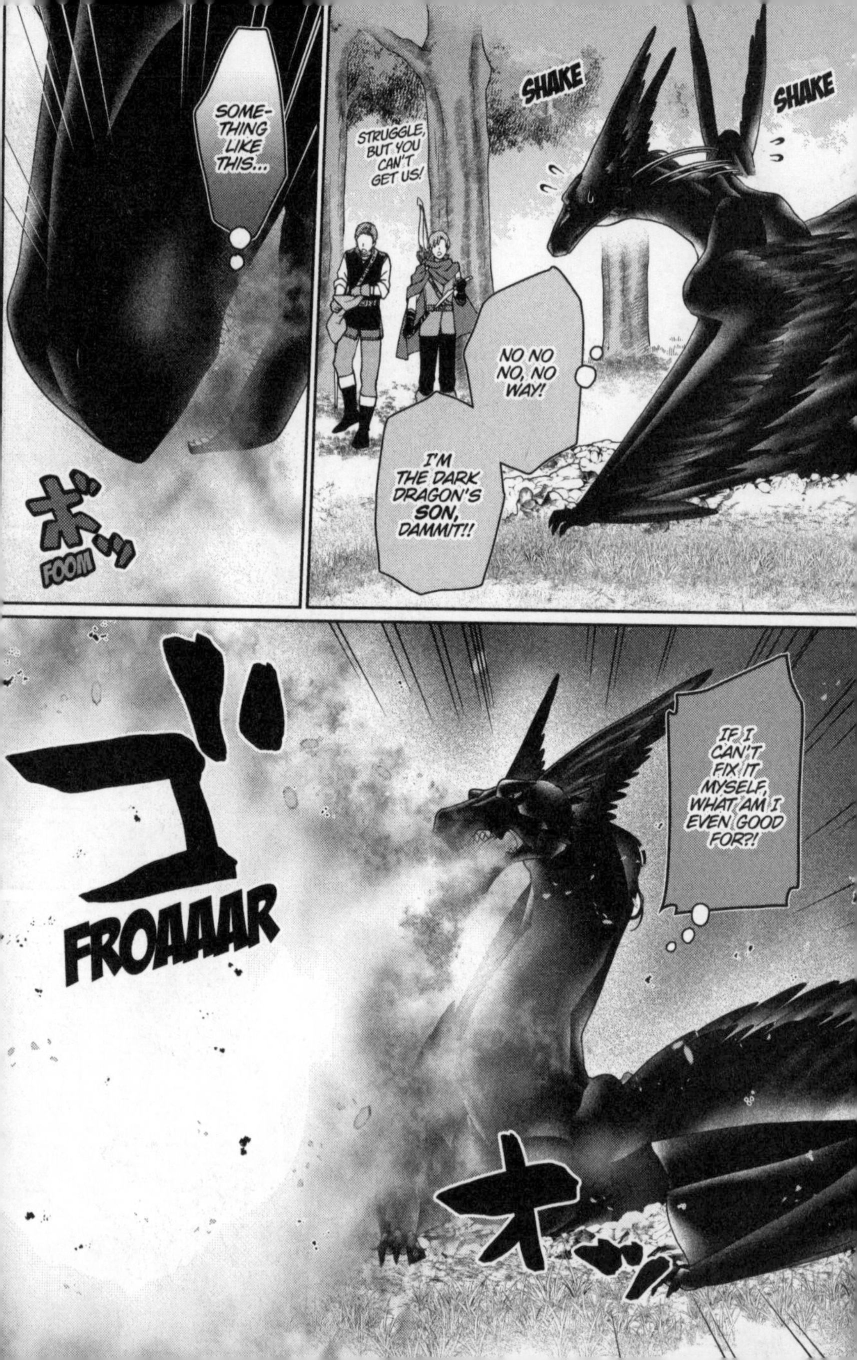
SHAKE
SHAKE
STRUGGLE, BUT YOU CAN'T GET US!
NO NO NO, NO WAY!
I'M THE DARK DRAGON'S SON, DAMMIT!!
SOME-THING LIKE THIS...
ボッ
FOOM
IF I CAN'T FIX IT MYSELF, WHAT AM I EVEN GOOD FOR?!
ゴオッ
FROAAAR

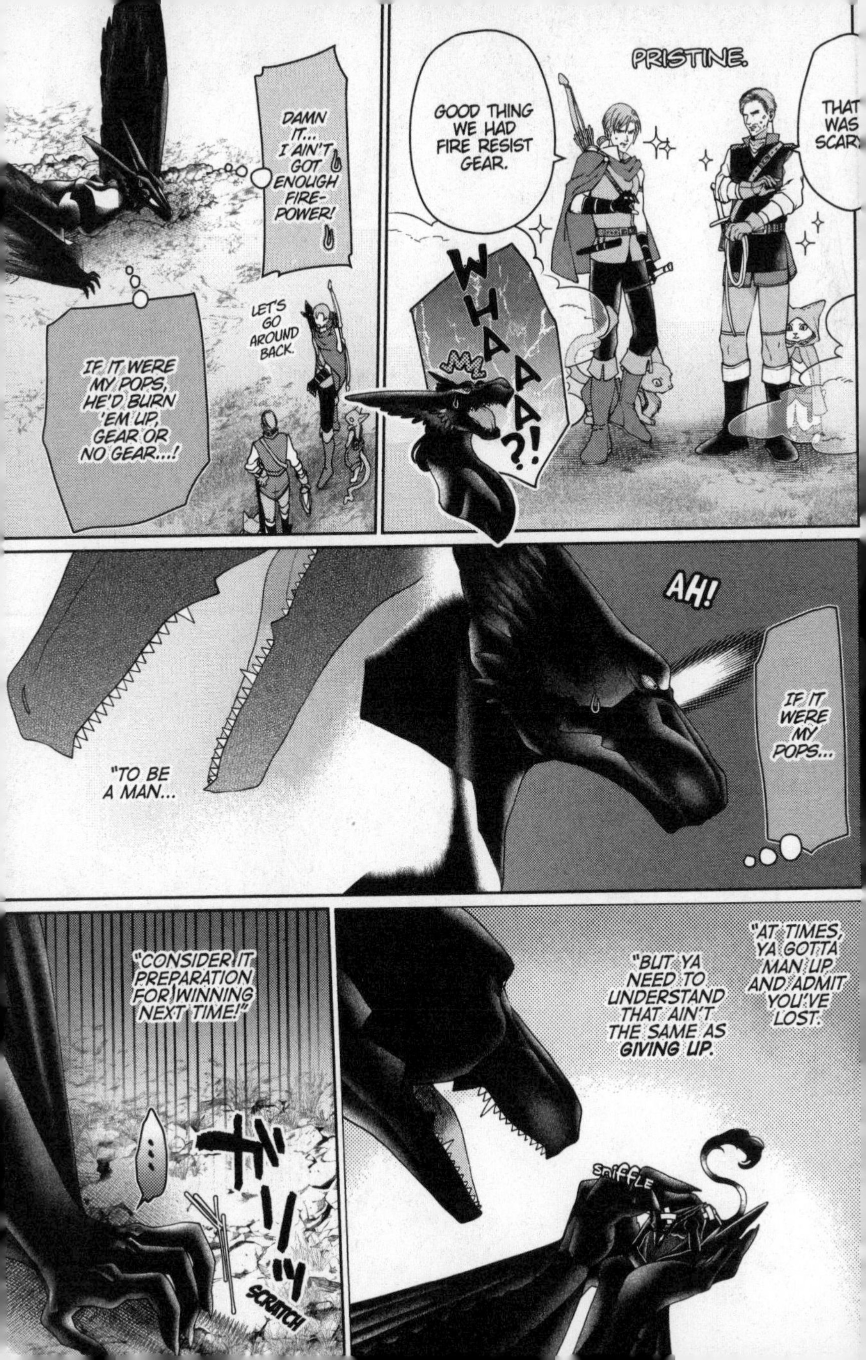
THAT WAS SCAR
PRISTINE.
GOOD THING WE HAD FIRE RESIST GEAR.
WHAAAA?!
DAMN IT... I AIN'T GOT ENOUGH FIRE-POWER!
LET'S GO AROUND BACK.
IF IT WERE MY POPS, HE'D BURN 'EM UP, GEAR OR NO GEAR...!
AH!
IF IT WERE MY POPS...
"TO BE A MAN...
"AT TIMES, YA GOTTA MAN UP AND ADMIT YOU'VE LOST.
"BUT YA NEED TO UNDERSTAND THAT AIN'T THE SAME AS GIVING UP.
SNIFFLE
"CONSIDER IT PREPARATION FOR WINNING NEXT TIME!"
...
SCRATCH

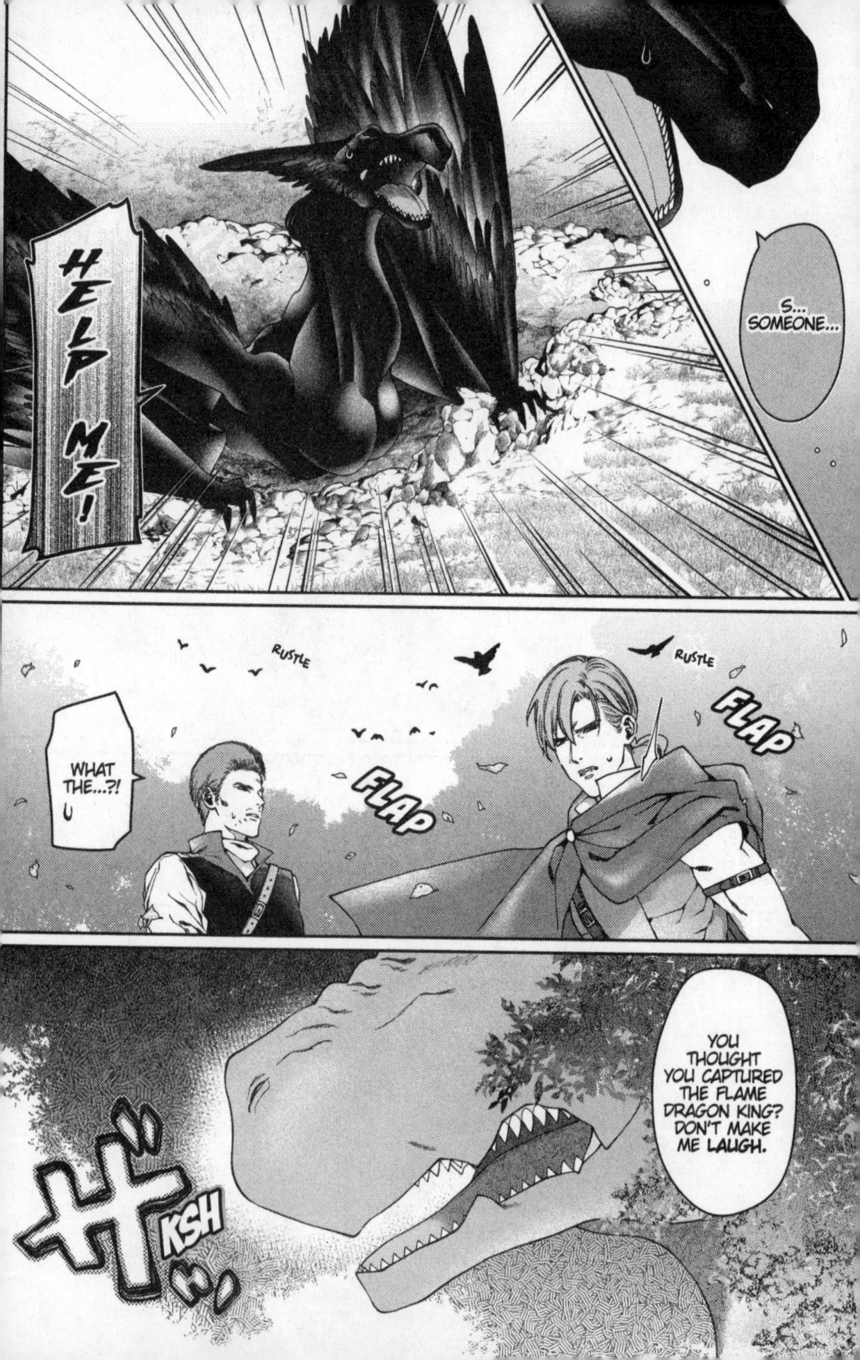
S... SOMEONE...
HELP ME!
RUSTLE
FLAP
RUSTLE
FLAP
WHAT THE...?!
YOU THOUGHT YOU CAPTURED THE FLAME DRAGON KING? DON'T MAKE ME LAUGH.
KSH

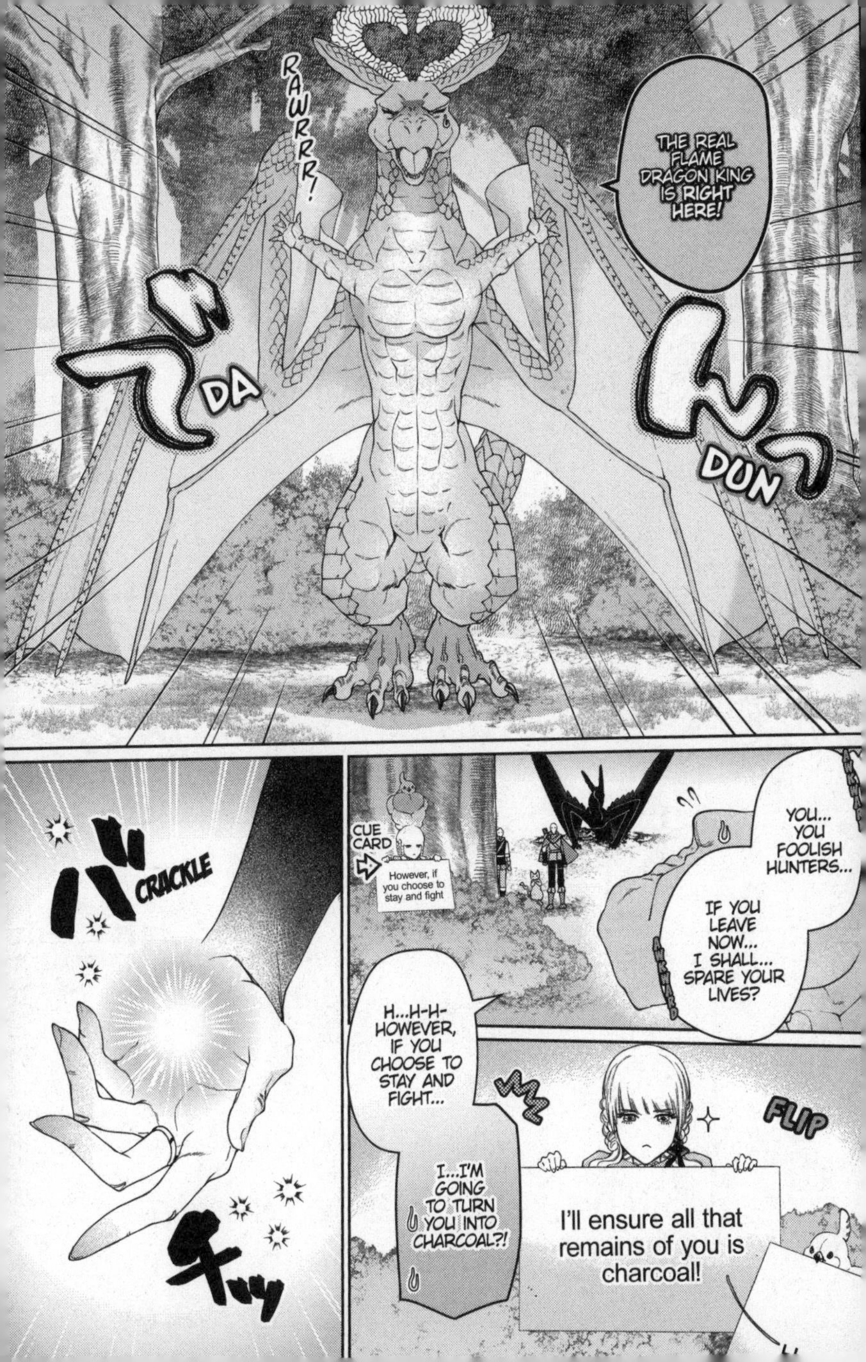
THE REAL FLAME DRAGON KING IS RIGHT HERE!
RAWRRR!
DUN
DA
AWKWARD
YOU... YOU FOOLISH HUNTERS...
IF YOU LEAVE NOW... I SHALL... SPARE YOUR LIVES?
AWKWARD
CUE CARD
However, if you choose to stay and fight
H...H-H-HOWEVER, IF YOU CHOOSE TO STAY AND FIGHT...
FLIP
I...I'M GOING TO TURN YOU INTO CHARCOAL?!
I'll ensure all that remains of you is charcoal!
CRACKLE

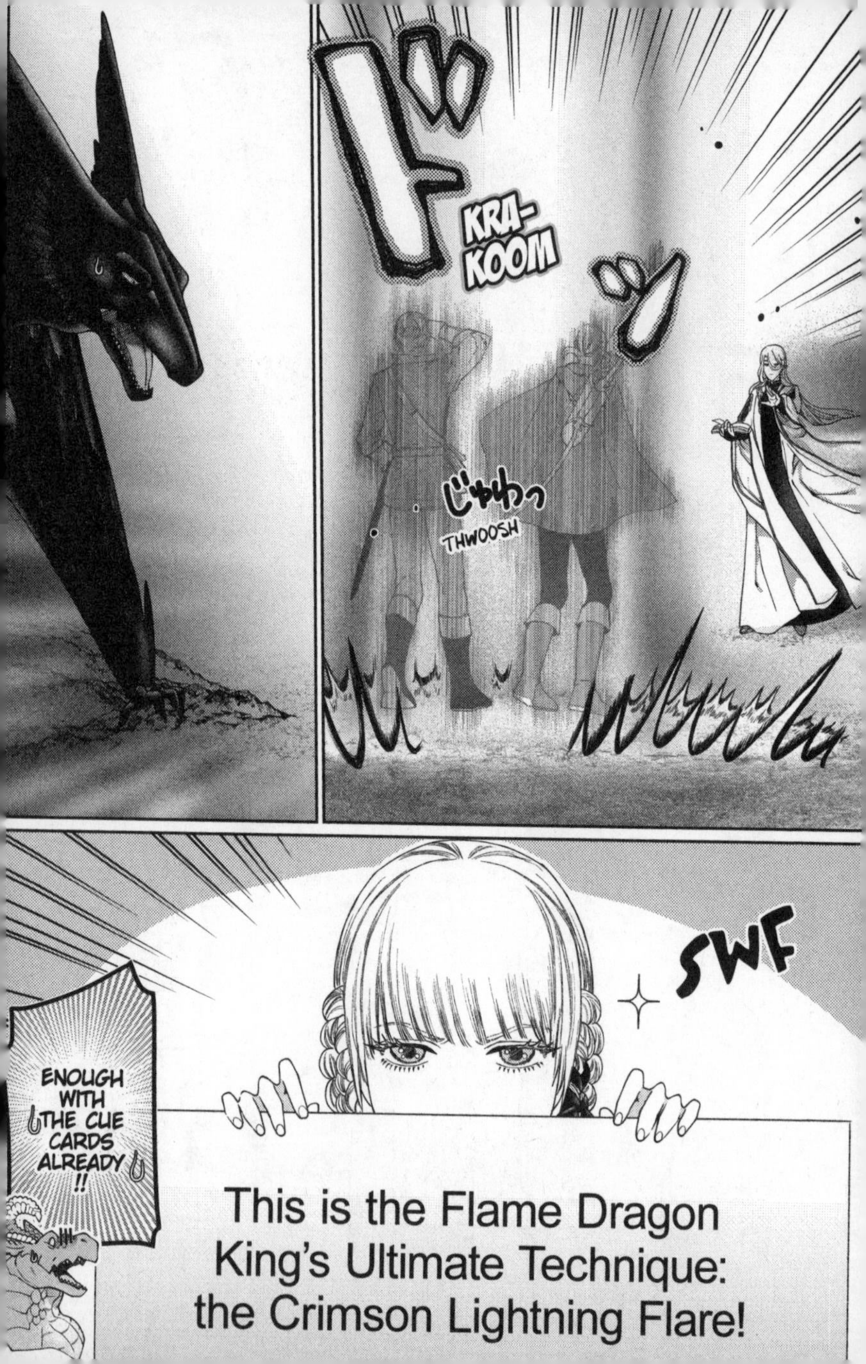

KRA-KOOM
じゅわっ
THWOOSH
SWF
This is the Flame Dragon King's Ultimate Technique: the Crimson Lightning Flare!
ENOUGH WITH THE CUE CARDS ALREADY!!

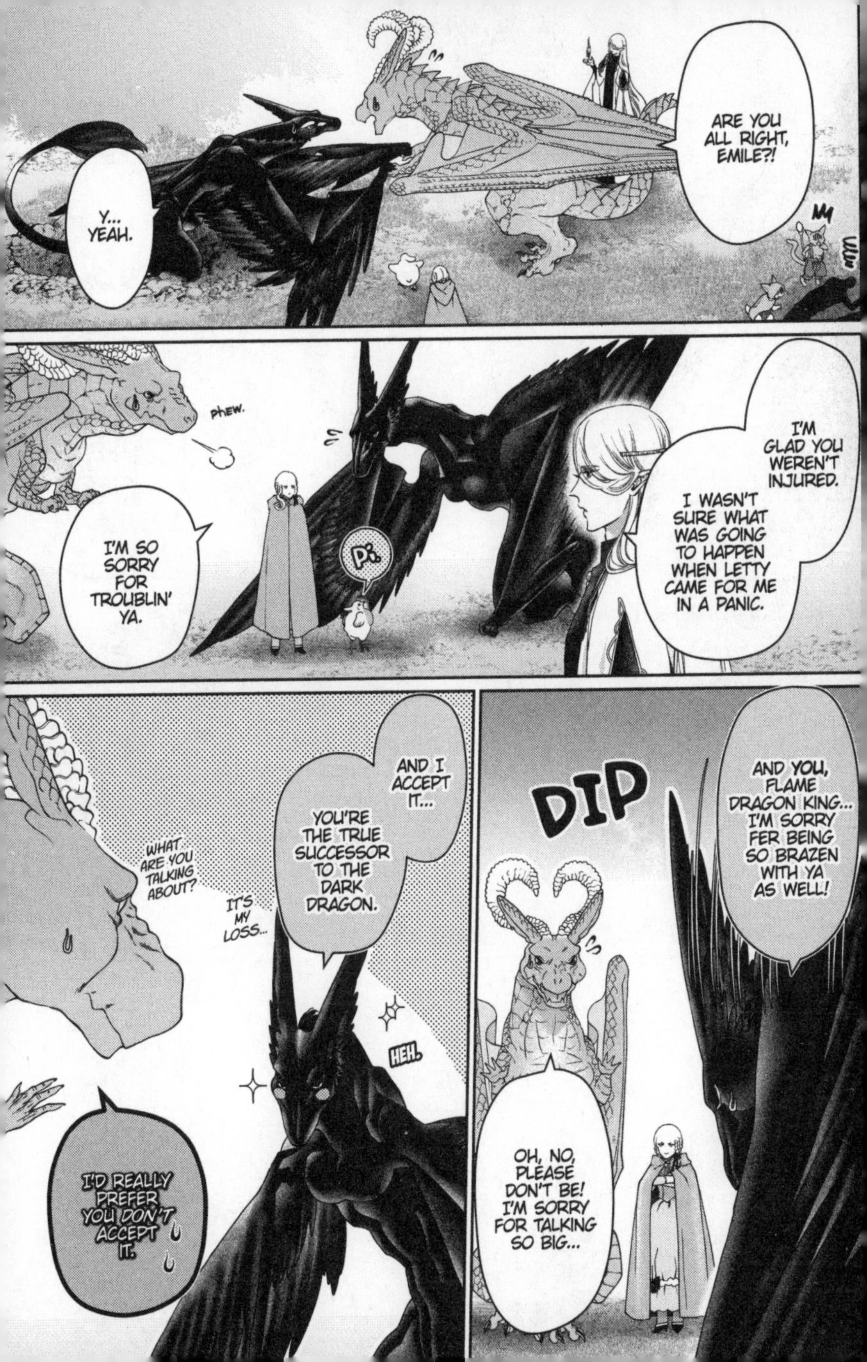
ARE YOU ALL RIGHT, EMILE?!
Y... YEAH.
I'M GLAD YOU WEREN'T INJURED.
I WASN'T SURE WHAT WAS GOING TO HAPPEN WHEN LETTY CAME FOR ME IN A PANIC.
PHEW.
Pi.
I'M SO SORRY FOR TROUBLIN' YA.
AND YOU, FLAME DRAGON KING... I'M SORRY FER BEING SO BRAZEN WITH YA AS WELL!
DIP
OH, NO, PLEASE DON'T BE! I'M SORRY FOR TALKING SO BIG...
AND I ACCEPT IT...
YOU'RE THE TRUE SUCCESSOR TO THE DARK DRAGON.
IT'S MY LOSS...
HEH.
WHAT ARE YOU TALKING ABOUT?
I'D REALLY PREFER YOU DON'T ACCEPT IT.

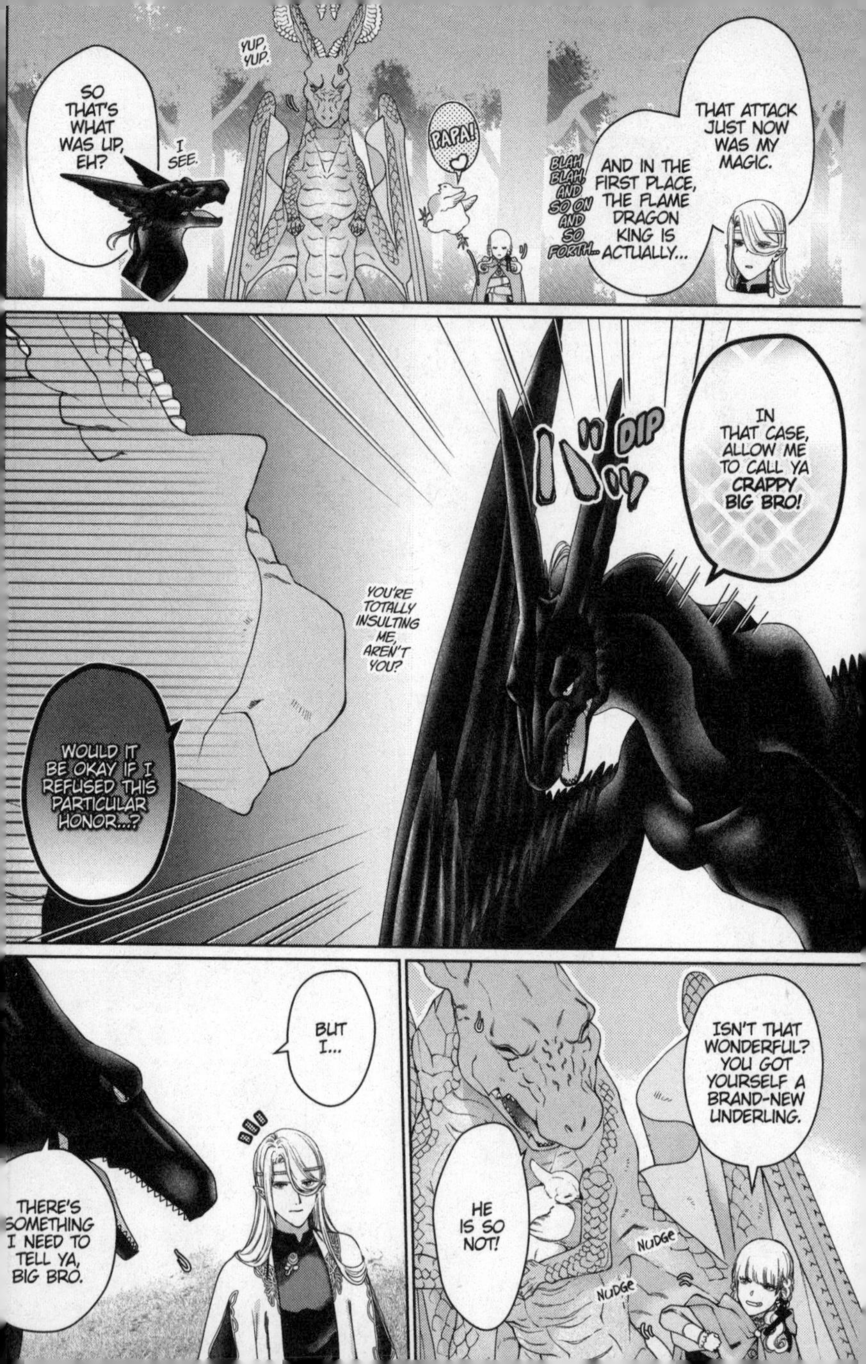
THAT ATTACK JUST NOW WAS MY MAGIC.
AND IN THE FIRST PLACE, THE FLAME DRAGON KING IS ACTUALLY...
BLAH BLAH, AND SO ON AND SO FORTH...
PAPA!
YUP, YUP.
I SEE.
SO THAT'S WHAT WAS UP, EH?
IN THAT CASE, ALLOW ME TO CALL YA CRAPPY BIG BRO!
DIP
YOU'RE TOTALLY INSULTING ME, AREN'T YOU?
WOULD IT BE OKAY IF I REFUSED THIS PARTICULAR HONOR...?
ISN'T THAT WONDERFUL? YOU GOT YOURSELF A BRAND-NEW UNDERLING.
NUDGE
HE IS SO NOT!
NUDGE
BUT I...
THERE'S SOMETHING I NEED TO TELL YA, BIG BRO.

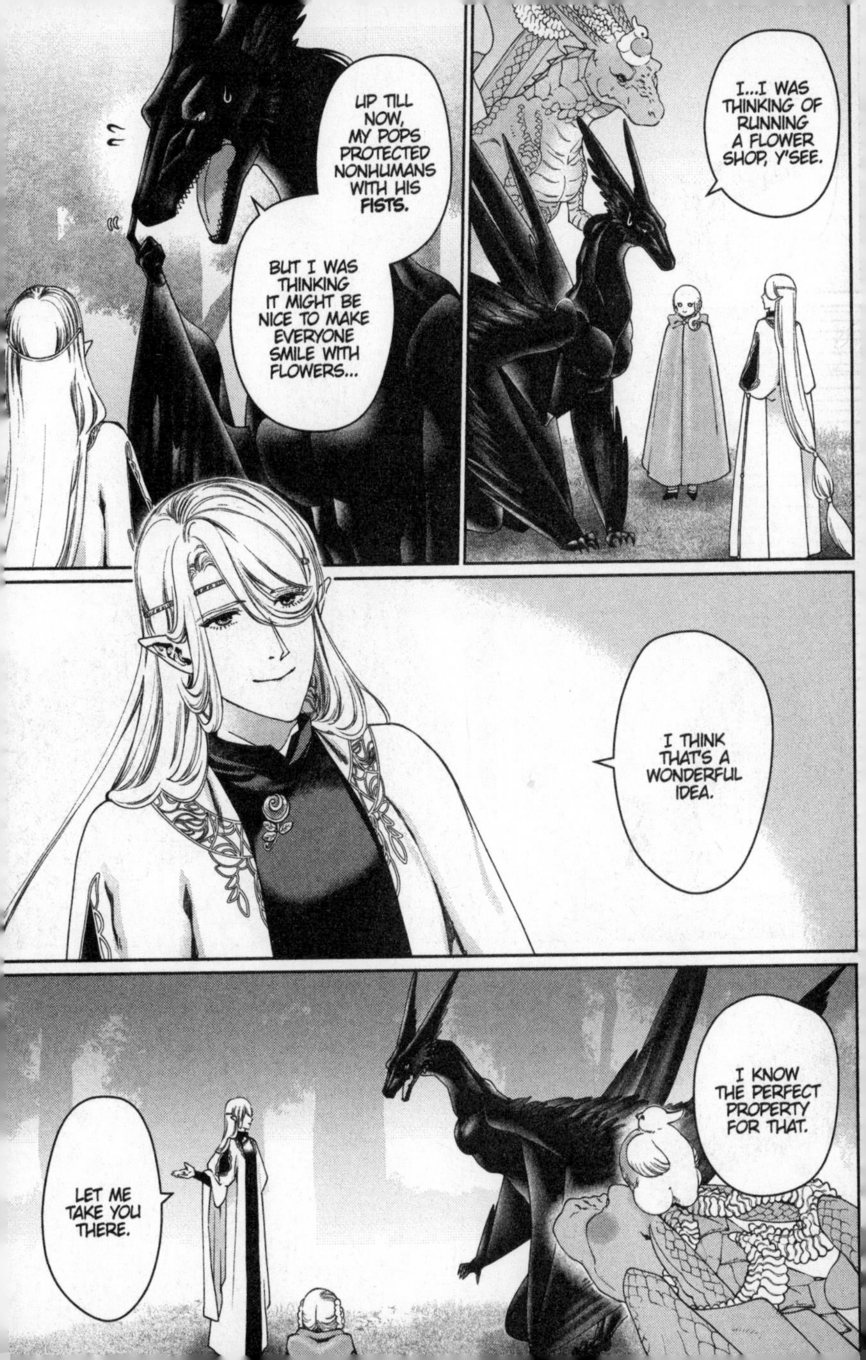
I...I WAS THINKING OF RUNNING A FLOWER SHOP, Y'SEE.
UP TILL NOW, MY POPS PROTECTED NONHUMANS WITH HIS FISTS.
BUT I WAS THINKING IT MIGHT BE NICE TO MAKE EVERYONE SMILE WITH FLOWERS...
I THINK THAT'S A WONDERFUL IDEA.
I KNOW THE PERFECT PROPERTY FOR THAT.
LET ME TAKE YOU THERE.

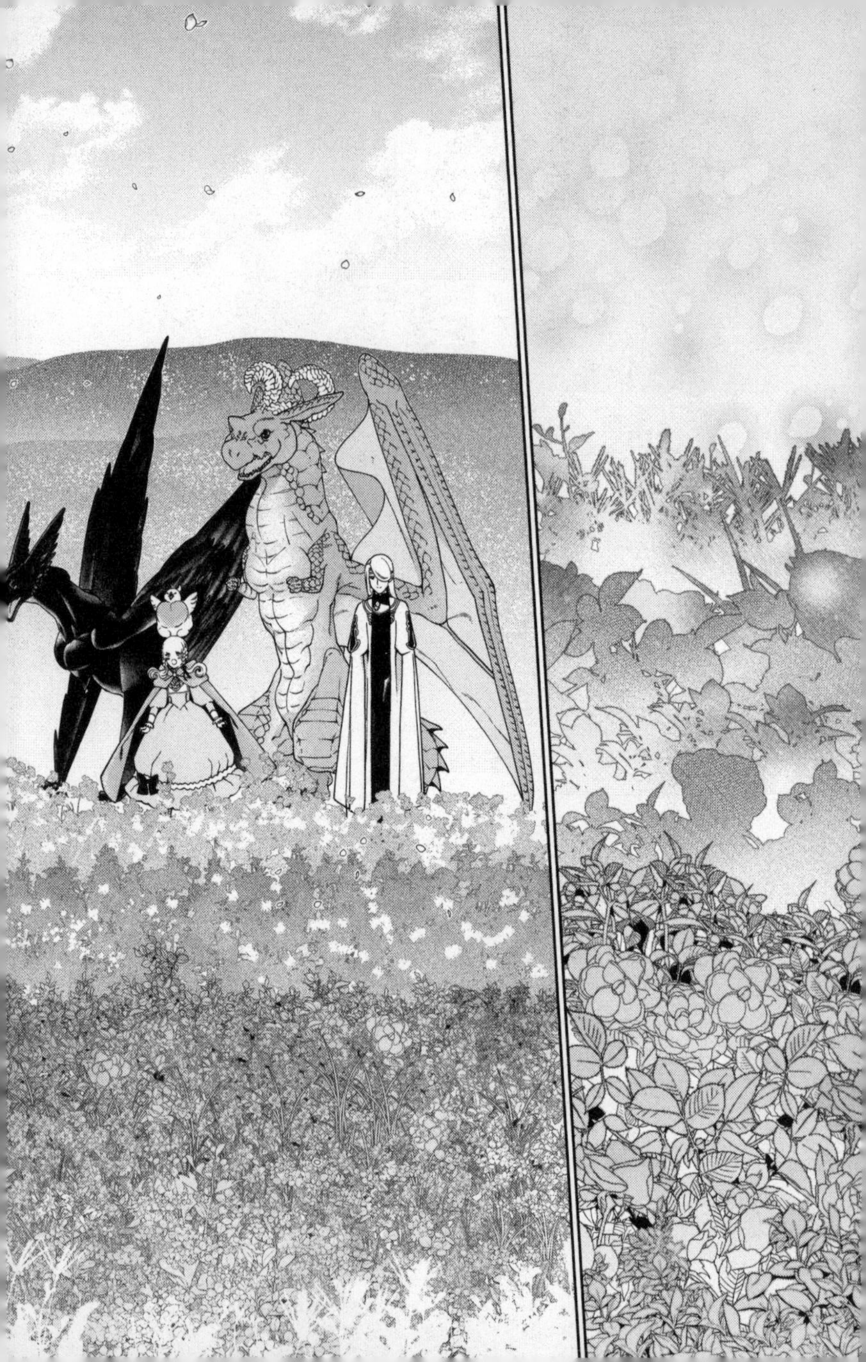

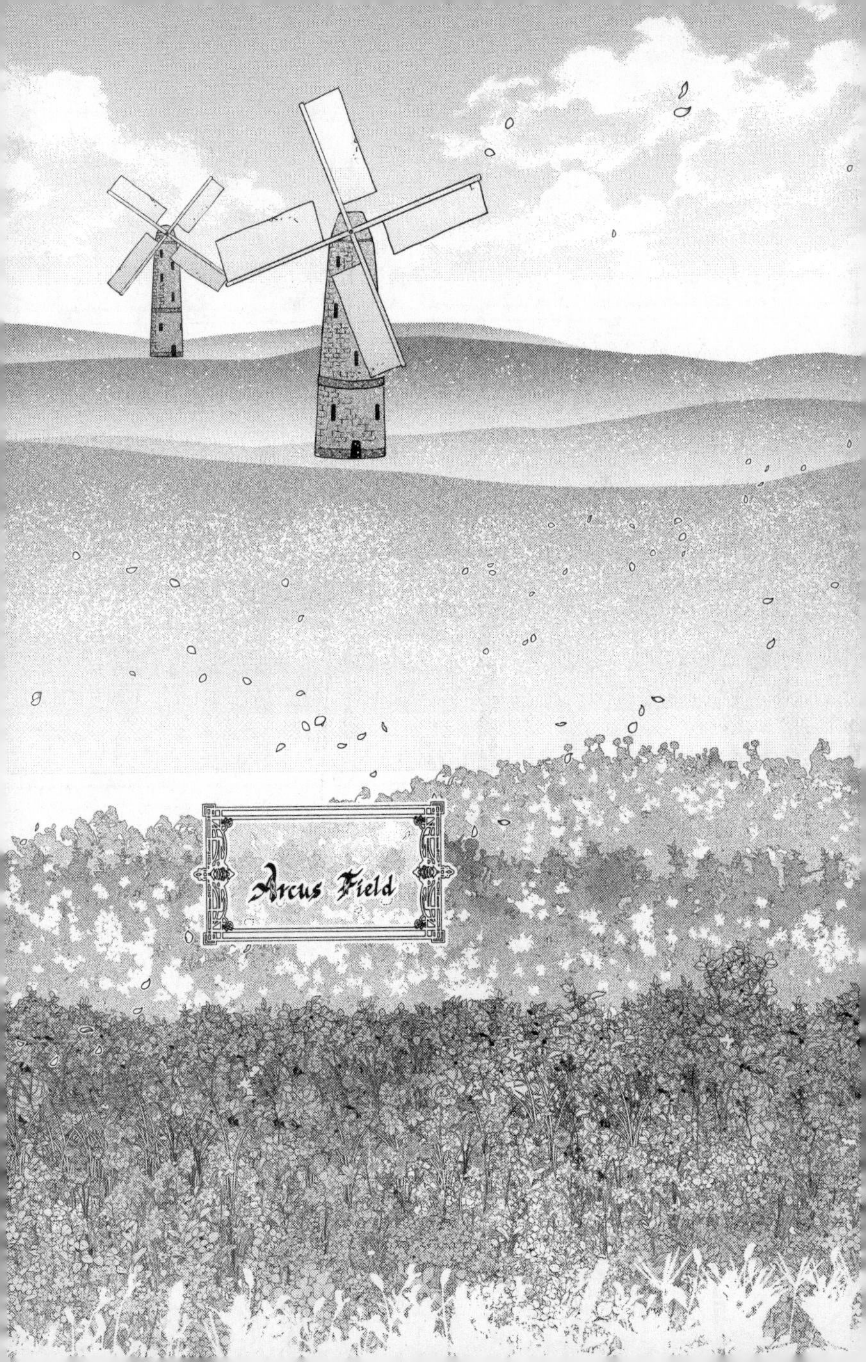
Arcus Field

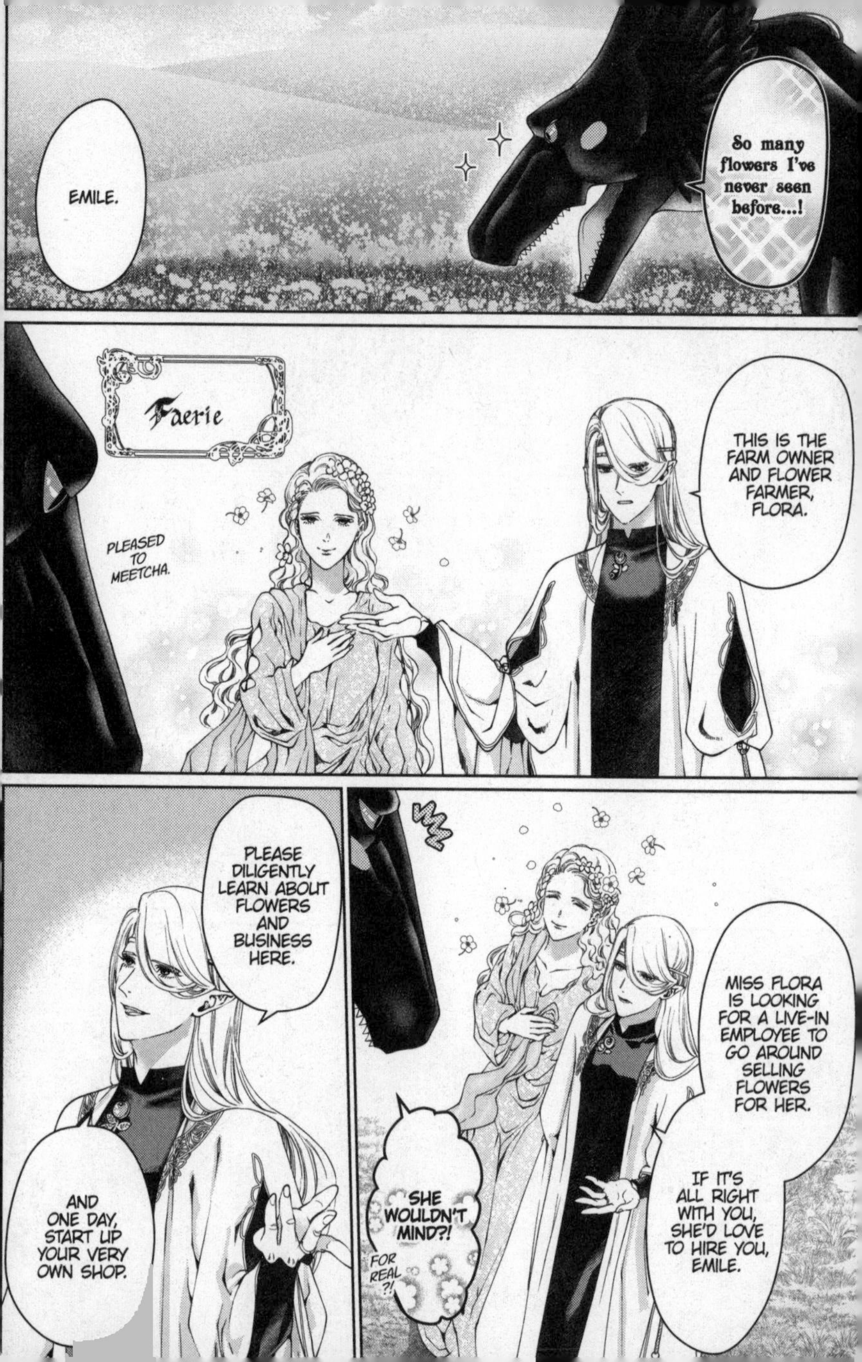
So many flowers I've never seen before...!
EMILE.
THIS IS THE FARM OWNER AND FLOWER FARMER, FLORA.
Faerie
PLEASED TO MEETCHA.
MISS FLORA IS LOOKING FOR A LIVE-IN EMPLOYEE TO GO AROUND SELLING FLOWERS FOR HER.
IF IT'S ALL RIGHT WITH YOU, SHE'D LOVE TO HIRE YOU, EMILE.
SHE WOULDN'T MIND?!
FOR REAL?!
PLEASE DILIGENTLY LEARN ABOUT FLOWERS AND BUSINESS HERE.
AND ONE DAY, START UP YOUR VERY OWN SHOP.

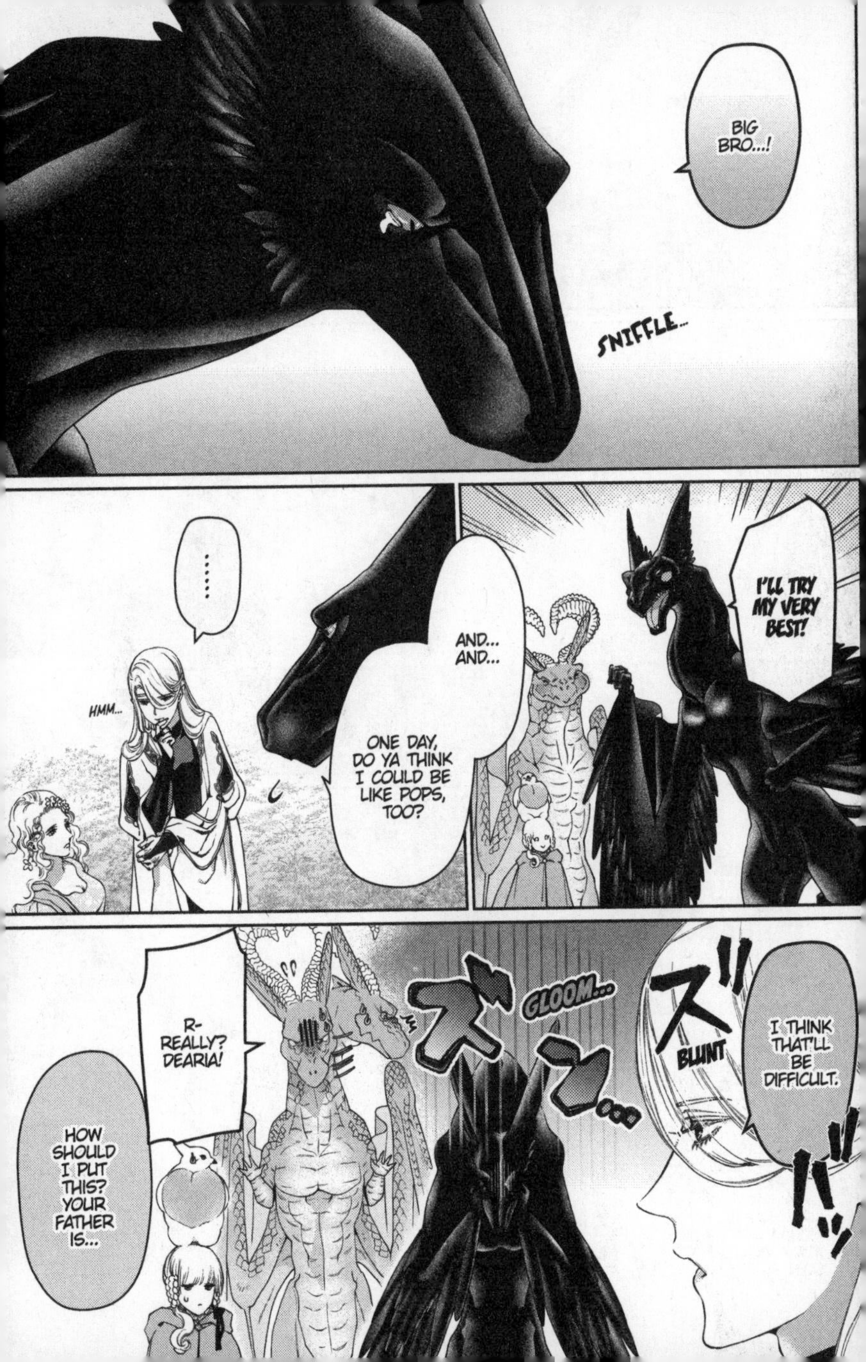
BIG BRO...!
SNIFFLE...
I'LL TRY MY VERY BEST!
AND... AND...
ONE DAY, DO YA THINK I COULD BE LIKE POPS, TOO?
......
HMM...
I THINK THAT'LL BE DIFFICULT.
BLUNT
GLOOM...
R- REALLY? DEARIA!
HOW SHOULD I PUT THIS? YOUR FATHER IS...

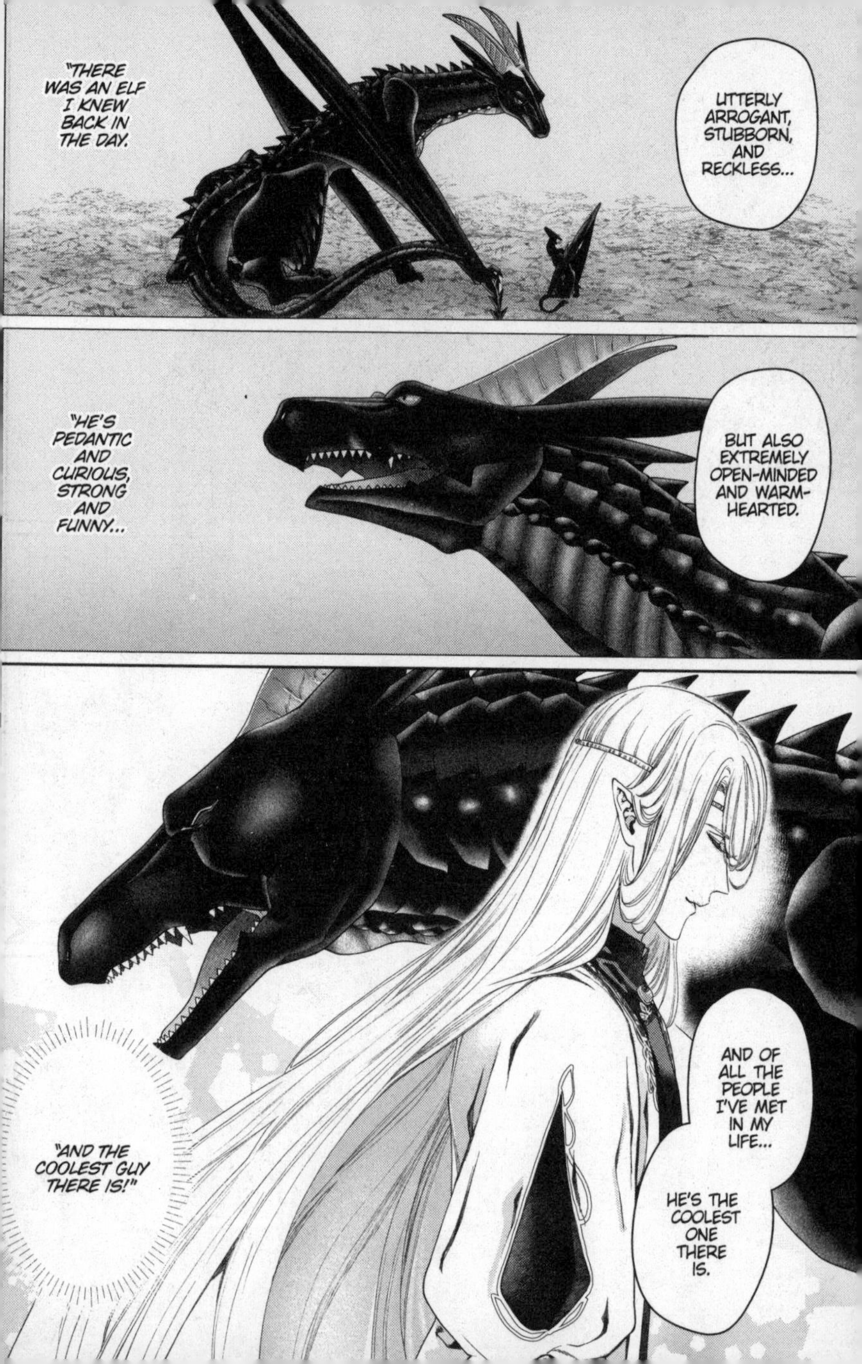
UTTERLY ARROGANT, STUBBORN, AND RECKLESS...
"THERE WAS AN ELF I KNEW BACK IN THE DAY.
BUT ALSO EXTREMELY OPEN-MINDED AND WARM-HEARTED.
"HE'S PEDANTIC AND CURIOUS, STRONG AND FUNNY...
AND OF ALL THE PEOPLE I'VE MET IN MY LIFE...
HE'S THE COOLEST ONE THERE IS.
"AND THE COOLEST GUY THERE IS!"

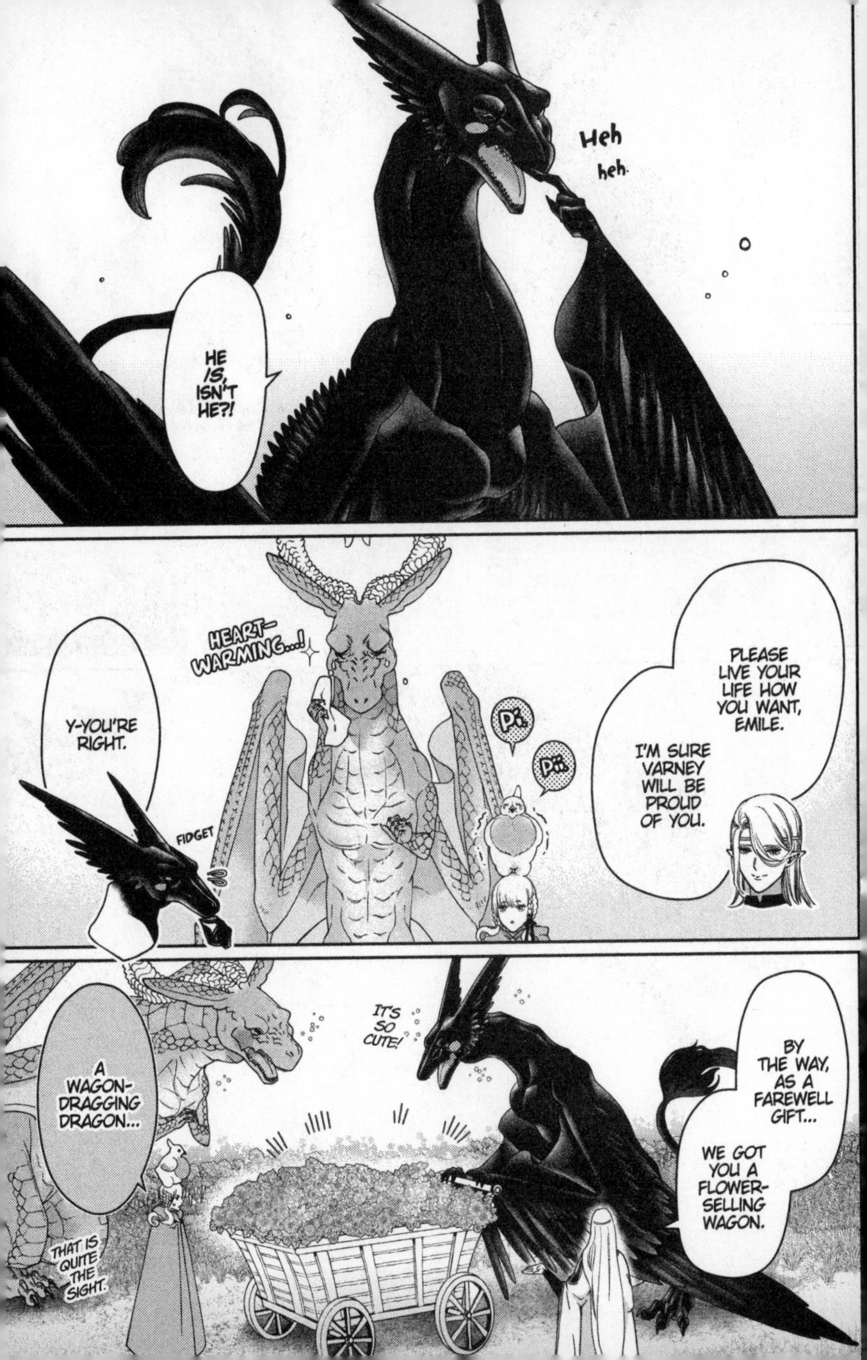
Heh heh.
HE IS, ISN'T HE?!
PLEASE LIVE YOUR LIFE HOW YOU WANT, EMILE.
I'M SURE VARNEY WILL BE PROUD OF YOU.
Pii
Pi
HEART-WARMING...!
Y-YOU'RE RIGHT.
FIDGET
BY THE WAY, AS A FAREWELL GIFT...
WE GOT YOU A FLOWER-SELLING WAGON.
IT'S SO CUTE!
A WAGON-DRAGGING DRAGON...
THAT IS QUITE THE SIGHT.

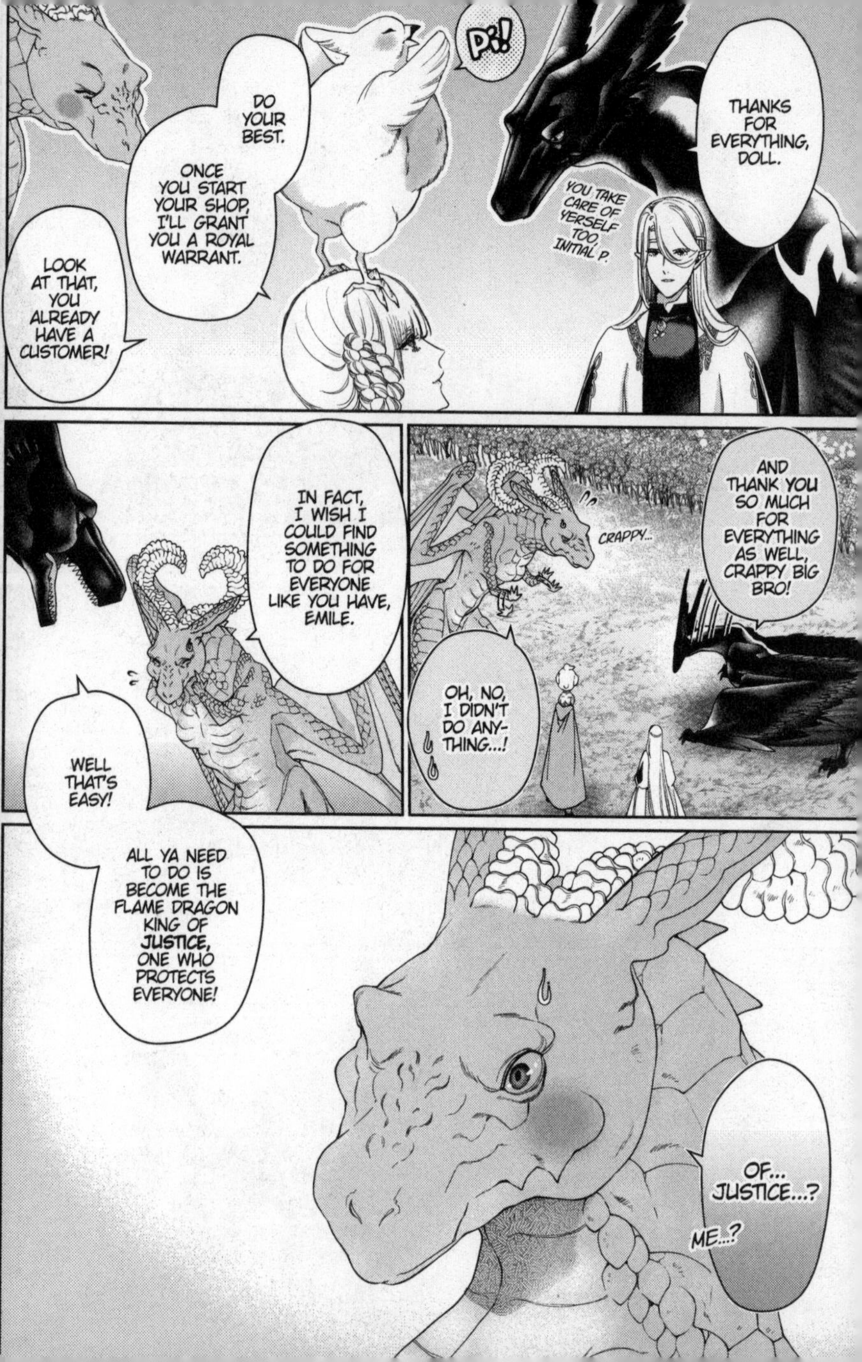
THANKS FOR EVERYTHING, DOLL.
YOU TAKE CARE OF YERSELF TOO, INITIAL P.
Pi!
DO YOUR BEST.
ONCE YOU START YOUR SHOP, I'LL GRANT YOU A ROYAL WARRANT.
LOOK AT THAT, YOU ALREADY HAVE A CUSTOMER!
AND THANK YOU SO MUCH FOR EVERYTHING AS WELL, CRAPPY BIG BRO!
CRAPPY...
OH, NO, I DIDN'T DO ANY-THING...!
IN FACT, I WISH I COULD FIND SOMETHING TO DO FOR EVERYONE LIKE YOU HAVE, EMILE.
WELL THAT'S EASY!
ALL YA NEED TO DO IS BECOME THE FLAME DRAGON KING OF JUSTICE, ONE WHO PROTECTS EVERYONE!
OF... JUSTICE...?
ME...?

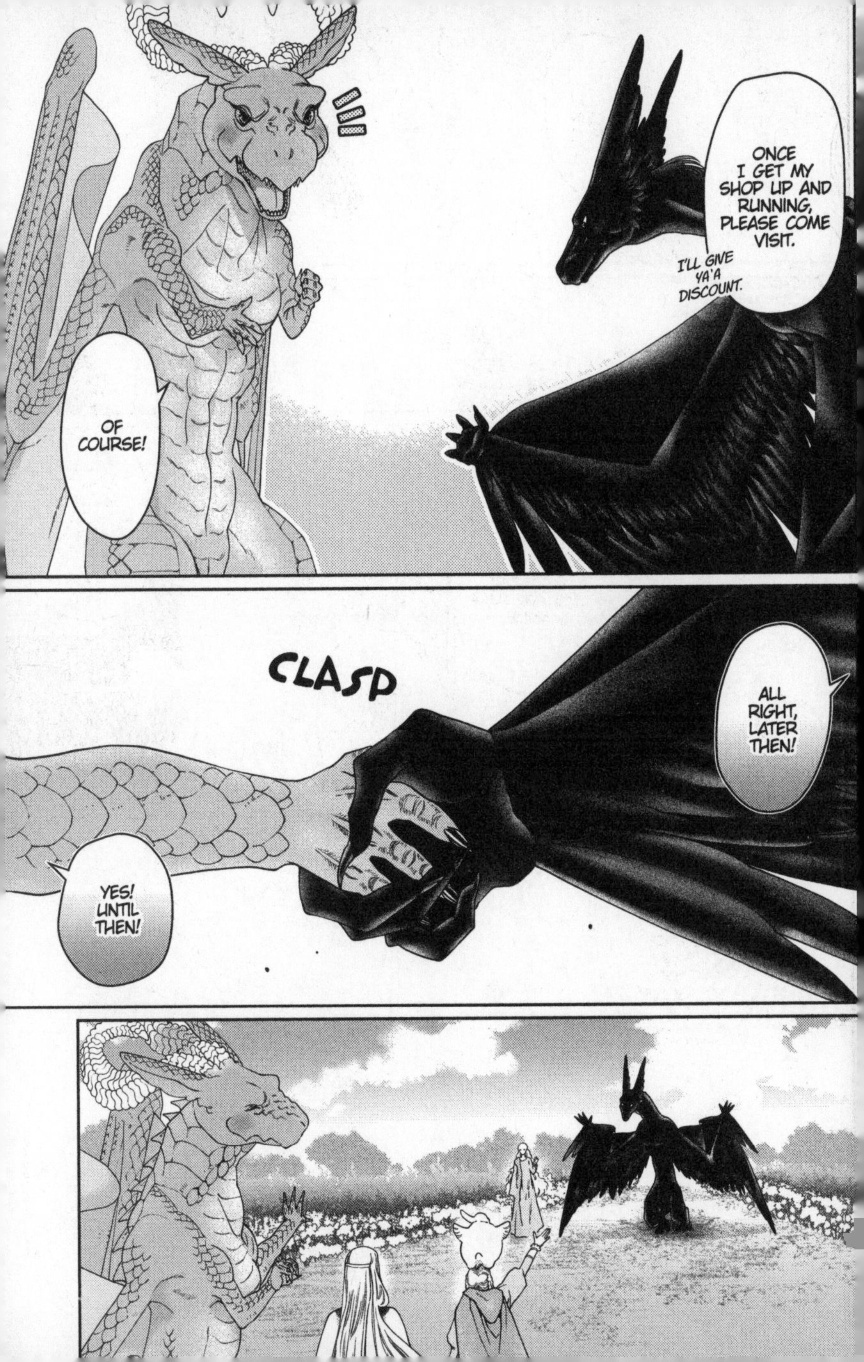
ONCE I GET MY SHOP UP AND RUNNING, PLEASE COME VISIT.
I'LL GIVE YA' A DISCOUNT.
OF COURSE!
ALL RIGHT, LATER THEN!
CLASP
YES! UNTIL THEN!

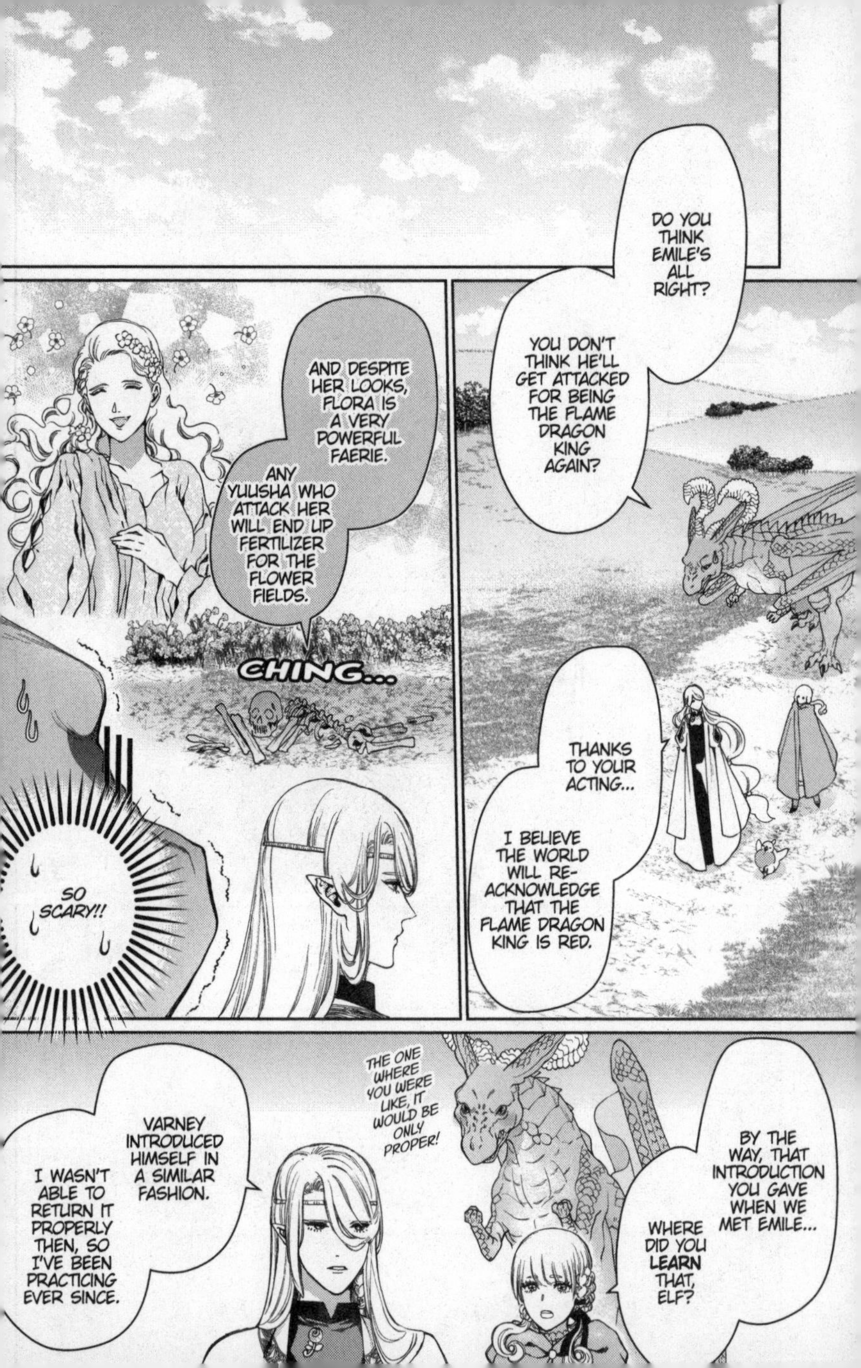
DO YOU THINK EMILE'S ALL RIGHT?
YOU DON'T THINK HE'LL GET ATTACKED FOR BEING THE FLAME DRAGON KING AGAIN?
THANKS TO YOUR ACTING...
I BELIEVE THE WORLD WILL RE-ACKNOWLEDGE THAT THE FLAME DRAGON KING IS RED.
AND DESPITE HER LOOKS, FLORA IS A VERY POWERFUL FAERIE.
ANY YUUSHA WHO ATTACK HER WILL END UP FERTILIZER FOR THE FLOWER FIELDS.
CHING...
SO SCARY!!
BY THE WAY, THAT INTRODUCTION YOU GAVE WHEN WE MET EMILE...
WHERE DID YOU **LEARN** THAT, ELF?
THE ONE WHERE YOU WERE LIKE, IT WOULD BE ONLY PROPER!
VARNEY INTRODUCED HIMSELF IN A SIMILAR FASHION.
I WASN'T ABLE TO RETURN IT PROPERLY THEN, SO I'VE BEEN PRACTICING EVER SINCE.

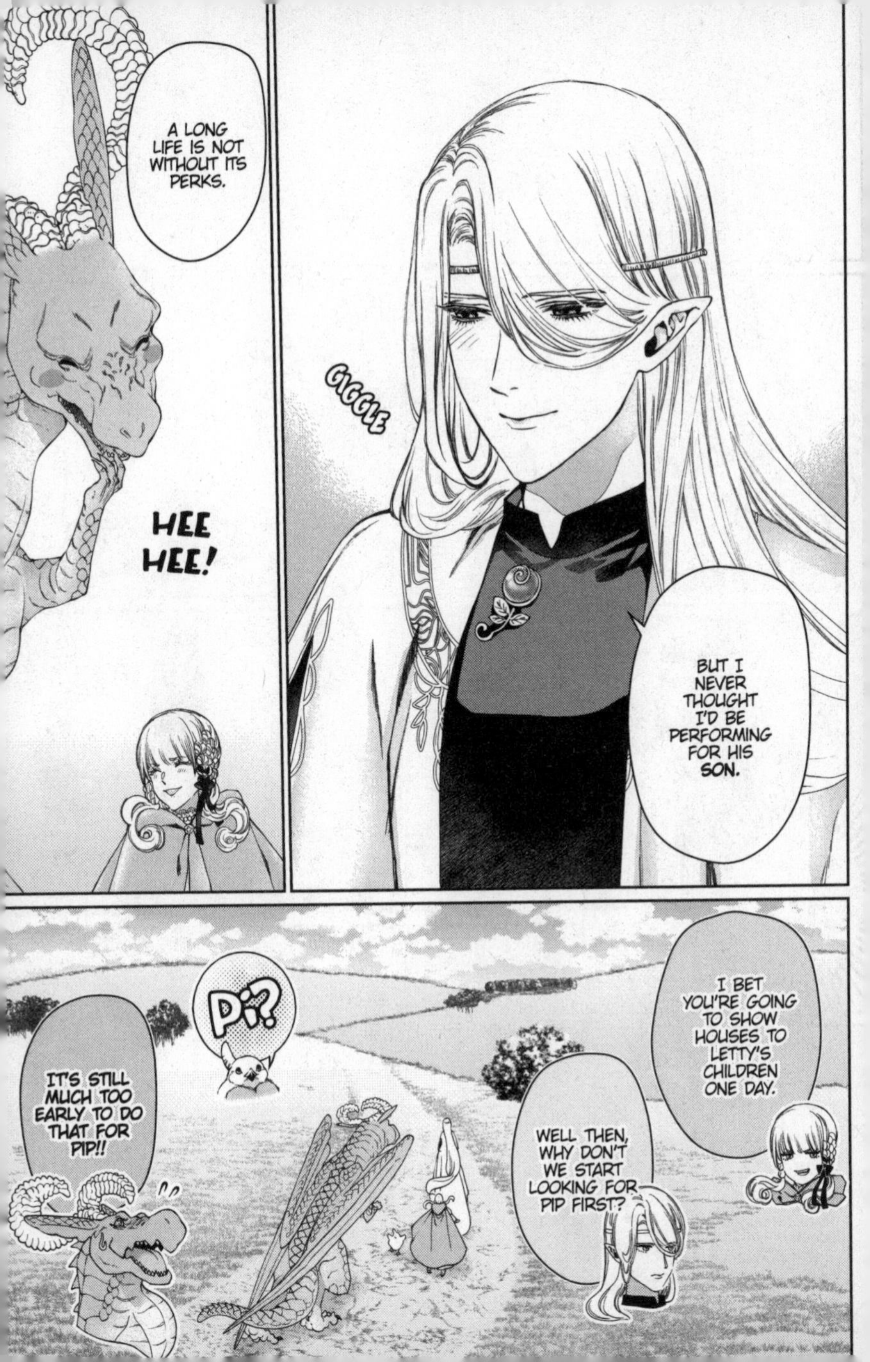
GIGGLE
BUT I NEVER THOUGHT I'D BE PERFORMING FOR HIS SON.
A LONG LIFE IS NOT WITHOUT ITS PERKS.
HEE HEE!
I BET YOU'RE GOING TO SHOW HOUSES TO LETTY'S CHILDREN ONE DAY.
WELL THEN, WHY DON'T WE START LOOKING FOR PIP FIRST?
Pi?
IT'S STILL MUCH TOO EARLY TO DO THAT FOR PIP!!

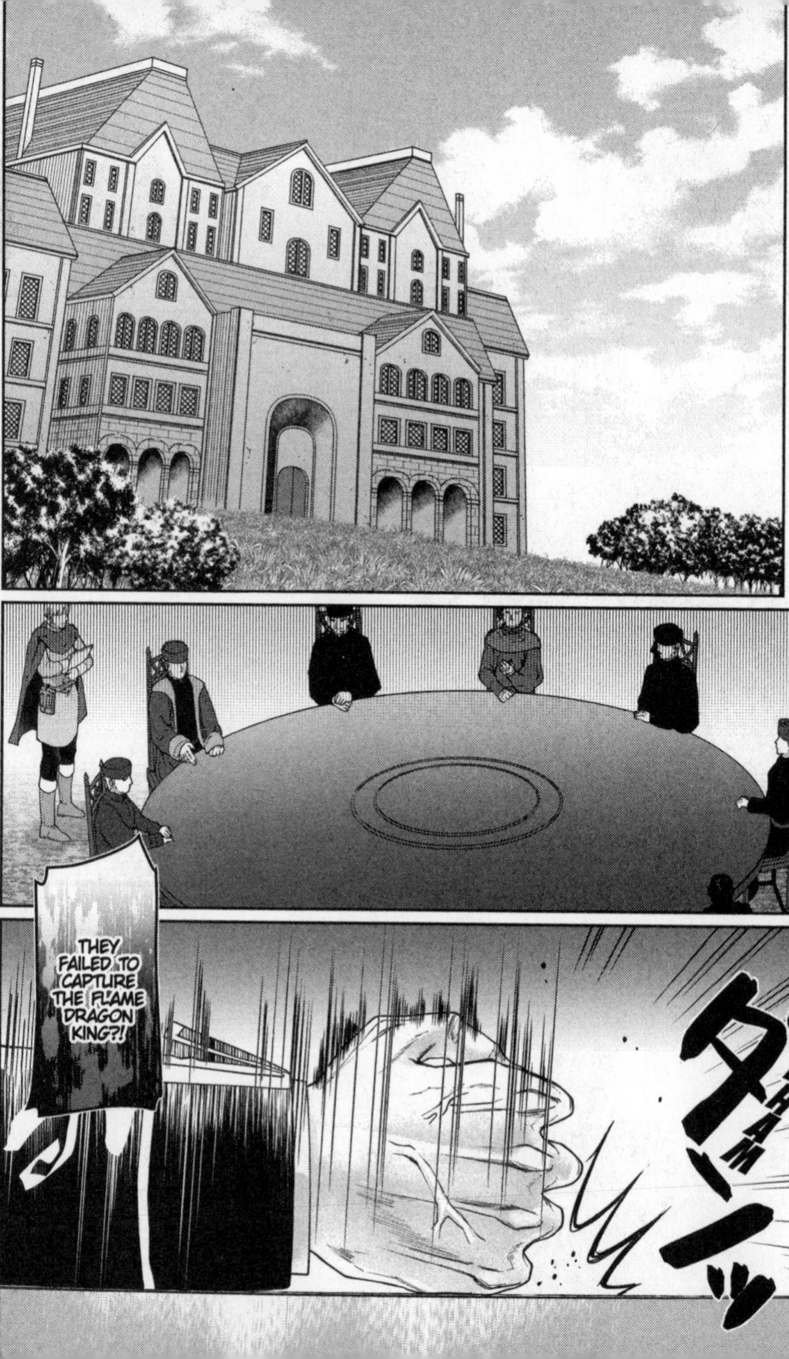
THEY FAILED TO CAPTURE THE FLAME DRAGON KING?!
WHAM

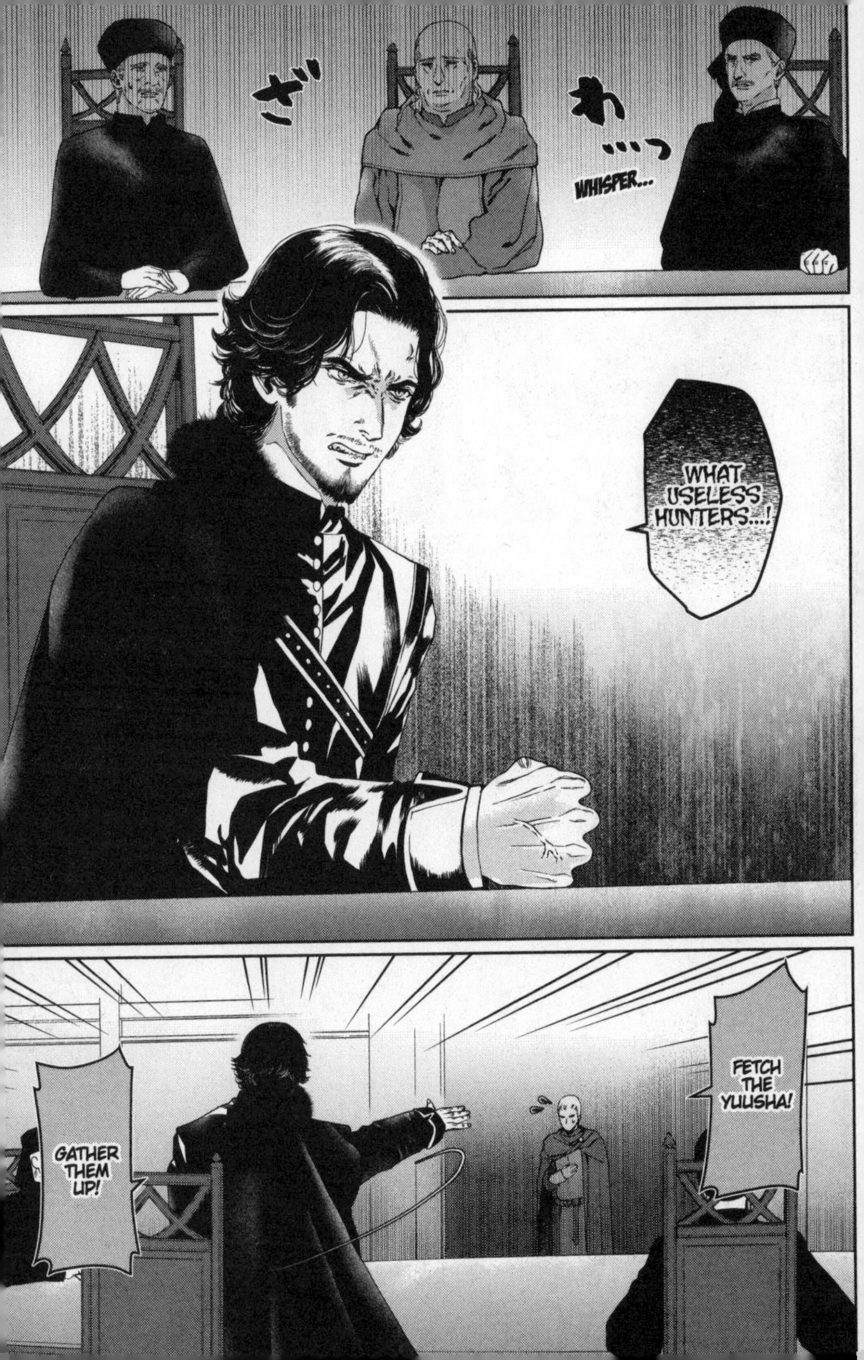
WHISPER...
WHAT USELESS HUNTERS...!
FETCH THE YUUSHA!
GATHER THEM UP!

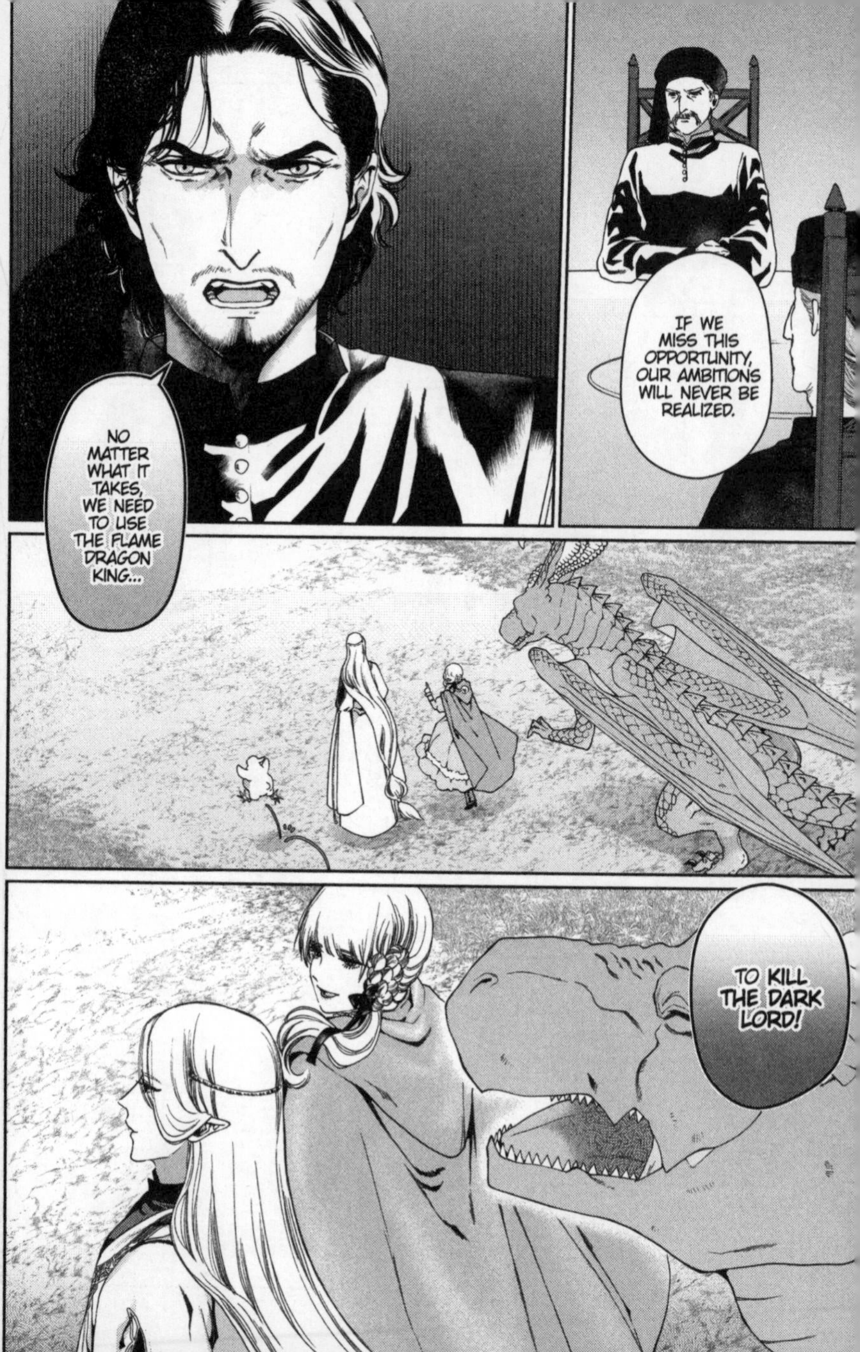
IF WE MISS THIS OPPORTUNITY, OUR AMBITIONS WILL NEVER BE REALIZED.
NO MATTER WHAT IT TAKES, WE NEED TO USE THE FLAME DRAGON KING...
TO KILL THE DARK LORD!

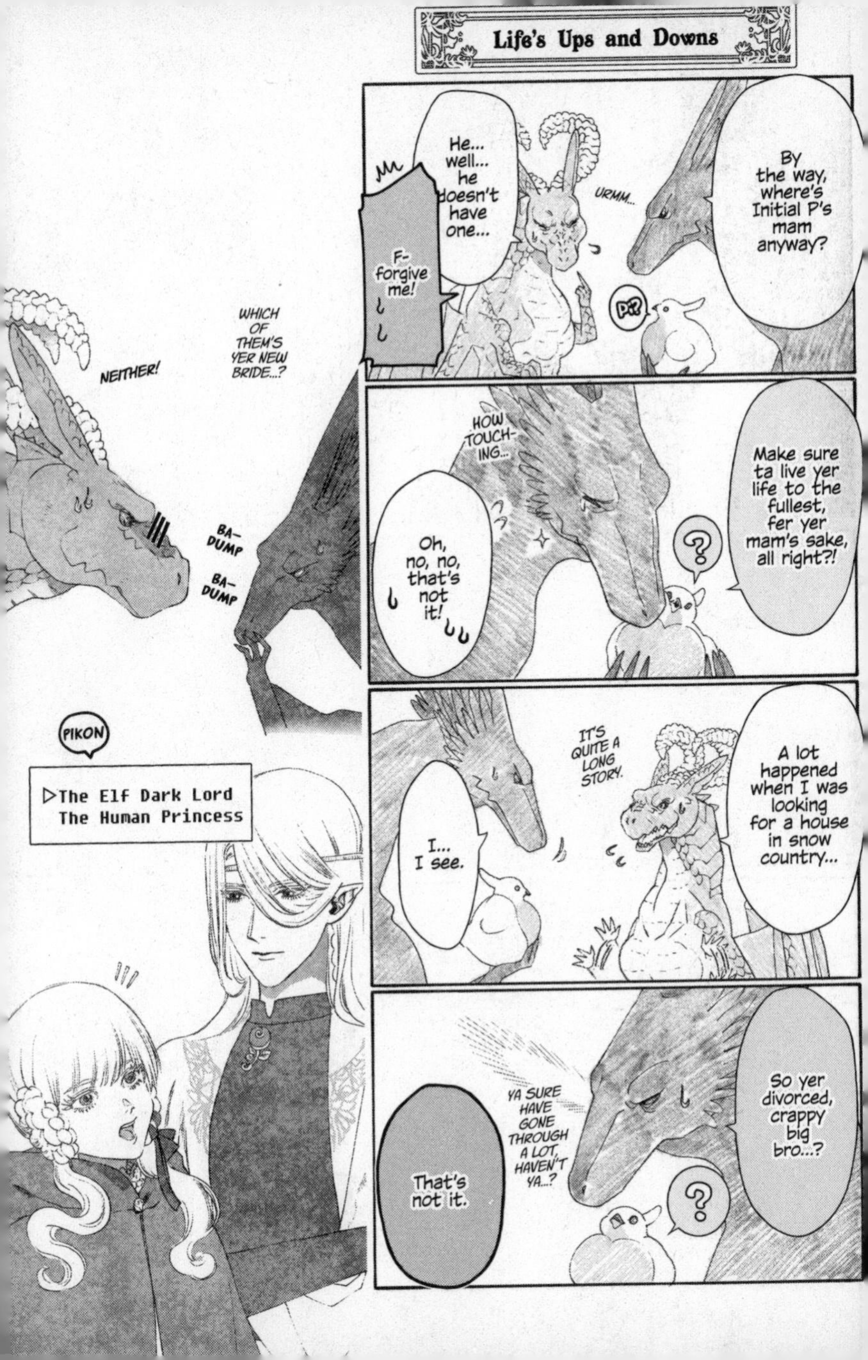
Life's Ups and Downs
By the way, where's Initial P's mam anyway?
P?
URMM...
He... well... he doesn't have one...
F-forgive me!
Make sure ta live yer life to the fullest, fer yer mam's sake, all right?!
?
HOW TOUCHING...
Oh, no, no, that's not it!
A lot happened when I was looking for a house in snow country...
IT'S QUITE A LONG STORY.
I... I see.
So yer divorced, crappy big bro...?
?
YA SURE HAVE GONE THROUGH A LOT, HAVEN'T YA...?
That's not it.
WHICH OF THEM'S YER NEW BRIDE...?
NEITHER!
BA-DUMP
BA-DUMP
PIKON
▷The Elf Dark Lord
The Human Princess

Dragon Goes House-Hunting

Side Story: A Day in the Life of Nell

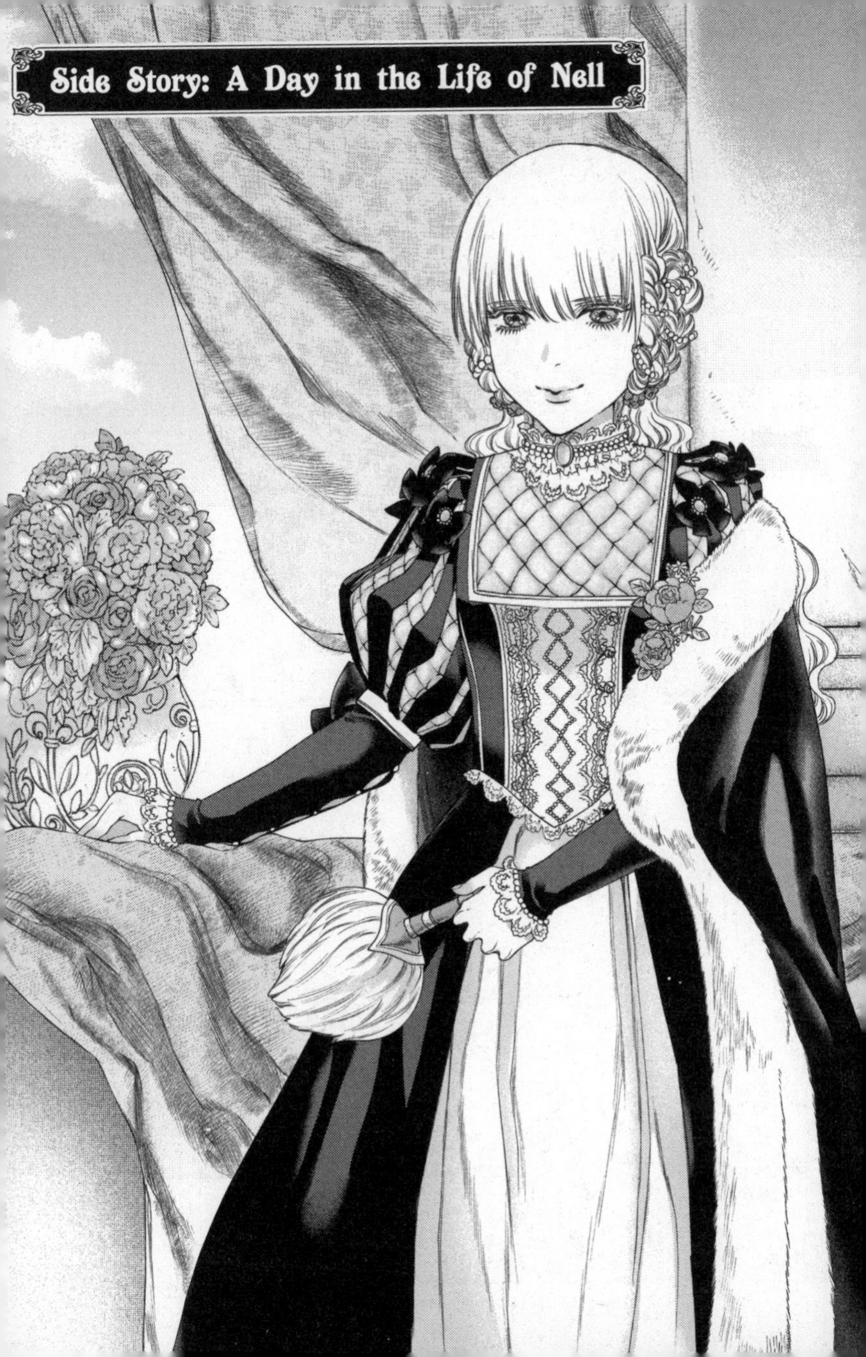

A Certain Princess's Day

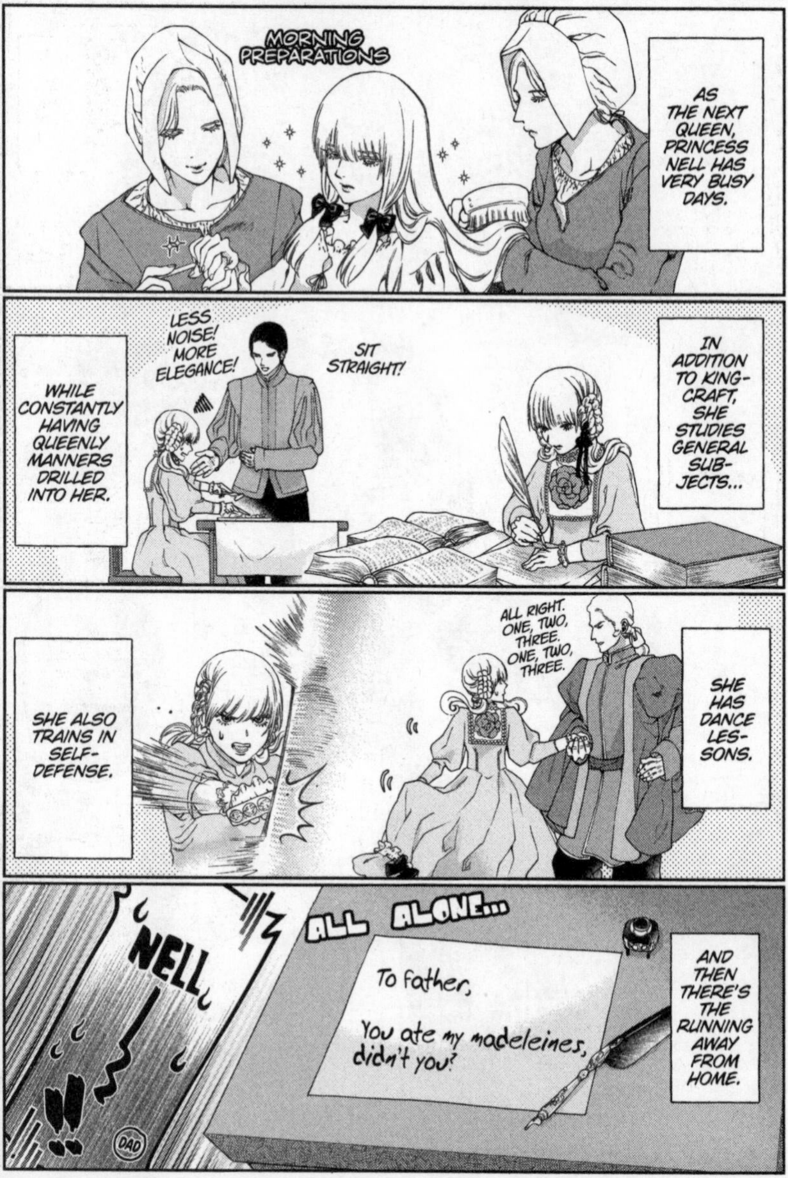
AS THE NEXT QUEEN, PRINCESS NELL HAS VERY BUSY DAYS.
MORNING PREPARATIONS
IN ADDITION TO KING-CRAFT, SHE STUDIES GENERAL SUB-JECTS...
SIT STRAIGHT!
LESS NOISE! MORE ELEGANCE!
WHILE CONSTANTLY HAVING QUEENLY MANNERS DRILLED INTO HER.
SHE HAS DANCE LES-SONS.
ALL RIGHT. ONE, TWO, THREE. ONE, TWO, THREE.
SHE ALSO TRAINS IN SELF-DEFENSE.
AND THEN THERE'S THE RUNNING AWAY FROM HOME.
To father,
You ate my madeleines, didn't you?
ALL ALONE...
NELL!
DAD

The Runaway Princess

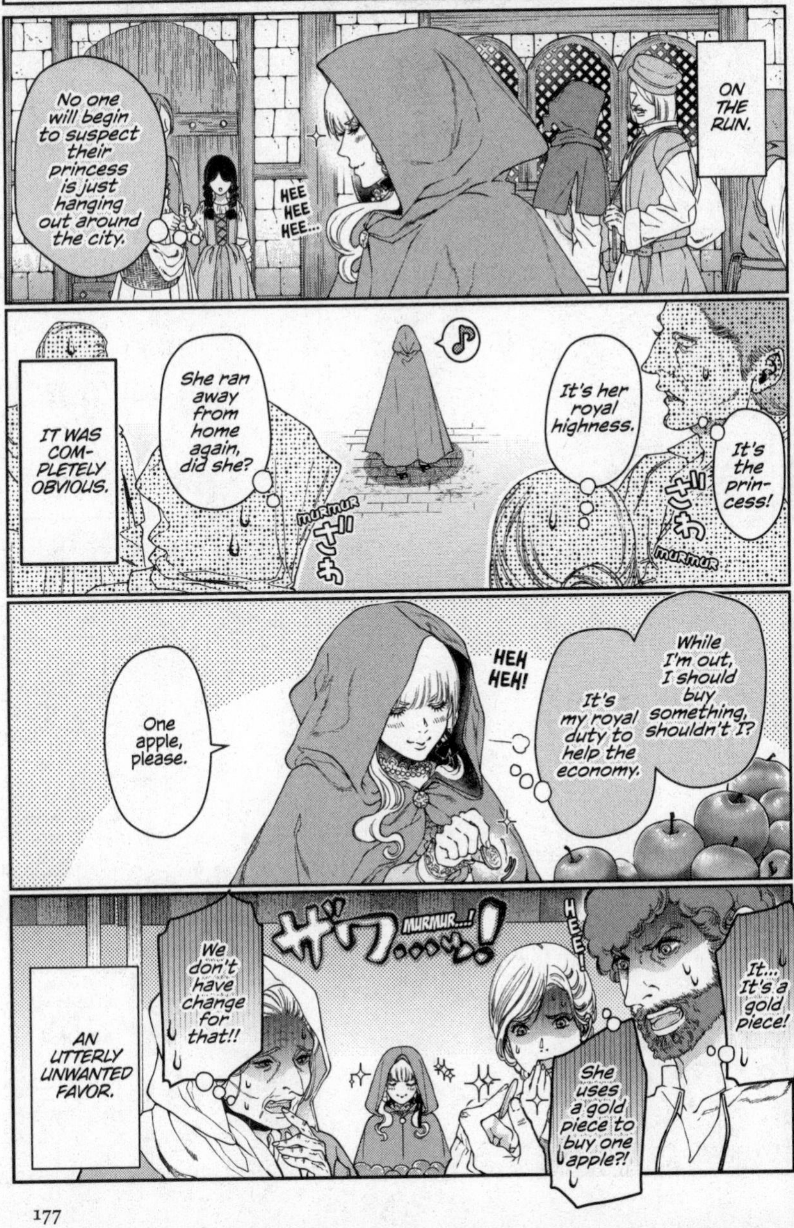
ON THE RUN.
HEE HEE HEE...
No one will begin to suspect their princess is just hanging out around the city.
It's the princess!
MURMUR
It's her royal highness.
She ran away from home again, did she?
MURMUR
IT WAS COMPLETELY OBVIOUS.
While I'm out, I should buy something, shouldn't I?
It's my royal duty to help the economy.
HEH HEH!
One apple, please.
It... It's a gold piece!
HEE!
She uses a gold piece to buy one apple?!
MURMUR...!
We don't have change for that!!
AN UTTERLY UNWANTED FAVOR.

A Sweet Trap

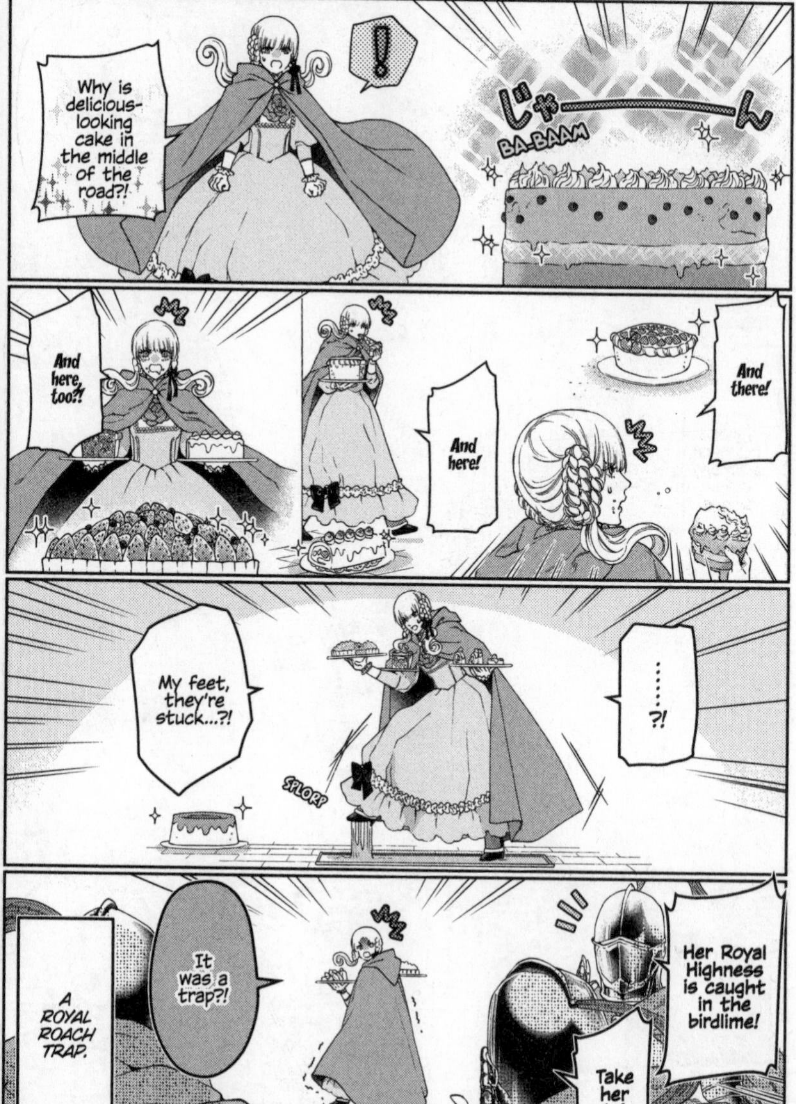

じゃーーーん
BA-BAAM
!
Why is delicious-looking cake in the middle of the road?!
And there!
And here!
And here, too?!
......?!
My feet, they're stuck...?!
SPLORP
Her Royal Highness is caught in the birdlime!
Take her in!
It was a trap?!
A ROYAL ROACH TRAP.

What She Learned

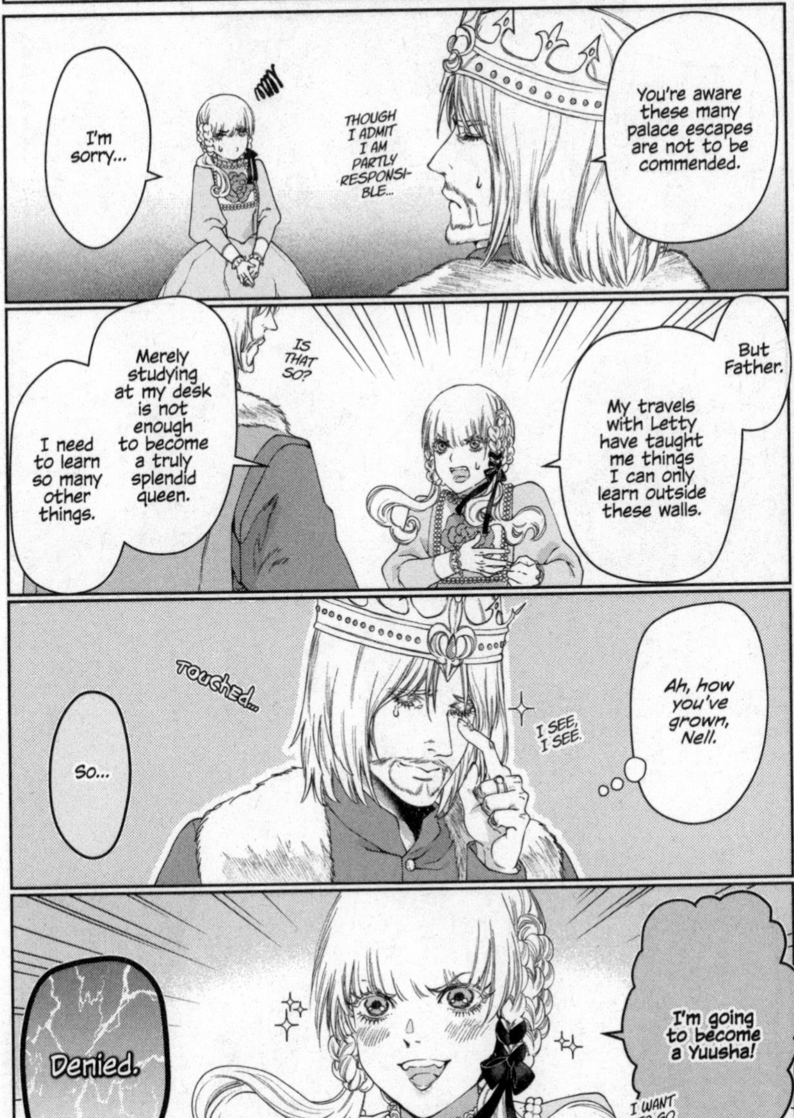
You're aware these many palace escapes are not to be commended.
THOUGH I ADMIT I AM PARTLY RESPONSIBLE...
I'm sorry...
But Father.
My travels with Letty have taught me things I can only learn outside these walls.
IS THAT SO?
Merely studying at my desk is not enough to become a truly splendid queen.
I need to learn so many other things.
Ah, how you've grown, Nell.
I SEE, I SEE.
TOUCHED...
So...
I'm going to become a Yuusha!
I WANT TO GO ADVENTURING!
Denied.

Her Required Specs

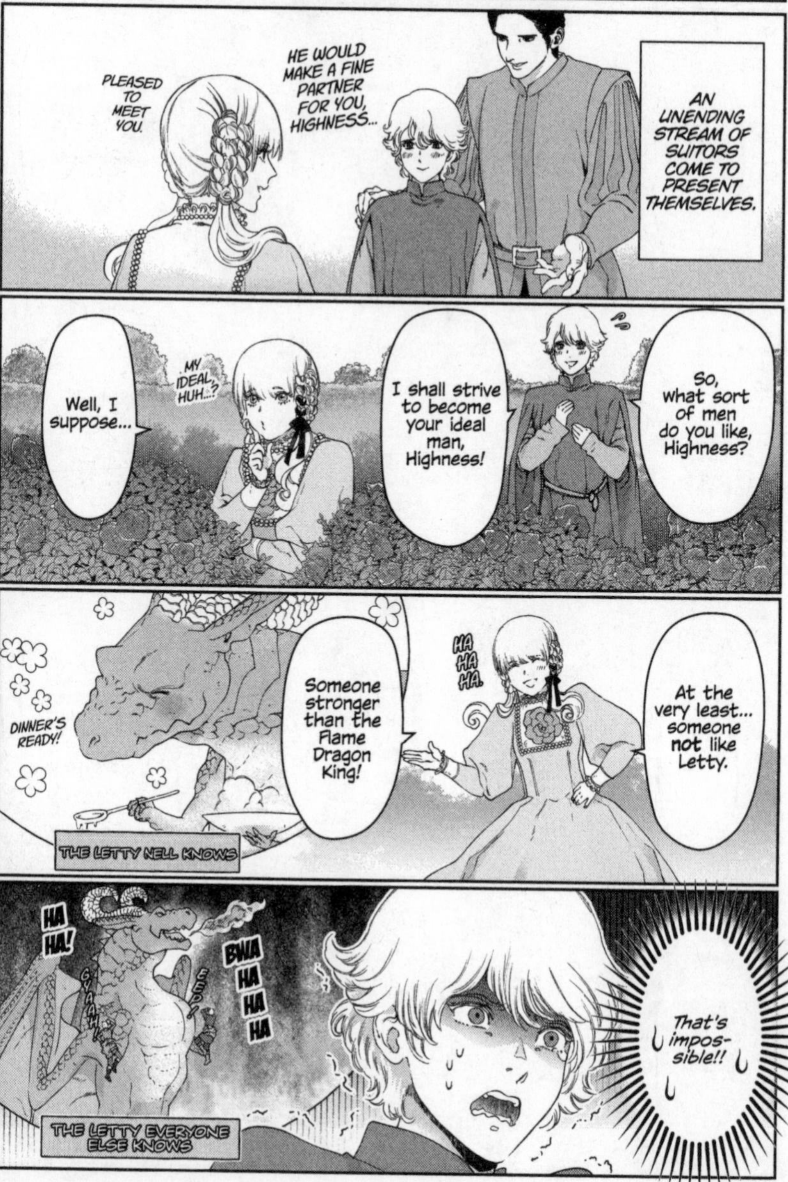
AN UNENDING STREAM OF SUITORS COME TO PRESENT THEMSELVES.
HE WOULD MAKE A FINE PARTNER FOR YOU, HIGHNESS...
PLEASED TO MEET YOU.
So, what sort of men do you like, Highness?
I shall strive to become your ideal man, Highness!
MY IDEAL, HUH...?
Well, I suppose...
At the very least... someone not like Letty.
HA HA HA.
Someone stronger than the Flame Dragon King!
DINNER'S READY!
THE LETTY NELL KNOWS
That's impos-sible!!
BWA HA HA HA
EEP!
GYAAAH!
HA HA!
THE LETTY EVERYONE ELSE KNOWS

My Darling Only Daughter

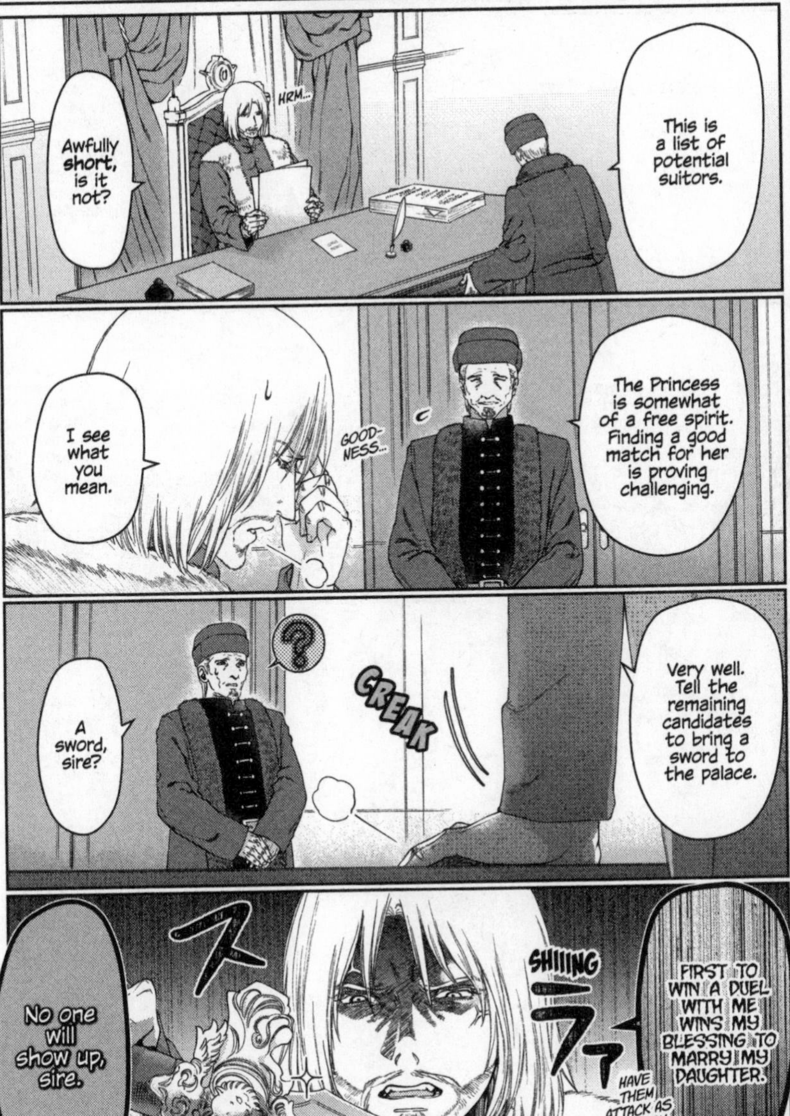
This is a list of potential suitors.
HRM...
Awfully short, is it not?
The Princess is somewhat of a free spirit. Finding a good match for her is proving challenging.
GOODNESS...
I see what you mean.
Very well. Tell the remaining candidates to bring a sword to the palace.
CREAK
?
A sword, sire?
FIRST TO WIN A DUEL WITH ME WINS MY BLESSING TO MARRY MY DAUGHTER.
HAVE THEM ATTACK AS THOUGH THEIR LIVES DEPENDED ON IT.
SHIIING
No one will show up, sire.

Too Far

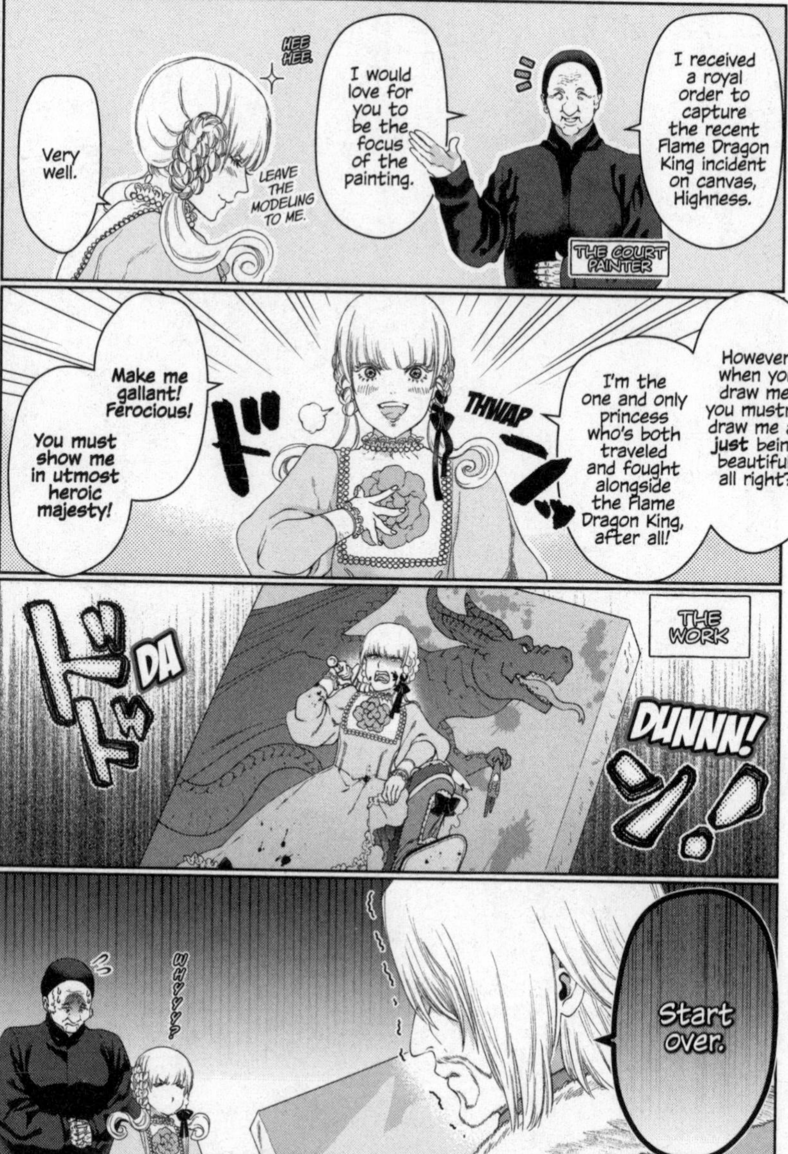

I received a royal order to capture the recent Flame Dragon King incident on canvas, Highness.
THE COURT PAINTER
I would love for you to be the focus of the painting.
HEE HEE.
LEAVE THE MODELING TO ME.
Very well.
However, when you draw me, you mustn't draw me as just being beautiful, all right?
I'm the one and only princess who's both traveled and fought alongside the Flame Dragon King, after all!
THWAP
Make me gallant! Ferocious!
You must show me in utmost heroic majesty!
THE WORK
DUNNN!
DA
Start over.
WHYYYY?

Taking A Shortcut

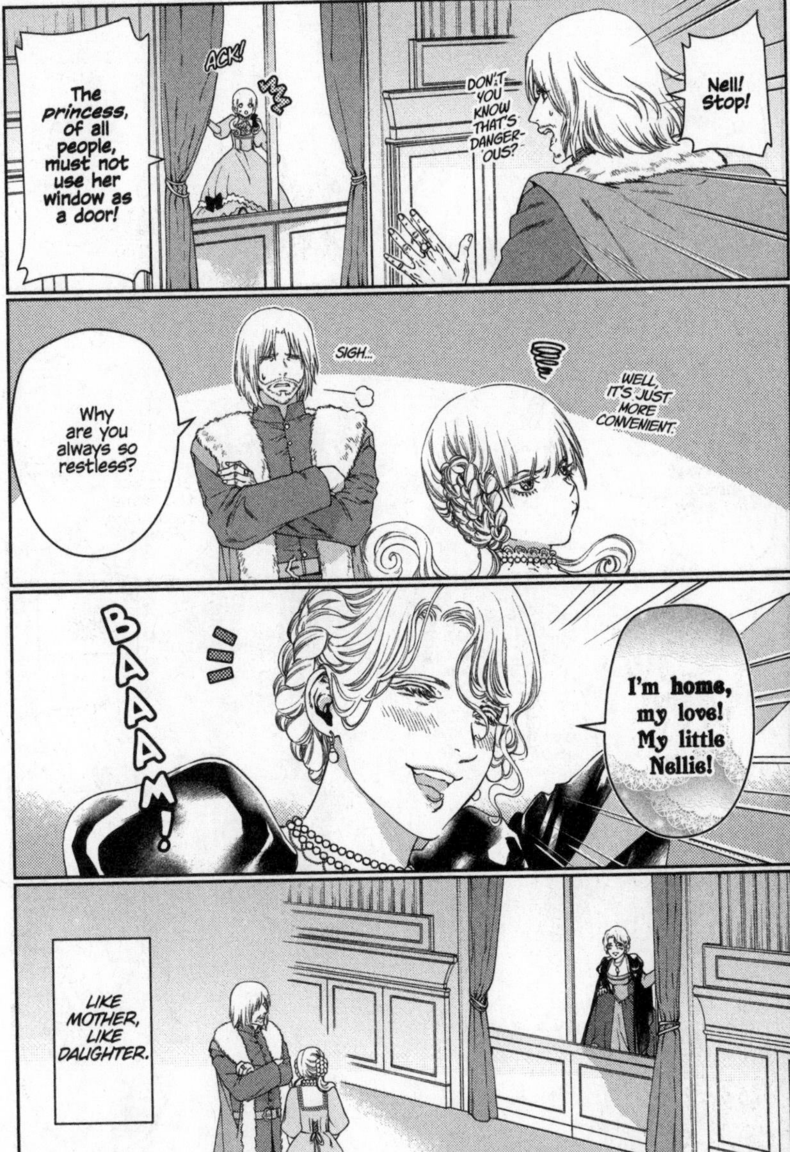
Nell! Stop!
DON'T YOU KNOW THAT'S DANGER-OUS?
ACK!
The *princess*, of all people, must not use her window as a door!
WELL, IT'S JUST MORE CONVENIENT.
SIGH...
Why are you always so restless?
I'm home, my love! My little Nellie!
BAAAM!
LIKE MOTHER, LIKE DAUGHTER.

A Gift

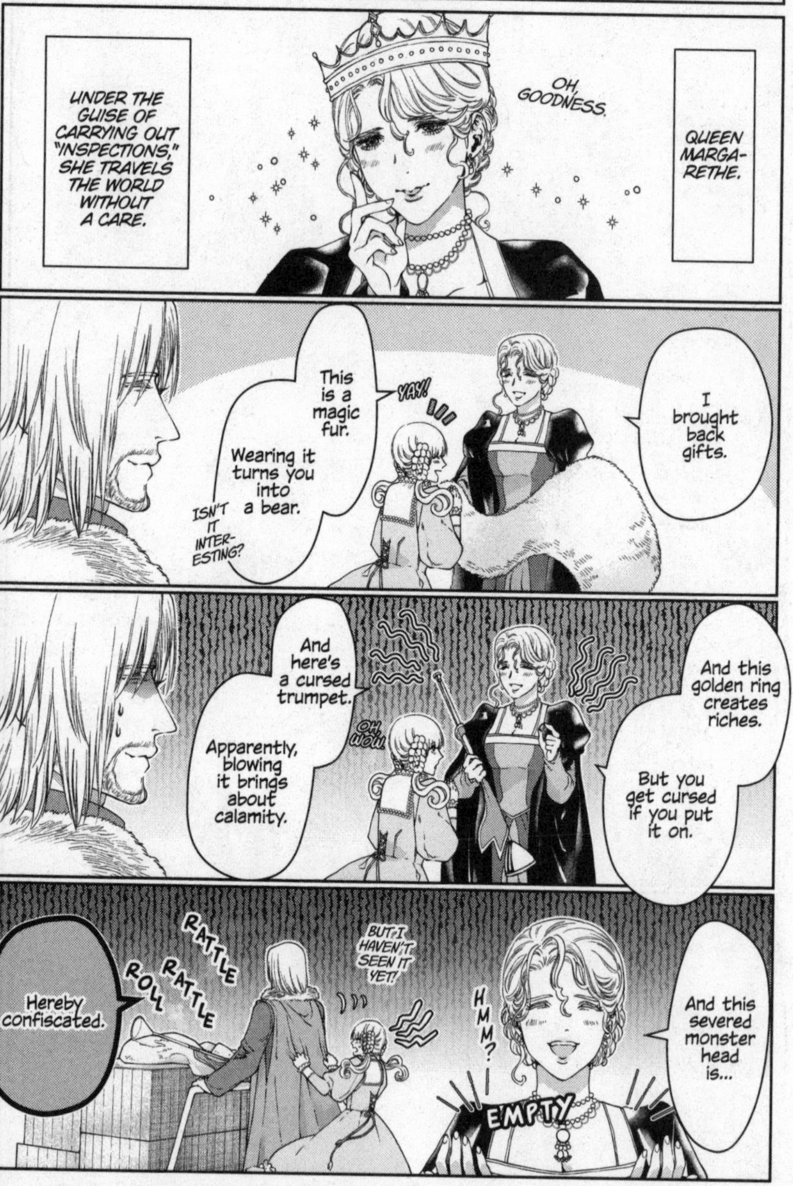
QUEEN MARGARETHE.
OH, GOODNESS.
UNDER THE GUISE OF CARRYING OUT "INSPECTIONS," SHE TRAVELS THE WORLD WITHOUT A CARE.
I brought back gifts.
YAY!
This is a magic fur.
Wearing it turns you into a bear.
ISN'T IT INTERESTING?
And this golden ring creates riches.
But you get cursed if you put it on.
OH, WOW!
And here's a cursed trumpet.
Apparently, blowing it brings about calamity.
And this severed monster head is...
EMPTY
HMM?
BUT I HAVEN'T SEEN IT YET!
RATTLE
RATTLE
ROLL
Hereby confiscated.

A Pinch

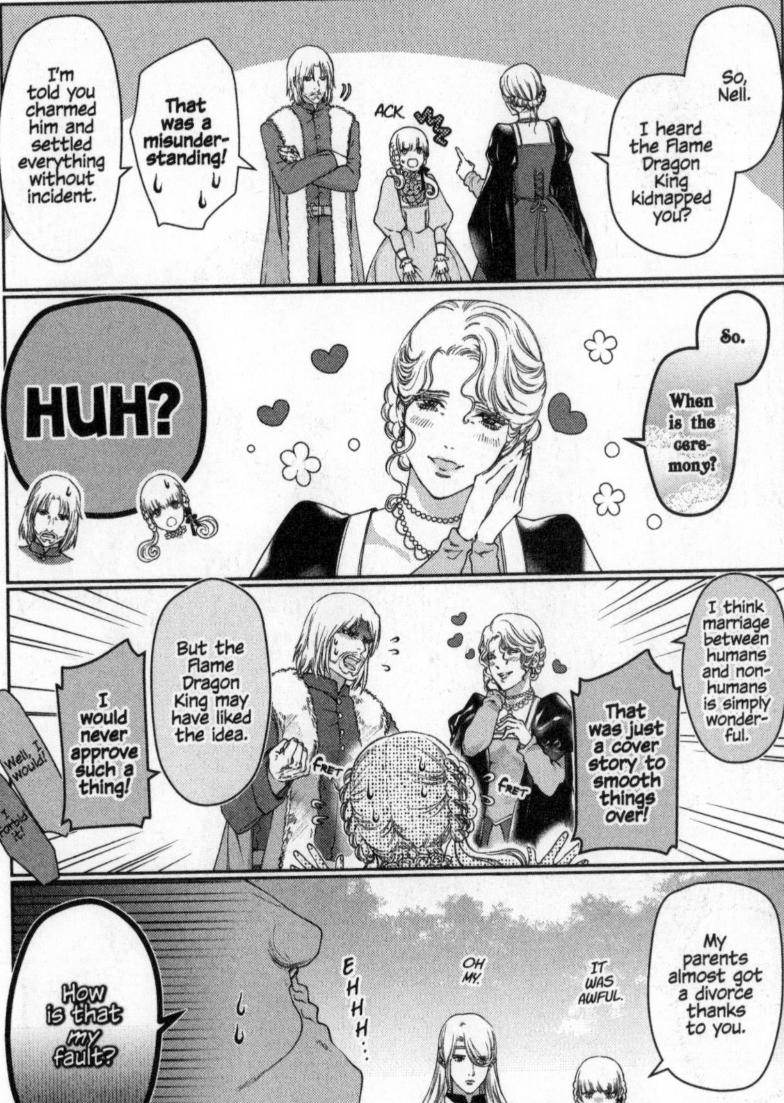
So, Nell.
I heard the Flame Dragon King kidnapped you?
ACK.
That was a misunder-standing!
I'm told you charmed him and settled everything without incident.
So.
When is the cere-mony?
HUH?
I think marriage between humans and non-humans is simply wonder-ful.
That was just a cover story to smooth things over!
FRET
FRET
But the Flame Dragon King may have liked the idea.
I would never approve such a thing!
Well, I would!
I forbid it!
My parents almost got a divorce thanks to you.
IT WAS AWFUL.
OH MY.
EHHH...
How is that my fault?

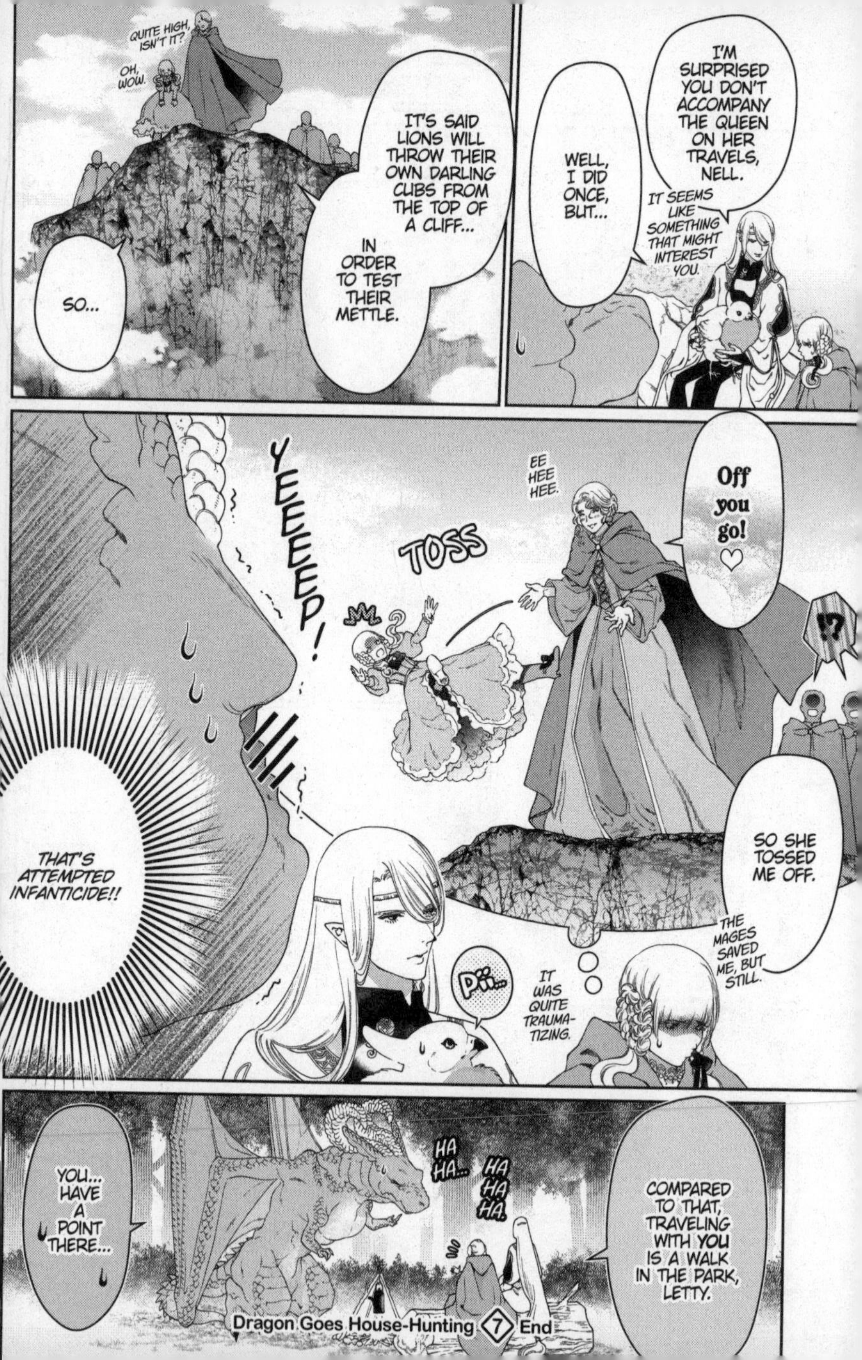
I'M SURPRISED YOU DON'T ACCOMPANY THE QUEEN ON HER TRAVELS, NELL.
IT SEEMS LIKE SOMETHING THAT MIGHT INTEREST YOU.
WELL, I DID ONCE, BUT...
QUITE HIGH, ISN'T IT?
OH, WOW.
IT'S SAID LIONS WILL THROW THEIR OWN DARLING CUBS FROM THE TOP OF A CLIFF...
IN ORDER TO TEST THEIR METTLE.
SO...
Off you go! ♡
EE HEE HEE.
!?
TOSS
YEEEEEP!
SO SHE TOSSED ME OFF.
THE MAGES SAVED ME, BUT STILL.
IT WAS QUITE TRAUMATIZING.
Pii...
THAT'S ATTEMPTED INFANTICIDE!!
COMPARED TO THAT, TRAVELING WITH YOU IS A WALK IN THE PARK, LETTY.
HA HA HA.
HA HA...
YOU... HAVE A POINT THERE...
Dragon Goes House-Hunting 7 End

A Fateful Meeting

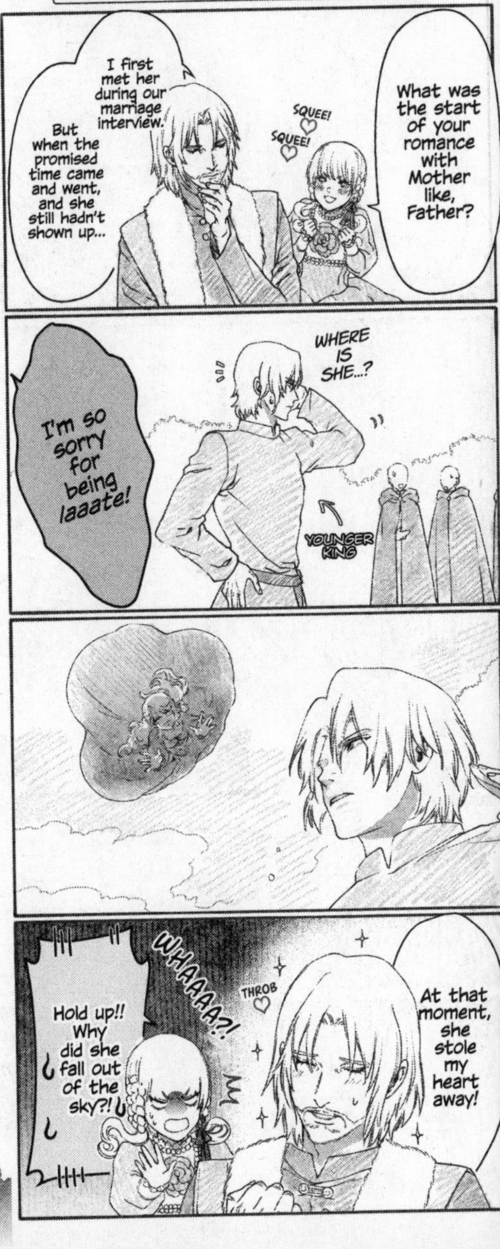
What was the start of your romance with Mother like, Father?
SQUEE! SQUEE!
I first met her during our marriage interview.
But when the promised time came and went, and she still hadn't shown up...
WHERE IS SHE...?
YOUNGER KING
I'm so sorry for being laaate!
At that moment, she stole my heart away!
THROB
WHAAAA?!
Hold up!! Why did she fall out of the sky?!

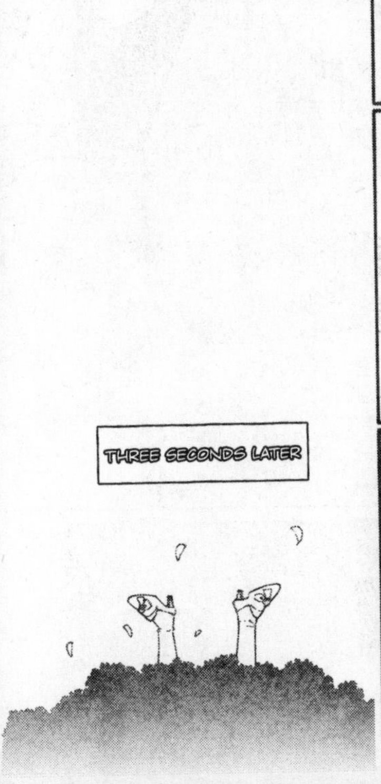
THREE SECONDS LATER

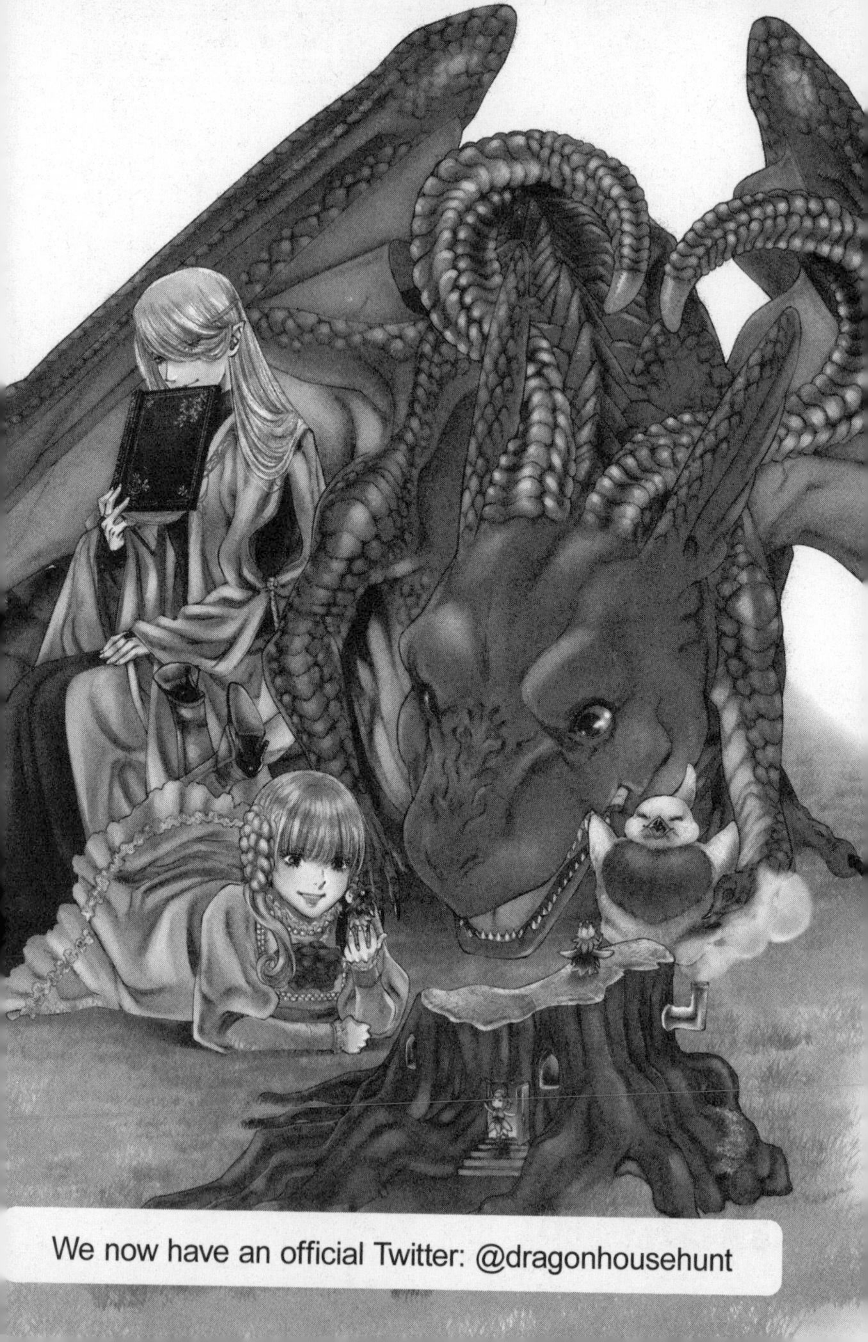
We now have an official Twitter: @dragonhousehunt

Dragon
Goes
House-
Hunting

Dragon Goes House-Hunting

SEVEN SEAS ENTERTAINMENT PRESENTS

VOLUME 7

Dragon Goes House-Hunting

story by **KAWO TANUKI** art by **CHOCO AYA**

TRANSLATION
Nan Rymer

ADAPTATION
T Campbell

LETTERING
Alexandra Gunawan

COVER DESIGN
Hanase Qi

PROOFREADER
Kurestin Armada
B. Lillian Martin

EDITOR
J.P. Sullivan

PREPRESS TECHNICIAN
Rhiannon Rasmussen-Silverstein

PRODUCTION MANAGER
Lissa Pattillo

MANAGING EDITOR
Julie Davis

ASSOCIATE PUBLISHER
Adam Arnold

PUBLISHER
Jason DeAngelis

Originally published in Japan in 2021 by MAG Garden Corporation, Tokyo.
English translation rights arranged through TOHAN CORPORATION, Tokyo.

Seven Seas press and purchase enquiries can be sent to Marketing Manager Lianne Sentar at press@gomanga.com. Information regarding the distribution and purchase of digital editions is available from Digital Manager CK Russell at digital@gomanga.com.

ISBN: 978-1-64827-329-2

Printed in Canada

First Printing: November 2021

10 9 8 7 6 5 4 3 2 1

FOLLOW US ONLINE: ***www.sevenseasentertainment.com***

READING DIRECTIONS

This book reads from ***right to left***, Japanese style. If this is your first time reading manga, you start reading from the top right panel on each page and take it from there. If you get lost, just follow the numbered diagram here. It may seem backwards at first, but you'll get the hang of it! Have fun!!

1
2
3
4
5
6
7
8
9

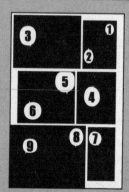